LIFE COURSE, HAPPINESS AND WELL-BEING IN JAPAN

Much of the existing literature on happiness in Japan has been produced in the field of economics and psychology and is quantitative in nature. Here, for the first time, a group of anthropologists and sociologists jointly analyze the state of happiness and unhappiness in Japan among varying social groups in its physical, interpersonal, existential and structural dimensions, offering new insights into fundamental issues.

This book investigates the connections between sociostructural aspects, individual agency and happiness in contemporary Japan from a life course perspective. The contributors examine quantitative and qualitative empirical data on the processes that impact how happiness and well-being are envisioned, crafted, and debated in Japan across the life-cycle. Therefore, the book discusses the shifting notions of happiness during people's lives from birth to death, analyzing the age group-specific experiences while taking into consideration people's life trajectories and historical changes. It points out recent developments with regards to demographic change, late marriage, and the changing labor market and focuses on their significant impact on the well-being of Japanese people. In particular it highlights the interdependencies of lives within the family and how families are collaborating for the purpose of maintaining or enhancing the happiness of its members.

Broadening our understanding of the multidimensionality of happiness in Japan, this book will be of interest to students and scholars of Japanese Studies, Anthropology, and Sociology.

Barbara Holthus is Assistant Professor at the Department of East Asian Studies, University of Vienna, Austria. Her most recent publications include *Parental Well-Being in Japan* (2015) and a co-edited volume on *Happiness and the Good Life in Japan* (Routledge 2017).

Wolfram Manzenreiter is Professor of Japanese Studies at the University of Vienna, Austria. His most recent publications include *Sport and Body Politics in Japan* (Routledge 2014) and the co-edited volume on *Happiness and the Good Life in Japan* (Routledge 2017).

The Nissan Institute/Routledge Japanese Studies Series
Series Editors:

Roger Goodman, Nissan Professor of Modern Japanese Studies, University of Oxford, Fellow, St Antony's College

J.A.A. Stockwin, formerly Nissan Professor of Modern Japanese Studies and former Director of the Nissan Institute of Japanese Studies, University of Oxford, Emeritus Fellow, St Antony's College

Other titles in the series:

Configurations of Family in Contemporary Japan
Edited by Tomoko Aoyama, Laura Dales and Romit Dasgupta

Ozawa Ichirō and Japanese Politics
Old versus new
Aurelia George Mulgan

Labour Market Deregulation in Japan and Italy
Worker protection under neoliberal globalisation
Hiroaki Richard Watanabe

Japanese Economic Development
Theory and practice
Third edition
Penelope Francks

Modern Japan
A social and political history
Third edition
Elise K. Tipton

Femininity, Self-harm and Eating Disorders in Japan
Navigating contradiction in narrative and visual culture
Gitte Marianne Hansen

Reconstructing Adult Masculinities
Part-time work in contemporary Japan
Emma E. Cook

The Democratic Party of Japan in Power
Challenges and Failures
Edited by Yoichi Funabashi and Koichi Nakano
Translated by Kate Dunlop

LIFE COURSE, HAPPINESS AND WELL-BEING IN JAPAN

*Edited by Barbara Holthus and
Wolfram Manzenreiter*

LONDON AND NEW YORK

First published 2017
by Routledge
2 Park Square, Milton Park, Abingdon, Oxon OX14 4RN

and by Routledge
711 Third Avenue, New York, NY 10017

Routledge is an imprint of the Taylor & Francis Group, an informa business

© 2017 selection and editorial matter, Barbara Holthus and Wolfram Manzenreiter; individual chapters, the contributors

The right of Barbara Holthus and Wolfram Manzenreiter to be identified as the authors of the editorial material, and of the authors for their individual chapters, has been asserted in accordance with sections 77 and 78 of the Copyright, Designs and Patents Act 1988.

All rights reserved. No part of this book may be reprinted or reproduced or utilised in any form or by any electronic, mechanical, or other means, now known or hereafter invented, including photocopying and recording, or in any information storage or retrieval system, without permission in writing from the publishers.

Trademark notice: Product or corporate names may be trademarks or registered trademarks, and are used only for identification and explanation without intent to infringe.

British Library Cataloguing-in-Publication Data
A catalogue record for this book is available from the British Library

Library of Congress Cataloging-in-Publication Data
A catalog record for this book has been requested

ISBN: 978-1-138-29057-0 (hbk)
ISBN: 978-1-138-29059-4 (pbk)
ISBN: 978-1-315-26611-4 (ebk)

Typeset in Bembo
by codeMantra

CONTENTS

List of figures   viii
List of tables   ix
List of contributors   x
Preface and acknowledgments   xiv
Series editors' preface   xvi

    Introduction: Making sense of happiness in "unhappy Japan"   1
    Barbara Holthus and Wolfram Manzenreiter

PART I
Childhood and youth

1   *Tanoshikatta ne?* Learning to be happy in Japanese preschools   31
    Eyal Ben-Ari

2   "Because I feel happy": Japanese first graders' views about schooling and well-being   45
    Yoko Yamamoto

3   "Unhappy" and isolated youth in the midst of social change: Representations and subjective experiences of *hikikomori* in contemporary Japan   57
    Sachiko Horiguchi

4 Anxious, stressed, and yet satisfied? The puzzle of
  subjective well-being among young adults in Japan 72
  Carola Hommerich

PART II
Adulthood

5 Being happy as a woman: The promise of happiness for
  middle-class housewives in Japan 97
  Ofra Goldstein-Gidoni

6 The well-being of single mothers in Japan 116
  James M. Raymo

7 Happiness at work? Marital happiness among Japanese
  housewives and employed wives 138
  Mary C. Brinton

8 The happiness of Japanese academics: Findings from job
  satisfaction surveys in 1992 and 2007 158
  Theresa Aichinger, Peter Fankhauser and Roger Goodman

9 Dilemma of fatherhood: The meaning of work, family, and
  happiness for salaried male Japanese workers 175
  Futoshi Taga

PART III
Old age

10 Happiness pursued, abandoned, dreamed of, and stumbled
   upon: An analysis of 20 Japanese lives over 20 years 189
   Gordon Mathews

11 Senior volunteers and post-retirement well-being in Japan 202
   Satsuki Kawano

12 Well-being and decision-making towards the end of life: Living wills in Japan 221
   Celia Spoden

13 Fear of solitary death in Japan's aging society 238
   Tim Tiefenbach and Florian Kohlbacher

14 Reconsidering the four dimensions of happiness across the life course in Japan 256
   Wolfram Manzenreiter and Barbara Holthus

Index 273

FIGURES

I.1	Academic publications on "life satisfaction," "happiness," and "well-being"	4
4.1	Life satisfaction across age groups	74
4.2	Life satisfaction by gender and age	76
4.3	General social trust across age groups	79
4.4	Having family to rely on across age groups	79
4.5	Having friends to rely on across age groups	80
4.6	Feelings of social affiliation across age groups	80
4.7	Experience of anxieties over the past six months across age groups	81
4.8	Experience of anxieties about the future	82
4.9	Future outlook across age groups	82
7.1	Marital happiness of Japanese wives	151
13.1	The number of solitary deaths in inner Tokyo from 1987 to 2013	241
13.2	Worries about solitary death over the life course	245

TABLES

4.1	OLS-regression on life satisfaction for age group subsamples	84
4.2	Descriptive statistics of demographic and socioeconomic indicators by age	89
4.3	Descriptive statistics for the items used to measure social affiliation	89
6.1	Descriptive statistics, by marital status	126
6.2	OLS results for models of happiness	128
6.3	OLS results for models of CES-D	130
6.4	Ordered logistic regression results for models of self-rated health	131
7.1	Changes in percent of Japanese women quitting work at marriage or first childbirth: Five cohorts	143
7.2	Determinants of marital happiness for older and younger wives	150
7.3	Characteristics of married women: Younger and older cohorts	154
8.1	Overall satisfaction with current job	162
8.2	Overall satisfaction with current work by age	162
8.3	Overall satisfaction with current job by rank	163
8.4	Overall satisfaction with current job by gender	163
8.5	Interpersonal dimension 1992–2007	165
8.6	Overall satisfaction with current job and collegial relationships	165
8.7	Overall satisfaction with current job	167
8.8	Distribution of income groups according to rank and age	168
8.9	Distribution of income groups according to institutional type	169
8.10	Correlations with key variables and overall job satisfaction among Japanese academics (2007)	169
13.1	Different worries and their correlation with happiness in the 2013 SQL	246
13.2	OLS regression predicting worries about solitary death (standardized)	248
13.3	Summary statistics	251
13.4	Loneliness predicting worries about solitary death	252

CONTRIBUTORS

Theresa Aichinger is a graduate student in Japanese Studies and political science at the University of Vienna. Her research interests are on Japanese folklore studies and political myth in Japan, gender, and political theory. In 2014/2015, she conducted fieldwork for her MA thesis on happiness research at Tokyo Metropolitan University. Since 2016 she works as research assistant for the Chair of Japanese Studies, University of Vienna.

Eyal Ben-Ari received his doctoral degree in Social Anthropology at the University of Cambridge, UK. Besides his research on Japan, within the last 30 years he focused on introducing an anthropological point of view on the Israeli army. One of his recent publications is "Militaries and the multiple negotiations of intervention" in G. Kuemmel and B. Griegrich (eds.) *The Armed Forces: Towards a Post-Intervention Era?* (Springer 2013). In 2011, he established the FEBA Research and Consultancy and since 2013 is a Senior Research Fellow at Kinneret Center, Israel. He is author of *Japanese Childcare: An Interpretive Study of Culture and Organization* (Kegan Paul International 1997).

Mary C. Brinton is Chair of the Department of Sociology at the Reischauer Institute of Harvard University. Her research focuses on gender stratification, education, labor markets, social demography, contemporary Japanese society and economy, economic sociology and comparative social stratification. Her recent publications include *Lost in Transition: Youth, Work and Instability in Postindustrial Japan* (Cambridge University Press 2010) and "School-work systems in postindustrial societies: Evidence from Japan" (*Research in Social Stratification and Mobility* 2010, with Zun Tang).

Peter Fankhauser, MA, is a graduate student in Japanese Studies at the University of Vienna and works as research assistant on a German Science Foundation project on Parental Well-Being (principal investigator: Barbara Holthus). His research interests include friendship, contemporary Japanese literature and sociology of youth. In 2015 he conducted fieldwork for his MA thesis entitled "Sharing is caring. Self-disclosure in friendships of Japanese students and the role of relational mobility," at Tokyo Metropolitan University.

Ofra Goldstein-Gidoni is Associate Professor at the Department of Sociology and Anthropology and East Asian Studies at Tel Aviv University. She earned her Ph.D. at the University of London. Her research focuses on gender, women and "new fathers" in Japan, on cultural globalization and the incorporation of New Age spirituality in Israeli mainstream. Among her publications are *Packaged Japaneseness: Weddings, Business and Brides* (Curzon Press and University of Hawai'i Press 1997) and more recently *Housewives of Japan: An Ethnography of Real Lives and Consumerized Domesticity* (Palgrave Macmillan 2012).

Roger Goodman holds the Nissan Chair of Modern Japanese Studies at Oxford University. Since 2008, he is also Head of Oxford's Social Sciences Division. His research over the past 30 years has been mainly on Japanese education and social policy. Furthermore, he does comparative work on South Korea and the United Kingdom. Among his many publications is *Children of the Japanese State: The Changing Role of Child Protection Institutions in Contemporary Japan* (Oxford University Press 2000). His latest edited book is *Higher Education and the State* (Symposium Books 2012).

Barbara Holthus holds two Ph.D. degrees (University of Trier, Germany and University of Hawaii at Manoa). Before joining the Department of East Asian Studies/Japanese Studies at the University of Vienna in 2013, she was Senior Research Fellow at the German Institute for Japanese Studies Tokyo (2007–2013). Her research is on marriage and the family, childcare, well-being, media and gender, as well as demographic and social change. She is principal investigator of a German Science Foundation (DFG) funded research project on comparing parental well-being in Germany and Japan (2014–2017). Her publications include *Parental well-being in Japan* (DIJ Miscellanea 19, 2015), the co-edited special issue *Mind the Gap: Stratification and social inequalities in Japan* (*Contemporary Japan*, 22 1/2, 2010), as well as the co-edited volume *Happiness and the Good Life in Japan* (Routledge 2017).

Carola Hommerich, Ph.D. in Sociology, is Associate Professor of Sociology at Hokkaido University. From 2008 to 2015 she was Senior Research Fellow at the German Institute for Japanese Studies Tokyo. Her research focuses on happiness and social inequality in Japan. Publications include *'Freeter' and 'Generation Internship' – Changing Working World? A German–Japanese Comparison* (Iudicium 2009, in German) and "Adapting to risk, learning to trust: Socioeconomic insecurities and feelings of disconnectedness in contemporary Japan" (*Asiatische Studien* 2013).

Sachiko Horiguchi is currently Assistant Professor of Anthropology at Temple University, Japan Campus in Tokyo. She is a social/medical anthropologist with a D.Phil. in Social Anthropology from the University of Oxford (2006). Her research interests lie in youth mental health issues and globalization of education in Japan, and her major publications include "Mental health and therapy in Japan: Conceptions, practices, and challenges" in Jeff Kingston (ed.) *Critical Issues in Contemporary Japan* (Routledge 2013) and "Hikikomori: How private isolation caught the public eye" in Roger Goodman et al. (eds.) *A Sociology of Japanese Youth* (Routledge 2012).

Satsuki Kawano is Associate Professor of Anthropology at the University of Guelph, Canada. She received a Ph.D. from the University of Pittsburgh. Before joining the University of Guelph she held positions at Harvard University (Center for the Study of World Religions) and the University of Notre Dame. Her research interests include ritual, death and dying, demographic change, aging, family and kinship, learning disabilities and childrearing. She is the author of *Ritual Practice in Modern Japan* (University of Hawai'i Press 2005) and *Nature's Embrace: Japan's Aging Urbanites and New Death Rites* (University of Hawai'i Press 2010). She is also the lead editor of *Capturing Contemporary Japan: Differentiation and Uncertainty* (University of Hawai'i Press 2014).

Florian Kohlbacher is an expert on global business and consumer trends, focusing on how to manage innovation, strategy, sustainability, and change. Currently he is the North Asia Director of The Economist Corporate Network, managing the Networks in Japan and South Korea. He is also an Adjunct Professor at Temple University, Japan Campus, and his research interests include aging and business, consumer behavior, marketing strategy, innovation management and sustainability. He is co-editor of *The Silver Market Phenomenon: Marketing and Innovation in the Aging Society* (Springer 2011, 2nd edition) and *Advertising in the Aging Society: Understanding Representations, Practitioners, and Consumers in Japan* (Palgrave 2016, with Michael Prieler).

Wolfram Manzenreiter is Professor of Japanese Studies at the Department of East Asian Studies at the University of Vienna. His research is mostly concerned with sociological and anthropological aspects of sports, emotions, work, and migration in a globalizing world. Currently he is working on migration networks and the Japanese diaspora in South America, happiness in sports, the transnationalization of security services, and gambling cultures. His most recent book-length publications include *Sport and Body Politics in Japan* (Routledge 2014), the co-edited volume *Migration and Development, New Perspectives* (ProMedia 2014, in German), and the co-edited volume *Happiness and the Good Life in Japan* (Routledge 2017).

Gordon Mathews, Ph.D. Cornell University, is Professor at the Department of Anthropology at the Chinese University of Hong Kong. His research interests are how individuals create senses of meaning in life and identity within different cultural and social contexts and how individuals culturally, socially, and economically locate themselves within the contemporary world of globalization. His recent publications include *Ghetto at the Center of the World: Chungking Mansions, Hong Kong* (University of Chicago Press 2011) and "Death and 'the pursuit of a life worth living' in Japan" in Hikaru Suzuki (ed.) *Death and Dying in Contemporary Japan* (Routledge 2013).

James M. Raymo is Professor at the Department of Sociology and Director of the Center for Demography and Ecology at the University of Wisconsin-Madison. His areas of interest include demography, marriage and family, aging and the life course, social stratification, methods, and contemporary and Japanese society. Among his most recent publications are "Educational differences in divorce in Japan" (*Demographic Research* 2013, with S. Fukuda and M. Iwasawa) and "Living arrangements and the well-being of single mothers in Japan" (*Population Research and Policy Review* 2012, with Yanfei Zhou).

Celia Spoden is research associate and lecturer at the Department of Modern Japanese Studies, Heinrich-Heine University, Duesseldorf, Germany. Her dissertation *Deciding About Death. Individual Interpretations and Social Realities of Living Wills in Japan* has been published in German in 2015. Her fields of interest include Okinawa and identity, bioethics, dementia and local care networks (German publication forthcoming in 2017). Her current research focuses on the independent living movement and social participation of people with disabilities in Japan, and the medical use of robot technology.

Futoshi Taga is Associate Professor at the Faculty of Letters of Kansai University since 2009. His research fields include sociology of education and gender with a special interest in masculinities. Among his recent publications are *Sociology of Masculinities: Changing Men's Life Courses* (Sekai Shisōsha 2006) and "Attitudes and behaviors of fathers who help children take entrance examinations for junior high schools" (*Educational Sciences Seminary* 2012, both in Japanese).

Tim Tiefenbach, Ph.D. in Economics, University of Bayreuth, is Senior Research Fellow at the German Institute for Japanese Studies Tokyo. His research interests are happiness economics, new institutional economics, and economic ethics. His recent publications include *The Contribution of Economic Theory on the Question of "The Good Life"* (NMP 2012, in German) and "Subjective well-being across gender and age in Japan: An econometric analysis," E. Eckermann (ed.) *Gender, Lifespan and Quality of Life* (Springer 2014, with Florian Kohlbacher).

Yoko Yamamoto is Adjunct Assistant Professor at the Department of Education at Brown University. In 2006, she earned her Ph.D. in Human Development and Education at the University of California, Berkeley. Her latest articles are "Social class and Japanese mothers' support for young children's education: A qualitative study" (*The Journal of Early Childhood Research* 2013) and "Cultural capital in East Asian educational systems: The case of Japan" (*Sociology of Education* 2010, with Mary C. Brinton).

PREFACE AND ACKNOWLEDGMENTS

幸せとはいつもちょっと先にある。
Shiawase to wa itsumo chotto saki ni aru.
Happiness always is just a bit ahead of you.

In 2008, the German Institute for Japanese Studies Tokyo (DIJ Tokyo) embarked on its new research focus: Happiness and unhappiness in Japan. At the time, Barbara was working at the institute and embarked on the study of women's magazine discourses on marital happiness and unhappiness in Japan. When the DIJ hosted Wolfram to give a talk at the institute in April 2010, the forging of an official partnership between the DIJ and the University of Vienna began. In August 2011, we were both assigned the jobs as convenors for the sociology/anthropology section of the European Association of Japanese Studies conference in Ljubljana, Slovenia, to be held in August 2014. When in February 2013 the official faculty agreement between our two institutions was signed, Wolfram had a visiting professorship for two weeks at the DIJ Tokyo. It was during that time that we began to plan the EAJS topic. With Wolfram a social anthropologist and Barbara a sociologist, we quickly figured out that exploring happiness in-depth through the perspectives of our disciplines as the EAJS theme was unique and timely.

But not stopping there, we also saw room enough to make happiness the theme of a joint conference for celebrating the newly forged partnership between the University of Vienna and the German Institute of Japanese Studies. The conference entitled "Deciphering the Social DNA of Happiness: Life Course Perspectives from Japan" then was scheduled for April 2014 in Vienna, and you will find several of the presenters from the conference also in this book.

From these endeavors, we eventually turned to making an assortment of these papers available to a larger audience, and thus out of these two events developed, over a considerable period of time, two books. Both of them are published with Routledge, one with the Routledge JAWS series, as it is more closely related to the EAJS conference. For this we solely chose scholars working qualitatively and looking through the anthropological lens. For the interdisciplinary perspective between anthropologists and sociologists, between qualitative and quantitative approaches, we chose the Nissan Institute/Routledge Japanese Studies Series.

Over the course of now three years discussing happiness and unhappiness between us, browsing through endless amounts of data and journal articles of different disciplines, as well as writing our own analyses of happiness and well-being in Japan, we sometimes feel that we are not even one inch closer to fully comprehending the topic. Once you feel you have grasped it, it feels like it has slipped through your fingers once again, something very frustrating and certainly not aiding us in achieving happiness through working on this project. Yet the happy moments outweigh the hard and difficult times of weekends spent in the office on the book rather than with our families, friends, and dog enjoying Vienna city life or its beautiful surrounding nature. Memories of the happy days even compensate for the outright unhappy moments we had when spending a tropical summer holiday and visits to the Japanese countryside huddled over our laptops, engrossed with editorial work for this book.

Funding for the conference came from a number of institutions, including the German Institute for Japanese Studies Tokyo (DIJ), the Japan Foundation, the University of Vienna, the Austrian Association of Japanese Studies (AAJ), the City of Vienna, and the Japanese Embassy in Austria and its then ambassador Taketoshi Makoto. Huge thanks also go to the former director of the DIJ, Florian Coulmas. He had been the driving force behind the happiness focus in the first place. Thanks also for the language-editing work by Ada Brant who helped clean a number of chapters by our non-native authors, and many thanks to Sebastian Polak-Rottmann for compiling the index.

In addition to the participants and audience at the workshop, we extend our thanks to our staff, in particular Angela Kramer and Philipp Unterköfler, our three interns Dijana, Lukas, and Regina, as well as the many graduate and undergraduate students who all diligently helped with the conference and proudly wore the conference t-shirts, with a slogan by Wolfram, featured at the beginning of this preface, and calligraphy by Junko Baba, Vienna-based artist.

The lovely atmosphere of our workplaces, the wonderful colleagues we have and have had, both in Vienna and Tokyo: We owe thanks to them as well. By now, for the time being, we share the same workplace, which has certainly made the collaborative effort for this book a whole lot easier. We hope that reading this edited book will increase your level of happiness (to the degree that an academic publication is ever capable of).

Kailua and Vienna, August 2016
Barbara Holthus and Wolfram Manzenreiter

SERIES EDITORS' PREFACE

This volume is the 100th in the Nissan Institute/Routledge Japanese Studies series, the first volume of which, Peter Dale's *The Myth of Japanese Uniqueness*, was published in 1986, exactly thirty years ago. The aim of the series has been to show the depth and variety of Japanese institutions, practices and ideas from a wide variety of social science and humanities perspectives. Much, of course, has changed in Japan over the past thirty years of the series. In many ways, the books in the series now can now be seen as providing a detailed commentary of that change. In the late 1980s, when the series was established, it was taken for granted that Japan would be the most powerful economy in the world by the end of that century, only for the economic 'bubble', as we came to see it, to burst and for the country to enter what subsequently became known as 'the lost two decades'. If Japan in the 1980s was seen as the country to which others looked for models of social reform, by the 2010s it has almost slipped into global obscurity. But how much has Japan really changed and what has been the impact of that change on the Japanese individual?

Happiness in Japan, edited by Barbara Holthus (a sociologist) and Wolfram Manzenreiter (a social anthropologist), encapsulates all the themes and approaches of the Nissan Institute/Routledge Japanese Studies series and provides us with an excellent sense of the subjective and objective experience of life in Japan today and also how it has changed over the past three decades. It combines qualitative and quantitative methodological approaches from (mainly) anthropologists and sociologists and examines the objective and subjective nature of happiness throughout the life course in Japan, from the experience of three-year-old preschoolers to those at the very end of their life. At all stages of this life course, these experiences are much more complex than the reader might expect.

As the editors of this volume point out, the concept of happiness is surprisingly difficult to pin down. In order to guide the structure of the chapters in this volume, therefore, each of the authors were asked to relate their research to a model proposed by Gordon Mathews and Carolina Izquierdo that relates the physical, interpersonal and existential dimensions of happiness to the material and immaterial forces of local and global institutions, what they call the 'structural dimension'. In doing so, Holthus and Manzenreiter say that they are pursuing three key objectives: to provide insight into what makes life worth living for different groups within Japan; to further an understanding of how cultural institutions, social relations, the economy and policy impact on both objective and subjective conditions of well-being; and to incorporate the example of Japan in the emerging debate on happiness in social science more globally.

As the chapters of this volume show, the 'happiness' of people in Japan is clearly closely related to many variables at both the macro and the micro level. The changing demography, economy and political situation all impact on the general sense of well-being at the same time as personal family, job and other circumstances affect the experience of individuals. Key themes which appear throughout the chapters which follow are the impact of key sociological variables such as class, gender, generation, region and educational background. It is also interesting to compare the rather low levels of self-reported happiness among the Japanese population as a whole with the sometimes rather higher levels of other populations which would appear, on objective levels, to have rather less, at least in material terms, to be happy about. Happiness, like poverty, is both an absolute and a relative concept.

The complex range of methods, examples, sources and approaches, as well as the clearly delineated theoretical context which holds all of the chapters together, renders this volume the most authoritative account of current state of happiness in Japan. We are very proud that it should be the 100th volume in what we believe is the largest series in the world on contemporary Japanese society.

Roger Goodman and Arthur Stockwin
Oxford, 2017

INTRODUCTION

Making sense of happiness in "unhappy Japan"

Barbara Holthus and Wolfram Manzenreiter

The happiness boom in public and academic discourses and its "white spots"

What makes people happy? What makes Japanese happy? How and why do perceptions of happiness change across the life cycle? How happy or unhappy is Japan as a society? These are just some of the fundamental questions that moved us to embark on this project of researching happiness in Japan. As we finalize this book in 2016, we cannot help but wonder about the amazing wealth and comfort of the industrialized world, despite political instabilities, poverty, terrorist attacks and wars going on in many areas of this world, large-scale migration within and between continents, and numerous natural and man-made technological disasters in Japan and elsewhere.

At the same time, seemingly in unison with a growing neoliberal ideology and technologies of self-governance, we see what we call a "happiness boom." Learning to be happy, as well as knowing how happy one is compared to others, is the new "in." The same goes for the marketing of almost any and all products: happiness sells. The marketability of happiness and of products promising happiness through consumption is not new but it certainly has been increasing over the last ten years. This boom cannot only be found to appeal to consumer industries and to be marketed to individuals. Governments in many countries are equally interested in learning about the well-being of their citizens and how their nations fare in comparison to others. The fact that Bhutan started the trend back in the 1970s with their policy of "Gross National Happiness" or GNH is well documented. GNH is intended to complement the solely materialistic focus of governments working to improve the GDP, the gross domestic product.

The happiness boom in public discourses

In the last five to ten years, the U.S., the U.K., Japan, and other countries have caught on to this trend by gathering information on the state of happiness of their citizens through large-scale surveys or an accumulation of macro-level data (see United Nations 2012). In the United States, for example, where the constitution explicitly mentions the pursuit of happiness as a fundamental right, the Gallup poll system launched a happiness survey collecting data on a national scale in 2008 (Gallup Healthways 2016). In the year 2011, the U.K. embarked on measuring national well-being (Office of National Statistics 2016). Nine months after the devastating triple disaster of Northeastern Japan, possibly better known internationally as the Fukushima catastrophe, the Cabinet Office published the report of the Commission on Measuring Well-being in Japan (Naikaku-fu 2011). Yet on the local level in Japan, interest in measuring happiness had started already in 2005, with the Gross Arakawa Happiness project, which was inspired by Bhutan's GNH concept (Kawahara 2013). The prefecture of Kumamoto in southwest Japan started indexing the Aggregated Kumamoto Happiness of its population on an annual basis in 2012. Both the governor of Kumamoto and the mayor of the Tokyo district of Arakawa have joined the so-called "happiness league" (shiawase rīgu), a conglomeration of more than 50 local politicians who aim to improve the well-being of the inhabitants of their districts (Hiroi 2015).

Joining this expanding interest on happiness and well-being were also the UN and OECD, elevating the interest to a more global level. The UN published its first *World Happiness Report* in 2012, followed by yearly updates. In the fourth *World Happiness Report* of 2016, 156 countries are surveyed for the "state of global happiness" (Helliwell, Layard and Sachs 2016). A further indicator of the popularity of happiness is the implementation of the International Day of Happiness, which the United Nations inaugurated as recently as 2013 and celebrates on March 20.

> The General Assembly of the United Nations in its resolution 66/281 of 12 July 2012 proclaimed 20 March the International Day of Happiness recognizing the relevance of happiness and well-being as universal goals and aspirations in the lives of human beings around the world and the importance of their recognition in public policy objectives.
> (United Nations 2013)

The hit song "Happy" by Pharrell Williams was used to help promote the second International Day of Happiness, a good example of how popular culture supports the spread of knowledge and information and raises interest for the general public. The OECD equally participated in the happiness trend and launched the "Better Life Index" in 2011 (OECD 2016), publishing regular reports on separate well-being measures, both in comparative perspective and on country-specific data.

We regularly see cities with the best quality of life receive broad media attention. We happen to be fortunate enough to live in Vienna, regularly ranked as "top spot for overall quality of living" in Mercer's annual study of foreign workers' overseas lifestyles (Neild 2016). In the 2016 ranking, four Japanese cities appear in the top 100 (Tokyo at 44, Kobe 46, Yokohama 49, and Osaka 58). Commercial and governmental surveys, as well as those from large international organizations like the UN and OECD, often use huge, usually macro-level indicators that still however tell us little about the well-being of individuals in each of the surveyed countries.

The ranking of cities, regions, countries, and individuals by their numerous indicators is the goal of many of these surveys. "Who is happier than everyone else?" seems to be the driving force behind these many different attempts of getting closer to our understanding of global, national, or regional happiness or well-being. However, culture specifics seem to be wiped clean and are not really considered in many of these multi-country comparisons.

The academic boom of happiness

Not all academic fields have seen an equal shift toward happiness research. Happiness was the focus of philosophical ponderings before economics and psychology (now the leaders in happiness research) began this work. Sociology and anthropology are even more recent newcomers. Anthropology's ambiguous relationship with happiness has been laid out in detail in Manzenreiter & Holthus (2017). Ruut Veenhoven paints the reasons for sociology's failure to fully embark on happiness research in his 2014 treatise. As the first and leading figure in the sociology of happiness, Veenhoven is the creator of the *World Database of Happiness*, an extremely ambitious project tying together survey data and references on the study of happiness from around the world.

Veenhoven (2014) points out that introductory sociology textbooks do not even list the word "happiness" in their glossaries, and happiness is not a topic often found in mainstream sociology journals, but rather is an altogether "neglected subject for sociology" (Veenhoven 2014: 554). He tries to explain this with sociology's "preoccupation with misery" (Veenhoven 2014: 545; for the same argument in anthropology see Thin 2005) and the fact that many scholars are more committed to the study of objective rather than subjective measures of well-being.

In respect to Japan, we see similar shortcomings of the burgeoning literature on happiness. Most research has been produced in the fields of economics and psychology and is of a quantitative nature, often lacking a clear understanding of how happiness is enhanced or restrained by social systems and institutions. We argue that sociology and anthropology are uniquely positioned to address these issues and simultaneously place structure and agency at the center of their inquiries.

Two academic journals specifically focus on happiness research; both are more or less interdisciplinary and feature quantitative research: *Social Indicators Research,*

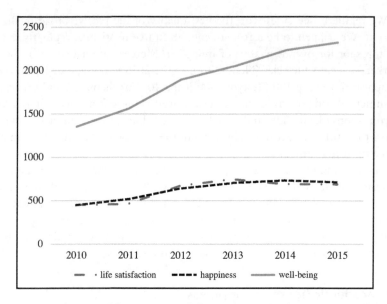

FIGURE I.1 Academic publications on "life satisfaction," "happiness," and "well-being"

Source: Number of publications listed in the University of Vienna online library catalogue (for life satisfaction, well-being, and happiness). Search was limited to scholarly articles with any of the search terms in the title.

founded in 1974, and the *Journal of Happiness Studies,* founded in 2000. Taking a look at the academic publishing market on happiness for the most recent years, we searched two databases: the Vienna University library holdings and the SocIndex database (Social Science Citation Index) for publications with happiness and happiness-related terminology in the title: namely "life satisfaction" and "well-being." "Quality of life" is another highly related term, though not featured in Figure I.1. These related terms and their differences are addressed later in this introduction.

The term "happiness" is less common in academic titles than we predicted; "well-being" is by far more widely used in academic publications. "Happiness" is more catchy and thus more popular within public and (most importantly) commercial discourse. Additionally, we have noticed that despite different connotations and meanings, as briefly explained below, a single paper may use two or even all three terms interchangeably (for more on the fuzziness of terms, see the introduction to Manzenreiter and Holthus 2017). So, even though academic and public discourse might partially use different terminology, we also see an increase in academic output in the areas of "happiness research."

How happy is Japan in comparison?

The question is, now, how Japan fares in all of these multi-country comparisons of happiness, life satisfaction, and well-being. How happy is Japan in comparison? In Adrian White's "World Map of Happiness," a meta-data construct from numerous survey data sources, Japan ranks 90th out of 178 countries (2016). In the United Nations' Human Development Index (HDI) on the other hand, which only looks at three indicators—life expectancy, education, and per capita income—Japan ranks 26th out of 188 countries (UNDP 2015) and thus fares quite well. In the OECD Better Life data from 2016, Japan's life satisfaction score (on a scale from 0 as lowest to 10 as highest) averages at 5.9, which lies below the OECD 20 country average of 6.5 (OECD Stat 2016). According to the *World Happiness Report*, Japan ranks 53rd out of 157 countries for the years 2013–2015. Japan's happiness ranking has greatly decreased between 2005 and the most recent surveys (Helliwell, Layard and Sachs 2016).

The "white spots" and this volume

What the numbers of just some of these multinational datasets reveal is that Japan as a highly industrialized country is not faring as well as could be expected. Culture-specific patterns should be taken into consideration (see Uchida & Ogihara 2012) when evaluating the meaning, importance, and understanding of happiness per se, as well as the different structural and socio-economic circumstances of Japan and other countries in large-scale comparisons. These surveys tend to homogenize the citizens of these countries, glossing over any diversity. Because the results of a study of middle-class urban salaried workers and housewives were generalized to all Japanese people, sociological research on Japan has long been riddled with problems of homogenization. Paying attention to plurality and diversity is not simply a strategy to counter prevalent views of Japan as a homogeneous entity. It is also a significant correction of the holistic approach to quantitative cross-cultural comparisons.

Now, for the first time, these fundamental questions are jointly addressed by anthropologists and sociologists, among them today's leading scholars on Japan. This book is unique in that it integrates the varying strengths of quantitative and qualitative research methodologies of both disciplines to understand the multidimensionality of happiness in Japan. In addition, throughout the chapters, the life course approach is employed to integrate the interdisciplinary analysis of specific age groups. The book discusses the shifting notions of happiness during people's lives from birth to death, analyzing the experiences of varying age groups and their cohort-specific life trajectories and life events. To provide theoretical coherence among the chapters, all contributions attend to the same compound model of happiness that relates its physical, interpersonal, existential dimensions to the material and immaterial forces of local and global institutions: the structural dimension (Mathews & Izquierdo 2009). In particular, the book pursues three objectives: to enhance insight into what makes life worth living for different age groups within specific social milieus; to aid in scholarly understanding of how cultural institutions, social relations, the economy, and policy making impact upon objective conditions of well-being and the subjective perceptions of their significance; and finally to contribute to the emerging debate on happiness among social scientists globally by using Japan as a prominent case study.

Outline of the introduction

This introduction subsequently touches upon the following elements: an outline of the cultural contexts of happiness, discussed in regards to the universality and particularity of the concept. We then briefly outline life course theories and research in general and as they pertain to the study of happiness. The multidimensionality of happiness, drafted by Mathews and Izquierdo (2009), is a cornerstone of all chapters and is explained in detail. As happiness is not timeless, but rather has to be understood and reflected against the social, structural, demographic, and economic situation, we provide some condensed background information about Japan's most pertinent social, structural, demographic, and economic changes of the 21st century. Finally, this introduction provides a short outline of the main arguments of each of the 13 chapters of this volume.

Universality and particularities of happiness

As mentioned above, happiness research faces fundamental problems, such as the precise definition of happiness in contrast to or in relation with similar key terms of the academic debate, including life satisfaction, well-being and quality of life. Quality of life is often associated with the objective factors needed to stabilize or enhance individual life chances. By contrast, life satisfaction, subjective well-being and happiness are based on individuals' subjective judgment and self-assessment. Among these three concepts, life satisfaction is regarded as the one that is most closely linked with cognition, and happiness as the one that is seen as an affect or emotion. The conceptualization of well-being, which sometimes includes an emotional dimension, usually exceeds the hedonist dimension of positive emotions and includes activities and realms of life that may not be purely pleasurable but give meaning to one's life.

In this volume, we do not sharply discriminate between happiness and subjective well-being. This does not mean that we are unaware of the sometimes not-so-subtle differences between happiness as ephemeral affect or as lasting mood or among the emotional and cognitive processes contributing to happiness. However, few of the studies in this volume are based on research that was primarily or exclusively interested in the question of happiness. We deliberately use the terminology interchangeably whenever referring to what this volume is primarily interested in: the overall positive appreciation of life results and prospects.

Another open issue is the debate on happiness as a phenomenon of universal or specific dimension. As a preconscious and ephemeral affect, happiness is very likely part of the human condition. Experimental studies have demonstrated the panhuman capabilities of identifying facial expressions of happiness across ethnic, gender, or age groups. We also have evidence of happiness as an anthropogenic constant in regard to the crucial role of negative and positive emotions for patterning human behavior. People's usual ability to reflectively identify their mood and rate their state of subjective well-being or dissatisfaction with life in general supports the assumption that the interplay between mood and cognition fulfills some important function in human behavior. Similar to other positive emotions, happiness, if experienced frequently enough, provides capacities to cope with adversities, relate to others, and contribute to the production of common goods in communal life and civil society (Scoffham and Barnes 2011: 540). In that regard, we have ample reason to think of happiness as a universally shared element of the human condition.

However, happiness, as social scientists try to grasp and measure it, is by nature fundamentally different from the immediate experience of one's emotional state. Happiness surveys usually aim at capturing the quantified assessment of respondents' overall satisfaction with life. Differences in outcome are explained by control variables and the variation of aggregated input factors. As independent variables, the surveys feature items considered essential for basic needs gratification and the realization of material or immaterial wants in response to external stimulants. Some studies such as the Human Developmental Index or the Happiness Ranking of Japan's 47 prefectures (Sakamoto 2011) rely solely on social indicators as objective factors that identify the existence of key resources and their scope for the quality of life at the societal level. Others like the National Survey on Lifestyle Preferences (*Kokumin seikatsu senkōdo chōsa*) by the Cabinet Office (Naikaku-fu 2010) or the Bank of Japan Survey on the General Public's Views and Behavior (*Seikatsu ishiki ni kan suru ankēto chōsa*; BoJ 2016) put their focus on the subjective evaluation of the importance that key resources such as income level and employment have for the respondent, and quite a few use a combination of social indicator measures and self-reporting (e.g. Ōtake, Shiraishi and Tsutsui 2010). A typical example of a mixed approach is the OECD Better Life Initiative. To grade national levels of happiness, this survey asks for housing, income, jobs, social relatedness, education, environment, civic engagement, health, life satisfaction, safety, and work-life balance. Other national and international studies use a similar mixed array of determinants, which arguably address key issues shared across nations of different developmental levels and cultural traditions. Yet their relative weight differs considerably between nations and cultures, indicating that happiness may mean different things to different people at different times.

According to the authors of the *World Happiness Report*, questions that address happiness in the sense of life satisfaction yield responses that are quite different from answers to questions addressing happiness as emotion (Helliwell, Layard and Sachs 2013: 3). As national differences of emotional evaluation ("how happy are you right now?") are smaller than differences in life evaluation ("how satisfied are you overall with your life?"), some scholars argue that first, human beings are better qualified to accurately evaluate domain-specific well-being than overall happiness (e.g. Helliwell et al. 2010), and second, that cultural differences are negligible for the sociological analysis of happiness (Veenhoven 2012). Countering the assumption that happiness is a cultural construct, Veenhoven points out that self-reported happiness "is systematically higher in nations that provide a decent material standard of living, freedom, equality, solidarity and justice"

(Veenhoven 2012: 347). Layard, after comparing populations of individualistic and collectivist orientations, similarly concludes from the data that "happiness seems equally familiar in all cultures" (2003: 19).

Yet there is ample reason to take these conclusions with a grain of salt. First of all, research has provided evidence that cultural scripts play an active role in shaping the regulation and experience of emotions. Research on happiness has "consistently shown that individuals sharing Eastern cultural heritage report less frequent and intense positive affect and lower levels of life satisfaction than those sharing a Western cultural heritage" (Wirtz et al. 2009: 1168). Many studies in happiness refer to such a categorical differentiation of Western and Eastern cultures, which are associated with different degrees of individualization and autonomy of the self. Within this framework, happiness appears to be of an unquestionable positive value only in the West, if at all, where the roots of happiness are seen in the modern self's capacity and responsibility for self-fulfillment (Jugureanu, Hughes and Hughes 2014: 4; Joshanloo et al. 2015: 1188). Cultures that valorize individuals' interdependence over independence may disregard the gratification of personal desires and the amplification of individual achievement; instead they seek beauty in social relations, the fulfillment of role obligation, and prosperity of the collective (Lu and Gilmour 2004: 276). In its extreme form, happiness can be seen as a potential source of disruption and detrimental for social harmony. For that reason, people may even be adverse to happiness (Wirtz et al. 2009: 1169; Joshanloo and Weijers 2014: 712). The "fear of happiness" seems to be more strongly endorsed in non-Western cultures, even though similar views are not completely unknown to Western cultures (Joshanloo and Weijers 2014: 728). It results in culturally specific display rules of emotions and probably also in experience rules due to the difference in cultural folk theories people command over to construct and reconsider their life experiences (Uchida and Kitayama 2009). The Japanese "habit of hesitation" toward happiness (Minami 1971: 34), for example, may be traced back to the ancient Yin–Yang philosophy, which takes a cosmological view that everything from the cosmos to human life is a never-ending, cyclic process of change, between good and bad, happiness and misery, well-being and ill-being.

Also, and closely related to the first point, most studies do not make explicit that they assess happiness as it is understood in advanced industrialized societies of the West (Coulmas 2009: 6). Since research on happiness originated in these countries, the countries' underlying heuristics were taken for granted and widely applied in cross-cultural comparisons and cultural settings. But there are substantial regional differences in the key variables used to explain international differences in happiness scores, with correspondingly large effects on average happiness (Oishi 2010). The items measured in cross-cultural contexts may not even refer to the same experiential dimension. For example, institutions such as marriage, work, and education are likely to have acquired specific forms, functions, and meanings in response to cultural context. Most scholars will agree that education is crucial for overall well-being, as it satisfies the basic need of learning and provides the elementary social skills, advanced qualifications, and knowledge needed for social upward mobility. Hence, access to general education is likely to raise well-being in society, and widespread access to higher education further increases societal happiness. However, such an equation ignores that even within the same national education system there is a considerable variation of school types, teaching styles, and pedagogic philosophies. A university degree has different weight depending on the type of university or the subject of study. As an educational status marker, it also fails to reflect whether a particular educational career has been more or less likely to instill a sense of autonomy, creativity, and other skills needed for self-realization. When comparing educational systems across borders, it is even more critical to take into account the very practical value of alumni networks and the relationship between educational credentials, labor market access, and status positions. A one-dimensional measure such as "highest achieved educational grade" therefore seems inadequate for grasping the significance of education for happiness.

Happiness surveys hence have their methodological biases and limitations. As they rely on self-reporting of subjective evaluations of general moods, they are based on questionable assumptions, such as the inherently contingent range of emotions and satisfaction (oscillating between two possible extremes of a minimum and maximum), the possibility of differentiating clearly and consistently between subtle numerical gradients, and the qualitative congruency of quantified subjective responses. In our view, the dominant quantitative approach used in psychology and happiness economics for cross-cultural comparison is characterized by a lack of awareness to marked differences in the culturally shared understanding of happiness and its overall moral appreciation. Cultural psychologists have for some time been aware of the methodological flaws deriving from an artificially flattened and essentially wrong understanding of happiness as culturally universal (e.g. Marcus and Kitayama 1998; Oishi et al. 2013; Uchida, Ogihara and Fukushima 2015). In their recent book *Cultures of Well-Being* (White and Blackmore 2016), the editors argue that research methods also have their own cultures in that they produce a generalized view of the world. The rules of the game, as they call it, command over specific key terms, reference points, criteria for truth and core routines, rituals and practices that ultimately do not map the world but rather draw a map of the world they are interested in. The mixed method approach this volume contains is an attempt to benefit from the strengths of qualitative and quantitative perspectives for a comprehensive examination of happiness, as requested by Hommerich and Klien (2012: 295). Yet it is inevitable that the single studies of our volume do not only produce complementary stories but also results that confirm or contrast each other.

Tackling the supposed U-shape of well-being over the life course

As explained above, this book applies a life cycle perspective for the analysis of happiness and well-being in Japan. It is our fundamental assumption that levels of happiness and its indicators and contributing elements change over the course of a person's life. A so-called "tripartite life course model" (Hagestad and Dykstra 2016: 137, based on Kohli 1986 and Cain 1964) identifies three phases: the first prepares the individual through schooling, while in the second the individual is involved with work and family. The third and last phase of life is the post-work/retirement period. Accordingly, the three main subsections of this book are Childhood and Youth, Adulthood, and Old Age.

The fundamental elements in life course research

The study of the life course is a growing, interdisciplinary field, with sociology, epidemiology, and psychology as its main disciplines (Shanahan, Mortimer and Johnson 2016b: 1–2). Two comprehensive handbooks, one published as recently as 2016, pay tribute to the developing academic focus on the life course (Mortimer and Shanahan 2003; Shanahan, Mortimer and Johnson 2016a). What the life course denotes is both a succession of life events an individual passes through and several social roles an individual holds over his or her lifetime at a certain historical period of time, influenced by social structures, institutions, and their respective stakeholders (Brynner 2016: 50). "Traditionally, the concept of the life course refers to the age-graded roles that structure (or create patterns in) biography" (Shanahan, Mortimer and Johnson 2016b: 3).

A look at the structure of the handbook by Mortimer and Shanahan (2003) already points to the main elements in life course research, as there are: "institutional structuring of life course trajectories," "transitions," "turning points," and "agency." Institutions that structure the life course include childcare institutions, educational institutions, the workplace, and family, but also the law and government, to name just a fundamental few. Transitions and turning points hint at the not necessarily linear development of life courses. Certain rites of passages, such as graduation, marriage, and divorce can serve as transitions from one life stage to another or can be seen as turning points. Extraordinary experiences such as disasters can serve as turning points within the life cycle as well.

With the focus in life course research on individual lives within their structural contexts and considering social change, time is a crucial element in life course research. Time can be distinguished into three elements: (1) the individual's birth year, meaning one's chronological age, (2) cohort membership as "historical markers of social change" (Elder and George 2016: 59), and (3) historical time, as large-scale social, political, technological, and economic changes most certainly have an influence on the existence and life of the individual. Yet the multicollinearity among age, time, and cohort make the analysis very difficult (Von Landeghem 2012).

The other crucial element in life course research is that of agency, signified by the choice and action of individuals. Structures surrounding the individual are seen to restrict his or her choices and actions throughout his or her life. Dannefer et al. (2016: 91–92) however problematize the oftentimes uncritical usage of counterposing "agency" with "structure," a fundamental concept in sociology. They write:

What this means is that the role of social structure is not merely to constrain agency, thereby defining and limiting the options among which an otherwise "free" actor may choose. Rather, what social structure does is to shape and define the individual's consciousness, within which intentions and purposes are externalized into agentic action. This is, of course what occurs continuously beginning in very early life and continuing on through the life course, through the learning of language and culture of one's habitus. (93)

A fuzzy concept such as that of agency, which cannot be evaluated outside of the structures around it, is difficult to operationalize for quantitative studies. Hitlin and Kwon (2016: 431) argue for concrete empirical measurements of competences of self-efficacy, personal control, and future orientations as expressions of agency. The discussion of our understanding of agency versus structure has not been put to rest.

Further important elements in life course research are the focus on the socially constructed character of age and life (Mortimer and Moen 2016: 111) and the degree to which life course is gendered (Moen 2016). The methodologies applied by life course scholars are for the most part cohort analysis, event history analysis, structural equation modeling, panel data analysis, latent structures, or life story narratives. The majority of life course research is quantitative, and there is a fundamental need for longitudinal data.

Our volume, therefore, can only be considered an "approximation" of a life course study of diverse subgroups of Japanese. Due to the lack of available datasets and researchers, we substituted the lack of longitudinal data with inferences about generational changes made in all papers, however not with direct longitudinal data. Each paper refers to the larger social changes that have influenced the choices and decision-making processes of the individuals they studied. Only one of our 13 authors, Gordon Mathews, has unique, longitudinal, qualitative data that qualifies to be called adequate life course analysis data. Mathews was able to re-interview Japanese men and women after a 20-year interval. As all other papers only study contemporary age cohorts, strictly speaking this book concerns itself only with age-related stages of well-being. During each stage of life, a person is shaped by the institutions he or she interacts with most, from schools to family, the labor market, and institutions (medical and governmental) regulating the end of life. Lives are studied in the context of social networks, of cohorts, families, and work colleagues.

Relationship of age and happiness

Research on the importance of age for happiness, or in other words the relationship between the life cycle and well-being has been the subject of heated debate for quite some time. Depending on the type of analysis, variables used, and statistical methods applied, researchers have contradicting results, ranging from a so-called U-shaped effect of age on happiness, to the opposite, the inverted curve. The U-shaped effect of age on happiness means that at the first and last stages of one's life, satisfaction with life or employment (Clark, Oswald and Warr 1996) is highest, whereas in the middle of one's life, satisfaction is lowest. Fischer's (2009) study of 30 OECD countries has even identified a "hyperbolic age-happiness relationship" for about a third of the countries, meaning that satisfaction is high in childhood and decreases throughout the middle of the life cycle only to increase again with a peak in the early 80s, with a subsequent decline again thereafter. Fischer identifies Japan as one of the OECD countries with this kind of relationship.

Most researchers arguing for a U-shaped effect of age on happiness believe this to be the standard in international scholarship (Von Landeghem 2012, Tiefenbach and Kohlbacher 2015). Research on the importance of age for people's happiness and well-being has been nicely summarized in the review of happiness indicators by Tiefenbach and Kohlbacher (2015: 337). They point out that although the international literature supports age's U-shaped effect on subjective well-being, Japan-related studies have shown contradictory and inconclusive results, ranging from U-shaped to inverted U-shape to decline in well-being over the life course.

Explanations for the U-shaped relationship between age and happiness or life satisfaction are also diverse. Blanchflower and Oswald (2004; see also Frey and Stutzer 2002, Von Landeghem 2012) identify evolving aspirations as the contributing factor. When aspirations are high but largely unmet, namely in the midst of life, they lower satisfaction. When one gives up or lowers one's aspirations in later life, there is a positive effect on well-being. Schwandt (2015), using the related term "expectations," attributes the U-shape relationship to unmet expectations. Analyzing SOEP data, Schwandt looks at the relationship between current and expected life satisfaction and finds that people make systematic mistakes in predicting how satisfied they will be in five years: Young people overestimate their future life satisfaction; the elderly underestimate. This finding is said to be stable across time, within cohorts, and across socio-economic groups. Those feeling the regret from unmet expectations experience a further reduction of life satisfaction.

Easterlin (2006) is one of the most prominent advocates of an inverted (bell-shaped) relationship between age and happiness. Using U.S. General Social Survey data, Easterlin looks at four major life domains: family life, financial situation, work, and health. He identifies life cycle happiness as the net outcome of satisfaction in those principal life domains, with satisfaction in each separate domain being the product of both objective conditions and goals or aspirations in that domain. "The finding that life cycle happiness is the net outcome of disparate movements in the four life domains implies [...] there is no 'iron law of happiness'" (Easterlin 2006: 478). What Easterlin however did not sufficiently consider is how cultural differences play into these four life domains and whether these are the four most important life domains for all cultures. Furthermore, it is not clear what level of importance each of these four domains has for one's overall life cycle happiness. Are certain domains more important than others at certain stages in one's life and how does that vary across cultures?

It is our fundamental assumption that levels of happiness and well-being and their indicators change over the course of a person's life. The shortcomings of quantitative studies alone have been pointed out by Clark (2014), by Frijters et al. (2014) in his introduction to the studies on age and life satisfaction, and Layard et al. (2014). Despite using large numbers of variables in their regression analyses, both achieved only quite small predicting values for happiness.

It is our goal to provide further insight into what makes life worth living for different age groups within specific social milieus through a conglomeration of qualitative and quantitative studies on happiness and well-being. This is to aid in scholarly understanding of how cultural institutions, social relations, the economy, and policy making impact on objective conditions of well-being and the subjective perceptions of their significance.

A model of well-being

In this section, we introduce the compound model of well-being that we have used to systematically organize core topics of happiness and that runs like a red thread through this volume. Among the various approaches toward formulating a comprehensive understanding of happiness that have been made so far we selected the model drafted by Mathews and Izquierdo (2009) for the purpose of making the diverging conceptions and experiences of happiness in different settings cross-culturally comparable. While the model resulted from a comparative reflection on the findings of the studies the anthropologists had compiled in an edited volume, we have taken their synthesis as the starting point for the discussion on happiness in contemporary Japan. The strategy of "soft comparison," which they saw based on description and ethnographic investigation, is equally appealing to our objective of understanding the diversity of happiness within Japanese society. Mathews and Izquierdo note that happiness is shaped by social structures and culture, but also by individual agency and past experiences, which fits neatly into our suggestion of using life course theory to generate a less superficial and more appropriate understanding of happiness in Japan.

Mathews and Izquierdo argue that happiness can be schematically divided into four experiential dimensions: the physical (e.g., corporeal sensualities, health, physical abilities), the interpersonal (e.g., family relations, social networks, organizational contexts), the existential (i.e., ideas and value systems that give people a sense of the meanings of their life), and the structural (an overarching dimension of cultural institutions at the national level and global forces giving shape and structure to the conception, perception, and experience of happiness in the three previously mentioned dimensions). Each and any of these four dimensions, as Mathews and Izquierdo convincingly argue, is retracted by the prism of culture, which does not determine, but to some degree at least gives shape to their dominant meaning and appreciation among members of a given society. We will shortly demonstrate the general applicability of the model by a step-by-step explanation of the four dimensions.

The physical dimension takes into account that human beings experience the world through their body and with their bodily senses. The warmth of sunrays felt on the skin, the touch of a hand, the delicateness of silk as a comforting combination of smooth and cool, the appealing scent in the entrance to a temple hall, the delicious taste of fresh food, or the skillful mastering of drilled routines in sport contests are all tied to the sensuality of the experiencing body. To varying degrees, they contribute to an immediate and likely short-term sense of well-being, in marked contrast to the more permanent quality of health and the concurring capabilities of living without pain and physical constraints. The fact that all cultures have developed ways of body decoration (including skin art, fashion, trimming, or plastic surgery) or devised certain style scripts for presenting the bodily self for specific occasions clearly shows that the subjective appreciation of the body in self-reflection and through the eyes of society is always shaped and structured by cultural forces.

Human beings are fundamentally interdependent on each other, which is at the backbone of the interpersonal dimension. There is good reason to assume that happiness is in many instances the result of collective action, as the (un)happiness of (at least significant) others cannot be seen as unconnected to an individual's sense of subjective well-being. In that regard, families are culturally universal of a particular social formation, which among other objectives is geared toward guaranteeing the primate of the well-being of its members. Of course, this is more of an ideal and families, as Tolstoi famously remarked in the opening lines of *Anna Karenina*, are as much a source of unhappiness. Furthermore, there are many variations of family types in different cultures and within modern societies, and the amount of social groups and associations in complex societies providing people with additional and alternative patterns in which they can develop and sustain meaningful relationships with dearly valued others, is sheer unlimited. Sociologists as well as cultural anthropologists have a natural propensity for putting particular emphasis on the sociality of their study objects. From their analytical angle, it is fully conceivable that sharing, relating, and experiencing acceptance and gaining recognition by significant others are all of fundamental importance for the happiness of human beings as social animals.

The existential dimension refers to another seemingly universal feature to be found in the common capacity of reflecting on ethical and moral questions that make individuals' lives meaningful and give direction to human behavior. Religion, ideologies, aesthetics, and traditional values can be seen as different sources for a moral compass or guidebook that effectively enables the meaningful interaction between members of the same community. Happiness may be enhanced or diminished by such principles, depending on the relative significance of autonomy and freedom that we think are tantamount for the independent capability to act on one's will, or shortly, agency. These then may be potentially conflicting value systems. But it is an open question whether agency comes closer to being an inert need or just an additional element within the cognitive belief structure resulting from past experiences and socially shared perceptions. While the physical dimension is at least partially leaning toward the hedonist nature of happiness, the existential is likely to coming closer to its eudaimonic interpretation.

These three dimensions are essentially bound to the experiencing self, which is in everyday life situated within patterns and structures that have a unifying impact on the way in which individuals sensualize, relate, and reflect. Social institutions, national policies and the forces of globalization are providing the structural framework in which the individual is positioned to achieve happiness or aspires to it. Most of the chapters in this volume originated from studies on such principal institutions as schooling, work, or marriage in Japan.

Changing Japan

Japan in the 1980s was looking back on a remarkable ascent from the ashes of the defeat in war to the world's forefront of industrialization and national wealth. Back then, virtually all families had members that vividly remembered the scarcity of the wartime period and the following years of poverty and struggles to overcome hardship. Having gone through the period of reconstruction, industrialization, and a sequential chain of economic growth cycles, each postwar generation was distinctly faring better than the previous. No end of the "Japanese Dream" (a neo-corporatist path of development that benefitted entire birth cohorts) was in sight when Japan reached an unprecedented level of national wealth, economic power, and political aspirations in the mid 1980s. When Japan willingly agreed to back up the ailing American economy by depreciating the dollar against the yen, no one realized that the combined effects of the export-led growth model, excess liquidity in the banks, and financial deregulation would set in motion a spiral that propelled stock and real estate prices to spectacular heights, only to collapse into a giant crash of the bubble economy in 1990. Since then the country has gone through a lasting crisis of its financial system with severe repercussions on national fiscal policy, industrial productivity, the labor market, and household incomes. With the tightening of money supply, many corporations searched for relief from debts by cutting personnel expenses and shifting their manufacturing plants overseas. Stagnating wages had a suppressing effect on prices and household consumption. Japanese and international media alike have dubbed the following years of economic stagnation the "lost decades" for the apparently inapt attempts of powerless governments to find a suitable solution against the forces of deflation and a way out of the crisis.

In marked contrast to previous cohorts, generations that graduated from school since then could no longer build their futures on the patterned premises of a gendered life path model. Access to the labor market became tighter when industries shifted their production plants to offshore locations and new corporate governance models enforced a radical change of the employment system. Irregular and precarious employment patterns rapidly increased in response to capital's demand for flexible, cheap labor. A university degree no longer guaranteed immediate and permanent employment. Unemployment came to be considered a social problem for the first time, as well as the initially juvenile, but over time aging, social group of working poor that struggle hard to make a living from reduced wages. Against the backdrop of the traditional conservative ideal of distribution of labor between the sexes, the widespread loss of employment stability and future prospects diminished the economic appeal of many male Japanese as breadwinner. While more women than ever graduated from university, fewer of their male peers could meet their expectations as marital partners. These developments apparently fueled the demographic crisis of a shrinking population, even though the delay of marriage and the decrease in number of children born per woman to a level beyond reproduction had started much earlier.

In the past five years, Japan lost about one million of its formerly 128 million people. According to projections by the National Institute of Population and Social Security Research (IPSS 2012), the country is expected to shrink by a third within the next five decades. Without drastic interventions, which are unlikely to happen or to yield notable results, the share of the elderly aged 65 and above will rise from its current 25 percent to 40 percent, while the working population will decrease by a fifth in these years. The repercussions of the aging society are already felt across all sectors, including public health due to medical expenses over-proportionally increasing with high aging, social welfare and public pension systems that were structured for a society with more or less universal marriage and childbirth at times of economic prosperity. Japan will become poorer when the financial burden of supporting a growing number of elderly cuts into the disposable income of ever fewer workers and inflates the debt burden of future generations. The country's fiscal debt stands at 250 percent of its GDP, and with the inverted population pyramid it is impossible to envision a scenario of a tax base allowing Japan to repay its debt while caring for its elderly. Only a tiny minority of the Japanese (14%; Gao 2014) expects the next generation to be financially better off, which in international comparison represents one of the most pessimistic views about the future. Even though *kibō* (hope) emerged as buzzword in political slogans and media discourse, at that time, its widespread usage much rather epitomized the lack of hope and growing anxieties about the future.

Discussions about social inequality, which so far had hardly been raised even by leftist political parties and sympathizing intellectuals, appeared within the mainstream media at the onset of the 2000s. The widening gap between the poor and the well-off, neatly summarized in another keyword of the time, *kakusa shakai* (gap society), has shaken the widespread belief in the equality of chances and outcomes that was at the backbone of the dominant image of homogeneous middle-class society (Holthus and Iwata-Weickgenannt 2010). However, even though precarity, structures of inequality, and social class reentered public debates, no political force emerged as a critical challenger to the neoliberal politics that continued to characterize governmental politics.

The loss of productivity, market leadership, and balanced distribution of wealth has also been accompanied by the deteriorating competitive edge Japan once held against other Asian exporters, most notably China. From a Japanese perspective, seeing China rising from a poor and underdeveloped country to the world's second largest economic power had a particularly sour taste. Japan saw its own stagnating economy outpaced by a fast-growing China that took over as the regional economic power in this period. The change of rank order also occurred in the field of international politics where China commanded more influence on a regional and global level. Opinion polls among the Japanese have shown a growing concern about peace and security, as well as widespread mistrust of China. China's geopolitical strategies and the massive build-up of its military forces were seen as a threat to the peace and stability in the region that had long rested on the hegemonic power of the United States. Feelings of safety in Japan were also curbed by North Korea's ballistic missile launches and its nuclear weapon program as well as by Japan's gradual expansion of the international peacekeeping missions of its self-defense forces. Territorial disputes among Japan, South Korea, China, and Russia continuously remind the Japanese of troubling issues that neither historians nor international courts can solve and of the fragility of peace in their region.

Probably nothing is more capable of expressing the nagging sense of anxiety and uncertainty than the triple disaster spurred by the most powerful earthquake ever to hit Japan in March 2011. A magnitude 9.0 earthquake off the shore of northeastern Japan caused a giant tsunami of more than 30 meters in height to flood long stretches of the shoreline and destroy coastal towns and villages, leaving 340,000 without homes and claiming more than 16,000 lives. An earthquake of this magnitude and the giant tsunami convey even to disaster-prepared Japan a major blow and enormous challenge to provide survivors with shelter, food, water, medicine, and fuel. The humanitarian tragedy, however, was further engraved by the nuclear disaster occurring at the Fukushima Daiichi Nuclear Power Plant complex where the tsunami had damaged three reactors. The meltdowns contaminated wide areas and forced hundreds of thousands of local residents to evacuate their homes. Radiation, the threat of serious health damages, and energy saving programs following the immediate shut-down of all remaining nuclear reactors (for examination purposes) affected the lives of many more in a much larger area that included the urban agglomeration of Greater Tokyo and surrounding prefectures. Because of the hesitant way in which TEPCO, the operator of the power plant, and the government released news on the scope of the nuclear disaster, many Japanese came to question the accuracy and veracity of official information and turned to other sources.

The overall impression of hapless crisis management led to the reinstallment of the Liberal Democratic Party in political power. Its overall conservative stance and attempts to mobilize the nation for the revitalization of a "beautiful Japan" propelled a new wave of nationalism that showed its ugly face in street rallies against Korean minorities and hate speeches. The initial wave of civil activism by concerned citizens who started to measure radiation by themselves, collected information on food security, or even openly protested against the government, eventually slowed down. But nonetheless Japan's invisible civil society has gained some momentum. Civil protests, political demonstrations, and social movements have fought against the legislation of the continuing expansion of roles of the military forces, against renewed attempts to rewrite the Constitution, and against the infamous Public Information Disclosure Law, seen by many as blunt censorship of critical voices, despite evidence of the waning interest in politics in general in Japan.

These short deliberations on changing Japan have shown how political and economic problems have come to exert impact on social institutions and how all of these together depressed the general future outlook of many Japanese. Whereas some institutions have undergone considerable changes, such as the labor market with the increases in precarious employment, other institutions, such as families, are slower to see change and thus clash with these labor market developments. The fact that gender equality in many areas of public and private life remains far from being realized adds to this clash. Institutions and their demands on people are found to significantly influence the levels of well-being, as will be shown in the subsequent chapters.

Outlining the volume

The chapters of this book are organized in three blocks, reflecting the major age-related stages of the life course. Section one is entitled "Childhood and Youth" and features four chapters that analyze the lives of children from age three up to young people in their 20s and 30s. As Eyal Ben-Ari in his chapter rightfully points out, research on the happiness of children, and in particular preschool children, is limited. Research conducted by UNICEF on the well-being of children is one of the laudable exceptions. This quantitative research, attempting to make child well-being internationally comparative among 31 countries, identifies five dimensions of child well-being, namely material well-being, health and safety, education, behaviors and risks, and housing and environment (UNICEF 2013).

Overall, Japan fares comparatively well, occupying rank 6 out of 31 countries. But the results are rather diversified, if looking at the different dimensions, and provide a much more complicated picture. For "material well-being," the child poverty rate is an important indicator. Here Japan fares exceptionally poorly, ranking only 21st out of 31: not only do 14.9 percent of Japanese children up to the age of 17 live below the poverty rate, but the depth of the poverty in which they live is severe. In regards to "health and safety," Japan is 16th; for "housing and environment," 10th; yet for both "education" and "behaviors and risks," Japan ranks highest. This is what UNICEF calls a "mixed performance of Japan," calling the findings "perplexing" (UNICEF 2013: 3). UNICEF itself writes that data on very young children are lacking, not just in Japan, in order to better understand the development of children in their early years. Studies on

Japanese children are also comparatively rare, and studies on child well-being in Japan even more so. So we are very happy to have two contributions on young children and their well-being in this book, one on preschool children and one on elementary school children.

Eyal Ben-Ari has conducted research for many years in Japanese daycare centers. In this chapter he fills a major gap in the literature by looking at how children learn to be happy, how happiness is culturally constructed, and how the institution of daycare centers and the daycare center teachers socialize the children in that regard. Ben-Ari's focus is on how happiness is internalized, a focus on the processual or developmental nature of how happiness is developed. He argues that it is in these early stages of life that happiness is learned to be "adequately" expressed, as well as has implications for the later stages of life. In his detailed anthropological study of free play and group activities in Japanese daycare centers, of the interaction of the children among themselves and with the teachers, Ben-Ari uses the concept of "flow" to describe the children's deep absorption into the all-consuming, enjoyable play experiences. During these flow experiences, happiness is not reflected upon. Yet through *hansei*, an institutionalized and important activity throughout the educational system, emotions are taught to be verbalized. This chapter, which predominantly focuses on the physical dimension of well-being, also points to the meta-skills learned by the children, namely that experiences of happiness first and foremost occur within the group.

Yoko Yamamoto's study focuses on elementary school first graders, by interviewing 100 Osaka students from diverse socio-economic backgrounds through the so-called story-completion method. In her quantitative and qualitative analysis, Yamamoto finds students having mostly very positive feelings toward schooling, yet they verbalize them with a different terminology from that of adults. Children hold complex views on the purpose of learning; most importantly they connote learning with happiness and not learning with unhappiness, because not learning equates to failure and not meeting social expectations. These discourses point to the existential dimension of well-being due to the values and meanings of learning expressed by the first-graders as well as the interpersonal dimension such as social benefits deriving from learning.

The remaining two chapters in this section on "Childhood and Youth" focus on young adults mostly in their 20s and early 30s. Sachiko Horiguchi's chapter concentrates on *hikikomori*, who are generally defined as "youth in isolation," meaning people who have withdrawn from society at some point and symbolize "youth ill-being." Due to a significant media focus on them, Japanese youth are stereotypically seen as unhappy, despite the fact that this particular group of youth withdrawing from society is a minority. In her mixed-method approach, looking at media discourses, ethnographic data from participating observation in support organizations, and her interview data with *hikikomori* and psychiatrists, Horiguchi looks at all four dimensions of well- and ill-being in relation to *hikikomori*. Physical violence, low quality of sleep, lack of exercise and sexual encounters, poor hygiene, and often a reversed day and night schedule from others in society contribute to a heightened sense of physical ill-being. The retreat from interpersonal relations for various reasons is arguably the most commonly known and most identifying element of *hikikomori* and is *the* issue support organizations try to tackle. Existentially, *hikikomori* could be positively understood as a form of resistance against social norms and questioning the meaning of life in contemporary society; however, an extended period of that behavior is not given room, as Japanese society continues its inflexibility of life cycle transitions and normative values of productivity. Instead, *hikikomori* also become a mental health issue with negative feelings of shame, anxieties, and fears.

Carola Hommerich also focuses at the outset of her paper on the social changes that negatively affect young Japanese of the same age group. Growing inequality, unemployment, weakened social bonds, increased social risks and anxieties, high stress levels, low self-esteem, and strong anxieties with regard to finding employment, their current jobs, their financial situations, and their future are said to ail this cohort. Using quantitative data from a 2009 survey and running OLS regressions, Hommerich shows that these factors indeed affect the well-being differently across age groups: for the group of 20-to-34-year-olds, seemingly contradictory findings are (1) that general social trust yielded a significant positive effect on life satisfaction, whereas one's immediate social network in times of crises did not, and (2) that anxieties about the present and future reduce life satisfaction, whereas not having positive expectations toward the future corresponds to higher levels of life satisfaction. This resonates well with the findings by Gordon Mathews, as described below, who finds parents not ambitious about their children's future to fare better and to be happier. So, low expectations for the future lead to elevated levels of happiness for youth as well as for their parents.

Section 2 focuses on the most researched group of Japanese, adults, both in their work and family contexts. The fact that this section features five chapters supports the importance that this segment of the Japanese population has been given in academic study thus far. Research remains quite gender segregated. Three of the chapters focus exclusively on Japanese women, while two focus on Japanese men. The focus on Japanese women lies on middle-class housewives (Goldstein-Gidoni), on single (and mostly employed) mothers (Raymo), and on the comparison between housewives and employed wives (Brinton). The remaining two chapters look at male as well as female academics, in particular at their job satisfaction (Aichinger, Fankhauser and Goodman), and at salarymen (Taga). This is the only paper that consciously tries to link work and family satisfaction.

Ofra Goldstein-Gidoni's anthropological study focuses on privileged, suburban, middle-class housewives in the Kansai area, who were born between 1966 and 1970, a cohort for whom the quest for happiness is still largely embodied in marriage, the male breadwinner and female homemaker gendered separation of work and family, and standardized life courses with strictly fixed life stages. Goldstein-Gidoni argues that the changes we nonetheless see in the idealized housewife image and what the promises of happiness are for housewives are cultural constructions, "scripts," influenced by such powerful stakeholders as the media and the corporate sector. She points to the particularly important role of women's magazine discourses in creating a new tribe of happy and fashionable housewives.

In contrast to the posh lives of housewives, the lives of single women are highly disadvantaged. James Raymo uses the National Survey of Households with Children from 2011 and 2012 that surveyed more than 4000 mothers and oversampled single mothers. Using regression analyses, Raymo shows that the socially and economically disadvantaged circumstances of single women, who still are a small minority among mothers in Japan, have great negative influence on their well-being, indicated through high levels of stress, poor physical and emotional health, depression, and despair. For the case of single mothers, high levels of employment coupled with insufficient income, significantly suppress their well-being, indicated in this study first and foremost through mental and physical health.

Mary Brinton's chapter then focuses on the interpersonal dimension of well-being of Japanese women up to age 50 through the analysis of the marital satisfaction of Japanese housewives in comparison to married, working wives. Running regression analyses with 2000 and 2009 data from the National Survey of Families and Economic Conditions, Brinton distinguishes between older and younger wives, thus pointing to cohort-related social changes. She finds age and in that respect a cohort effect to significantly matter for the correlations between husband's income and the gendered division of household labor with marital satisfaction. Whereas Japanese older housewives, particularly those whose husbands' income is high, are the most satisfied in most instances, only a small segment of younger, full-time employed, university-educated women are equally if not even more satisfied with their marriages. The gendered division of household labor, a stable occurrence throughout all marriages, seems only to shift slightly among those dual-employed full-time working couples, further aiding in the wives' levels of marital satisfaction.

Cohort changes are also the focus of the chapter by Theresa Aichinger, Peter Fankhauser, and Roger Goodman in their aggregate data analysis of employment satisfaction of one particular segment of Japanese society, namely academics. The authors examine three major surveys of job satisfaction, which were undertaken in 1992 and 2007. These surveys are unusual in that they allow, to an extent, for the comparison of both how job satisfaction among Japanese academics, male and female, has changed over time and how it compares with the job satisfaction of academics in other countries. Despite the problems the dataset and the partially contradictory published findings display, the analyses of the three authors show the interplay between the institutional changes of the Japanese higher education system since the early 1990s and the satisfaction they derive from their work life.

The structures surrounding people working in academia have greatly changed, and the authors do a good job in pointing out the most important changes that affect the well-being of academics. Age, respectively the cohort-factor, is one of the most significant indicators for differences in employment well-being, with older academics being significantly more satisfied than their younger colleagues. The same goes for male academics in that they are more satisfied than female. Both variables are highly influenced by the structural, institutional changes over time. Older male academics have had the privilege of more favorable working conditions than women or younger colleagues, who find themselves in working situations that are more precarious. These divides among gender and age are the fundamental explanatory elements between the differences in the physical, interpersonal, and existential dimensions of job satisfaction of academics.

The final chapter in this section by Futoshi Taga solely concentrates on male employees, the so-called salarymen. Salarymen have been equally subjected to the rapid socio-economic changes that Japan experienced since the early 1990s. While this led to changing discourses and related pressures and value changes, work realities however have not significantly changed, other than having become less stable and potentially even more stressful. For his study, Taga interviewed 20 regular employees, born in the 1960s and early 1970s. For this new generation of married salarymen, the definitions of work and family life have broadened and diversified, as Taga convincingly shows. Salarymen are faced with an increasing dilemma of trying to balance work and family life, with the increase in choices having led to the de-standardization and subsequent decline of happiness.

The final section of this volume is entitled "Old Age," covering a broad range of foci. The main life event signifying the transition to old age is that of retirement, either of oneself or of one's spouse. This is an important topic in Gordon Mathews' chapter in his longitudinal interview study of 21 older Japanese, looking at the areas of family and work in regards to their feelings of happiness. He compellingly shows how social and value changes, as well as the (in)flexibility of social and institutional structures, correlate with people's feelings of happiness. He argues that if society were to become more flexible in its demands on individuals, this might create more optimal conditions for happiness. On the other hand, new flexibilities and increased freedom do not automatically mean greater happiness, but can cause an increase in uncertainties and instabilities and suppression of happiness. Mathews examined marital expectations, employment, and retirement as sources of happiness or its lack. He has found that changing marital ideals have left some of the people less than happy in their marriages, that Japanese corporate life has been consistently unfulfilling for many, and that retirement is a source of hope that may or may not actually be fulfilling.

Retirees are also the focus in Satsuki Kawano's chapter on senior volunteers and post-retirement well-being. She studies seniors' post-retirement volunteering experiences and their senses of well-being. The loss of employment status reduces well-being for men in significant ways. Volunteering offers the development of new identities and a renewed sense of well-being, fostered through appreciation from non-family others during volunteer activities. Volunteering benefits the physical, existential, and interpersonal dimensions of well-being of seniors. They volunteer for the Grave-Free Promotion Society, which helps them to create the new freedom to choose mortuary practices, which further contributes to their existential well-being and fulfillment.

The last two chapters of this book concern themselves with the end-of-life stage and processes of death and dying. Celia Spoden has conducted narrative interviews with ten women and men between the ages of 45 and 88. They all have signed Living Wills, for times of serious disease when they are no longer able to make end-of-life decisions themselves. Interviewees see it as unlikely that a state of well-being can be achieved in circumstances of irreversible loss of consciousness and a prolonged process of dying. The Living Will is used to avoid situations of personal non-well-being, restore agency and a sense of well-being to the self as well as to protect the well-being of the social group. This option of a Living Will has only been possible due to changes in the institutional framework of medical decision making so that making decisions about the process of dying could become an individual matter.

Tim Tiefenbach and Florian Kohlbacher in the final chapter of this volume provide a quantitative analysis on fears and worries about *kodokushi*, solitary death, by using data from the 2013 Survey of Quality of Life. Their findings show that within an environment in which media discourses on solitary deaths, particularly afflicting the elderly, increase and become sensationalized, social isolation and feelings of loneliness are the main drivers of worries, especially for the middle aged. A particular correlation can be found in the fact that the less satisfied people are with their neighborhood, the more they worry about dying alone. Contrary to their hypothesis, worries about solitary death decrease in old age. It is particularly the young and the middle aged who experience subjective feelings of loneliness and social isolation, which are then directly linked to feelings of unhappiness.

In closing the book, we point at similarities and dissimilarities emerging from the analysis of happiness across the life course in Japan. Summarizing findings from the single studies, we demonstrate that happiness in a Japanese context is largely to be understood as relational and interdependent on the well-being of others. A Japanese sense of happiness therefore is closely linked to the institutionalized values and norms that regulate social behavior and to conscious reasoning about the purpose of life and living. Highlighting the role of the family as framework for collective experiences, role development and adjustment to change, we argue for a "happy life" course perspective that projects the ideas of interdependent lives, synchronized time, and agency onto the notion of happiness as a socially co-produced state of being.

References

Blanchflower, David. G., and Andrew J. Oswald. 2004. "Well-Being over Time in Britain and the USA." *Journal of Public Economics* 88/7–8:1359–1386.

BoJ/Nippon Ginkō. 2016. "Seikatsu ishiki ni kan suru ankēto chōsa" [Survey on the general public's views and behavior]. http://www.boj.or.jp/research/o_survey/index.htm/. Retrieved July 25, 2016.

Brynner, John. 2016. "Institutionalization of Life Course Studies." pp. 27–58 in *Handbook of the Life Course. Vol II*, edited by M. Shanahan, J. T. Mortimer and M. Kirkpatrick Johnson. Heidelberg and New York: Springer.

Cain, Leonard D. 1964. "Life Course and Social Structure." pp. 272–309 in *Handbook of Modern Sociology*, edited by R.E.L. Faris. Chicago: Rand McNally.

Clark, Andrew E. 2014. "Son of My Father? The Life-Cycle Analysis of Well-Being: Introduction." *Economic Journal* 124/580:F684-687.

Clark, Andrew E., Andrew Oswald and Peter Warr. 1996. "Is Job Satisfaction U-Shaped in Age?" *Journal of Occupational and Organizational Psychology* 69:57–81.

Comparing Japan, Report Card 11, UNICEF Office of Research, Florence. https://www.unicef-irc.org/publications/709/. Retrieved April 19, 2016.

Coulmas, Florian. 2009. "The Quest for Happiness in Japan." *DIJ Working Paper* 09/1. http://www.dijtokyo.org/publications/WP0901_Coulmas.pdf. Retrieved February 11, 2012.

Dannefer, Dale, Jessica Kelley-Moore and Wenxuan Huang. 2016. "Opening the Social: Sociological Imagination in Life Course Studies." pp. 87–110 in *Handbook of the Life Course. Vol II*, edited by M. Shanahan, J. T. Mortimer and M. Kirkpatrick Johnson. Heidelberg and New York: Springer.

Easterlin, Richard A. 2006. "Life Cycle Happiness and Its Sources: Intersections of Psychology, Economics, and Demography." *Journal of Economic Psychology* 27:463–482.

Elder, Glen Jr., and Linda George. 2016. "Age, Cohorts, and the Life Course." pp. 59–86 in *Handbook of the Life Course. Vol II*, edited by M. Shanahan, J. T. Mortimer and M. Kirkpatrick Johnson. Heidelberg, New York: Springer.

Fischer, Justina A. 2009. "Happiness and Age Cycles - Return to Start…?: On the Functional Relationship between Subjective Well-Being and Age." *OECD Social, Employment and Migration Working Papers*, No. 99. Paris: OECD Publishing.

Frey, Bruno S., and Alois Stutzer. 2002. *Happiness and Economics*. Princeton: Princeton University Press.

Frijters, Paul, David Johnston and Michael Shields. 2014. "Does Childhood Predict Adult Life Satisfaction? Evidence from British Cohort Surveys." *Economic Journal* 124/580:F688-719.

Gallup Healthways. 2016. "Gallup Healthways Well-Being Index." http://www.well-beingindex.com/. Retrieved August 3, 2016.

Gao, George. 2014. "6 Facts about Japan's Downbeat Economy." PEW Research Center News in the Numbers. http://www.pewresearch.org/fact-tank/2014/11/25/6-facts-about-japans-downbeat-economy/. Retrieved July 26, 2016.

Hagestad, Gunhild, and Pearl Dykstra. 2016. "Structuration of the Life Course: Some Neglected Aspects." pp. 131–160 in *Handbook of the Life Course. Vol II*, edited by M. Shanahan, J. T. Mortimer and M. Kirkpatrick Johnson. Heidelberg, New York: Springer.

Helliwell, John et al. 2010. "International Evidence on the Social Context of Well-Being." pp. 291–327 in *International Differences in Well-Being*, edited by E. Diener, D. Kahneman and J. Helliwell. New York: Oxford University Press.

Helliwell, John, Richard Layard and Jerry Sachs. 2013. *World Happiness Report*. New York: United Nations.

Helliwell, John, Richard Layard and Jerry Sachs. 2016. *World Happiness Report 2016, Update (Vol. I)*. New York: Sustainable Development Solutions Network.

Hiroi, Yoshinori. 2015. "Tokushū. Jūmin no 'kōfukudo' kōjō. Jichitai kara no apurōchi" [Special issue: Enhancing the people's level of happiness. Approaches taken by local governments]. *Gabanansu* 56/2:12–38.

Hitlin, Steven and Hye Won Kwon. 2016. "Agency across the Life Course." pp. 431–450 in *Handbook of the Life Course*. Volume II, edited by M. J. Shanahan, J. T. Mortimer, M. Kirkpatrick Johnson. Heidelberg and New York: Springer.

Holthus, Barbara, and Kristina Iwata-Weickgenannt. eds. 2010. *Contemporary Japan 22. Mind the Gap: Stratification and Social Inequality in Japan*. New York and Berlin: De Gruyter.

Hommerich, Carola, and Susanne Klien. 2012. "Happiness: Does Culture Matter?" *International Journal of Wellbeing* 2:292–298.

IPSS. 2012. "Population Statistics." http://www.ipss.go.jp/p-info/e/Population%20%20Statistics.asp. Retrieved July 27, 2016.

Joshanloo, Mohsen and Dan Weijers. 2014. "Aversion to Happiness across Cultures: A Review of Where and Why People Are Averse to Happiness." *Journal of Happiness Studies* 15/3:717–735.

Joshanloo, Moshen et al. 2015. "Fragility of Happiness Beliefs across 15 National Groups." *Journal of Happiness Research* 16:1185–1110.

Jugureanu, Alexandra, Jason Hughes and Kahryn Hughes. 2014. "Towards a Developmental Understanding of Happiness." *Sociological Research Online* 19/2:2.

Kawahara, Kentaro. 2013. "A Case Study of Happiness Index by Local Government: Gross National Happiness in Arakawa City." *Waseda Kyōiku Hyōron* 27/1:67–82.

Kohli, Martin. 1986. "The World We Forgot: A Historical Review of the Life Course." pp. 271–303 in *Later Life: The Social Psychology of Ageing*, edited by V. W. Marshall. Beverly Hills: Sage.

Layard, Richard 2003. "Happiness: Has Social Science a Clue?" In *Lionel Robbins Memorial Lectures 2002–3*, March 3–5, 2000. London, UK. http://eprints.lse.ac.uk/47425/. Retrieved June 12, 2014.

Layard, Richard et al. 2014. "What Predicts a Successful Life? A Life-Course Model of Wellbeing." *Economic Journal* 124/580:F720-738.

Lu, Luo, and Robin Gilmour. 2004. "Culture and Conceptions of Happiness: Individual Oriented and Social Oriented Subjective Well-Being." *Journal of Happiness Studies* 5/3:269–291.

Manzenreiter, Wolfram, and Barbara Holthus, eds. 2017. *Happiness and the Good Life in Japan*. London, New York: Routledge.

Marcus, Hazel R. and Shinobu Kitayama. 1998. "The Cultural Psychology of Personality." *Journal of Cross-Cultural Psychology* 29/1:63–87.

Mathews, Gordon, and Carolina Izquierdo. 2009. "Towards an Anthropology of Well-Being." pp. 248–266 in *Pursuits of Happiness. Well-Being in Anthropological Perspective*, edited by G. Mathews and C. Izquierdo. New York and Oxford: Berghahn Books.

Minami, Hiroshi. 1971. *Psychology of the Japanese People*. Toronto: University of Toronto Press.

Moen, Phyllis. 2016. "Work over the Gendered Life Course." pp. 249–275 in *Handbook of the Life Course*, Volume II, edited by M. J. Shanahan, J. T. Mortimer, M. Kirkpatrick Johnson. Heidelberg and New York: Springer.

Mortimer, Jeylan T., and Phyllis Moen. 2016. "The Changing Social Construction of Age and the Life Course: Precarious Identity and Enactment of 'Early' and 'Encore' Stages of Adulthood." pp. 111–130 in *Handbook of the Life Course. Vol II*, edited by M. Shanahan, J. T. Mortimer and M. Kirkpatrick Johnson. Heidelberg, New York: Springer.

Mortimer, Jeylan T., and Michael J. Shanahan, eds. 2003. *Handbook of the Life Course*. Heidelberg, New York: Springer.

Naikaku-fu. 2010. "Heisei 22nendo kokumin seikatsu senkōdo chōsa" [National survey on lifestyle preferences]. http://www5.cao.go.jp/seikatsu/senkoudo/senkoudo.html. Retrieved July 22, 2016.

Naikaku-fu. 2011 *Measuring National Well-Being: Proposed Well-Being Indicators.* http://www5.cao.go.jp/keizai2/koufukudo/koufukudo.html. Retrieved August 3, 2016.
Neild, Barry. 2016. "World's Best City for Expats Revealed." *CNN Online* http://edition.cnn.com/2016/02/23/travel/best-cities-for-expats-2016-mercer/index.html?iref=obnetwork. Retrieved May 24, 2016.
OECD. 2016. "Better Life Initiative: Measuring Well-Being and Progress." http://www.oecd.org/statistics/better-life-initiative.htm. Retrieved August 3, 2016.
OECD Stat. 2016. "Better Life Index – Edition 2016." http://stats.oecd.org/Index.aspx?DataSetCode=BLI#. Retrieved August 4, 2016.
Office for National Statistics. 2016. *Measuring National Well-Being: Happiness.* http://www.ons.gov.uk/peoplepopulationandcommunity/wellbeing/datasets/measuringnationalwellbeinghappiness. Retrieved August 3, 2016.
Office of National Statistics. 2016. "Well-Being." https://www.ons.gov.uk/peoplepopulationandcommunity/wellbeing, Accessed August 10, 2016.
Oishi, Shigehiro. 2010. "Culture and Well-Being: Conceptual and Methodological Issues." pp. 34–69 in *International Differences in Well-Being,* edited by E. Diener, D. Kahneman and J. F. Helliwell. New York: Oxford University Press.
Oishi, Shigehiro et al. 2013. "Concepts of Happiness across Time and Cultures." *Personality & Social Psychology Bulletin* 39/5:559–577.
Ōtake Fumio, Sayuri Shiraishi and Yoshirō Tsutsui, eds. 2010. *Nihon no kōfukudo: Kakusa, rōdō, kazoku* [Happiness in Japan. Social inequality, work, family]. Tokyo: Nihon Hyōronsha.
Sakamoto, Kōji. 2011. "47 todōfuken kōfukudo ranking [Happiness ranking of 47 prefectures]." http://www.hosei.ac.jp/documents/koho/photo/2011/11/20111110.pdf. Retrieved December 12, 2014.
Schwandt, Hannes. 2016. "Unmet Aspirations as an Explanation for the Age U-Shape in Wellbeing." *Journal of Economic Behavior & Organization,* 122:75–87.
Scoffham, Stephen, and Jonathan Barnes. 2011. "Happiness Matters: Towards a Pedagogy of Happiness and Well-Being." *Curriculum Journal* 22/4:535–548.
Shanahan, Michael J., Jeylan T. Mortimer and Monica Kirkpatrick Johnson, eds. 2016a. *Handbook of the Life Course. Vol II.* Heidelberg, New York: Springer.
Shanahan, Michael J., Jeylan T. Mortimer and Monica Kirkpatrick Johnson. 2016b. "Introduction: Life Course Studies: Trends, Challenges, and Future Directions." pp. 1–26 in *Handbook of the Life Course. Vol II,* edited by M. Shanahan, J. T. Mortimer and M. Kirkpatrick Johnson. Heidelberg, New York: Springer.
Thin, Neil. 2005. "Happiness and the sad topics of anthropology." *ESRC Research Group on Wellbeing in Developing Countries WeD Working Paper,* 10. www.welldev.org.uk/research/workingpaperpdf/wed10.pdf. Retrieved March 3, 2014.
Tiefenbach, Tim, and Florian Kohlbacher. 2015. "Happiness in Japan in Times of Upheaval: Empirical Evidence from the National Survey on Lifestyle Preferences." *Journal of Happiness Studies* 16:336–366.
Uchida, Yukiko, and Shinobu Kitayama. 2009. "Happiness and Unhappiness in East and West: Themes and Variations." *Emotion* 9/4:441–456.
Uchida, Yukiko, and Yuji Ogihara. 2012. "Personal or Interpersonal Construal of Happiness: A Cultural Psychological Perspective." *International Journal of Wellbeing* 2/4:354–369.
Uchida, Yukiko, Yuji Ogihara and Shintaro Fukushima. 2015. "Cultural Construal of Wellbeing: Theories and Empirical Evidence." pp. 823–837 in *Global Handbook of Quality of Life: Exploration of Well-Being of Nations and Continents,* edited by W. Glatzer et al. Heidelberg: Springer.

UNDP. 2015. "Human Development Report 2015: Work for Human Development." http://hdr.undp.org/en/content/human-development-index-hdi. Retrieved August 4, 2016.

UNICEF Office of Research. 2013. "Child Well-Being in Rich Countries: A Comparative Overview." *Innocenti Report Card* 11. Florence: UNICEF Office of Research. https://www.unicef-irc.org/publications/pdf/rc11_eng.pdf. Retrieved January 17, 2015.

United Nations. 2012. "Happiness: Towards a Holistic Approach to Development. Draft Note." http://www.un.org/esa/socdev/ageing/documents/NOTEONHAPPINESS FINALCLEAN.pdf. Retrieved July 20, 2016.

United Nations. 2013. International Day of Happiness March 20. http://www.un.org/en/events/happinessday/background.shtml. Retrieved May 24, 2016.

Van Landeghem, Bert. 2012. "A Test for the Convexity of Human Well-being over the Life Cycle: Longitudinal Evidence from a 20-Year Panel." *Journal of Economic Behavior & Organization* 81:571–582.

Veenhoven, Ruut. 2012. "Cross-National Differences in Happiness: Cultural Measurement Bias or Effect of Culture? "*International Journal of Wellbeing* 2/4:333–353.

Veenhoven, Ruut. 2014. "Sociology's Blind Eye on Happiness." *Comparative Sociology* 13/5:537–555.

White, Adrian. 2006. "World Map of Happiness." http://www.le.ac.uk/ebulletin-archive/ebulletin/news/press-releases/2000-2009/2006/07/nparticle.2006-07-28.html. Retrieved May 24, 2016.

White, Sarah C., and Chloe Blackmore, eds. 2016. *Cultures of Well-Being. Method, Place, Policy*. Houndmills, Basingstoke: Palgrave Macmillan.

Wirtz, Derrick et al. 2009. "What Constitutes a Good Life? Cultural Differences in the Role of Positive and Negative Affect in Subjective Well-Being." *Journal of Personality* 77/4:1167–1196.

PART I
Childhood and youth

1

TANOSHIKATTA NE? LEARNING TO BE HAPPY IN JAPANESE PRESCHOOLS

Eyal Ben-Ari

Introduction

Reflecting back on two in-depth studies of daycare centers in Kyoto (four months in 1988 and six months in 2005) and on visits to tens of other such institutions, my unqualified impression—bolstered by observations of other scholars such as Tobin (2005)—was that Japanese children, like children around the world, seem to love attending their preschools. Not only did children tell me that they enjoyed their experiences there, but the smiling faces, cheerful demeanors, and contented body stances that I repeatedly observed reinforced my impressions. Given the questions posed by the editors of this volume, I began to ask additional questions: what is it that makes the children happy? How do children learn or better acquire the ability to take pleasure in certain activities? What does socialization to happiness entail? And indeed, what is specifically Japanese about happiness in preschools?

A turn to the scholarly literature on happiness does not seem to help. Most research on "happiness" and "well-being" focuses—like much of the social sciences—on adults. Even when children's well-being is investigated, youngsters are habitually seen as *objects* of adult views, care, or normative prescriptions. In fact, one such example is the international project on indicators of the well-being and development of children (Ben-Arieh 2008). Another instance is a long line of research that asks if adults with children are happier than childless couples are (Demo and Cox 2000; Hansen 2011). Similarly, a sustained attempt has been made to consider the effect of marital discord on the happiness of children (Cummings and Davies 2002). Such worthwhile efforts are part of a wider bias at the base of our disciplines entailing the perspective of fully developed, adult actors (often middle-class). Indeed, when children are studied, the questions tend to be overwhelmingly about whether they are happy or not, or what makes them happy (Luthar and Latendresse 2005; Morrow 1999; Chu et al. 2010). Scholars, however, have not systematically analyzed how children *learn* to be happy. Against this background, I use the case of daycare centers in Japan to shift the scholarly inquiry to one that explores the actual experiences of children in institutions of early childhood. Such a move allows us to ask not only what happiness is and why it is important, but *how* it is achieved and internalized. In other words, I hope to explore questions of a more processual or developmental nature than have been previously asked.

I focus on early childhood institutions for a number of reasons. First, almost all Japanese children attend daycare centers that are under the direction of the Ministry of Health and Welfare or kindergartens supervised by the Ministry of Education. Second, while one can argue that a focus on children should concentrate on the needs of families, as Holthus (2010) convincingly does by examining caregiving patterns, if we want to examine the direct impact of the state on youngsters, then it is in early childhood institutions that the first sustained effects of official policies can be found. Third, given the developmental stages of childhood (marked by multiple transformations), a careful analysis of how children learn to enjoy and be contented in certain contexts has implications for later life. In other words, we can perhaps see some of the origins of long-term effects of early childhood education for happiness.

The data I use is primarily taken from my studies of two medium-sized daycare centers in Kyoto (Ben-Ari, 1997a, 1997b, 2009, 2012) while referring to other studies published during the past decades. I focus especially on daycare centers because this allows me to explore happiness not only in regard to curricular matters, but also to a plethora of other activities, such as sleeping, eating, or toilet training.

Official views and institutional life

In general, what is of interest to teachers and caretakers is the local daycare institution where they work, specifically for this is the place that is creating an enjoyable environment and pleasurable experiences for the children in their care. The more abstract notions of happiness or well-being (as part of what can be termed developmentally appropriate trajectories) are frequently found in official pronouncements and policies (Ben-Ari 1997b). Thus, a broad overview (Ochanomizu University 2004: 14; emphasis added) provides the overall frame for such institutions where the emphasis is on:

> [a] form of early childhood care and education that is based on nurturing the human relationships within the group: The main objective is for children to learn the basic routines of daily life and study habits. Activity times consist of slots that are put together by the teacher, and slots that the child can use with relative freedom, without instructions from the teacher. During free play times, children are encouraged to play with other children or

turn their attention to, and relate with, one another, rather than spending time on their own.... Teachers are *affectionate* toward the children, avoid becoming authoritarian, behave calmly, and build a *warm* relationship with the children...

The teacher is *warm* and *cheerful*, and adapts his or her approach to each individual child. Some positive features that are shared by all these diverse forms of early childhood education include "saying 'Good Morning,'" "closeness," "unhurried time," "responsibility of children," and "physical activity."

Thus official views focus on what Mathews and Izquierdo (2009: 259–260) label the interpersonal dimension of well-being, since at the heart of such policies are the experiences of children with others: teachers and peers. Even when the physical dimension is mentioned—namely children's experiences of their bodies in the world—it is seen as subservient, as contributing to the interpersonal dimension. The ongoing activities of the daycare centers take place against this backdrop. To provide readers with the flavor of what goes on, let me sketch out a few relevant examples from periods of free play framing each day (held during mornings and afternoons) and from the planned activities held each morning.

Art class (taken from my study in 1988; from Ben-Ari 1997a: chapter 4). As the group of four-year old children enter the hall with the two class teachers (and me), the children are welcomed by the art education teacher. She invites the youngsters in by greeting them with cries of "*irasshaimase*." Explaining that this is the word used in welcoming customers to shops and stores, she informs the children that today "we are going to play as though we have a shop here, a shop selling machines." "We will make them by pasting things on boxes and by pasting boxes together." She goes on to show the children what she had prepared (boxes, straws, or magic markers). The children, who had been anticipating this activity since morning assembly, assault the boxes. Scattering equipment around them, groups of two to five children sit together and talk occasionally but work by themselves. From time to time, teachers inquire about what they are making and in most cases, the children—busy cutting, attaching, pasting and coloring— answer that they "don't know." Some kids have problems in cutting and pasting the thick cardboard boxes and although aware of these difficulties, the teachers do not intercede and only help youngsters once they go through (what seemed to me to be an excruciating) effort at tackling the problem by themselves. The children then begin to name the machines they have prepared and add additional features (extra switches from bottle-caps, for instance) in order to fit what they had designated as cars, ships, and refrigerators. Having finished his vehicle, one boy begins to drive it around the hall, and soon some of the other boys follow him.

Rhythmic class (2005). The five-year old children enter the central hall with their two teachers. Once they are arrayed in a semi-circle, one of the teachers tells them that they are going to have fun today. Putting music on with a cassette player at the side of the hall and joining the children, the teachers variously walk, run, and skip around the hall. They lead the children in various animal versions of walking and running: turtles, rabbits, and frogs (see also Ben-Ari 1997a: chap 4). The youngsters are then divided into twosomes (based on who is standing next to whom) and carry out the animals' running styles together. The children seem to be enjoying themselves very much. A number of times three or four exuberant boys run off to the side of the hall, and one of the teachers urges them back with a smile.

Teacher-initiated game during free play (2005). When I enter the room of the five-year old children, one of their teachers is telling them a story using story cards about a machine that grants all sorts of wishes to animals: a lion who asks for a crown since he is the king of the animals, a monkey that has a cold and wants some medicine. It ends with a female raccoon-dog (*tanuki*) who asks for friends. The machine replies that one cannot ask for friends, and by the end of the story she meets a male raccoon-dog and they become friends. The children listen intently and from time to time ask questions. When storytelling ends, the teacher asks the children if they want to play catfish, and they noisily retort that they do. She hands out short threads of wool, which they stick under their noses to resemble moustaches. When a male teacher enters, the first teacher asks him to go out again and come in and guess what they are doing. Upon entering, he tries all sorts of speculations but in the end the children answer that they are catfish. Spontaneously he grabs a plastic bucket and says that like in an aquarium he will hand out food to the fish. The children lie on the floor to catch the imaginary fish he is throwing at them. He then widens his legs and the children "swim" underneath him as though he is a bridge. From time to time he sings a song about a bridge falling and falls on the children swimming underneath him to everyone's laughter.

Playing in open grounds surrounding the daycare centers (1988 and 2005). Both centers being urban institutions have small grounds surrounding them but are still sites of an abundance of activities. Here children make mud pies and cookies, ride small tricycles, push prams, play catch or climb, and slide down slides (see also Adis Tahan 2015). In these games the children enjoy each other's company, become connected, and learn to trust and feel comfortable with each other. Teachers often join the children, either by being invited in or by helping organize dances or games of hide-and-seek or by looking and commenting on how children mastered ever-more complex uses of jungle-jims. In contrast to the structured morning programs, all of these games go on simultaneously and with "permeable" boundaries. Children are free to move into and out of any activity, under the proviso that they keep to the rules of the action. As in other places in Japan (Burke 2013; Che et al. 2007; Tobin et al. 2004), games very often involve mixed-age groups. In October 2005, two four-year old girls spontaneously took up the role of caretakers while two more children (from the group of three years) and I "played" the children. The two girls offered us a short performance with dolls that they had brought from home. A teacher from the group of six-year old children joined and suddenly became an MC using a small plastic block as a microphone and asking everyone to introduce themselves.

Playing house during free play (2005): Walking into the room of the six-year-old group, I find two girls playing house (*mamasan gokko*). They take white toy plates and cups, clear plastic jars and a purple kettle from open shelves and place them on a table. One brings some water in the kettle, and they both proceed to pour it back and forth into the jars and cups. One girl invites me over and shows me a small cloth used for cleaning up when water spills and then explains that the jars have a line on them showing the children how much water to pour in so that none is spilled. She then explains that they are making tea and invites me to join them. Her friend takes a saucer with small rounded stones and using plastic tweezers places them on the plates. She does not integrate me into her game.

While one can easily (and correctly) interpret these events in developmental terms (as preparation for the housewife role, mastering motor skills, or learning about friendship), I underscore the following points as a basis for my analysis. First, in all or parts of the games and play, children are deeply engaged in "the action," in "another" world. While many occurrences of play have relatively porous boundaries, all are characterized by profound absorption as indicated by the fascination on youngsters' faces, the seeming lack of attention to outside cues (including those of authority figures) while playing, or the emergent character of many episodes where new elements were introduced almost seamlessly into the created worlds.

Second, the deep absorption of the children—say when making the machines out of cardboard, placing ever-smaller beads on plastic cords, or dancing in more and more complex patterns—is very often related to tasks that are difficult for them. Accordingly, play is not only agreeable but involves ever-greater challenges for the youngsters. In fact, such episodes—involving minute tests of abilities—are not only limited to games as Tobin (Tobin et al. 2009) explains. In the preschool he studied, a five-year-old boy took a two-year-old boy and taught him to pee while standing. Tobin shows that the older child seemed to enjoy the act of teaching with its intricate explanations about posture and self-control and subsequently took pride in a job well done. In a related manner, Cave (2007: 199) explains that, after some elementary school children spent a day with preschoolers, he "had rarely seen Japanese primary school children so full of spontaneous pleasure and enthusiasm at a school event."

Third, activities often included various amalgamations of twosomes, threesomes, or small groups. To follow Adis Tahan (2015), the absorption and challenges of games and play are collective actions that create a space of togetherness as a result of a sort of non-locatable body of children and teachers (and occasionally of the anthropologist). By this experience I do not refer to the Japanese notions of *skinship* (I only saw rare instances of skin-to-skin contact) but of a more general feeling of a shared space of play.

So what is happening here? What can be learned from these fascinating clusters of engagement, challenge, and group contexts?

"Active" and "passive" enjoyment

My starting point is, following the psychologist Csikszentmihalyi (1975), that we approach enjoyment through the concept of flow, this particular experience that is so engrossing and enjoyable that it becomes of value for its own sake even though it may have no consequence outside itself. Flow involves

> [a] sense of that one's skills are adequate to cope with the challenges at hand in a goal directed, rule bound action system that provides clear clues as to how one is performing. Concentration is so intense that there is no attention left over to think about anything irrelevant or to worry about problems. Self-consciousness disappears, and the sense of time becomes distorted. An activity that produces such experiences is so gratifying that people are willing to do it for its own sake, with little concern for what they will get out of it, even when it is difficult or dangerous.
> (Csikszentmihalyi 1975: 71)

While the clearest instance of flow experiences are those found in music, sports, games, or religious rituals, they may also appear during work, study, or even driving. Indeed Csikszentmihalyi (1996, 1997) found that happiness depends on whether people are able to derive flow from whatever they do, when they feel they are thoroughly involved in something that is enjoyable and meaningful to them. Flow experiences are central, I found, to the life of preschoolers.

A number of qualities mark the flow experience, each of which can be found in my data. First, flow is somehow separate from the routines of everyday life and is created by cues, such as walking into a sport event or a religious ceremony or internally by focusing attention on a set of stimuli with their own rules, such as composition of music or writing. This property is most evident in events organized by teachers when children enter a situation marked by verbal or non-verbal cues (like arts class), but is also found in times of free play either by participants' declarations ("Shall we play house?") or more informally (often spontaneously) by joining together in a space of their own (three children playing catch in a corner of the grounds). Second, time seems to stop, as flow entails involvement in an activity so demanding that no surplus attention is left to monitor any stimuli irrelevant to the task at hand. The utter absorption, the deep engagement, of the children (and at times the teachers) in games and play are indicators of this quality. Indeed, so rapt was the attention of some children in what they were doing that it took some effort on the part of others to bring them back to "reality." Third, the experience often involves a sense of effortless performance that is made possible only because the skills and techniques have been learned and practiced so well that they have become automatic. Climbing and going down slides is one example. Only once youngsters have enough control of their bodies and are no longer afraid of the slide can they take pleasure in the recurring event in ever more "daring" ways. Thus, greater control allows ever-more sophisticated modes of sliding: lying on one's back or stomach or sliding down head first.

Fourth, what is important here is that the challenge not be something beyond a child's ability or not so simple as to become uninteresting. Thus when the slide no longer provides a challenge to the child's skills it may become boring, or when it is too difficult it may bring on anxiety: when there is a balance between ability and challenge the action "just flows out by itself" (Csikszentmihalyi 1997). A case in point is the game teachers (in 2005) had children play by walking along a plank suspended 15–20 centimeters above the ground: as the children gradually mastered the task they could run across the plank with increasing speed. During the flow experience people (and children are, after all, people) are not necessarily happy because they are too involved in the task to have the luxury of reflecting on their subjective states. Being happy would be a distraction, an interruption of the flow. But afterward, when the experience is over, people report having been in as positive a state as it is possible to feel. Moreover, the experience itself is so enjoyable that people will do it even at great cost, for the sheer sake of doing it (Csikszentmihalyi 1975).

The flow experience, however, does not encompass the full range of experiences related to happiness and enjoyment. Another range of activities is related to more passive, reflective (as opposed to flow's active) states of pleasurable experiences (Csikszentmihalyi 1999). I refer here to a set of experiences in which children come to embody comfortableness, delight, or amusement, without much effort and especially without the efforts of others. Such activities and pastimes include reading books or listening to stories, going to movies, watching television, or listening to music.

While lack of space precludes a more sustained analysis of these kinds of more passive pleasures, let me briefly provide a few cases. One type of such experience entails children taking pleasure in the jokes others tell or the way others may make fun of the teachers. Here delight is derived from the (sometimes passive, sometimes more active) participation in the witticisms, obscenities, jokes, and general mischief that form an essential part of any child's life (Ben-Ari 1997a). In a related way, appreciating the aesthetics of food presentation can be seen in similar ways (Ben-Ari 1997a; Burke 2013). In some of the preschools I studied and visited, the cooks emphasized the visual presentation of food, explaining that it was important that the youngsters learn to appreciate the different colors and textures of the fare. Another kind of activity involves sleep (in daycare centers) where children learn to fall asleep in the deep comfort during the period before actual slumber. In this case, a link is created between the physical side of fatigue and the deep pleasure of sinking into sleep in secure surroundings (Ben-Ari 1996). Finally in some preschools, gardening or tending to animals is a pursuit that involves both a direct, situational enjoyment—the texture and colors of plants or the touch of a small animal's fur—and a longer-term pleasure of seeing things grow and develop. From an analytical point of view, it appears that the informal agenda of the centers includes a very strong emphasis on what Mathews and Izquierdo (2009: 259–260) call the physical dimension of well-being and especially the short-term physical experience of pleasure in bodily activities.

Verbalization: Differentiation and reflection

A focus on these variegated activities—the more active or the more passive—underscores the bodily aspects of happiness and enjoyment involving all of the children's faculties and senses in the process of socialization to happiness, entailing sensual, embodied experiences. But things are complex, since the analysis I have been sketching out till this point could be true of any age group. In thinking about the peculiarity of early childhood, I was struck by the prominence of verbalized questions about pleasure and enjoyment. Teachers and caretakers constantly asked questions such as "Wasn't that enjoyable?" (*Tanoshikatta, ne*), "Was that nice?" (*Yokatta no?*) or "Was that tasty?" (*Oishikatta?*). Given the developmental trajectory of youngsters in preschools, proper feelings toward one's experiences (and of one's peers) are contextualized and labeled through verbal cues. These processes of verbalization help the children reinforce and elucidate existing sentiments and motives. Questions and statements as these associate the emotions the children sense—enjoyment, pleasure, delight, contentment—to the specific circumstances in which they occur or have occurred. Thus, phrases like "What would you feel if you were hit?" work toward marking the emotions of due consideration of others through empathy.

As Bruner (1986: 16) explains, the point in this social contextualization of emotions is not one of "[...] calling up some prepared emotions, but consists, rather, of helping the child contextualize initially undifferentiated feelings into highly differentiated social situations that give these feelings their affective signature." But there is more here. By saying that I have enjoyed or am enjoying myself, I may, in fact, be producing a motive, or more likely deepen and clarify an existing motive (Lutz 1987: 301). In this way the children's understanding of motives and of emotions is enabled or enhanced by social discourse: "In hearing what we ourselves and others say about emotions, we come to understand better (or create) our goals and other perceptions" (Lutz 1987: 301). Thus throughout any given day, I observed numerous instances of teachers helping children verbalize their emotions and link them to motives via anticipation of future events: for instance, in telling the children that the main morning event of a given day would be dances or art work, things they had enjoyed in the past, teachers were cultivating their eagerness for such activities.

The climax of verbalization in Japanese preschools can be found in the periods called *hanseikai* (literally meetings for reflection), which may take anywhere between two and ten minutes and in which the day's events are discussed and thought about. In these periods, both emotions and motivations may become "objects" for deliberation and discussion. On the one hand, like sports coaches working with athletes in improving performance, so *hanseikai* are used by teachers to comment and elaborate on ways to better participate in play or games. On the other hand, the children themselves are active participants in creating their emotions and motivations by re-experiencing the pleasurable aspects of various activities.

Flow and enjoyment in a group

Since one can see the things I have been sketching in any preschool around the world, we are still left with a question: what is Japanese about all of this? Here I follow Mathews and Izquierdo (2009: 254) who argue for human universals in the pursuit of well-being that come to the fore differently in different societies. In my case their point means linking flow and more passive enjoyments to one of the most important educational goals of Japanese daycare centers and kindergartens: the fostering of group life (as evident in a line of scholarly studies—Cave 2007; Kelly 2001; Lewis 1995; Peak 1989—and official pronouncements—Muto 2006; Ochanomizu University 2004). In other words, what we find in Japanese institutions is the shaping of experiences of happiness *toward* collective life.

One of the most common practices is one where teachers constantly suggest to—but do not coerce—children to join group games and activities. Take a game for the six-year old children (1988) in which they had to match three cards to form a complete picture with the word of the picture (e.g., ship, sled, peach) in *hiragana* at the bottom. While involving writing, these occasions seemed to be directed more toward other aims. The children were helped at the beginning by the teachers but later encouraged to help each other or to match the cards by themselves. Again, the lesson was one about social cooperation and the individual ability to concentrate and enjoy oneself within groups. Again, during one rhythmic class after running around the hall, the children went on to, in turn, walk on all fours, move on their toes, sit on their bottoms and advance forward, and hold hands in twosomes or groups of three and run around the hall. With the teachers' encouragement, these activities were accompanied by loud cries of encouragement to "Everyone, give it all you've got!" (*minnasan gambare*).

In a complementary manner, Tobin and his colleagues (2009; also Burke 2008) show that there is a cultural emphasis on articulating loneliness as the reverse of well-being and completeness in groups. Thus among the many ways in which children in Japanese preschools learn to express, experience, and reflect on emotions one of the most important is that of *sabishisa* (loneliness). Teachers draw attention to feelings of loneliness to promote a desire in young children for social connection built on expressions of dependency needs and empathy for others. As they explain, feeling lonely motivates people to seek the company of others, and demonstrations of loneliness are supposed to rouse an empathic response of inviting the lonely person to join the group. During both stints of fieldwork, I witnessed time and again how children would adopt a posture of appeal while standing on the sidelines of some game. They would tilt their heads slightly forward, focus their gaze on the playing children, and try to initiate eye contact with them. The youngsters who were playing would often open their ongoing activity to the new participant directly (Ben-Ari 1997a: chapter 4), or, if the entreaties did not work, teachers would often gently suggest that it would be nice if they included their peers. On the basis of my observations, I concur with Peak (1989: 116) who observes that unwillingness to join group activities is particularly "threatening to preschool teachers, who are well socialized members of Japanese group-oriented culture." In fact, caretakers sometimes keep a whole class waiting while persuading a recalcitrant youngster to take part in the goings-on. To be sure, an emphasis on flow and enjoyment in groups does not preclude experiences at the individual level. Children in Japanese preschools do have choice, especially in regard to free play, but this leeway for choice is seen as crucial in creating a constructive and secure engagement with the group.

I now understand what the teachers were trying to tell me about creating a happy environment for the children. As I explained above, teachers create conditions that make possible flow and more passive experiences of pleasure, even though they would not necessarily formulate it in these terms. They use almost any opportunity—brushing teeth, setting tables, cleaning rooms and hallways, as well as filling in coloring books and completing puzzles—to create happy experiences. Of course, the majority of preschools are run according to rather exact schedules as attested to by the plethora of forms detailing yearly, monthly, weekly and daily plans (Ben-Ari 1997b). But what teachers are especially aware of is the importance of planning for and creating ad-hoc those moments—in American parlance, the magic moments—when children are fully engaged and to try to embed them in group contexts.

Meta-abilities—to flow and to enjoy along the life course

The final layer of my analysis entails a proposition about the life course, about the long-term effects of the children's experiences. My argument is that over time the children learn not only the (relatively) more inactive forms of enjoyment but also that to be happy it is necessary to find flow in activities that are complex and challenging: namely, activities that provide potential for growth over a life span, allow the emergence of new opportunities for action and reflection, and stimulate development of new skills (Csikszentmihalyi 1999). What I am trying to get across here is something I encountered many years ago. After completing my first fieldwork in Japan (1981–1983), I became fascinated with the question of how Japanese people learn "to group": to feel comfortable within, to find identification with, and to master the ground rules for joining groups. I proposed that such learning is not so much a matter of learning to be a member of a specific group, but rather of acquiring the more general set of abilities "to group:"

> Most (middle-class) Japanese acquire through their socialization a learned capacity to move from and relate to a succession of groups throughout their lifetime. This [learned capacity] is related to the complex processes of socialization (direct, anticipatory and vicarious), and to an individual's procession - from childhood to old age - through a whole range of formal and informal groups.[...]

> In rather abstract terms, middle-class Japanese acquire - through a process Bateson (1972: 167) terms deutero- or meta-learning - a capacity to move from one frame to another. [...] They learn, then, to relate to groups on a meta-level. That is, they learn to relate to a constant 'idea' or 'construct' of a group although they may move successively or concurrently through many concrete or actual groups.
>
> (Ben-Ari 1997a: 188–189)

Sometimes called meta-skills or meta-competencies, the idea here is that just as people learn to learn or learn to group, so they learn *how* to be happy. Meta-competencies refer to how well and quickly someone develops competencies that in our case involve the ability to seek and enter experiences of flow and more reflective forms of enjoyment. Earlier I proposed that it is by not only asking what happiness is or why it is important, but also *how* it is achieved (attained or accomplished), that new questions can be asked. We realize that happiness involves skills and abilities to search for and recognize potentially satisfying and pleasing occasions, to learn how to enter such situations, to concentrate long enough within them to "step out of time," and to derive pleasure from either reflection or matching abilities to challenges.

While meta-abilities are universal, they are always culturally constructed. In the case of Japanese preschools' particular forms of playful interaction, teacher involvement, and participation in games, or the creation of a special space for play all transmit quite clear "notices" to the children that the pleasures of games and play (and often of more "solitary" pursuits) are (also) the pleasures of being in a group. Furthermore, once internalized, these orientations become self-validating. Children exposed to flow and reflective enjoyment become skilled over time and are able to verbalize their experiences and actively seek new, similar ones. Faced by a new situation, they continue under the assumption that enjoyment—undergoing a pleasurable experience—also involves cooperating, taking others into consideration, and being identified and committed to the social framework. The point is that these self-validating premises are learned and maintained throughout one's lifetime so that they form a set of unquestioned assumptions, shared by many (if not most) members of Japanese (middle-class) culture, that permeate their experiences.

Conclusion

By way of conclusion let me underscore two points. First, Mathews and Izquierdo (2009: 257) rightly argue for the need to understand the *diversity* of senses of well-being within societies refracted through class, age (in my case, children), and gender. I suggested that it may be worthwhile to complement the analysis of these diverse experiences with a focus on *how* one accomplishes happiness and how this achievement is *culturally constructed*. In other words, I attempted to unpack the experience of happiness by focusing on the processes of acquiring certain meta-competencies. In this view these processes—never certain, never uni-directional, nor ever complete—of abilities or capacities are the basis for the long-term effects of preschools on happiness. Thus understanding how children acquire abilities to be happy is only possible in terms of those largely ephemeral and highly situation-specific actions through which these practices are internalized. Socialization to happiness thus usually takes place through an exposure to parts and pieces of experiences and images that are not always directly explicated, but that over the long run result in the skills acquired.

Second, along these lines, perhaps I can add a note to the discrepancy between my observations on the one hand and findings that point to Japanese adults being comparatively unhappy on the other (introduction to this volume). My processual view focuses on the personal and interactional processes that are part of enjoyment—of being happy, of embodying happiness—but perhaps more important, on the process by which one can learn to be happy; to acquire the skills necessary to be happy. In this sense, childhood experiences are *potentiating* mechanisms: they create individual potential to be happy. But whether these potentials are actually achieved is dependent on a whole range of other variables. Thus if one wants to understand why Japanese adults report that they are relatively unhappy—as many essays in this volume do—then I suggest looking for the factors that shape their lives rather than at the experiences they underwent as youngsters.

References

Adis Tahan, Diana 2015. *The Japanese Family: Touch, Intimacy and Feeling*. London: Routledge.

Bateson, Gregory. 1972. *Steps to an Ecology of Mind*. New York: Ballantine.

Ben-Ari, Eyal. 1996. "From Mothering to Othering: Culture, Organization and Nap Time in a Japanese Preschool." *Ethos* 24/1:136–164.

Ben-Ari, Eyal. 1997a. *Body Projects in Japanese Childcare: Culture, Organization and Emotions in a Preschool*. London: Curzon.

Ben-Ari, Eyal. 1997b. *Japanese Childcare: An Interpretive Study of Culture and Organization*. London: Kegan Paul International.

Ben-Ari, Eyal. 2009. "Transnational Similarities, Ethno-theories and "Normal" Child Development: Early Childhood Education in Japan." pp. 231–250 in *The Production of Educational Knowledge in the Global Era*, edited by J. Reznick. Amsterdam: Sense Publishers.

Ben-Ari, Eyal. 2012. "Israeli Soldiers, Japanese Children: Fieldwork and the Dynamics of Participant-Observation and Reflection." pp. 65–80 in *Serendipity in Anthropological Research: The Nomadic Turn*, edited by H. Hazan and E. Hertzog. Furnham, Surrey: Ashgate.

Ben-Arieh, Asher. 2008. "The Child Indicators Movement: Past, Present, and Future." *Child Indicators Research* 1:3–16.

Bruner, Jerome. 1986. *Actual Minds, Possible Worlds*. Cambridge, MA: Harvard University Press.

Burke, Rachael. 2008. "Becoming Individuals Together: Socialization in the Japanese Preschool." *Sites* 5/2:135–157.

Burke, Rachael. 2013. *Bodies in Context: A Comparative Study of Early Childhood Education in New Zealand and Japan.* Doctoral Dissertation in Social Anthropology, Massey University, Albany.

Cave, Peter. 2007. *Primary School in Japan: Self, Individuality and Learning in Elementary Education.* London: Routledge.

Che, Yi, Akiko Hayashi and Joseph Tobin. 2007. "Lessons from China and Japan for Preschool Practices in the United States." *Educational Perspectives* 40:7–12.

Chu, Po Sen, Donald A. Saucier and Eric Hafner. 2010. "Meta-Analysis of the Relationships between Social Support and Well-Being in Children and Adolescents." *Journal of Social and Clinical Psychology* 29/6:624–645.

Coulmas, Florian. 2008. *The Quest for Happiness in Japan.* German Institute for Japanese Studies, Tokyo. Working Paper 09/01.

Csikszentmihalyi, Mihaly. 1975. *Beyond Boredom and Anxiety.* San Francisco: Jossey-Bass.

Csikszentmihalyi, Mihaly. 1996. *Creativity: Flow and the Psychology of Discovery and Invention.* New York: HarperCollins.

Csikszentmihalyi, Mihaly. 1997. *Finding Flow.* New York: Basic Books.

Csikszentmihalyi, Mihaly. 1999. "If We Are So Rich, Why Aren't We Happy." *American Psychologist* 54/10. http://www.owlnet.rice.edu/~erinm/Mihaly.html. Retrieved February 4, 2014.

Cummings, Mark E., and Patrick T. Davies. 2002. "Effects of Marital Conflict on Children: Recent Advances and Emerging Themes in Process-oriented Research." *Journal of Child Psychology and Psychiatry* 43/1:31–63.

Demo, David H., and Martha J. Cox. 2000. "Families with Young Children: A Review of Research in the 1990s." *Journal of Marriage and Family* 62/4:876–895.

Hansen, Thomas. 2011. "Parenthood and Happiness: A Review of Folk Theories versus Empirical Evidence." *Social Indicator Research.* http://link.springer.com/article/10.1007/s11205-011-9865-y#page-1. Retrieved February 8, 2015.

Holthus, Barbara. 2010. "Parental Evaluation of Institutionalized Childcare: Survey Results from Japan." Child Research Net http://www.childresearch.net/projects/ecec/2010_06.html. Retrieved February 23, 2015.

Kelly, Victoria E. 2001. "Peer Culture and Interaction: How Japanese Children Express Their Internalization of the Cultural Norms of Group Life." pp. 170–204 in *Japanese Frames of Mind*, edited by H. Shimizu and R. A. Levine. Cambridge: Cambridge University Press.

Lewis, Catherine C. 1995. *Educating Hearts and Minds: Reflections on Japanese Preschools and Elementary Education.* Cambridge: Cambridge University Press.

Luthar, Suniya S., and Shawn J. Latendresse. 2005. "Children of the Affluent: Challenges to Well-Being." *Current Directions in Psychological Science* February 14:149–153.

Lutz, Catherine. 1987. "Goals, Events, and Understanding in Ifaluk Emotion Theory." pp. 290–312 in *Cultural Models in Language and Thought*, edited by D. Holland and N. Quinn. Cambridge: Cambridge University Press.

Mathews, Gordon, and Carolina Izquierdo. 2009. "Towards an Anthropology of Well-Being." pp. 248–67 in *Pursuits of Happiness: Well-Being in Anthropological Thought*, edited by G. Mathews and C. Izquierdo. New York and Oxford: Berghahn Books.

Morrow, Virginia. 1999. "Conceptualising Social Capital in Relation to the Well-Being of Children and Young People: A Critical Review." *The Sociological Review* 47/4:744–765.

Ochanomizu University Research Center for Child and Adolescent Development and Education. 2004. *Early Childhood Education Handbook.* Tokyo: Ochanomizu University. (Internal publication).

Peak, Lois. 1989. "Learning to Become Part of the Group: The Japanese Child's Transition to Preschool Life." *Journal of Japanese Studies* 15/1:93–124.

Tobin, Joseph. 2005. "Quality in Early Childhood Education: An Anthropologist's Perspective." *Early Childhood and Development* 16/4:421–434.

Tobin, Joseph, Yeh Hsueh and Mayumi Karasawa. 2009. *Preschool in Three Cultures Revisited*. Chicago: Chicago University Press.

Tobin, Joseph, Mayumi Karasawa and Yeh Hsueh. 2004. "Komatsudani Then and Now: Continuity and Change in a Japanese Preschool." *Contemporary Issues in Early Childhood* 5/2:128–144.

2
"BECAUSE I FEEL HAPPY"

Japanese first graders' views about schooling and well-being

Yoko Yamamoto

> QUESTION: What's good about going to school?
> CHILD: I can study a lot.
> INTERVIEWER: What's good about studying a lot?
> CHILD: Everyone would say great (*sugoi*)!
> INTERVIEWER: Why is it good if everyone says great?
> CHILD: I feel happy (*ureshī*) and [that means] I am smart (*kashikoi*).

From a young age, Japanese children understand that attending school is a critical part of their life. They are also aware that school learning will promote their future life chances and prepare them to be "good adults." Theories and empirical studies have demonstrated that children are capable of expressing their emotions and thoughts when they are quite young (Li 2004; Li et al. 2010). Children are also capable of constructing ideals related to their well-being as they actively interpret their lives and processes (Fattore, Mason and Watson 2007). However, when it comes to understanding children's well-being, objective indicators assessed and evaluated by adults are widely used. According to the Organization for Economic Cooperation and Development (OECD), indicators of well-being for children aged 0 to 17 are focused on themes such as fulfilling basic needs and survival: material well-being; housing and environment; health and safety; risk behaviors; education; and quality of school life (OECD 2009). In psychological studies, researchers have assessed children's socioemotional, behavioral, and academic outcomes as indicators of their well-being, and these methods tend to rely on reports and assessments by adults, such as parents, teachers, and scholars (Goodman et al. 2000).

While these objective measures inevitably help us understand children's experiences, developmental processes, and outcomes, in addition to their environments and the conditions affecting their well-being, well-being observed at this level tends to be restricted to the conceptual framework of adults. Children's subjective views and understandings of happiness, or well-being, could differ from those shared among adults. Thus, it is imperative to examine children's subjective experiences. It is especially challenging to understand children's well-being across different societies because conceptualizations of happiness are likely to differ across cultures (Mathews and Izquierdo 2009). As part of the socialization process, children are expected to internalize norms and values in the culture from a young age (LeVine and White 1986). Examining children's beliefs related to antecedents and components of well-being will help us understand the dominant ideology of well-being that is passed down from adults to children in the society.

For children living in industrial societies such as Japan, schooling is a fundamental and important part of life. In Japan, school-age children spend more than six hours at school on weekdays, and nine years of education is mandatory. Most Japanese people spend more than 12 years in school as approximately 97 percent of students attend high school after the compulsory education, and approximately 55 percent of students further attend a two- or four-year college (Ministry of Education, Culture, Sports, Science and Technology 2013). While the purposes of schooling may differ across societies, in general schools are expected to prepare children to become competent adults by teaching important skills for and knowledge of society. Furthermore, the level of education strongly affects occupational prospects and future income in Japan as in many other industrial societies (Brinton 2010; Hashimoto 1999; Ishida and Slater 2010). Under such conditions, schooling is likely to have a strong influence on Japanese children's understanding and experiences of well-being, even though school and academic life is only one aspect that constitutes children's lives and well-being. In this chapter, I examine Japanese first graders' views on well-being in the domain of schooling and school learning.

Are Japanese students happy or unhappy? Conflicting images

Scholars outside Japan have often highlighted positive pictures of Japanese education and students. According to these studies, Japanese students, in general, enjoy learning and attending school, are motivated to learn, and demonstrate high academic performance in international academic tests (Cave 2007; Stevenson and Stigler 1992). Compared to American students, Japanese students spend longer hours in school, do more homework, and also attend extra-curricular academic schools (Chen and Stevenson 1989). Scholars have pointed out positive elements that promote students' well-being, such as competent and involved teachers, egalitarianism, and practices that promote healthy socioemotional development in kindergarten and primary school (Cave 2007; Holloway and Yamamoto 2003; Lewis 1995; Stevenson and Stigler 1992). Contrary to such findings, inside Japan, images of Japanese education and students are increasingly negative and pessimistic. Media and critics have highlighted continuous and growing issues such as academic pressure on children, bullying at school (*ijime*), and increasing numbers of students who refuse to go to school (*futōkō*). Media have also featured the changing school environment for students; they have reported increasing numbers of "monster parents" who make unreasonable requests of schools as well as the phenomenon of *gakkyū hōkai*, meaning classrooms that do not function as a learning environment for students due to children who have behavioral and discipline issues (Onoda 2013; Takahashi 1999). Especially highlighted is the "first grader problem" (*shōichi puroburamu*), the rapid increase in first graders who are unprepared for learning at school and cannot pay attention to teachers' instructions (Takada 2008). The media have accentuated images of unhappy students and a changing school environment that does not support students' positive learning and well-being.

Neglected here are children's subjective school experiences and their views about school learning, especially at an early stage. Increasingly, scholars have examined the subjective school experiences of Japanese adolescents and youth. These studies have demonstrated variations and diversity in students' perspectives on and experience of schooling. Middle-class youth tend to hold strong educational aspirations by foreseeing the role of education in their future well-being, but working-class youth tend to demonstrate rebellion and disinterest in school learning (Brinton 2010; Chinen 2012; Slater 2010). A quantitative study conducted by Kariya (2004) demonstrates that fifth-grade attendees of *juku* display significantly higher academic motivation than those who do not attend these extra-curricular academic schools. His study suggested socio-economic factors affecting students' academic motivation. However, little is known about whether particular students' negative attitudes toward schooling and learning begin at the onset of schooling or develop as they attend school. Because there is a persistent socio-economic gap in students' academic motivation and performance (Hashimoto 1999; Kariya 2004; Yamamoto and Brinton 2010), it is also critical to understand how young students from various family backgrounds view school learning, including the purpose and meaning of schooling in relation to their well-being. Even though it is challenging to conduct research with young children, developmental theories and evidence have validated children's ability to report their thoughts and ideas as early as their preschool period when appropriate methods are used (Greig, Taylor and MacKay 2007; Li 2004).

In this study, I examine views about schooling and learning among Japanese first graders from both middle-class and working-class backgrounds. I aim to understand (1) young students' subjective experiences of schooling and learning, (2) students' views about schooling in relation to their well-being, and (3) any difference in students' experiences of and views about schooling depending on their family backgrounds.

The first-grade study

Data for this study were drawn from the Japan-US cross-cultural study on students' beliefs about learning. In Japan, 100 first graders aged six or seven who attended public school in Osaka prefecture participated in this study in 2013 and 2014, along with their mothers. Several public schools, located in both working-class and middle-class neighborhoods, helped to distribute a letter to parents to solicit their participation in this study. Interested parents signed a consent form, and both children and parents participated in the study. Half of the student participants were boys and half were girls. The family backgrounds of the children were diverse as their parents' occupations ranged from researcher, physician, and computer technologist to factory worker, carpenter, and painter; about one-third of the children had parents both of whom had graduated from a university while 38 percent had parents without university education. Interviews were conducted from June through July, a few months after the students began first grade.

To grasp children's own narratives and perspectives, I employed a story-completion interview method that was developed to elicit young children's beliefs and views (Li 2004). In an individual interview, each child was asked about his or her school life and learning experiences. Then the child listened to two story beginnings while looking at a black-and-white picture that presented the image of each story. The two story beginnings used in this study related to school attendance but involved opposite scenarios. One began with a story of a student who was eager to go to school and the other with a story of a student who did not want to go to school. For each beginning, the child was asked to continue the story. Whenever the child mentioned any schooling or learning-related ideas, a follow-up question of "Why is it good to …?" or "What's good about…?" was asked to probe the child's response. Following up with the exact words and responses given by the child helps him or her express and explain thoughts and ideas that are difficult to elicit otherwise. All interviews were audio-recorded and transcribed in Japanese. For this chapter, I focused on examining themes related to children's experiences, views, and conceptualizations about well-being in the domain of schooling. I mainly examined children's narratives qualitatively. However, I also performed quantitative analyses to examine frequencies of coded response as well as socio-economic differences by running t-tests. Survey data collected from the children's mothers also allowed me to compare children's report of their school lives to their mothers'.

Happiness and schooling: First graders' views

Do first graders enjoy attending school?

The majority of first graders (93%) in this study reported that they enjoyed attending school. What students enjoyed at school varied from the academic to the non-academic. About 40 percent of the children reported enjoying recess, especially playing with other children, and about half reported "studying" or learning a specific subject as their favorite time at school. When it came to enjoyment of studying academic subjects such as math and Japanese language arts (*kokugo*), the rate of subjective enjoyment dropped. However, 80 percent of the children reported that they enjoyed studying math and about 75 percent did so for Japanese language arts. The children's reports were significantly and highly correlated with their mothers' responses in the parent survey, indicating the overall validity of the children's report of enjoyment.

In the story-completion interviews, about 80 percent of the children voluntarily mentioned positive feelings toward schooling and learning. For example, one boy continued the story of a child who does not want to attend school by stating, "School is fun, so he starts to feel like going to school"; these children highlighted fun and enjoyable experiences at school. In general, the children conveyed excitement and positive feelings toward schooling. When children described their happy and unhappy feelings and moments in the stories, they did not use words such as *shiawase* (happiness), *fushiawase* (unhappiness), or *manzoku suru* (satisfied), which are frequently used in the assessment of adults' subjective well-being. First graders in this study voluntarily mentioned words such as *ureshii* (feeling glad or happy), *tanoshii* (enjoyable), and *suki* (like) to describe their happiness. When students mentioned unhappy feelings and moments, they used terms such as *kanashii* (feeling sad), *gakkari* (disappointing), *iya na kimochi* (unpleasant feeling), and *hazukashii* (feeling ashamed). The children in this study did not report anger, frustration, or aggression when describing unhappy moments or feelings as American people commonly do (Uchida and Kitayama 2009).

Because participation in this study was voluntary, there is a possibility that only parents whose children had positive attitudes toward schooling signed up. It is also possible to interpret that most Japanese students enjoy attending school and learning school subjects in the very beginning of formal schooling. At the time of the interview, a few months after the beginning of first grade, children were learning very basic content such as simple addition for mathematics and the basic alphabet in Japanese (*hiragana*). School learning was likely to be easy and fun after the initial entry, as some students reported so. However, it also warrants attention that one in four or five children in this study reported not enjoying the study of mathematics or Japanese language arts after the initial transition to formal schooling. I did not find a significant socio-economic difference in children's enjoyment in schooling and learning. Regardless of socio-economic backgrounds, most first graders in Japan reported positive feelings about attending and learning at school.

School learning is essential for well-being

The children's voluntary narratives demonstrated that first graders have already developed complex and unique ideas about well-being in the domain of school learning. Most of the first graders described why schooling was important and how it would help them become competent adults. Almost all of the children demonstrated strong value judgments by mentioning that it is good to go to school. However, they demonstrated diverse reasons for and meanings of attending school. The same children also demonstrated multifaceted views about the meanings and purposes of attending school, as the following interview reveals:

> INTERVIEWER: What's good about going to school?
> CHILD: She can study a lot, can answer any questions, and she can do everything.
> INTERVIEWER: What's good about studying a lot, answering any questions, and doing everything?
> CHILD: She can say many things when she is adult, and she can tell the meaning of difficult words to her baby.
> INTERVIEWER: What's good about that?
> CHILD: Then she can be smart!
> INTERVIEWER: What's good about being smart?
> CHILD: She can go up a path to be an adult more and more. She doesn't go down and down. She doesn't want to hear her school teacher say, "I will send you back to a kindergarten by express mail (*takkyūbin*)."
> INTERVIEWER: What's good about being adult?
> CHILD: I can wear cute shoes and cute clothing when I am adult. I can work as an idol singer (*aidoru*). If I have a lot of money, I don't need to cook and can go to restaurants. I can do shopping.
> INTERVIEWER: Do you like Erika in this story?
> CHILD: Yes!
> INTERVIEWER: Why do you like her?
> CHILD: She wants to study. She listens to adults, or may listen to adults, and it's really good to go to school. Erika is great (*erai*).

In this story-completion interview, seven-year-old Yuka (pseudonym) mentioned various benefits of attending school. Yuka believed that school is a place to learn and described various benefits of school learning, such as gaining knowledge, being smart, and learning to "do everything." For her, school learning is critical to become a competent adult and thus is a necessary path to follow. A competent adult has a job and earns money, which allows her to get what she wants. Yuka also believed that learning would help her contribute to other people, such as her future baby. Even though the children mentioned diverse ideas related to the purpose and meaning of attending school, common themes indicated their conceptualization of well-being.

First of all, first graders viewed being smart and acquiring knowledge and skills as critical for them and their future, as 75 percent of the children mentioned such a theme. As Yuka demonstrated in her interview, "being smart" (*kashikoi*) or "bright" (*atama ga ii*) appeared as a common response when the children talked about reasons for attending school. Significant numbers of children further described specific knowledge and skills such as learning Chinese characters, understanding addition and subtraction, and reading difficult books. First graders viewed school learning as helping them acquire critical skills and knowledge.

As one of the children stated, "You can't be an adult if you didn't study;" this demonstrates that the young children tended to view school learning as a step to becoming a competent adult.

Second, the children mentioned an interpersonal dimension of well-being (Mathews and Izquierdo 2009), such as contribution to others from school learning. About half of the children mentioned themes related to social well-being associated with school learning. Examples included "teaching directions to old people," "reading books to her sister," or "answering other children's questions." Not bothering others (*meiwaku o kakenai*) and not making other people worry also appeared as reasons for learning and attending school. Such comments indicated the children's close relationships with peers, teachers, and parents. For example, one boy continued the story of the student who did not want to go to school by saying that "his teacher is waiting" and not wanting to go to school is not good because "everyone will be worried." There was no socio-economic difference in the children's mention of social benefits. However, the children who lived in a downtown working-class neighborhood (*shitamachi*) mentioned more social benefits than the children who lived in a newly developed community, even after controlling for socio-economic status. As some mothers reported that people are friendly and maintain close relationships in *shitamachi*, children in *shitamachi* may have close contact with people, including elders, and may develop ideas more oriented to others around them.

However, children's articulations of social benefits were sometimes intertwined with the idea of benefits for oneself. For example, some children said that praise would make them feel happy. A sense of achievement, independence, and confidence appeared in relation to ideas about social benefits. For example, one girl stated that it is good for her to be able to read by herself because she will not take her mother's time and not bother her. While mentioning the benefit to her mother, she also mentioned a benefit to herself by stating, "It's good because it means I can do it by myself" (*hitori de*), which reflected a sense of independence and accomplishment. Social benefits and benefits for oneself may co-exist in children's minds as elements contributing to their own and others' well-being.

Finally, about 30 percent of the children talked about future well-being such as material and status benefits. Children mentioned that school learning would help them "earn money," "have a good life," or acquire status such as "being famous" or respected (*erai hito*). These themes demonstrate the complexity of the subjective and multidimensional views about the purpose of learning shared by children, which may or may not fit into socially and culturally emphasized ideas in Japan.

Obligation and unhappy consequences

Not all of the children mentioned that school is a fun place and learning is enjoyable. School experiences may not always be positive. As much as they talked about the importance of attending school and positive feelings toward school, many of them also perceived school attendance as an obligation. Some children perceived that attending school and learning at school is a requirement for school-age children; for example, one boy stated, "On school days, you have to go to school." To the question of "Why is it good to go to school?," some first graders did not articulate reasons for attending school but simply responded "because you have to go to school!" These comments indicate that the children had internalized a sense of obligation to attend school by the time they began formal schooling.

First graders also frequently reported negative consequences of not attending school and not learning. Young students sometimes described unhappy feelings and moments such as failure to learn, a lack of ability or knowledge, and unpleasant feelings. In the story of a child who did not want to go to school, six-year-old Akira described a sense of obligation and hypothetical unhappy consequences as follows:

> CHILD: His mother says, "No, you have to go," and the child says, "I don't want to," and they argue (*kenka*). And he gets scolded, and maybe he is slapped (*binta*), and then he gives up and goes to school.
> INTERVIEWER: Is that good or not good?
> CHILD: Not good. Because he has to go to school once he becomes a first grader. It's better to go to school.
> INTERVIEWER: What's good about going to school?
> CHILD: If he goes to school, he can learn a lot. At preschool, he can't study much. So, he can't do calculation, and then it's his loss (*son suru*) in the future.
> INTERVIEWER: What's not good about not being able to do calculation?
> CHILD: If he can't calculate, he can't sell desks when he works at a shop. He would feel ashamed (*hazukashii*) when he becomes adult. He would feel ashamed and sad (*kanashii*).

In this story, Akira described the unhappy consequences of not attending and learning at school. He imagined parental demands and punishment. Like Yuka, he believed that school is a place to learn. Akira foresaw the role of school learning in his future work. He imagined a situation in which a person could not perform his job due to a lack of competency. As to the differences between preschoolers and first graders, in Akira's mind, school attendance was required once a child "becomes a first grader." Akira's narrative demonstrates various negative consequences of not learning, such as a lack of skills, failure, and resulting unhappy feelings.

Like Akira, significant numbers of children mentioned that not attending school and not learning would lead to negative and unhappy consequences in the future. These negative consequences included not learning expected content, being in trouble, and not catching up with classmates. In some narratives, the children's fear of not meeting expectations appeared. Some of the children described social sanctions and punishment such as being laughed at, others' recognition of failure, or feeling ashamed (*hazukashii*). Here a motivator for learning included shame. In a previous study that examined American children, fear of not achieving did not appear as a significant theme in young children's narratives (Li et al. 2010). It is possible that expectations for learning are high and emphasized in children's socialization processes in Japan, and young children may develop a fear in which not attending school and not learning is a social failure that would bring unhappy consequences to them. As 55 percent of the children in this study also voluntarily mentioned the value of schooling and learning, students may consider attending school and learning at school a moral obligation placed on them. About 90 percent of the children liked the student who wanted to attend school in the story, while only about 18 percent liked the student who did not want to go to school.

Discussion and conclusion

In previous studies, scholars have observed that Japanese kindergarten and primary schools maintain nurturing, cooperative, and creative learning environments (Cave 2007; Lewis 1995; Stevenson and Stigler 1992). Comparative studies mainly conducted around the 1980s identified the overall positive feelings toward school shared among Japanese primary students. One may wonder whether Japanese students have changed over the last few decades and become unmotivated and unengaged, as highlighted in recent discourses within Japan.

First graders in this study generally reported positive feelings about schooling and academic learning even though it must be mentioned that participation in this study was not random. In story-completion interviews that elicited the children's voluntary and subjective feelings and ideas, many of the first graders narrated excitement and enjoyment in the process of schooling. Children also expressed an existential dimension of well-being such as the value and meaning of their school life and an interpersonal dimension such as social benefits (Mathews and Izquierdo 2009), in addition to a sense of obligation related to school learning. As Mathews and Izquierdo (2009) argued, the importance of national institutions and global forces in shaping these dimensions of well-being, educational policies, and practices play a critical role in children's conceptualization of well-being in the domain of schooling. Fundamentally, the existence of compulsory education in the nation itself reflects the message that schooling is a critical part of children's lives and well-being. The majority of Japanese children interviewed in this study demonstrated multifaceted views about how school learning contributes to their current and future well-being. While not all the children mentioned future benefits, Japanese first graders commonly articulated various benefits that school learning would bring to their future. For young children, growing up and being a competent adult is an ultimate developmental goal, even though their views about "a good adult" and pictures of happiness differ. Thus, it is not surprising that children articulated short-term and long-term benefits of school learning. Children may tend to highlight future well-being more than adults because of their unique developmental stages that encourage them to foresee their future.

Overall, these narratives suggest that children understand that schooling has important meaning in their lives. Even though academic competition and pressure are accentuated in the Japanese media, the first graders in this study did not mention much about competition among peers or display signs of academic pressure. The children talked about the negative consequences of not learning and the fear of not achieving, but their fear seemed to emerge from their understanding of general social expectations and the possibility of not meeting standards. Scholars have observed that Japanese parents place little pressure on children to learn before they start elementary school, yet once the children enter school both parents and children work hard to maximize educational success (Stevenson and Stigler 1992). The children in this study were recruited from both middle-class and working-class backgrounds, and significant numbers of working-class parents responding to the survey did not aspire to a college education for their children. However, at the primary school level, parents, especially working-class parents, emphasize the importance of not lagging behind other children (Yamamoto 2015). As expectations for fulfilling a prescribed role are strong in Japanese society (De Vos 1996; Holloway 2010), adults may emphasize the role of students and the importance of meeting standards once children enter school. The children's comments suggested that they internalized the message in which failure, or a sense of failure, can lead to unhappiness.

I did not find socio-economic differences in the children's enjoyment of school experiences and academic learning or their views related to schooling. The value that the children placed on schooling, their sense of obligation to learn, and their conceptualizations about benefits of schooling also did not differ across socio-economic groups unlike previous findings demonstrated in the U.S. (Li et al. 2010). It is possible that attending school and learning create a fundamental and common path expected for children in Japan and most children are exposed to positive messages about schooling, regardless of their socio-economic background, especially at the primary-school level. It is also possible to interpret that emphasis on egalitarianism and social relations in Japanese primary schools helps children develop positive emotion toward schooling, regardless of students' academic performance or socio-economic backgrounds (Cave 2007; Tsuneyoshi 2001). However, findings of this study have to be interpreted with caution as participation in this study was voluntary and these children were interviewed only a few months after they entered first grade. Moreover, this study focused on the domain of attending and learning at school rather than actual learning processes and behaviors. Future studies should examine children's conceptualizations related to academic processes, strategies, and engagement (e.g., what it takes to learn) depending on socio-economic status.

One important question remains. Shared values regarding education and idealized views about school learning may help children develop positive feelings about and attitudes toward schooling at the initial learning stage. However, what happens when students face difficulties in meeting the ideal of being a dedicated and competent student or when they find school learning not as enjoyable in the future? Examining the changing views related to schooling among students and the relations between student beliefs and experiences will allow us to understand more complex learning processes as they relate to children's well-being. Furthermore, as some mothers in my previous study stated that educational success would not necessarily bring happiness to their children (Yamamoto 2015), the role of schooling in children's well-being may be questioned in the changing and diversifying lives of Japanese people. The focus on schooling, rather than daily routines such as eating and bathing, may be one reason that the physical dimension of well-being did not appear in children's narratives in this study. Additional examination of children's subjective well-being outside of school life, such as their relationships with family and friends and their health conditions, would in sum present a more comprehensive picture of young students' well-being in Japan.

Acknowledgments

This research was assisted by a grant from the Abe Fellowship administered by the Social Science Research Council and the American Council of Learned Societies in cooperation with and with funds provided by the Japan Foundation.

References

Brinton, Mary C. 2010. *Lost in Transition: Youth, Work, and Instability in Postindustrial Japan*. New York: Cambridge University Press.
Cave, Peter. 2007. *Primary School in Japan: Self, Individuality, and Learning in Elementary Education*. London and New York: Routledge.
Chen, Chuansheng, and Harold W. Stevenson. 1989. "Homework: A Cross-cultural Examination." *Child Development* 60:551–561.
Chinen, Ayumu. 2012. "Yanchana kora no gakkō keiken: Gakkō bunka e no ika to dōka no jirenma no naka de [The school experience of Japanese lads: Dilemma of differentiation from an integration into school culture]." *The Journal of Educational Sociology* 91:73–94.
De Vos, George A. 1996. "Psychocultural Continuities in Japanese Social Motivation." pp. 44–84 in *Japanese Childrearing: Two Generations of Scholarship*, edited by D. W. Shwalb and B. J. Shwalb. New York: Guilford Press.
Fattore, Toby, Jan Mason and Elizabeth Watson. 2007. "Children's Conceptualisation(s) of Their Well-Being." *Social Indicators Research* 80:1–29.
Goodman, Robert et al. 2000. "The Development and Well-Being Assessment: Description and Initial Validation of an Integrated Assessment of Child and Adolescent Psychopathology." *Journal of Child Psychology and Psychiatry* 41:645–655.
Greig, Anne D., Jayne Taylor and Thomas MacKay. 2007. *Doing Research with Children: A Practical Guide*. London: Sage Publications.
Hashimoto, Kenji. 1999. *Gendai nihon no kaikyū kōzō: Riron, hōhō, keiryō bunseki* [Class structure in modern Japan: Theory, method, and quantitative analysis]. Tokyo: Tōshindo.
Holloway, Susan D. 2010. *Women and Family in Contemporary Japan*. New York: Cambridge University Press.

Holloway, Susan D., and Yoko Yamamoto. 2003. "Sensei! Early Childhood Education Teachers in Japan." pp. 181–207 in *Contemporary Perspectives in Early Childhood Education: Studying Teachers in Early Childhood Setting*, edited by O. Saracho and B. Spodek. Greenwich, CT: Information Age Publishing.

Ishida, Hiroshi, and David H. Slater. 2010. *Social Class in Contemporary Japan: Structures, Sorting and Strategies*. London and New York: Routledge.

Kariya, Takehiko. 2004. "Gakuryoku no kaisōsa wa kakudai shita ka" [Has the educational gap increased?]. pp. 127–151 in *Gakuryoku no shakaigaku*, edited by T. Kariya and K. Shimizu. Tokyo: Iwanami Shoten.

LeVine, Robert A., and Merry I. White. 1986. *Human Conditions: The Cultural Basis of Educational Developments*. New York and London: Routledge Kegan & Paul.

Lewis, Catherine C. 1995. *Educating Hearts and Minds: Reflection on Japanese Preschool and Elementary Education*. Cambridge, UK: Cambridge University Press.

Li, Jin. 2004. "I Learn and I Grow Big: Chinese Preschoolers' Purposes for Learning." *International Journal of Behavioral Development* 28/2:116–128.

Li, Jin et al. 2010. "'Why Attend School?' Chinese Immigrant and European American Preschoolers' Views and Outcomes." *Developmental Psychology* 121:9–25.

Mathews, Gordon, and Carolina Izquierdo, eds. 2009. *Pursuits of Happiness: Well-Being in Anthropological Perspective*. New York and Oxford: Berghahn Books.

Ministry of Education, Culture, Sports, Science and Technology 2013. "Gakkō kihon chōsa. Heisei 25nendo kekka no gaiyō" [Basic school survey 2013]. http://www.mext.go.jp/b_menu/toukei/chousa01/kihon/kekka/k_detail/1342607.htm. Retrieved December 11, 2014.

OECD. 2009. *Doing Better for Children*. Paris: OECD Publishing.

Onoda, Makoto. 2013. *Futsū no kyōshi ga futsū ni ikiru gakkō: Monsutā parento ron o koete* [Schools where ordinary teachers can live normally: Beyond monster parent debates]. Tokyo: Jiji Tsūshinsha.

Slater, David H. 2010. "The 'New Working Class' of Urban Japan: Socialization and Contradiction from Middle School to the Labor Market." pp. 137–169 in *Social Class in Contemporary Japan: Structure, Sorting and Strategies*, edited by H. Ishida and D. Slater. London and New York: Routledge.

Stevenson, Harold W., and James W. Stigler. 1992. *The Learning Gap: Why Our Schools Are Failing and What We Can Learn from Japanese and Chinese Education*. New York: Touchstone.

Takada, Kazuhiro. 2008. "Shōichi puroburamu ankēto bunseki" [Survey analyses of first grader problems]. pp. 47–62 in *Ōsaka no kodomotachi 2008 nendo ban*, edited by Ōsaka-fu Jinken Kyōiku Kenkyūkai. Osaka: Ōsaka-fu Jinken Kyōiku Kenkyūkai.

Takahashi, Shotaro. 1999. "Chaos in Elementary Classrooms." *Japan Quarterly* 46:78–82.

Tsuneyoshi, Ryoko. 2001. *Japanese Model of Schooling: Comparisons with the U.S.* New York: Routledge.

Uchida, Yukiko, and Shinobu Kitayama. 2009. "Happiness and Unhappiness in East and West: Themes and Variations." *Emotion* 9/4:441–456.

Yamamoto, Yoko. 2015. "Social Class and Japanese Mothers' Support for Young Children's Education: A Qualitative Study." *Journal of Early Childhood Research* 13/2:165–180.

Yamamoto, Yoko, and Mary C. Brinton. 2010. "Cultural Capital in East Asian Educational Context: The Case of Japan." *Sociology of Education* 83/1:67–83.

3

"UNHAPPY" AND ISOLATED YOUTH IN THE MIDST OF SOCIAL CHANGE

Representations and subjective experiences of *hikikomori* in contemporary Japan

Sachiko Horiguchi

Hikikimori is a category coined in the late 1990s to refer to "youth in isolation," and has been considered a social problem in Japan since the 2000s afflicting (mostly male) youth. *Hikikomori* literally means "withdrawal" and generally refers to those who stay at home for a long period of time without taking part in any social activities, such as attending school, working, or socializing with friends outside the home. *Hikikomori* refers to the condition of withdrawal as well as to the person/people experiencing the condition. The common feature is said to be lack of interaction with others (Shiokura 2002[1999]: 23), and by definition, it is usually distinguished from mental diseases.

This chapter examines what well-being means for youth in Japan by positing *hikikomori* as an issue that symbolizes youth *ill-being*, relying on Mathews and Izquierdo's (2009) four-dimensional model of well-being. In so doing, I draw on examinations of media discourses, ethnographic data from participant observation conducted in support organizations for withdrawn youth, and interviews with those who identify themselves as *hikikomori*, parents or siblings of recluses, psychiatrists, and others providing support. I begin with an overview of the *hikikomori* issue as it is represented in media discourses. Based on this overview, I discuss ways in which youth isolation is problematized in its physical dimension (Mathews and Izquierdo 2009: 261–62), focusing in particular on the perceptive levels of pleasure and health experienced by the socially withdrawn youth. I then examine the interpersonal dimension of well-being (Mathews and Izquierdo 2009: 261–63), highlighting how youth in withdrawal distance themselves from interpersonal relations and what they expect from interpersonal communication in the process of recovery. This is followed by a discussion of ways in which they make sense of and question the meaning of life in light of the existential dimension of happiness (Mathews and Izquierdo 2009: 261, 263).

Finally, with respect to the fourth dimension of institutional forces structuring well-being (Mathews and Izquierdo 2009: 261, 263–264), I analyze how problematization of *hikikomori* at the national level reflects structural changes at local, national, and global levels.

Representations in the media and official discourses

At the level of general media discourse, *hikikomori* is an ethnicized, gendered, and classed phenomenon. First, it is generally believed that *hikikomori* is unique to contemporary Japanese society (Saitō 2001: 124–133) due to its particular characteristics. This does not necessarily mean, however, that socially withdrawn youth in reality exist at a larger scale in Japan than in other societies, since there is no equivalent term available outside Japan and it is difficult to make precise comparisons. Saitō Tamaki, the psychiatrist who coined the term *hikikomori*, in the early years of discussing *hikikomori* stated that the issue may be seen as unique to Japan. He (Saitō 2001: 124–133) gave an in-depth analysis through developing Doi Takeo's theory of dependence (*amae*) and argued (2001: 127) that the existence of *hikikomori* is in itself living evidence to *Nihonjinron* or discourses of Japanese uniqueness. This type of culturalist argument relies on popularized discourses about Japanese families arguing that it is acceptable for adult-age children to live with parents (see Horiguchi 2011) whereas in the "West" this arrangement is discouraged. My view is that youth social withdrawal is likely to remain hidden in other societies where such an arrangement is discouraged due to stigma. I have met a number of people from the U.S., the U.K., Brazil, France, and other countries who, upon hearing about my study of the *hikikomori* issue, confided to me that they know relatives under a similar condition but had never discussed this with others because of a lack of language to articulate the issue and for fear of potential stigma. Furthermore, there are signs that values around home-leaving are changing in the "West;" American and British media (Davidson 2014; Koslow and Booth 2012) have widely reported a "growing trend" in the "West" of adult-age children labeled "the boomerang children / generation" (Parker 2012) who live with their parents after a short period of living on their own.

Hikikomori is often presented as a youth issue (Saitō 2013[1998]), as can be seen in the title of the *Guidelines of intervention in local mental health activities for social hikikomori mainly among those in their teens and twenties* by the Ministry of Health, Labor and Welfare (MHLW 2001, 2003). A nationwide survey (MHLW 2003) revealed that the average age was 26.7, though the age ranges widely from 13 to over 30. A more recent survey conducted by a nation-wide association of parents' groups (Sakai et al. 2013) noted the average age of 33.1, pointing to the "ageing" of *hikikomori*. However, it is impossible to arrive at an accurate age range from these reported cases. Yet the numbers show that among the withdrawn, those in their twenties or thirties are viewed as problematic and hence reported.

Mass media seems to agree that there are more male than female *hikikomori* cases (Hisada 1999), and surveys confirm this tendency (see Saitō 2013

[1998]: 31; 2002: 31–32). Again, rather than being "real numbers," these data show how male cases are more likely to be reported (Shiokura 2000: 68). Journalist Shiokura (2000: 268–269) writes that the reason for this gender difference at the level of representation is generally explained through more pressures put on males than females to achieve "social participation," primarily in the labor market.

Hikikomori has been said to be a middle-class phenomenon. The mass media rhetoric sees it as a potential problem for "most" Japanese families (Shiokura 2000: 239–240). Saitō (2013[1998]: 50) suggests that the phenomenon is frequently found in families in the middle-class or above, with a university-educated father in the executive post in a large corporation and a professional housewife (*sengyō shufu*) mother. This does not mean, however, that withdrawal only occurs in middle-class families: throughout my fieldwork, I have seen cases of withdrawn youth of various family backgrounds. Yet upper-middle-class families are the ones more likely to seek support. With growing attention to child poverty in recent years, there are new discussions on *hikikomori* as being symbolic of poverty. It may be said, nevertheless, that sustaining the condition of withdrawal requires certain socio-economic resources, for without such resources the socially withdrawn would starve to death. Or, perhaps more likely, they would be forced to engage with the outside world to fulfill basic needs.

Hikikomori in its physical dimension

In this section, I discuss how socially withdrawn youth survive in isolation while fulfilling basic needs and will discuss problematic consequences in the physical sense, with particular attention to the perceptive levels of pleasure and health experienced by the individuals. *Hikikomori* is defined as social isolation, and yet it is impossible for those isolating themselves to survive without existence of people and institutions that provide them with food and shelter.

The majority of socially withdrawn youth are said to spend much of their time in a house with their parents, with varying levels of interactions with their family members or the outside world. While a widely popularized image of a *hikikomori* is a complete shut-in never stepping outside his/her room, many of the experiences I came across in my fieldwork entail life outside the individual's rooms or his/her house, though with very limited meaningful communication with the outside world. *Hikikomori* is not the same as *tojikomori*, a "shut-in," in the physical sense. One of the features of the withdrawn lifestyle is said to be a reversed day and night shift (*chūya gyakuten*), where the person stays up all night when society is "resting" and falls asleep as the morning starts (Saitō 2013[1998]: 141–142). In acute cases, a mother may leave a tray with some dinner dishes outside the door of the child's room. The child brings the tray into his/her room later in the evening to avoid contact with the mother and puts the tray back outside the door for the mother to pick up in the morning after finishing the meal. In other cases, the child may come to the kitchen when the other family members are asleep and help himself/herself with the meal. He/she may also go out on his/her own to nearby convenience stores (often by bicycle to avoid eye contact with neighbors) late at night to buy some prepared food or cup noodles. Whilst having different meal routines from other family members is common, there are also cases where the withdrawn child maintains a high level of communication and happily dines together with the family, or he/she performs domestic roles and cooks for the family. If the socially withdrawn persons live on their own, they buy or prepare food for themselves; the financial resources necessary to maintain life in solitude are typically provided by parents or through social welfare (often with diagnoses of depression or other mental disorders).

The physical dimensions of withdrawal entail not only this reversed schedule for sleeping and eating but other "problem behaviors" as well. Physical violence in the home (*kateinai bōryoku*), particularly to parents, is not necessarily seen in all cases but is seen as a typical occurrence (MHLW 2003). Even if there is no violence, the "unproductive" (in a capitalist sense) and asocial lifestyle itself usually appears puzzling and "problematic" to "normal" people. Withdrawn youth often suffer from low quality of sleep despite many hours spent in bed/ *futon*. Throughout the night when they are awake, they may spend a lot of time playing video games (online or offline), watching TV, reading books and manga, or surfing the Internet in their rooms, depending on the availability of devices required for these activities. These behaviors make *hikikomori* appear "lazy" or "avoidant of social pressures" in the eyes of productive members of society. But psychologically, they constantly suffer from high levels of anxiety so that these daily activities become unpleasurable and are merely a means to let time pass. At the same time, they find "life out there" even more threatening and therefore prolong their lifestyle in isolation. Moreover, they often note their anxiety over life after their parents pass away, associated with fears of losing food and shelter. Retreat from society may be seen as a form of temporary escape, but as I discuss below, it does not free the afflicted from long-term consequences of isolation. In their attempts to protect themselves from shame, they go out of the home if they need to after the sun sets to avoid drawing attention from neighbors, typically to convenience stores, 100 yen shops, second-hand bookshops, or local libraries. Many members of support groups I have talked to say that they hesitate to ask their parents for pocket money and therefore try to minimize their expenses for their daily activities, which further limits their activities outside the home. Saitō (2002) actually encourages parents to give pocket money to their withdrawing children in the process of recovery as incentive to reconnect with society.

Withdrawing from society may bring health problems, but at the same time, there are those who attempt to maintain their physical well-being. In cases where they spend 24 hours a day in their rooms for years (which were rare among the cases I have seen during my fieldwork), they often grow their hair and beards long and develop strong odor due to lack of showering/bathing. Some exhibit symptoms of obsessive-compulsive disorders (MHLW 2003), which poses difficulties in public spaces, or have eating disorders, particularly among female cases (Kondō 1999: 25). Yet others worry about becoming overweight or unhealthy and therefore include exercises in their daily routine. Ex-*hikikomori* Moroboshi (2003: 71–79) writes comically about how he started taking walks in the neighborhood every evening and working out indoors after becoming overweight due to stress-induced overeating and inactivity. Similarly, one ex-*hikikomori* mentioned to me that in order to keep fit, he used to exercise everyday with dumbbells he bought at a 100-yen shop and regularly went running and cycling late in the evenings. He joked that isolated youth are not flattered when they are told that they "look young" or they "have beautiful skin" since such phrases point to their lack of life experiences or maturity. He explained that they simply look pale because they spend too much time indoors.

While a withdrawn lifestyle seems to meet the minimal physical needs of food and sleep and a certain level of health, it significantly lacks in the pleasure that comes with intimate sexual encounters with a significant other, which is often seen as a rite of passage for youth (see Ueyama 2001: 151). Moroboshi (2003: 103–107) writes that in his pre-*hikikomori* years as an undergraduate college student, he did not worry about his inexperience of sex. But after graduating from college and realizing that his peers, both male and female, would have had the experience, his inferiority complex as someone lacking in both maturity and masculinity grew. He acknowledges having sexual desires, but fears entering a physically intimate relationship due to the lack of masculine confidence. This *dōtei* complex (virgin complex) made him uncomfortable to listen to pop songs or to watch "trendy dramas," many of which take up romance as a core theme (Moroboshi 2003: 106–107).

To conclude, a *hikikomori*'s individual bodily experience is characterized by isolation and significant lack of engagement with others or with society at large. They often go through emotional anxieties, shame, and guilt in response to their physical state of withdrawal. And yet, their physical isolation is temporarily enabled by their (financial) connectedness with family members or social welfare, which they may lose as they grow old.

Hikikomori in its interpersonal dimension

A key characteristic of *hikikomori*, as noted earlier, is retreat from interpersonal relations. It is therefore important to examine how withdrawn individuals conceive, perceive, and experience their relation with others. Psychiatrist Saitō (2013[1998]: 77–89; 2002: 72–75) hypothesizes a "*hikikomori* system," in which he explains how a vicious circle prolongs withdrawal. In the "healthy model," the individual, the family, and society all share contact with each other. In the "*hikikomori* system," however, contact is lost between the withdrawn, their families, and society. Once individuals begin withdrawing, they develop self-hatred, which in turn prolongs the isolation. The family members also become increasingly anxious and impatient, with shame and stigma attached to having a withdrawn person in the family. There are cases where not only the socially withdrawn youth but family members as well stop attending events with their extended family, for fear of being asked about how they are doing and being compared with other "successful" relatives. The withdrawn feel pressure to start taking some form of action, which exacerbates their anxiety and irritation, leading to further withdrawal.

At the social level, withdrawal is often triggered by issues in interpersonal relations. One common trigger is *ijime* (bullying) from peers in school (Saitō and NHK 2004: 81), and indeed, bullying featured as a cause in many cases I have come across in fieldwork. Sociologist Ogino (2008: 129–33) lists four lines of argument made by psychiatrists and sociologists on *hikikomori* and interpersonal relations:

1. Youth retreat because they lack the skills or mental strength to deal with complexities and conflicts in building and maintaining interpersonal relations.
2. Socially withdrawn persons have a perfectionist view of friendship where they want to be completely understood by their friends, and they are disappointed by the "real" interpersonal relations, which fail to meet their expectations.
3. In an era where young people increasingly have superficial relationships that value *nori* (keeping pace with others), *hikikomori* expect a deeper level of "understanding" and hence retreat from interpersonal relations.
4. Contemporary youth have such low esteem that they try their best to maintain an excessively empathetic mode of communication and avoid doing harm to each other, while withdrawn youth find themselves unable to get over these psychological pressures for maintaining communication that requires a high level of empathy.

Ogino (2008) finds in his study of 48 ex-*hikikomori* narratives that the majority expressed distress in interpersonal relations, which provides evidence for the first line of argument above. Most ex-*hikikomori* I have talked to also mentioned that they have found it hard to deal with interpersonal relations since their childhood, often noting their experiences of having been bullied. Ogino (2008) is critical of the second line of argument, noting that no narratives pointed to a longing for complete understanding in communication, and in relation to the third and fourth arguments, Ogino (2008) notes some narratives that point to the superficiality of human relations among youth and the importance of mutual acceptance in identity construction and self-esteem. In my own fieldwork, whereas I have only heard of the longing for full understanding from a leader of a support organization, many ex-*hikikomori* expressed their wish to make "true" friends who accept and understand each other at a "deep" level. One such individual mentioned that since he was bullied in his childhood, he learned to superficially follow trends and to behave similarly with his peers in his adolescent years and came to be heavily distressed with the constant pressure to perform and the inability to build deep, intimate relations with others.

It is also important to examine the effect of the Internet and other social media on socially withdrawn youth, which allow them to be physically withdrawn while staying socially connected with others. At the same time, the superficiality of media communication means that it is also difficult to achieve a complete level of mutual understanding or intimacy in online communities (Takayama 2008: 267). Anonymity in online communication can have the positive effect of allowing stigmatized individuals to connect with each other but can, at the same time, easily create negativity that may damage the self-esteem of these individuals. Online media may be a great resource of information on communities and networks or counselling services for socially withdrawn youth and their parents (Takayama 2008: 266) as in the case of *"Hikikomori* Support Net" (Tokyo Metropolitan Government 2015), but can cause Internet addiction and exacerbate withdrawal, and the immediacy of communication required in emerging social media (such as LINE) may be a source of stress for youth.

In this section thus far, I have examined how withdrawal entails lack of well-being in the interpersonal dimension. It is also important to consider ways in which support organizations help the isolated youth get over the distress experienced in interpersonal relations and what these youth expect from support organizations. Saitō (2002: 128–31) suggests that the goal of the treatment is having three or more friends, noting the importance of recovering interpersonal relations.

A three-step model of *hōmon* (visiting support), *ibasho* (literally "a place to be," referring to a type of community space), and *shūrō* (employment support) is conceived as an effective approach by the government (MHLW 2010) as well as privately run lay support organizations with a long experience of supporting socially withdrawn youth (Nakamura and Horiguchi 2008). Below I outline ways in which these steps are practiced.

Visiting support is available from public health centers or privately run support organizations, with a range in approaches, frequency, and duration. First, the supporter typically has contact with parents and negotiates strategies to gain access to the child without intimidating him/her (Nakamura and Horiguchi 2008: 194). Once they are able to meet, they may enjoy playing games, chatting, reading *manga*, or watching TV together; the supporter may take the child outside to cinemas, events, and cafes and practice taking public transport in the later stages.

Ibasho, which literally translates as "a place to be," is a key term used to describe the foundation of *hikikomori* support groups. It is attached to a space where people can simply be, without being expected to fulfill specific roles. The term also describes a place of belonging in its abstract sense and implies the expectation that the person will see it as a place to return to. Much of what is done at an *ibasho* is left to the participants themselves. Flexibility in time and space management is often ensured to make it a comfortable and secure (*anshin*) place outside of the home (Kaneko 2006; Ogino 2013). Events are organized by staff or members, including seasonal outings like summer festivals or end-of-year parties. These outings provide members with shared social experiences as a basis for building mutual interpersonal relations (see Ogino 2013). It is important to note, however, that for socially withdrawn youth, getting over their trauma with interpersonal relations from their past and attempting to make friends is usually a struggle. As one male member in his late 20s said in an interview with me, it can be particularly difficult to build sustainable friendships with other ex-*hikikomori* who are overly sensitive or do not know how to maintain a healthy distance from each other.

The employment support may include programs where members actually gain some job experience and earn a salary, or skills-training programs focusing on preparing them for job hunting. Ex-*hikikomori* over the age of 30 mention the difficulty of getting a job without any previous experience, partly due to the age limits in most job descriptions. Thus they have high expectations for the job opportunities within the support organizations. The nature of the employment support at one group is to let members work at their own pace, without time pressure. There are also groups that emphasize discipline to prepare members for work in a "real" environment and others that provide job opportunities in local companies with individualized support provided by both the employer and the members.

This three-step model is designed to help the withdrawn youth to become psychologically and economically independent while reconstructing connections with larger society. While some find this approach helpful for recovery, others are critical, suggesting that it is too linear and downplays the will of the youth themselves. It is often the case that the individuals go back and forth between isolation and social participation (often part-time for a short span). Some suggest that self-help groups—rather than support groups—cater better to their needs by providing a forum to share anxieties with others of similar backgrounds in a safer environment. One interviewee mentioned that he prefers a supporter who accompanies him while he seeks a way out over one that puts him on a certain route, and another said she is reluctant to work with someone with a strong *shien-shū* ("odor of a supporter") and an "arrogant" attitude.

In summary, this section outlined how withdrawal may be seen as behavior lacking in the interpersonal dimension of well-being and the ways in which support groups approach their target group in an attempt to re-integrate them into interpersonal relationships and larger society.

Hikikomori and the existential dimension of happiness

As hinted above, one of the reasons why support for isolated youth can be difficult is that the socially withdrawn individuals may be asking fundamental questions about the meaning of work. As Ishikawa (2007) suggests, these questions comprise part of a larger set of existential questions about meanings of life: Why does one have to be a productive member of society? Why does society require people to communicate with others? Does my own existence entail any value?

Individuals in isolation often continue to ask these questions throughout their withdrawal period and beyond.

Retreat from society may be assessed positively as a period for contemplating the meaning of life. Some commentators suggest that young people in general need a period of solitude to develop their sense of identity to find pathways to life as part of a maturing process. Serizawa (2010), for example, provides a positive appraisal of withdrawal, noting that it is based on a fundamental human need. The length one needs for reflection can vary among individuals, and some ex-*hikikomori* argue that the withdrawn should not be disturbed or rushed during the stage of reflection. Maruyama (2014), an ex-*hikikomori* who currently runs a support organization, suggests that retreat from society reflects a subconscious need of the person to prepare himself/herself for rebirth as a renewed self. Maruyama uses the metaphor of a tunnel with no end to be seen, to explain the withdrawal as a period of negotiating the burdens of normative expectations in society with an elevated level of self-consciousness. Based on his own experience of "reaching the bottom" (*sokotsuki*) and eventually finding the energy to live on, he suggests that supporters should patiently wait until the withdrawn is fully re-energized to make his/her way out into society.

This necessary period of contemplation, however, is usually not experienced as a happy period. As noted earlier, the withdrawal is often experienced as a stressful, anxious period with a high level of distress. Furthermore, not everyone agrees that the socially withdrawn should be "protected" from pressures from the outside; one ex-*hikikomori* stated in an interview that he had not experienced energy gushing out when "reaching the bottom," and pointed to the dangers of over-emphasizing the need to wait. He noted that he had seen some unfortunate cases of socially withdrawn youth committing suicide, breaking through the "bottom" to death.

The existential questions outlined above lead isolated individuals to challenge social norms. Ueyama (2001), an ex-*hikikomori* writer and blogger, points to the importance of questioning normative social expectations. His writings display his fears of labor, money, or sex that symbolize mainstream social norms in his opinion. His argument sustains a critique of the unquestioned focus on labor as a means for survival in contemporary society, which suppresses individual autonomy or values. Katsuyama (2011), another ex-*hikikomori*, seeks alternatives to the normalized life courses. Katsuyama (2011: 178–91) questions the meaning of wage labor or the assumption that unwillingness to work is "laziness," and provides recipes for a "secure" (*anshin*) lifestyle withdrawn from society and free of a sense of guilt, by giving up competing against others and accepting downscaling. Katsuyama (2011: 225) also critiques support programs that focus on helping individuals adjust themselves to society, arguing for the need of socially withdrawn individuals and support organizations to challenge normative ideals and to transform society. To summarize, *hikikomori* in its existential sense may be seen as a form of resistance against social norms and questioning the meaning of life in contemporary society.

Hikikomori and national/global issues concerning youth

In this final section, I attempt to analyze how the issues with *hikikomori* reflect national and global concerns. In particular, I examine how the problematization of *hikikomori* at the national level (in policy and media discourses) is influenced by changes in labor market conditions.

In 2001 the government published its initial *Guideline* on coping with *hikikomori* cases (MHLW 2001) along with results of surveys conducted in health centers all over Japan, in response to a "moral panic" surrounding socially withdrawn youth (see Horiguchi 2012). Itō and Yoshida (2005: 17–20) suggest that this *Guideline* as well as media reports prompted awareness of *hikikomori* as a social problem and clearly designated the public mental health sector's responsibilities for support of *hikikomori*. The *Guideline* showed a marked shift in the government's approach, but the problem was still located within the private realm of the family and mental welfare, rather than in the public realms of education or the labor market (Itō and Yoshida 2005: 24). Higuchi (2004: 122) argued that few public organizations offer employment support, due to lack of networking with schools, private organizations, or job agencies that deal with labor issues. It should also be noted that compared to the governmental funding made available for NEET (youth not in education, employment, or training) support (see Toivonen 2013), only limited governmental funding has been made available for *hikikomori* support. A revised MHLW *Guideline* (2010), drafted by a team of mostly psychiatrists, continues to rely heavily on mental health and psychiatric approaches/treatments. But with an inclusion of a psychiatric social worker with experience in employment support programs on the team, it provides a more concrete model for employment support and points to the importance of networking with employment support agencies and welfare systems.

Despite the state's focus on *hikikomori* as a mental health issue, concerns in Japan have revolved around its being a labor market issue tied to anxieties about aging Japan and the deterioration of modern work ethics (Shiokura 2000: 187–188). The decline of work ethics has become generally associated with discussions of *furītā* (youth in irregular part-time work) since the late 1980s and NEET since the mid-2000s. It has been said that post-war institutions, such as schools, public agencies, and the mass media, intrude on family life with a homogenizing force that regularizes the life-cycle experience across occupations and family forms, making life-cycle transitions (e.g., school leaving, work entrance, marriage, child rearing) orderly and uniform (Kelly 1986: 611; Brinton 1993: 79). On the one hand, as Brinton (2011) finds, prior to the 1990s, youth in Japan had a relatively good chance of securing jobs, regardless of educational backgrounds or communication skills, supported by smooth school-work transition and an underlying stable economy. On the other hand, such rigid life-cycle transitions meant that individual failure or indecisiveness at the early stages in life could not be compensated for by further human capital investment later in the life cycle (Brinton 1993: 79). Indeed, in discussions of *hikikomori* in support groups, participants suggest that Japanese society should allow for youths' "trial and error" in finding their way until around age 30, implying that rigid life-cycle transitions are one of the causes of social withdrawal. With economic stagnation, along with the increasing participation of women in the work force, particularly after the Equal Employment Opportunity Law (1986), the rigidity of life-cycle transitions has been shaken (Brinton 1993: 229–234; Mathews 2003: 118). The "lost decades" since the 1990s have made it increasingly difficult for youth to secure stable jobs (see also Allison 2013). Furthermore, due to a relative decline in the manufacturing industry and the self-employed sector and a rise of the service sector, demands for a labor force with high interpersonal communication skills rose, deeming youth lacking in such skills as "problematic." While there are discourses that stamp these youth as "lazy," as discussed above, some ex-*hikikomori* question the normative work ethics, and commentators such as Ogi (2002) note the difficulty with which youth today find positive meaning in work due to the prolonged economic recession. Genda (2001) also argues that the blame for the rise of youth in unemployment or irregular labor should not be placed on youth but rather on the job protection for older workers and that new graduates have been pushed into non-standard work simply because firms have cut down on hiring new graduates. This negativity has been fueled by national concerns of a declining birth rate and aging, as well as by the estimate of one million *hikikomori* (Shiokura 2000: 188–189). If, indeed, there are as many who supposedly cannot "reproduce," it would be a huge challenge for a society where "social and welfare policies historically have been constructed so as to support the most productive elements of society" (Goodman 2002: 15).

These societal concerns frame existing and future policies surrounding Japanese youth. But it is also important to avoid painting a generalized picture of uniquely "unhappy Japanese youth." The one million "guesstimate" above has no empirical grounds (Horiguchi 2012: 127), and it is unlikely that the majority of Japanese youth withdraw from society. There is huge diversity in the experiences of Japanese youth just like young people in any other society, and generational conflicts between adults and youth can be found in any society at any point of time in history. In an attempt to critique adult-centered assessments of youth, sociologist Furuichi (2011) challenges popularized portrayals of "unhappy" youth faced with rising inequality or an impoverished labor market and argues in his best-selling book *Zetsubō no kuni no kōfuku na wakamonotachi* (The happy youth of a desperate country) that young people today are "happier" with their lives than their previous generation. Furuichi suggests contemporary Japanese youth live in a society with the highest level of affluence and peace in post-war Japan, and despite or because of the uncertainties for their future, they find themselves content with their lives here and now.[1] The youth examined in this chapter are hardly satisfied with their lives in the past or present, but they are also not representative of Japanese youth as a whole.

Furthermore, youth precarity should be situated as a global phenomenon rather than a uniquely Japanese problem. Precarious labor market conditions and high unemployment rates among youth are problems experienced in other OECD countries and elsewhere (see Means 2015). Youth precariousness in this global context is understood as one of the symptoms of neoliberalism, characterized by state pull-back and increased marketization, the impact of which on the everyday lives of youth across the globe has been documented (Allison and Piot 2014). This implies that Japanese youth are not alone in being faced with flexibilization of life-cycle transitions and uncertainties about the future. The "rise" of the "boomerang generation" of adult-age children living with parents due to the economic downturn in the U.S. and the U.K. is symbolic of this trend. Youth around the globe are also affected by the spread of the Internet and social media, which, as discussed above, may potentially have an impact on youth sociality anywhere. With the recent translation of Saitō's classic (2013[1998]) on *hikikomori* into English it can be expected that social isolation of youth will be more widely discussed beyond Japan. In short, this section has outlined ways in which *hikikomori* has been discussed in state policies and discourses as a national problem, while pointing to the possibility of situating the precarity of youth as a "global" issue, potentially afflicting youth beyond Japan.

Conclusion: "Happy" or "unhappy" Japanese youth?

Through examining *hikikomori* as symbolizing ill-being and unhappiness of contemporary Japanese youth in its physical, interpersonal, existential, and structural dimensions, this chapter has shed light on the extent to which youthhood is experienced as a "happy" period of life, with hopes and/or anxieties for the future, at the individual and social levels. *Hikikomori* in its physical dimension entails isolation from society in time and space, which often reflects and intensifies anxieties about the outside world. Retreat from interpersonal relations, often due to trauma induced by past failures to develop a "complete" friendship, characterizes *hikikomori*, and much of *hikikomori* support attempts to help withdrawn youth recover the joy of relating with others and larger society. While asking existential questions about the meaning of life may be seen as a necessary process for youth in general and can potentially be a key for human development and human happiness, it may also become a source of distress and an obstacle for withdrawn youth's re-integration into society. Structurally, media representations of *hikikomori* as a social "problem" reflect domestic concerns around youth precarity and more broadly, structural social changes faced by an aging society. In the above discussions, I have shown ways in which socially withdrawn youth make sense of their struggles against the backdrop of these changes and social norms that emphasize "productivity" and "interpersonal skills" while stigmatizing "unproductive" and "uncommunicative" youth. The reader should be reminded that social withdrawal does not impact the whole population of Japanese youth, nor is it uniquely Japanese, and that despite uncertainties lingering in the future, many Japanese youth are "happily" enjoying their lives.

Note

1. See Fujimura et al. (2016) for a quantitative study conducted by a group of Japanese sociologists on happiness among contemporary Japanese youth, which provides a partial critique of Furuichi's theses.

Acknowledgements

Part of the research conducted for this chapter was supported by Grant-in-Aid for Scientific Research (No. 22720333). I would like to thank all the individuals and institutions that have supported me during the course of this research.

References

Allison, Anne. 2013. *Precarious Japan*. Durham, NC: Duke University Press.
Allison, Anne, and Charles Piot. 2014. "Editors' Note on 'Neoliberal Futures'." *Cultural Anthropology* 29(1):3–7. http://dx.doi.org/10.14506/ca29.1.02. Retrieved July 19, 2015.
Brinton, Mary C. 1993. *Women and the Economic Miracle*. Berkeley and Los Angeles: University of California Press.
Brinton, Mary C. 2011. *Lost in Transition*. Cambridge: Cambridge University Press.
Davidson, Adam. 2014. "It's Official: The Boomerang Kids Won't Leave." *The New York Times Magazine* (June 20, 2014). http://www.nytimes.com/2014/06/22/magazine/its-official-the-boomerang-kids-wont-leave.html. Retrieved July 19, 2015.
Fujimura, Masayuki, Tomohiko Asano and Ichigo Habuichi, eds. 2016. *Gendai wakamono no kōfuku: Fuankan shakai no ikiru* [Happiness of Japanese youth today: Living in a society with a sense of insecurity]. Tokyo: Kōseisha.
Furuichi, Noritoshi. 2011. *Zetsubō no kuni no kōfuku-na wakamonotachi* [The happy youth of a desperate country]. Tokyo: Kodansha.
Genda, Yūji. 2001. *Shigoto no naka no aimai na fuan* [A nagging sense of job insecurity]. Tokyo: Chūō Kōron Shinsha.
Goodman, Roger. 2002. "Anthropology, Policy, and the Study of Japan." pp. 1–28 in *Family and Social Policy in Japan: Anthropological Approaches*, edited by R. Goodman. Cambridge: Cambridge University Press.
Higuchi, Akihiko. 2004. "Dare ga hikikomori o kea suru no ka: kazoku ni okeru jendā kōsei no shiten kara mita hikikomori shien no kōzu" [Who takes care of *hikikomori*?: The structure of *hikikomori* support from the perspective of gender fairness in the family]. pp. 120–127 in *Gender Policies of the State and Local Governments* (F-GENS Publications Series 3). Tokyo: Ochanomizu University.
Hisada, Megumi. 1999. "Seikimatsu no yamai "hikikomori" hyakumannin no higeki" [An illness at the end of the century: *Hikikomori*, a tragedy of a million]. *Bungei Shunjū* 7/8:286–299.
Horiguchi, Sachiko. 2011. "Coping with *Hikikomori*: Socially Withdrawn Youth and the Japanese Family." pp. 216–235 in *Home and Family in Japan: Continuity and Transformation*, edited by R. Ronald and A. Alexy. London: Routledge.
Horiguchi, Sachiko. 2012. "Hikikomori: How Private Isolation Caught the Public Eye." pp. 122–138 in *A Sociology of Japanese Youth: From Returnees to NEETs*, edited by R. Goodman, Y. Imoto and T. Toivonen. London: Routledge.
Ishikawa, Ryōko. 2007. *Hikikomori no "gōru": "Shūrō" demo naku "taijin kankei" demo naku* [The goals of *hikikomori*: Neither employment nor interpersonal relations]. Tokyo: Seikyūsha.

Itō, Junichiro, and Kōji Yoshida. 2005. "*Hikikomori gaidorain no hankyō to igi*" [The impact and meanings of the guideline for *hikikomori* support]. *Kokoro no Kagaku* 123:17–24.
Kaneko, Sachiko. 2006. "Japan's 'Socially Withdrawn Youths' and Time Constraints in Japanese Society: Management and Conceptualization of Time in a Support Group for '*Hikikomori*'." *Time & Society* 15/2–3:233–249.
Katsuyama, Minoru. 2011. *Anshin hikikomori raifu* (Secure *hikikomori* life). Tokyo: Ota Shuppan.
Kelly, William. 1986. "Rationalization and Nostalgia: Cultural Dynamics of New Middle-class Japan." *American Ethnologist* 13/4:603–618.
Kondō, Naoji. 1999. "Hikikomori kēsu no genjō to seishin-igakuteki rikai" [The current situation and psychiatric understanding of *hikikomori* cases]. pp. 10–45 in *Hikikomori no rikai to enjo* [Understanding and supporting *hikikomori*], edited by N. Kondō and T. Hasegawa. Tokyo: Hōbunsha.
Koslow, Sally, and Hannah Booth. 2012. "Generation Boomerang: Children Who Go Back to Mum and Dad." *Guardian* (March 15, 2012). http://www.pewsocialtrends.org/2012/03/15/the-boomerang-generation/. Retrieved July 19, 2015.
Maruyama, Yasuhiko. 2014. *Futōkō/hikikomori ga owaru toki* [When school refusal/withdrawal ends]. Yokohama: Life Support-sha.
Mathews, Gordon. 2003. "Can 'a Real Man' Live for His Family?: *Ikigai* and Masculinity in Today's Japan." pp. 109–25 in *Men and Masculinities in Contemporary Japan: Dislocating the Salaryman Doxa*, edited by J. Roberson and N. Suzuki. London: Routledge.
Mathews, Gordon, and Carolina Izquierdo, eds. 2009. *Pursuits of Happiness: Well-Being in Anthropological Perspective*. New York and Oxford: Berghahn Books.
Means, Alexander. 2015. "Generational Precarity, Education, and the Crisis of Capitalism: Conventional, Neo-Keynesian, and Marxian Perspectives." *Critical Sociology*. http://crs.sagepub.com/content/early/2015/01/07/0896920514564088.refs. Retrieved July 19, 2015.
MHLW (Ministry of Health, Labor and Welfare). 2001. *Jūdai/nijūdai o chūshin to shita "shakaiteki hikikomori" o meguru chiiki seishin hoken katsudō no gaidorain* [Guidelines of intervention in local mental health activities for "social hikikomori" mainly among teenagers and those in their twenties (provisional version)]. Tokyo: Kokuritsu Seishin/Shinkei Center.
MHLW (Ministry of Health, Labor and Welfare). 2003. *Jūdai/nijūdai o chūshin to shita "shakaiteki hikikomori" o meguru chiiki seishin hoken katsudō no gaidorain* [Guidelines of intervention in local mental health activities for "*social hikikomori*" mainly among teenagers and those in their twenties (complete version)]. Tokyo: Kokuritsu Seishin/Shinkei Center. http://www.mhlw.go.jp/topics/2003/07/tp0728-1.html. Retrieved July 19, 2015.
MHLW (Ministry of Health, Labor and Welfare). 2010. *Hikikomori no hyōka/shien ni kan suru gaidorain* [Guideline of *hikikomori* assessment/support]. http://www.ncgmkohnodai.go.jp/pdf/jidouseishin/22ncgm_hikikomori.pdf. Retrieved July 19, 2015.
Moroboshi, Noa. 2003. *Hikikomori, seki-ra-ra-ra* [Naked *hikikomori*]. Tokyo: Sōshisha.
Nakamura, Yoshitaka, and Sachiko Horiguchi. 2008. "Hōmon/ibasho/shūrō shien: 'Hikikomori' keikensha e no shien hōhō" [Visiting support/place to be/ employment support: Methods of support for ex-*hikikomori*]. pp. 186–211 in *"Hikikomori" e no shakaigakuteki apurōchi: Media, tōjisha, shien katsudō* [Sociological approaches to *hikikomori*: Media, those who identify as *hikikomori*, support activities], edited by T. Ogino et al. Kyōto: Minerva Shobō.
Ogi, Naoki. 2002. "Wakamono ga kibō wo motenai shakai ni mirai wa nai" [There is no future in a society to which young people cannot hold hope]. *Sekai* 697:232–239.

Ogino, Tatsushi. 2008. "Hikikomori to taijin kankei: Yūjin wo meguru konnan to sono katari ['Hikikomori' and interpersonal relations: Difficulties with friendship and narratives]." pp. 127–158 in *"Hikikomori" e no shakaigakuteki appurōchi: Media, tōjisha, shien katsudō*, edited by T. Ogino et al. Kyōto: Minerva Shobō.

Ogino, Tatsushi. 2013. *Hikikomori mō ichido, hito o suki ni naru* [Retreating, and then coming to like people again]. Tokyo: Akashi Shoten.

Parker, Kim. 2012. "The Boomerang Generation: Feeling OK about Living with Mom and Dad." Pew Research Center (March 12, 2012). http://www.pewsocialtrends.org/files/2012/03/PewSocialTrends-2012-BoomerangGeneration.pdf. Retrieved July 19, 2015.

Saitō, Tamaki. 2001. "'Hikikomori' no hikaku bunkaron" [Comparative cultural analyses of '*hikikomori*']. *Chūō Kōron* 1401:124–133.

Saitō, Tamaki. 2002. *Hikikomori kyūshutsu manyuaru* [How to rescue your child from *hikikomori*]. Tokyo: PHP Kenkyūjo.

Saitō, Tamaki. 2013 [1998]. *Hikikomori Adolescence without End* (trans. Jeffrey Angles). Minneapolis, Minnesota: University of Minnesota Press.

Saitō, Tamaki, and NHK. "Hikikomori Support Campaign" Project, eds. 2004. *Hikikomori@NHK: Hikikomori*. Tokyo: Nihon Hōsō Shuppan Kyōkai.

Sakai, Motohiro et al. 2013. *"Hikikomori" no jittai ni kan suru chōsa hōkokusho 10* [A survey report of realities of social withdrawal, volume 10]. http://www.khj-h.com/pdf/12hikikomori.pdf. Retrieved July 19, 2015.

Serizawa, Shunsuke. 2010. *Sonzaironteki hikikomoriron: Watashi wa "watashi" no tame ni hikikomoru* [Existential theories of *hikikomori:* I withdraw for "myself"]. Tokyo: Kirara Shobō.

Shiokura, Yutaka. 2000. *Hikikomori*. Tokyo: Village Center Press.

Shiokura, Yutaka. 2002 [1999]. *Hikikomoru wakamonotachi* [Withdrawing youth]. Tokyo: Asahi Shinbunsha.

Takayama, Ryūtaro. 2008. "'Hikikomori' wa intānetto no sei?" [Is *hikikomori* due to the internet?]. pp. 266–67 in *'Hikikomori' e no shakaigakuteki appurōchi: Media, tōjisha, shien katsudō*, edited by T. Ogino et al. Kyōto: Minerva Shobō.

Toivonen, Tuukka. 2013. *Japan's Emerging Youth Policy: Getting Young Adults Back to Work*. London: Routledge.

Tokyo Metropolitan Government. 2015. *Hikikomori Support Net*. http://www.hikikomori-tokyo.jp/. Retrieved July 19, 2015.

Ueyama, Kazuki. 2001. *"Hikikomori" datta boku kara* [From me, who was "*hikikomori*"]. Tokyo: Kōdansha.

4

ANXIOUS, STRESSED, AND YET SATISFIED? THE PUZZLE OF SUBJECTIVE WELL-BEING AMONG YOUNG ADULTS IN JAPAN

Carola Hommerich

Introduction

Over the past two decades, Japan has seen growing inequality triggered by an increase of precarious employment, rising numbers of unemployed, and a retrenchment of company and government welfare (Chiavacci and Hommerich 2017; Ishida and Slater 2010; Shirahase 2010; Yamada 2009). At the same time, social bonds hitherto provided by family, neighbors, or the company have weakened, meaning that there is less of a network to fall back on for support than used to be the case. Both the increase in social inequality and the decline in social capital have been widely discussed by academic scholars and the media (Hommerich 2015; NHK 2010; Tachibanaki 2010). One of the main protagonists of this widespread academic and public discourse are Japanese youth, as young Japanese in their twenties and thirties are especially affected by these structural changes and an increase of social risks. They entered the labor market in times of recession after the end of the bubble economy at the beginning of the 1990s or were hit by its repercussions in their first years of employment (Brinton 2011; Genda 2003). At the same time, they cannot rely on the institutionalized networks that were available to their parents to give life structure and meaning, let alone reach financial independence (Yamada 2013). With regard to the future, the young generation can expect to shoulder the financial burden that comes with the demographic aging of Japanese society, while at the same time, they are insecure about whether their own livelihood in old age will be covered by the current pension system (Hommerich 2013). As a result, many face economic and social uncertainties and have trouble finding their place in society (Miyamoto 2012).

Amidst these developments, an increasing number of young Japanese seem unable to cope with their daily lives. For some this leads to social withdrawal (Horiguchi in this volume; Kawai and Uchida 2013; Zielenziger 2006) or mental disorders like clinical depression (Denda 2009; NHK Shuzaihan 2013), with cases of both having increased over the past two decades. For others, the daily struggle becomes unbearable enough for them to decide to end their own lives. Since the early 1990s, the suicide rate of the 15- to 39-year-olds has been on the rise and has become the most frequent cause of death in this age group (Cabinet Office 2014a: 5). The share of suicides related to trouble at work specifically is higher than in older age groups (Cabinet Office 2012: 78–79).

While these are rather extreme cases, which only concern a small minority of young people, the recent developments do seem to have taken their toll on the mental health of broader shares of the Japanese youth. While an increase of anxieties can be observed across all age groups since the early 1990s,[1] recent government reports emphasize that it is especially young adults who display comparatively high stress levels (MHLW 2014). Asked whether they experienced uncertainty or distress, 79.4 percent of the 20- to 39-year-olds answered "always" or "sometimes" (ibid.: 98ff). The share was somewhat lower for the 40- to 64-year-olds (71.4%) and lowest for the over-64-year-olds (59.6%). Anxieties in the youngest age group were mainly related to the future (50.8%), to income, household budget, or debt (48.1%), to work in general (38.1%), and to problems with co-workers in particular (30.5%).

Results of the *Heisei 25-nendo Wagakuni to shogaikoku no wakamono no ishiki ni kan suru chōsa* (International Survey on Youth Attitudes) from 2013 indicate that such high anxieties are by no means typical for this specific stage in the life course. Compared to their peers from the U.S., the U.K., Germany, France, Sweden, and Korea, young Japanese display low levels of self-esteem and strong anxieties with regard to finding employment, their current job, their financial situation and their future (Cabinet Office 2014c). The share of young Japanese who stated that they felt sad, depressed, or unmotivated in the past week was larger than in the countries of comparison. 38.4 percent did not have hope for their future, by far the largest share of the countries compared (U.S. 8.9%, U.K. 10.2%, Germany 17.6%, France 16.7%, Sweden 9.2%, and Korea 13.6%). At the same time, the share who felt the future of their country was bright was the smallest of all countries (28.8%) in Japan, as opposed to U.S. (57%), U.K. (59.6%), Germany (66.3%), France (36.7%), Sweden (67.8%), and Korea (43.1%)).

The rather bleak outlook for the future and high uncertainties experienced by young Japanese intuitively lets one expect them to be rather unhappy and dissatisfied with their lives. This, however, does not seem to be the case, as young sociologist Furuichi Noritoshi discusses in his book *Zetsubō no kuni no kōfuku na wakamonotachi* (The happy youth of a desperate country), which became a nationwide bestseller after its publication in 2011.[2] Looking at young Japanese in their twenties, he quotes longitudinal government statistics showing that the share of 20- to 29-year-olds who consider themselves satisfied[3] with their life has increased since the 1970s and by the turn of the century has outstripped those Japanese in their thirties, forties, or fifties[4] (Figure 4.1). Similar results can also be retrieved from the Survey on Japanese Attitudes (*Nihonjin no ishiki chōsa*), which has been carried out every three years by public broadcaster NHK since 1973 (NHK Hōsō Bunka Kenkyūjo 2015: 176).

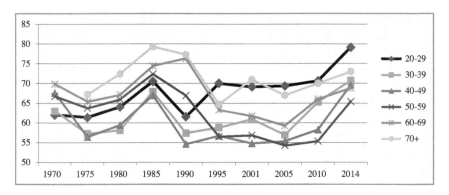

FIGURE 4.1 Life satisfaction across age groups
Note: Assembled by the author from the *Kokumin seikatsu ni kan suru yoron chōsa* (Public Opinion Survey on the Life of the People) carried out annually by the Cabinet Office (2014b). Shares of respondents who answered "satisfied" or "rather satisfied" are shown.

These high levels of life satisfaction seem to contradict the difficult structural context and poor mental constitution of young Japanese. By way of an explanation, Furuichi agrees that Japanese youth experience anxieties and are dissatisfied with the society they live in. He argues that instead of striving for a future goal, they are content to live in the "here and now" (*ima, koko*), an attitude he calls "consummatory" (Furuichi 2011: 104–105, in reference to a term created by Talcott Parsons[5]). What counts for young people at the end of the two "lost decades" (*ushinawareta nijūnen*), an era of economic stagnation that followed the burst of the Japanese asset price bubble in 1991, is that they have friends (*nakama*) to rely on. Their evaluation of their own "small world," he claims, is detached from the "big world," namely society as a whole. Based on an argument developed by Toyoizumi (2010) and Ōsawa (2011), Furuichi further suggests that not having positive expectations for the future will actually result in higher levels of life satisfaction in the present, because there is no positive point of comparison in the future. In this sense, the fact that young Japanese have low hopes for the future should have a positive effect on their life satisfaction in the present.

The seemingly contradictory experiences of young Japanese—who have low self-esteem, are highly anxious, are pessimistic about their own as well as their country's future, yet still report to be satisfied with their lives—imply that measuring and understanding individual well-being is by no means a straightforward task. Happiness, this indicates, is not simply "one thing," but needs to be imagined as a multidimensional concept. To grasp the "diversity of senses of well-being," Mathews and Izquierdo (2009: 257)—leaning on Colby (2009)—suggest four dimensions to be considered when analyzing individual well-being: (1) a material or physical dimension of well-being, which relates to how individuals conceive and experience themselves in the world; (2) an interpersonal dimension that comprises an evaluation of relationships with others; (3) an existential dimension, which is about how individuals comprehend the values and meanings of their lives; and (4) an overarching dimension of institutional context that shapes all other three dimensions (Mathews and Izquierdo 2009: 261). While they develop this concept for cross-national and cross-cultural comparisons of well-being, they emphasize that senses of well-being might also differ within one society, "refracted through social class, age, and especially gender" (Mathews and Izquierdo 2009: 257).

With this in mind, it seems plausible, that the "structure of well-being" of young Japanese diverges from that of older generations, with the different dimensions contributing to differing degrees to their general subjective well-being. As Furuichi (2011) bases his argument on a comparison of simple distributions of different survey data, the assumptions made in his book remain purely hypothetical. The same can be said of numerous other publications, which focus on the objective living circumstances of young Japanese and discuss the precariousness of their existence with regard to both economic and social capital, but do not analyze the actual impact of the latter on young people's subjective well-being.

In this chapter, I take a first step toward reaching a more comprehensive understanding of what matters for the subjective well-being of young Japanese, in order to solve the puzzle of their reported high levels of life satisfaction. Using data from a nationwide postal survey from 2009, I analyze whether the structure of well-being of young Japanese differs from that of older generations. I include measures for the material, the interpersonal, as well as the existential dimension of well-being and test their impact on evaluations of well-being across age with multiple regression models. Results are discussed in light of the institutional context in which the different age groups find themselves.

Data

The data used for analysis were collected in a nationwide postal survey in September 2009.[6] Two-stage stratified random sampling was used to draw an original sample of 5000 respondents from the population registry. With a response rate of 32.7 percent, 1633 questionnaires were collected for analysis. Appendix 1 sums up the socio-demographic distribution of the sample population. Comparison with the original sample as well as with the data of the 2005 Japanese Census shows that the realized sample gives a good model of Japanese society in terms of gender, age, and region.

Distribution of subjective well-being

From the time series data of the Cabinet Office quoted earlier (Figure 4.1), it becomes apparent that a higher share of young Japanese are satisfied with their lives at the beginning of the 21st century than in the 1970s. The survey here uses the same standard item to measure general life satisfaction. Respondents were asked to rate the item "Overall, I am satisfied with my life as it is" on a 7-point scale from 1 "does not apply to me at all" to 7 "strongly applies to me" (mean = 4.43, SD = 1.48).

To compare the distribution of life satisfaction across age, respondents were divided into four groups. These were formed to represent different cohorts as well as different stages in the life course, which are accompanied by differences in institutional embeddedness and financial responsibilities—something that might affect evaluations of social context and life as a whole.

The 20- to 34-year-olds are entering the labor market or are in the early stages of their careers and most often are not yet restricted by family obligations. This cohort has grown up during what has come to be called Japan's two "lost decades." For them, the transition into the labor market is more difficult than for earlier cohorts. They have lower chances of entering regular employment and are oftentimes forced to take on precarious jobs, which makes it difficult to achieve financial independence or plan a future (Brinton 2011; Genda 2003).

The 35- to 49-year-olds are in the midst of their careers and have taken on responsibility, e.g. by getting married, starting a family, or taking on a loan to buy a home. This group still profited from the era of high growth when entering the labor market but will also have felt the effects of economic stagnation as companies have cut back on bonuses and welfare benefits.

The 50- to 64-year-olds have established themselves in work and family life. While this cohort will not have been affected much by Japan's economic downturn in their work life, they worry about their financial situation in old age, especially after a scandal of lost pension records shook trust in the old age pension system (Coulmas 2007: 137ff; Takayama 2009).

The over-64-year-olds have retired from work and will be least affected by the recent changes of the socio-economic climate. However, with the breakup of the three-generation-household an increasing share of the elderly lives alone (MHLW 2010). As expectations to live with their children and grandchildren were still strong in this cohort, it seems possible that interpersonal well-being is low in this group.

For ease of comparison, respondents were grouped according to whether they were "rather not satisfied" (scale points 1–3), "undecided" ("neither/nor" = 4), or "rather satisfied" (5–7)[7] with their lives, with results displayed in Figure 4.2.

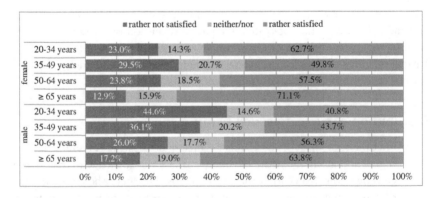

FIGURE 4.2 Life satisfaction by gender and age

Note: A Chi-Square test of independence indicated a significant association between age and life satisfaction for both men and women (p = .000).

The shares in Figure 4.2 do not indicate that all young Japanese are "happy," as suggested by Furuichi's book title. With a little over half of the youngest age group being satisfied with their life (52.9 percent when considering men and women together), this share is not as high as in the Public Opinion Survey on the Life of the People quoted above (Figure 4.1, Cabinet Office 2014b). This might in part be due to the placement of the middle category on the questionnaire.[8] Results are, however, close to those of another government survey, the *Kokumin seikatsu senkōdo chōsa* (National Survey on Lifestyle Preferences) from 2008 (Cabinet Office 2009). The distribution of life satisfaction across age groups shows a U-shape, with life satisfaction being lower for the middle aged but increasing again for the two oldest age groups.[9]

What we do not know from these simple distributions is what causes these differences between the age groups. If these distinctions relate to a certain generational "mindset," as suggested by Furuichi, then we should find that the structure of subjective well-being is different for younger, middle-aged, or elderly Japanese, meaning that different dimensions of well-being impact to differing degrees.

Determinants of subjective well-being

To test whether the assumption worded above is supported by the data, the four age groups were used as subsamples for OLS-regressions. As possible determinants of life satisfaction, I included gender and indicators of socio-economic status to measure the *material dimension* of well-being. The *interpersonal dimension* was measured as resources of social capital in form of tangible relationships with family and friends and feelings of belongingness to society. To represent the *existential dimension* of well-being, measures of how well respondents coped with their lives as apparent through experiences of anxieties and the optimism or pessimism of their future outlook were included. Before discussing the results of the regression models, the control variables with their distribution across the four age groups are introduced.

Material dimension of well-being

In addition to gender, educational level, income, the existence of savings, and employment status were included to control for the impact of the socio-economic context—a sociological take on what Mathews and Izquierdo (2009) call the material dimension of well-being. The descriptive statistics of the demographic and socio-economic indicators for the whole sample as well as across age groups are displayed in the appendix (Table 4.2).

Gender was coded as 0 for males and 1 for females. Educational levels were assessed by asking for the highest educational level achieved, ranging from middle school as the lowest and post-graduate education as the highest level. High school education was used as reference category, as only a small number of the youngest cohort had not continued their education after graduating from middle school, making this category less relevant as a point of comparison for the 20- to 34-year-olds. The self-reported annual household income was adjusted for household size with an elasticity of 0.5 to reflect the individual financial situation (Förster and D'Ercole 2009: 7–8). Four income groups were formed in relation to the equivalized median annual household income of 2,240,000 yen published by the MHLW for 2009 (2010). This approach was chosen in order to capture the social strata to which respondents belong (Atkinson and Brandolini 2011). The lowest income group earns less than 1,120,000 yen. This corresponds to less than 50 percent of the official median disposable income in 2009, which is the threshold set by the Japanese government to define relative poverty (MHLW 2010). Respondents who fall into this category are highly likely to face socio-economic difficulties. Middle incomes are divided into two groups with incomes ranging from 1,120,000 to 2,240,000 yen (50–100 percent of median income) categorized as lower middle, and incomes ranging from 2,240,000 to 3,360,000 yen (100–150 percent of median income) grouped as upper middle of the income range. The highest income group earns over 3,360,000 yen, which equals more than 150 percent of the median income. Dummy variables were formed with the lowest as the reference category.

To control for the effect of different forms of employment and non-employment, respondents were grouped as regular employee (reference group); non-regular employee; self-employed; unemployed, but actively looking for work; and unemployed, but not actively looking for work or deliberately not working. The latter includes respondents who were still in education, full-time homemakers, or retirees.

Interpersonal dimension of well-being

To measure this dimension, two aspects of interpersonal connectedness were included: subjectively perceived resources of social capital in the form of tangible relationships with family and friends on the one hand and feelings of belongingness to society as a whole on the other. The former is measured as trust in others and in the existence of a social network of family and friends to fall back on in times of need (Coleman 1988; Dasgupta and Serageldin 2000; Granovetter 1973; Uslaner 2002). The latter refers to the feeling of being a respected and valued member of society (Hommerich 2015; Bude and Lantermann 2006). Including an evaluation of both, tangible relationships on the one hand and a broader, more abstract social context on the other, allowed for a test of Furuichi's argument that being part of a close social network, namely having close friends, is especially important for the life satisfaction of young Japanese, whereas the more abstract concept of "society" is something they see as detached from their personal well-being.

To measure general trust, respondents were asked to rate the statement "I can trust most people" on the same 7-point-scale as subjective well-being

Subjective well-being among young adults **79**

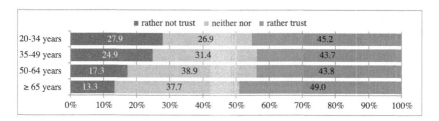

FIGURE 4.3 General social trust across age groups

Note: A Chi-Square test of independence indicated a significant association between age and general social trust, χ^2 (6, n = 1,577), p = .000.

(mean = 4.32, SD = 1.19). Distributions across age groups are displayed in Figure 4.3, grouping respondents into those who "rather not trust" (scale points 1–3), who were undecided ("neither/nor" = 4), or who "rather trust" (5–7). This reveals that shares of respondents who stated that they generally trust others did not differ much by age. However, in the two younger age groups, there were larger shares of respondents who stated that they rather do not trust. In mean scores,[10] this translates into significantly lower levels of general social trust in the two younger age groups.

Two additional items measure how young Japanese evaluate their immediate social network. The first item measures whether respondents felt that they had family to rely on in times of need (1 = yes and 0 = no) (Figure 4.4). As Furuichi (2011) claims a strong impact of close friends for the well-being of young Japanese, a second item asks about the existence of friends to rely on in times of need (Figure 4.5). With regard to family, the age groups did not differ significantly. Overall, 86.1 percent answered that they have family to rely on. The share for friends was considerably smaller (56.7%). Here, differences across age groups were significant, with the youngest group displaying the largest share of respondents indicating they have friends to rely on (73.5%).

To test whether young people evaluate their subjective well-being detached from society as a whole, a scale was included to assess respondents' level of social affiliation, namely how respondents evaluate their place in and value for society

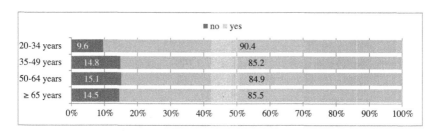

FIGURE 4.4 Having family to rely on across age groups

Note: A Chi-Square test of independence indicated no significant association between age and having family to rely on.

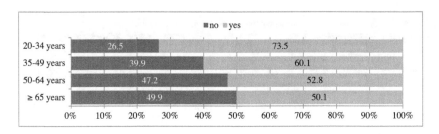

FIGURE 4.5 Having friends to rely on across age groups
Note: A Chi-Square test of independence indicated a significant association between age and having friends to rely on, χ^2 (3, n = 1,621), p = .000.

(Lantermann et al. 2009; Bude and Lantermann 2006). The scale consists of the following six statements measuring overall feelings of not belonging to the social whole, fears of not being recognized as a contributing member of society, up to an experience of subjective exclusion, which were rated on the same 7-point-scale as the life satisfaction item (Cronbach's α = 0.91):

1. I am worried that society leaves me behind.
2. Society does not care about me.
3. I feel like I do not really belong to society.
4. I do not see a place in society in which I am being taken seriously.
5. I feel that nobody needs me.
6. I feel excluded from society.

The six items were combined into an unweighted index and used as an aggregate measure of social affiliation, with means ranging from 1 (= low feeling of social affiliation) to 7 (= strong feeling of social affiliation, mean = 4.88, SD = 1.15).[11] Shares of respondents who did not feel to be fully integrated into the social whole were largest in the youngest age group (18.2%), followed by the over-64-year-olds (15.8%) (Figure 4.6, respondents were divided into those who felt "socially affiliated" ($\geq$ 4) and those who displayed "low social affiliation" (< 4)).

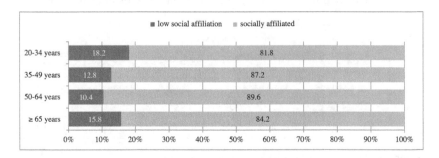

FIGURE 4.6 Feelings of social affiliation across age groups
Note: A Chi-Square test of independence indicated a significant association between age and social affiliation, χ^2 (3, n = 1,532), p = .013.

Existential dimension of well-being

This dimension of well-being is concerned with the meaning of life and thus touches the core of human existence. Mathews and Izquierdo (2009: 263) concur that this is a comparatively difficult aspect of well-being to explore, as "people don't tend to talk about it readily with others." To go about this problem, an indirect approach was taken, in looking at how well individuals seem to cope with their lives in the sense of experiencing them as coherent, meaningful, and manageable, an aspect also hinted at as central to this dimension by Colby (2009: 60). Here, this is measured through an experience of anxieties and the optimism or pessimism of expectations of the future.

As discussed above, various surveys indicate young Japanese have strong anxieties regarding the present as well as the future. Intuitively, one would expect this to impact negatively on their subjective well-being. Furuichi, however, argues that young Japanese display high levels of satisfaction despite these anxieties, because they only consider a very small and directly tangible context of their daily life when evaluating their well-being. This seems to imply that an experience of uncertainty in the present as well as of anxieties regarding the future do not impact their life satisfaction. To test this assumption, two items were included. First, respondents were asked whether they experienced anxieties over the past six months ("never" (1), "hardly ever" (2), "sometimes" (3), "often" (4), to "very often" (5), mean = 2.75, SD = .94).[12] The distribution across age groups shows a linear relationship, with the youngest group experiencing anxieties most frequently (76.1%) and the frequency decreasing with age (Figure 4.7).

The second item assessed anxieties about the future. Respondents were asked to rate the statements "I feel anxious about my future" on the same 7-point scale used for subjective well-being (mean = 4.73, SD = 1.49).[13] Future-related anxieties were stronger among the young than among the old (Figure 4.8, respondents were grouped as "rather not anxious" (scale points 1–3), ("neither/nor" = 4), and "rather anxious" (5–7)).

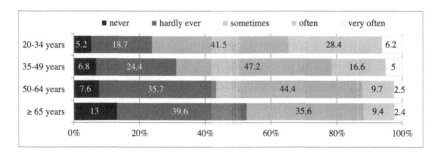

FIGURE 4.7 Experience of anxieties over the past six months across age groups

Note: A Chi-Square test of independence indicated a significant association between age and anxieties, χ^2 (12, n = 1,584), p = .000.

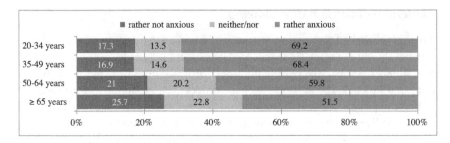

FIGURE 4.8 Experience of anxieties about the future

Note: A Chi-Square test of independence indicated a significant association between age and anxiety toward the future, χ^2 (6, n = 1,568), p = .000.

A positive expectation for the future implies having something to look forward to, something worth working toward. It means that there is something that gives life meaning. The expectation that one's fate will change for the worse, on the other hand, might result in disillusionment and a notion of futility, something that intuitively would be expected to lower subjective well-being. Furuichi, however, argues that not having positive expectations toward the future will impact positively on subjective well-being in the present. To test whether his assumption can be supported and whether the relationship is the same across age, an item was included to assess future expectations. Respondents were asked how they expect their standard of living to develop over the next few years as compared to the present ("gets worse," "is unchanged," and "gets better"). Shares of respondents with positive expectations were generally small, with the youngest age group displaying the largest share of respondents who expected their standard of living to improve in the future (Figure 4.9).

Multivariate analysis

To test whether the structure of well-being differs across age with different importance being attached to the dimensions of well-being measured here, the four age groups were used as subsamples. Two OLS-regression models were run

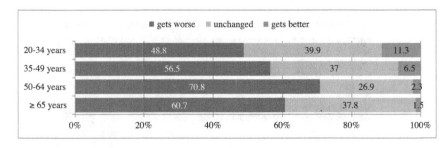

FIGURE 4.9 Future outlook across age groups

Note: A Chi-Square test of independence indicated a significant association between age and future outlook, χ^2 (6, n = 1,629), p = .000.

per group with overall life satisfaction as dependent variable. The first model includes only gender and the socio-economic indicators. To model 2, respondents' evaluation of their social well-being, their experience of anxieties, and future outlook were added. This allowed for an investigation of the extent to which material aspects can explain differences in life satisfaction, before testing possible additional explanatory power of subjective evaluations of interpersonal relationships and the future.

Results

Results are summed up in Table 4.1. While the analysis yields various interesting differences among the four age groups, discussion here concentrates on special characteristics of the youngest group.

For the youngest group, only 11 percent of the variance in levels of life satisfaction is explained by differences in gender and socio-economic status, while shares of explained variance are slightly larger in the other age groups. This indicates that the material dimension of well-being is of less importance for young Japanese than for members of the older age groups.

The gender gap in life satisfaction was largest in the youngest age group[14] and slightly smaller for the 35- to 49-year-olds. For the 50- to 64-year-olds, there was no significant gender difference at all. In the oldest group, levels of life satisfaction were again significantly higher among women. The result of higher levels of life satisfaction among women is in line with the data of the National Survey on the Lifestyle of the People, as well as with previous findings from international surveys (Graham and Chattopadhyay 2012). That this relationship might not be constant across age, however, is an interesting finding.

Levels of life satisfaction did not differ by education for the 20- to 34-year-olds.[15] Regarding employment status, only unemployed who were actively looking for work had significantly lower levels of life satisfaction than regular employees. There was no significant difference among respondents who were in regular or non-regular employment. This implies that for young Japanese—as long as the respondents had a job—the precarity of the employment per se did not impact on their subjective well-being. With regard to income, only young respondents in the highest income group were significantly more satisfied with their lives than were their peers in the lowest income category. Having savings to fall back on in times of need had a positive effect. These results were similar for the other three age groups, with a slightly stronger impact of income differences for the 35- to 49-year-olds and the over-64-year-olds.

When controlling for respondents' social well-being, anxieties, and future outlook, the share of explained variance increased to 35 percent for the youngest group, indicating that the interpersonal and existential dimensions of well-being are of greater importance for the general well-being of young Japanese than the material dimension was. This interpretation is supported by the fact that in model 2 none of the items controlling for socio-economic status (educational

TABLE 4.1 OLS-regression on life satisfaction for age group subsamples

	20–34		35–49		50–64		65 and older	
	B (SE)	B (SE)	B (SE)	B (SE)	B (SE)	B (SE)	B (SE)	B (SE)
Constant	3.287***(.247)	6.634***(.639)	3.107***(.211)	6.412***(.526)	3.578***(.179)	5.801***(.480)	4.584***(.181)	6.657***(.430)
Gender (1 = female)	.742***(.192)	.613***(.171)	.422**(.181)	.309*(.160)	-.022(.137)	.031(.128)	.230*(.118)	.194*(.113)
Education								
Middle school	-.124(.543)	-.520(.470)	-.266(.378)	-.300(.332)	-.292(.192)	-.143(.178)	-.359***(.131)	-.153(.124)
High school	Ref.	Ref.	Ref.	Ref.	Ref.	Ref.	Ref.	Ref.
University	.143(.199)	-.026(.172)	.116(.11)	.032(.132)	-.058(.139)	-.143(.130)	-.232(.163)	-.247(.154)
Employment								
Regular	Ref.	Ref.	Ref.	Ref.	Ref.	Ref.	Ref.	Ref.
Non-regular	.174(.223)	.206(.195)	-.052(.209)	-.010(.183)	.254(.166)	.198(.154)	-.354*(.210)	-.300(.196)
Self-employed	-.314(.784)	-.293(.677)	-.836***(.317)	-.695**(.277)	.162(.214)	.175(.196)	.018(.248)	.044(.233)
Unemployed (active)	-.612*(.346)	-.110(.305)	-.411(.375)	.287(.336)	-.571(.351)	-.410(.322)	-.821**(.368)	-.629*(.341)
Unemployed (inactive)	.057(.306)	.261(.269)	-.236(.271)	.127(.249)	.347(.254)	.338(.238)	-.759***(.221)	-.447**(.209)
Not in the labor force	.933(.192)	.374(.617)	.823**(.398)	.567(.354)	.620***(.213)	.546***(.198)	-.150(.163)	-.035(.152)
Income								
Below 50%	Ref.	Ref.	Ref.	Ref.	Ref.	Ref.	Ref.	Ref.
Lower middle	.116(.258)	-.043(.224)	.040(.265)	-.316(.234)	-.071(.218)	-.037(.204)	.062(.188)	-.003(.177)
Upper middle	.207(.273)	-.202(.241)	.635***(.206)	.312*(.183)	.273(.183)	.082(.169)	.364**(.143)	.210(.134)
Upper	.536**(.247)	.186(.216)	.693***(.195)	.292(.175)	.530***(.172)	.281*(.160)	.385**(.172)	.185(.161)
Savings (1 = yes)	.596***(.196)	.216(.172)	1.001***(.151)	.542***(.139)	.897***(.128)	.442***(.128)	.593***(.121)	.296**(.118)

	(1)	(2)	(3)	(4)
Social Well-being				
Social trust	.138** (.061)	.081 (.052)	.180*** (.054)	.110** (.051)
Family (1 = yes)	.348 (.284)	.209 (.185)	.525*** (.172)	.474*** (.159)
Friends (1 = yes)	.056 (.190)	-.065 (.138)	.113 (.123)	.076 (.117)
Social affiliation	.323*** (.078)	.153** (.071)	.077 (.062)	.133** (.055)
Anxieties and future outlook				
Anxieties past 6 months	-.217** (.096)	-.437*** (.077)	-.281*** (.074)	-.273*** (.066)
Anxious about the future	-.242*** (.062)	-.254*** (.053)	-.190*** (.047)	-.155*** (.046)
Future expectation (1 = positive)	-.637** (.258)	-.299 (.259)	.389 (.384)	-1.031** (.431)
Adj. R²	.11 / .35	.18 / .39	.17 / .32	.15 / .33
N	291	400	484	458

Note: *p<.10, ** p<.05, *** p<.01

level, type of employment, income, and savings) impacted significantly on the life satisfaction of the 20- to 34-year-olds. In the older age groups, differences by socio-economic status—especially with regard to savings—remained significant, even after controlling for the subjective indicators.

The gender effect, however, remained significant and strong in the youngest group, with women's life satisfaction being .61 scale points higher than men's. As this difference remains significant, even when controlling for socio-economic status, social capital, anxieties, and future expectations, other factors must lie behind this gender effect. Brinton (2011) suggests that the increasing dualization of the Japanese labor market affects young men in a special way, as the risk of not being able to enter stable employment is especially new to them: "In the context of a society where the male breadwinner ideology has been as strong as it has in Japan, the employment security of men in their twenties and thirties has broad echo effects" (Brinton 2011: 30). For an increasing share of young men, the "de-gendering of irregular employment" (Brinton 2011: 30) means that they cannot live up to what is still considered a "normal life course" and their responsibility to provide for a family. As a result, they might struggle to find their role and place in life and society in a way that is different from young women and which negatively affects their life satisfaction.

While the explanatory power of the interpersonal and existential dimension of well-being is high for young Japanese, it lends support to only *one* of Furuichi's hypotheses, while contradicting all others. Whereas general social trust has a positive impact, the life satisfaction of the 20- to 34-year-olds did not differ according to whether or not they felt they had family or friends to fall back on in times of need. This result is contrary to Furuichi's claim of a special importance of friends for the subjective well-being of young Japanese. In fact, friends had no significant impact on life satisfaction across all age groups.[16] Having family to rely on when needed had a large positive effect only on the life satisfaction of respondents of 50 years and older. For them, this might be connected to an—increasingly unfulfilled—expectation of living with their children and grandchildren in old age.

What was more decisive for the life satisfaction of the 20- to 34-year-olds was whether they were able to feel like valuable and accepted members of society. Higher levels of social affiliation resulted in higher life satisfaction. Comparing the strength of the regression coefficient across groups reveals that this effect is significantly larger for the 20- to 34-year-olds than for the two oldest groups.[17] Whereas the coefficient for the 35- to 49-year-olds also appears to be smaller, this difference is only significant at p< .20 (i.e., with 80% confidence). This means that for the 35- to 49-year-olds feeling like being part of society has a similarly strong impact on life satisfaction as for the youngest group. Contrary to Furuichi's argument, feeling like being part of the social whole matters, especially for the life satisfaction of the young.

An experience of anxieties over the past six months reduces life satisfaction significantly for all age groups. Here, the negative effect was especially large for the 35- to 49-year-olds.[18] Anxieties about the future also impacted negatively on life satisfaction, with no significant difference in effect size across age.

Having positive expectations for one's standard of living in the future had a negative effect on the life satisfaction of the 20- to 34-year-olds, making this the only hypothesis of Furuichi to be supported by the data. This seems to be an effect characteristic for the youngest age group, as it was neither confirmed for the 35- to 49-year-olds nor the 50- to 64-year-olds. It was significant for the oldest age group, but as only 7 respondents aged 65 and older stated they had a positive expectation for their standard of living in the future, this is not a reliable result.

Happy but without hope?

The results of the analysis presented here indicate that the structure of well-being does indeed differ across age. The different well-being dimensions contribute to differing degrees to the general subjective well-being of the four age groups. It turns out that for the 20- to 34-year-olds, socio-economic status has no direct impact on life satisfaction once interpersonal and existential aspects of well-being, having a substantial effect, are controlled for. However, not all aspects of interpersonal and existential well-being measured here were equally important. While general social trust yielded a significant positive effect on the life satisfaction of the 20- to 34-year-olds, having friends—or family—to rely on in times of trouble did not, thereby contradicting the argument brought forward by Furuichi (2011) that for young Japanese having close friends counts most to make them happy. The data also does not suggest that young Japanese evaluate their satisfaction levels detached from society as a whole. On the contrary, feeling like being part of the social whole proved to be especially important for the two youngest age groups. At the same time, and also running contrary to Furuichi's argument, anxieties experienced in the present as well as anxieties held toward the future reduced life satisfaction.

The data supported only one of Furuichi's hypotheses: Not having positive expectations for the future did indeed correspond to higher levels of life satisfaction in the youngest age group. While this effect could not be confirmed for older respondents, it was comparatively strong (-.637) for the 20- to 34-year-olds. But what does this tell us? Can it really be positive, when only slightly more than ten percent of a cohort feels able to hope for a better future? Is it enough to be content in the present, even when this might mean forfeiting one's future? To answer these questions, it seems necessary to consider another function attributed to hope in psychological and sociological theory: the motivation to take action (Genda 2010; Snyder 2000). Dahrendorf sees hope as the necessary ingredient that "motivates people to change their conditions, or their lives" (1976: 19). Durkheim even went as far as saying that when hope for a positive future is lost, "we may be sure that life itself loses its attractiveness, that misfortune increases, either because the causes of suffering multiply or because the capacity for resistance on the part of the individual diminishes" (1984 [1893]: 190). With this in mind, it seems that life satisfaction in the present cannot be the ultimate goal, at least not when it comes at the expense of the future development of younger generations and, thereby, eventually also the development of society as a whole (Yamada 2004: 194).

Taken together, the results presented here contradict rather than support the rather positive description of the "happy youth of a desperate country" offered by Furuichi in his book. While this chapter takes a first step toward a better understanding of the "structure" of the well-being of Japanese youth, the puzzle of their high levels of life satisfaction is by no means fully solved. It even seems questionable whether their high satisfaction levels can be interpreted as something positive. On the contrary, they seem to be indicative of a generation of youngsters who have arranged themselves with a society that does not give them room to grow, a generation who has given up on expecting more for themselves in the future and—as a result—does not speak up for their own rights or push for change.

In general, there still seems to be more to the equation than was possible to control for here. From a purely quantitative point of view, this calls for larger data sets, more variables, and more sophisticated measurement models, i.e., an exploration of possible indirect effects of socio-economic status on life satisfaction, as mediated by resources of social capital or an experience of anxieties. However, there is most possibly a limit to what quantitative research can tell us when it comes to subjective well-being. Only 35 percent of the variance in subjective well-being of the youngest age group could be explained, in spite of controlling for various impact factors. Whereas this is a high share for a quantitative study, it nevertheless means that 65 percent remains unexplained. This, again, points to the fact that subjective well-being is not simply "one thing" and that measuring it is by no means a straightforward task. We need to dive deeper. When contemplating how to achieve a more in-depth analysis of what shapes individual patterns of well-being, a combination of quantitative and qualitative methods seems promising, as each might be able to provide the information the other lacks (Hommerich and Klien 2012).

Appendix

TABLE 4.2 Descriptive statistics of demographic and socioeconomic indicators by age

% (n)	Total	20–34	35–49	50–64	65 and older
	100% (1633)	17.8% (291)	24.5% (400)	29.6% (484)	28.0% (458)
Gender					
Male	48.2% (787)	44.7% (130)	45.8% (183)	48.1% (233)	52.6% (241)
Female	51.8% (846)	55.3% (161)	52.4% (217)	51.9% (251)	47.4% (217)
Education					
Middle school	15.3% (244)	3.1% (9)	4.0% (16)	13.4% (64)	35.6% (155)
High school	45.1% (722)	35.1% (101)	41.4% (165)	53.5% (255)	46.1% (201)
University	39.6% (634)	61.8% (178)	54.6% (218)	33.1% (158)	18.3% (80)
Income					
<1.120.000 Yen	22.6% (331)	21.1% (52)	17.9% (67)	19.3% (88)	32.0% (124)
≥1.120.000 Yen <2.240.000 Yen	14.7% (216)	25.1% (62)	11.5% (43)	12.5% (57)	13.9% (54)
≥2.240.000 Yen <3.360.000 Yen	27.1% (397)	20.6% (51)	29.1% (109)	23.2% (106)	33.8% (131)
≥3.360.000 Yen	35.6% (522)	33.2% (82)	41.4% (155)	45.1% (206)	20.4% (79)
Employment status					
Regular	34.1% (519)	46.5% (131)	51.0% (198)	35.5% (157)	8.0% (33)
Non-regular	24.0% (366)	29.4% (83)	24.7% (96)	29.2% (129)	14.1% (58)
Self-employed	7.1% (108)	1.4% (4)	5.7% (22)	10.9% (48)	8.3% (34)
Unemployed (active)	4.7% (71)	8.9% (25)	4.4% (17)	3.6% (16)	3.2% (13)
Unemployed (inactive)	10.5% (160)	12.1% (34)	10.6% (41)	7.9% (35)	12.2% (50)
Not in the labor force	19.6% (299)	1.8% (5)	3.6% (14)	12.9% (57)	54.3% (223)
Savings					
Yes	47.6% (770)	37.8% (110)	39.4% (157)	54.6% (262)	53.6% (241)
No	52.4% (849)	62.2% (181)	60.6% (241)	45.4% (218)	46.4% (209)

TABLE 4.3 Descriptive statistics for the items used to measure social affiliation

Variable	n	Mean	SD	Min	Max
I am worried that society leaves me behind.	1567	3.37	1.44	1	7
Society does not care about me.	1559	3.38	1.36	1	7
I feel like I do not really belong to society.	1552	3.15	1.36	1	7
I do not see a place in society in which I am being taken seriously.	1560	3.24	1.39	1	7
I feel that nobody needs me.	1564	2.97	1.40	1	7
I feel excluded from society.	1561	2.50	1.28	1	7

Notes

1 Numbers from an annual survey by the Cabinet Office (2014b) confirm an increase of anxieties to be a long-term trend, starting in the early 1990s. Since then, the share of Japanese who experiences anxiety and uncertainty in their everyday life has steadily grown, from 47 percent in 1991 to 66 percent in 2013.
2 As the book came out in September 2011, it seems plausible to attribute some of its success to the wave of self-reflection Japan underwent in the first months after the triple disaster of March 11, 2011. Contrary to the general feeling at the time, however, Furuichi, does not anticipate a long-term change in societal values in the aftermath of the disaster. His impression was that most people who were not directly affected had already returned to their pre-disaster lifestyle (Furuichi 2011: 216–217). Survey results regarding an impact of the disaster on subjective well-being are mixed, with differences in well-being mostly depending on the proximity to the disaster area and affectedness (Hommerich 2012). The greater part of this literature does not point to substantial change (for an overview, cp. Tiefenbach and Kohlbacher 2015: 339; Uchida et al. 2014). The possibility of an impact of 3/11 on the subjective well-being of Japanese youth is, thus, not further explored in this chapter.
3 Furuichi uses the terms life satisfaction and happiness interchangeably. The data he shows, however, measure life satisfaction. Despite a strong correlation between the two, happiness and life satisfaction are not synonymous (Kobayashi, Hommerich and Mita 2015; Hommerich and Kobayashi 2014).
4 Furuichi is not the first to point this out. He quotes Toyoizumi (2010) and Ōsawa (2011) who had both discussed this puzzle earlier.
5 Furuichi here quotes Toyoizumi (2010) who introduces this term in relation to Japanese youth.
6 The survey was designed by the author and financed by the German Institute for Japanese Studies (DIJ). Data collection was carried out by Chūō Chōsa Sha.
7 Mean scores for life satisfaction across age groups were as follows: 20–34 = 4.23 (SD = 1.63), 35–49 = 4.16 (SD = 1.56), 50–64 = 4.44 (SD = 1.44), 65 and older = 4.8 (SD = 1.26).
8 In the survey used for analysis here, the middle category was placed in the middle of the scale, as is common practice. The survey quoted by Furuichi also offers a middle category ("neither/nor"), but in the questionnaire it was placed next to the actual scale, with the result that only very few respondents chose it.
9 For a discussion of a possible quadratic (U-shaped) relationship of age with subjective well-being in the case of Japan, cp. Tiefenbach and Kohlbacher (2015).
10 Mean scores across age groups for social trust are as follows: 20–34 = 4.20 (SD = 1.37), 35–49 = 4.21 (SD = 1.27), 50–64 = 4.32 (SD = 1.10), 65 and older = 4.49 (SD = 1.10).
11 Means and standard deviation of the single items can be found in the appendix (Table 4.3). Mean scores across age groups for the index are as follows (range 1–7): 20–34 = 4.77 (SD = 1.26), 35–49 = 4.94 (SD = 1.14), 50–64 = 5.01 (SD = 1.09), 65 and older = 4.76 (SD = 1.14).
12 Mean scores across age groups for anxieties in the past six months are as follows (range 1–5): 20–34 = 3.21 (SD = .96), 35–49 = 2.89 (SD = .93), 50–64 = 2.64 (SD = .86), 65 and older = 2.49 (SD = .92).
13 Mean scores across age groups for anxieties toward the future are as follows (range 1–7): 20–34 = 5.01 (SD = 1.55), 35–49 = 4.93 (SD = 1.46), 50–64 = 4.63 (SD =1.47), 65 and older = 4.46 (SD = 1.45).
14 A t-test was used to compare whether the size of coefficients differs significantly across the age groups. Here, it was significantly different at $p<.05$. In favor of readability this procedure is not mentioned for every comparison hereafter. Instead, the level of significance is merely stated in a footnote.

15 Education showed no significant relationship with life satisfaction, except for the over-64-year-olds, where life satisfaction was significantly lower among middle school graduates.
16 This result remained unchanged also when not controlling for the importance of family to rely on, implying that this is not a case of shared variance.
17 The size of the coefficient for the youngest group differs significantly from the two oldest groups (p<.05).
18 The size of the coefficient for 35- to 49-year-olds differs significantly from the other groups (p<.10).

References

Atkinson, Anthony B., and Andrea Brandolini. 2011. "On the Identification of the 'Middle Class'." ECINEQ Working paper 2011-217.
Brinton, Mary C. 2011. *Lost in Transition. Youth, Work, and Instability in Postindustrial Japan.* Cambridge: Cambridge University Press.
Bude, Heinz, and Ernst-Dieter Lantermann. 2006. "Soziale Exklusion und Exklusionsempfinden." *Kölner Zeitschrift für Soziologie und Sozialpsychologie* 58:233–252.
Cabinet Office. 2009. *Heisei 20-new do Kokumin seikatsu senkōdo chōsa* [National survey on lifestyle preferences 2008]. http://www5.cao.go.jp/seikatsu/senkoudo/senkoudo.html. Retrieved March 15, 2015.
Cabinet Office. 2012. *Heisei 24-nenban Jisatsu taisaku hakusho honbun* [White paper on suicide 2012]. http://www8.cao.go.jp/jisatsutaisaku/whitepaper/w-2012/pdf/index.html. Retrieved March 15, 2015.
Cabinet Office. 2014a. *Heisei 26-nenban Jisatsu taisaku hakusho* [White paper on suicide 2014]. http://www8.cao.go.jp/jisatsutaisaku/whitepaper/w-2014/pdf/index.html. Retrieved March 15, 2015.
Cabinet Office. 2014b, *Heisei 26-nen Kokumin seikatsu ni kan suru yoron chōsa* [Public opinion survey on the life of the people 2014]. http://survey.gov-online.go.jp/index-ko.html. Retrieved March 15, 2015.
Cabinet Office. 2014c. *Heisei 25-nendo Wagakuni to shogaikoku no wakamono no ishiki ni kan suru chōsa* [International survey of youth attitudes 2013]. http://www8.cao.go.jp/youth/kenkyu/thinking/h25/pdf_index.html. Retrieved March 15, 2015.
Chiavacci, David and Carola Hommerich, eds. 2017. *Social Inequality in Post-Growth Japan: Transformation during Economic and Demographic Stagnation.* London and New York: Routledge.
Colby, Benjamin N. 2009. "Is a Measure of Cultural Well-Being Possible or Desirable?" pp. 45–66 in *Pursuits of Happiness: Well-Being in Anthropological Perspective*, edited by G. Mathews and C. Izquierdo. New York and Oxford: Berghahn Books.
Coleman, James S. 1988. "Social Capital in the Creation of Human Capital." *The American Journal of Sociology* 94:95–120.
Coulmas, Florian. 2007. *Die Gesellschaft Japans: Arbeit, Familie und demographische Krise.* München: C. H. Beck.
Dahrendorf, Ralf. 1976. *Inequality, Hope, and Progress. Eleanor Rathbone Memorial Lecture.* Liverpool: Liverpool University Press.
Dasgupta, Partha, and Ismail Serageldin. 2000. *Social Capital: A Multifaceted Perspective.* Washington, D.C.: The World Bank.
Denda, Kenzo. 2009. *Wakamono no "utsu" – "shingata utsubyō" to wa nani ka* ["Depression" of young people – What is the "new type depression"?]. Tokyo: Chikuma Shobō.
Durkheim, Emile. 1984 [1893]. *The Division of Labor in Society.* New York: The Free Press.

Förster, Michael F., and Marco Mira D'Ercole. 2009. "The OECD Approach to Measuring Income Distribution and Poverty: Strength, Limits and Statistical Issues." Paper presented at the OECD/University of Maryland International Conference *Measuring Poverty, Income Inequality, and Social Exclusion: Lessons from Europe*.

Furuichi, Noritoshi. 2011. *Zetsubō no kuni no kōfuku na wakamonotachi* [The happy youth of a desperate country]. Tokyo: Kodansha.

Genda, Yūji. 2003. "Who Really Lost Jobs in Japan? Youth Employment in an Aging Japanese Society." pp. 103–133 in *Labor Markets and Firm Benefit Policies in Japan and the United States*, edited by S. Ogura, T. Tachibanaki and D. A. Wise. Chicago: University of Chicago Press.

Genda, Yūji. 2010. *Kibō no tsukurikata* [Building hope]. Tokyo: Iwanami Shinsho.

Graham, Carol, and Soumya Chattopadhyay. 2012. *Gender and Well-being around the World: Some Insights from the Economics of Happiness* (Working Paper Series No. 2012–010). Chicago: University of Chicago, Economic Research Center.

Granovetter, Mark S. 1973. "The Strength of Weak Ties." *The American Journal of Sociology* 78:1360–1380.

Hommerich, Carola. 2012. "Trust and Subjective Well-being after the Great East Japan Earthquake, Tsunami and Nuclear Meltdown: Preliminary Results." *International Journal of Japanese Sociology* 21:46–64.

Hommerich, Carola. 2013. "Adapting to Risk, Learning to Trust: Socioeconomic Insecurities and Feelings of Disconnectedness in Contemporary Japan." *Asiatische Studien/ Etudes Asiatiques* 67/2:429–455.

Hommerich, Carola. 2015. "Feeling Disconnected: Exploring the Relationship between Different Forms of Social Capital and Civic Engagement in Japan." *VOLUNTAS* 26:45–68.

Hommerich, Carola, and Susanne Klien. 2012. "Happiness: Does Culture Matter?" *International Journal of Well-being* 2/4:292–298.

Hommerich, Carola, and Jun Kobayashi. 2015. "Are Satisfied People Happy? Disentangling Subjective Well-being in Japan." pp. 201–216 in *Forschung fördern. Am Beispiel von Lebensqualität im Kulturkontext*, edited by G. Trommsdorff and W. R. Assmann. Konstanz: UVK.

Ishida, Hiroshi, and David H. Slater. 2010. *Social Class in Contemporary Japan. Structures, Sorting and Strategies*. London and New York: Routledge.

Kawai, Toshi, and Yukiko Uchida. 2013. *"Hikikomori" kō* [Analyzing "hikikomori"]. Osaka: Sogensha.

Kobayashi, Jun, Carola Hommerich and Akiko Mita. 2015. "Naze kōfuku to manzoku wa ichi shinai no ka? Shakai ishiki e no gōriteki sentaku apurōchi" [Why do happiness and satisfaction not coincide? A rational choice approach to social psychology]. *Bulletin of the Faculty of Humanities. Seikei University* 50:87–99.

Lantermann, Ernst-Dieter, Elke Döring-Seipel, Frank Eierdanz and Lars Gerhold. 2009. *Selbstsorge in unsicheren Zeiten. Resignieren oder gestalten*. Weinheim and Basel: Beltz Verlag.

Mathews, Gordon, and Carolina Izquierdo. 2009. "Conclusion - Towards an Anthropology of Well-being." pp. 248–66 in *Pursuits of Happiness: Well-being in Anthropological Perspective*, edited by G. Mathews and C. Izquierdo. New York and Oxford: Berghahn Books.

MHLW. 2010. *Heisei 22-nen Kokumin seikatsu kiso chōsa no gaikyō* [Results of the survey on the standard of living of the population]. http://www.mhlw.go.jp/toukei/saikin/hw/k-tyosa/k-tyosa10/2-7.html. Retrieved May 11, 2015.

MHLW. 2014. *Heisei 26-nenban Kōsei rōdo hakusho* [White paper on health, labor and welfare]. Tokyo: MHLW.

Miyamoto, Michiko. 2012. *Wakamono ga muenka suru. Shigoto, fukushi, komyuniti de tsunagu* [The youth are losing their bonds. Connecting through work, social security and the community]. Tokyo: Chikuma Shobō.
NHK. 2010. "Muen shakai. 'Muenshi' 32.000 nin no shōgeki" [Society without bonds. Unnoticed deaths: the shocking number of 32.000 people]. NHK "Muen shakai purojekuto" shuzaihan." Tokyo: Bungei Shunjū.
NHK Hōsō Bunka Kenkyūjo. 2015. *Gendai Nihonjin no ishiki kōzō, dai-8 kan* [The structure of Japanese attitudes today, 8th edition]. Tokyo: NHK.
NHK Shuzaihan. 2013. *Shokuba o osō "shingata utsu* [Attacking the work place: New type depression]. Tokyo: Bungei Shunjū.
Ōsawa, Masachi. 2011. "Kanō ni naru kakumei dai ikkai. 'Kōfuku da' to kotaeru wakamonotachi no jidai" [A possible revolution, part 1. The age of a youth who states 'I am happy']. *At plus*:114–127.
Shirahase, Sawako. 2010. *Ikikata no fubyōdō. Otagaisama no shakai ni mukete* [Inequality of lifestyles. Towards a society of reciprocity]. Tokyo: Iwanami Shoten.
Snyder, Charles R. 2000. *Handbook of Hope. Theories, Measures, & Applications*. San Diego: Academic Press.
Tachibanaki, Toshiaki. 2010. *Muen shakai no shōtai – ketsuen, chien, shaen wa ika ni hōkai shita ka* [The reality of a society without bonds – Have blood relations, regional relations, social relations been lost?]. Tokyo: PHP Kenkyūjo.
Takayama, Noriyuki. 2009. "On Fifty Million Floating Pension Records in Japan." *Project on Intergenerational Equality*, Progress Report 2009. Tokyo, Hitotsubashi University. http://www.ier.hit-u.ac.jp/pie/stage2/English/report/PR0906/3.1%20takayama.pdf. Retrieved June 25, 2015.
Tiefenbach, Tim, and Florian Kohlbacher. 2015. "Happiness in Japan in Times of Upheaval: Empirical Evidence from the National Survey on Lifestyle Preferences." *Journal of Happiness Studies* 16/2:333–366.
Toyoizumi, Shūji. 2010. *Wakamono no tame no shakaigaku. Kibō ni ashiba o kakeru.* [A sociology for the youth. Giving a foothold to hope]. Tokyo: Haruka Shobō.
Uchida, Yukiko, Yoshiaki Takahashi and Kentaro Kawahara. 2014. "Changes in Hedonic and Eudaimonic Well-being after a Severe Nationwide Disaster: The Case of the Great East Japan Earthquake." *Journal of Happiness Studies* 15/1:207–221.
Uslaner, Eric M. 2002. *The Moral Foundations of Trust*. Cambridge: Cambridge University Press.
Yamada, Masahiro. 2004. *Kibō kakusa shakai – 'makegumi' no zetsubōkan ga Nihon o hikisaku* [Society of split hopes – the despair of the losers rips Japan apart]. Tokyo: Chikuma Shobō.
Yamada, Masahiro. 2009. *Wākingu puā jidai. Sokonuke sēfutī netto o saikōchiku seyo* [The era of the working poor. Towards the renewal of a bottomless safety net]. Tokyo: Bungei Shunjū.
Yamada, Masahiro. 2013. *Naze Nihon wa wakamono ni reikoku na no ka? Soshite kakō idō shakai ga tōrai suru* [Why is Japan so heartless towards its youth? The coming of a society of downward mobility]. Tokyo: Tōyō Keizai Shinpōsha.
Zielenziger, Michael. 2006. *Shutting out the Sun. How Japan Created Its Own Lost Generation*. New York: Vintage Departures.

PART II
Adulthood

5

BEING HAPPY AS A WOMAN

The promise of happiness for middle-class housewives in Japan

Ofra Goldstein-Gidoni

> A woman can be beautiful, smart, fashionable, rich, and have a respectable career but nevertheless is considered *"unhappy as a woman"* (*onna toshite shiawase dewa nai*) if she is not married and does not have children [emphasis added].
> (Sakai 2003)

The book *The Howl of the Loser Dogs* (*Makeinu no tōboe*) by Junko Sakai published in 2003 soon became a best seller. Its publication has produced a heated debate in Japanese society that seemed eager to adopt the rigid division suggested by the popular writer between single women as "losers" and married women with children as society's "winners." As it is clearly articulated by Nakano in her study of those considered "losers" or "loser dogs,", for single women who generally wish to marry and have a family, the primary distinction between winners and losers in Japanese society is whether they have a "regular family" or not (Nakano 2011: 133). In other words, a woman's happiness in contemporary Japanese society seems to be defined by her access to being part of a "regular family."

What forms a "regular family" has a clear face to most women—and men—in Japan. The process of the "standardization" of the Japanese family pattern has been widely observed in relation to the postwar economic miracle (Allison 1996; Garon 1997; White 2002). This modern Japanese family or "postwar Japanese family system" (Ochiai 1996) is embodied in a nuclear family consisting of a salaryman husband, a full-time housewife, and their children. By the 1960s, the extent of the ideological force of this family pattern was so striking that it "overwhelmed" all other co-existing lifestyles and older forms in social discourse (Gordon 2000: 287).

The hegemonic status of the idea of "middle-class-ness" as both social experience and self-understanding (Gordon 2002: 116) was described by Ezra Vogel in his seminal work on the emergence of Japan's new middle class. As Vogel observed in the late 1960s, "for the rest of Japan the people who have been able to become salarymen are symbols of the *akarui seikatsu* (bright new life)" (Vogel [1963] 1991: 71). The idea of *akarui seikatsu*, a bright and happy life, was propagated in the mid-1950s with strong government support. The term, which had widespread impact, was promoted as a symbol and promise of Japan's future (Cwiertka 2006: 159). At the focus of this promise of a good life stood the salaryman and his family. The "bright life" actually implied a "modern" home with middle-class standard of living and "a nuclear family with a housewife at its center" (Partner 1999: 137). The salaryman, who became the symbol of hegemonic masculinity in Japan, thus came to symbolize the ubiquitous "everyman" (Dasgupta 2000; Miller 1995), and the housewife became almost synonymous with womanhood (Ochiai 1996: 35), the middle-class "everywoman."

The women who are the focus of this chapter are the daughters of that generation of women who symbolized the promise of bright life and happiness in postwar Japan. The chapter focuses on the ideas of happiness as they are grasped by middle-class housewives of today's Japan. Naturally, there have been changes in what forms the idea of happiness, certainly with the growing economic bubble and moreover after its burst in the early 1990s. However, as I will show in what follows, the ideas of happiness for contemporary middle-class housewives still are strongly related to the ideas or pursuit of stability. The quest of happiness for middle-class women is thus embodied in marriage as the idea of following a standardized life plan and forming a "standard family."

The sociocultural idea of happiness and its promise

As can be seen from the variety in the chapters in this volume, there are manifold ways to study "happiness." In this chapter I do not intend to try to offer any measurement of happiness (Colson 1962; 2012: 7–8). I do not even attempt to decipher whether the middle-class housewives I studied are happy. Also, albeit suggesting a connection between happiness and marriage, I am not interested here in the women's level of marital happiness (Holthus 2010). My focus is on the *sociocultural idea of what happiness is* or what can hold *the promise of happiness* as seen by the women I studied.

In their ambitious attempt to uncover what anthropology can contribute to the study of well-being or happiness, the volume edited by Mathews and Izquierdo (2009a) explores four main experiential dimensions. The first three are the physical, the interpersonal, and the existential. The fourth dimension, which is Mathews and Izquierdo's (2009b: 261) main addition to the study of happiness, structures all other dimensions. It involves how "national institutions and global forces" shape perceptions, conceptions, and experiences of well-being. What anthropology can offer to the study of happiness is, according to Mathews and Izquierdo, a "sociocultural contextualizing that can enable us to make sense of how people in different societies feel about their lives" (2009b: 259). Mathews and Izquierdo emphasize conceptions, perceptions, and feelings *about* happiness. In this chapter, I offer my interpretation to this "fourth dimension." I suggest viewing "happiness" mainly as a cultural construct. As such, "happiness" or the conception of happiness is naturally always deeply embedded in a particular socio-cultural context. As anthropologists we cannot see or observe "happiness;" what we can grasp is what is regarded by the people we study as "happiness" or as that which can make them happy.

The notion of happiness as suggested by Sara Ahmed (2007, 2010) is very useful in this sense. Happiness, Ahmed tells us, operates as "something that is hoped for, creating a political and personal horizon that gives us an image of the good life" (2007: 12). Happiness is "a wish, a will, a want" (2010: 2). Happiness is always associated with some life choices and not others (Ahmed 2010: 2). More than anything, it involves a promise, the promise that if you do this or if you have that, happiness will follow (Ahmed 2007: 12).

Marriage has been widely considered as one of the main social institutions that holds the promise of happiness. Recently it has even received "the imprimatur of hard science" in the new science of happiness that demonstrates a link between marriage and overall life satisfaction (Heather 2007: 53). In these recent studies, as suggested by Heather, the promise of happiness is largely related to the prospect of "normal family life." It can be thus argued that marriage has gained its position as one of the primary happiness indicators (Ahmed 2010: 6) since it is culturally regarded as the normative or "taken-for-granted" path of life, and because "happiness is expected to reside in certain places, those that approximate the taken-for-granted features of normality" (Ahmed 2007: 9).

Pierre Bourdieu (1977: 166, cited in Mathews 1996: 209–10) emphasized the power of normality with regard to how our social world shapes us to see its structures and the parallel structures of our minds as "natural" rather than as human-made and arbitrary. Gordon Mathews (1996) has observed the power of this taken-for-granted cultural perspective with relation to people's idea of *ikigai* (what makes life worth living) and more specifically to one's cultural fate. Comparing the accounts of American and Japanese men and women, Mathews depicted the power of the unconscious "taken-for-granted" in its shaping of the way in which people conceived of or discussed their goals in life. As another contribution to the anthropological study of the pursuits of happiness, Mathews (2009) uses the concept of *ikigai* in a cross-cultural perspective in an attempt to capture the existential dimension of well-being.

In my previous work (Goldstein-Gidoni 2012), I drew attention to the power of normality or taken-for-grantedness (*atarimae*) as related to the way modern Japanese women enter the social role of the full-time housewife upon marriage as part of the normative life plan that they follow as members of society. In the following, I will underline the strong link between the taken-for-granted normative life plan and the idea of happiness as it is conceived by housewives residing in a typical suburban middle-class neighborhood. I will also demonstrate how these concepts of happiness are for the most part shaped by significant agents of the state. The latter include the strong corporate sector, the media, and the market, which are vigorously involved in producing and endorsing the idea of happiness for women as residing in normative middle-class marriage and in particular in the promotion of the idea of the "happy housewife." The second part of this chapter relates more closely to the influence of women's magazines in forming and reproducing notions and images of the socio-cultural idea of "being happy as a woman."

The women of Royal Heights

Data for this chapter were collected between 2003 and 2011 and in 2013 and 2014 when I went back to the same women to further discuss their idea of happiness (*shiawase*). The majority of the over 50 women involved in this study reside in a typical middle-class neighborhood that I call Royal Heights, a suburban condominium complex (*manshon*) located in the Kansai area and at a convenient commuting distance from central Osaka.

The women who formed the largest age and social group in the neighborhood, and who made up the majority of the interviewees, were born between 1966 and 1970. They were in their 20s during the late 1980s and early 1990s, the last days of the bubble economy. This generation was described as a generation that celebrated the consumer lifestyle. Cultivating so-called individualistic and hedonistic ideas unknown to former generations of women in Japan, they were dubbed the "*Hanako* tribe" (*Hanako zoku*), after a women's magazine titled *Hanako*, whose advice on fashion, dining, and travel was almost religiously followed by its readers, most of them young women (Pollak 1993). The *Hanakos* were expected to make a change both in women's lives and in the nature of the Japanese family. However, as lamented by the family sociologist Ochiai Emiko, they broke this promise of social change, as reaching their 30s, "one after the other [they] married, had children and became housewives" (2005: 161).

When women in Royal Heights are asked to define their identity or status, whether it is for formal purposes like surveys or questionnaires or on any other occasion when a self-introduction (*jiko shōkai*) is required, they mostly use the label "*shufu*" (housewife). As suggested by Robin LeBlanc (1999: 28), for the women of suburban Japan, "'housewife' is a label for *public* identity." However, attentive listening to the women's narratives reveals some other factors that have affected their lives and more particularly their perspectives with regard to their idea of what constitutes a proper housewife, a proper woman, and consequently what can make a woman "happy as a woman." These include some usually neglected "thin" class differentiations, certain generational gaps, and other structural and personal characteristics. In the following, I will try to make some distinctions among the women I interviewed to give a fuller account of their background and their attitude toward their role as housewives and women.

Model housewives

A "model housewife" (*shufu no kagami*) can be described as a paragon of perfect role performance as a wife and a mother. She is in fact a somewhat modernized version of the "good wife, wise mother," who emerged in Japan at the end of the nineteenth century and at least until the 1980s epitomized the role of the married woman who devotes herself to taking care of the house and her husband and to raising her children.

Inoue-san[1] is considered such a model housewife. She is married to a university professor and is a mother of two girls, aged eight and nine at the time of interview. She worked as an office lady (OL) at an insurance company after graduating from junior college. Like most of her fellow OL, she quit her job upon marriage. Very similarly to other model housewives, Inoue-san talked about her lifelong yearning to become a housewife:

> From a very young age, my dream was to become a cute young wife (*kawaii oyomesan*). It wasn't as though my mother [clearly] told me so, but I was raised in such a family. My mother never worked after graduation. She did her bridal training (*hanayome shūgyō*), without working, and then got married. I was often told this story, so I thought I should follow her. Since I was a child, I was always told, "women should be women, men should be men," so I just thought this is how things should be.

This same alleged strong yearning to become a housewife seems to characterize other women who are considered model housewives in the neighborhood. In all these cases, the impact of their mothers on cultivating such childhood or adolescence dreams is evident. Sakai-san can be described as one of the prominent second-generation model housewives. She was raised in a model family: her father is a highly dedicated and successful corporate worker, and her mother has always been a perfect wife who followed her husband dutifully in all of his numerous job transfers. In an in-depth interview I conducted with her in 2003, Sakai-san talked about her longtime yearning to become a dedicated full-time housewife just like her mother. Furthermore, she said that she could hardly imagine any different kind of life:

> As my father was a salaryman, I could never imagine myself getting married to an owner of a small company or a store, nor with a craftsman. I can hardly imagine how they live.

Wannabes

In a society that has proclaimed itself to be a middle-class one, class distinctions are naturally too "thin" to be observed, let alone acknowledged. Nevertheless, within the context of the mass of narratives of the "standard" middle-class family background, the protected aristocracy of model housewives was not the only one to stand out. What I term as "wannabe" middle-class narratives were no less intriguing. Take for example two Royal Heights residents, Shibata-san and Yamada-san. Unlike Inoue-san and Sakai-san, neither was in any manner raised in a pampered environment. Yamada-san's father was in fact not a regular salaryman—he had his own small business, and her mother had to work as his income was irregular. Shibata-san's father was a salaryman, but he worked for a small company that allowed the family only a relatively meager middle-class lifestyle. In both cases, however, the parents made efforts to produce a middle-class environment or consciousness. Yamada-san recalls how her father always insisted that her mother would quit her job at some point in time, which is very typical of salarymen who wish to create the right middle-class image of the male breadwinner. Shibata-san's mother was so eager to play the proper role of a housewife that she did not work outside although the family needed the money, and instead she became intensely involved in typical full-time housewives' activities such as voluntary work and a demanding PTA participation.

Both Shibata-san and Yamada-san married atypically young, in their very early 20s, and they both left home before their marriage. Whereas after marriage both families were lucky enough to purchase an apartment in the comfortable *manshon* of Royal Heights, their husbands' definition as salarymen seems to relate to those stretches of the term that have come to cover almost any more or less regularly working man, especially in office jobs or in administration.

Unlike model housewives, Yamada-san and Shibata-san do not mention any memory of a yearning (*akogare*) to become a housewife at adolescence; nevertheless, they both convey a rather strong identification with the role of the housewife. Moreover, they hold to a very rigid and patriarchic concept of the division of gender roles.

As we will see later, their views of being happy as a woman differ from those of model housewives as well as from the new generation of housewives soon to be discussed. They cannot accept happiness that comes with consumption and "easy life." As Yamada-san explains, she cannot tolerate the "*shufu* of these days who have lunches at nice restaurants while their husbands (*otōsan*), who are working so hard, have the cheapest lunches." Likewise, Shibata-san has a strong aversion toward "new-type housewives," who forget their proper role of total dedication to house and child rearing, and is particularly disgusted by their latest tendency to "have their nails done."

The younger generation of "happy housewives"

Some of the women in the neighborhood pronounced "a kind of generation gap" when describing a group of slightly younger mothers, or mothers of younger children, who enjoy themselves much more than most other women did while raising their children. Some of these women in fact formed a "young" group of close friends who met daily and often held joint dinners with the young children or even drinking parties.

These women seem to represent a somewhat novel attitude toward the idea of the "good wife, wise mother," or even the basic ideal of the housewife. Whereas their life plan appears to have followed a very similar route to that of "regular" housewives, they seem to have never had any clear aspirations to become "model housewives." However, their position is not a result of any inferiority they may feel toward perfect housewives. This new image of the housewife, who does not necessarily have to be hard working, suffer (*kurō*), or endure (*gaman*), has been defined as the "new orientation of housewives" (*shin sengyō shufu shikō*). This new wife and mother is allowed to enjoy herself, to pursue her own hobbies and interests, and, very importantly, after finding the "right" husband, she knows how to use him and his money to do so (Ogura 2003).

Another "new" characteristic of this group of women is that they tend to talk openly about their interest in shaping their (female) bodies, often in ways once considered right for unmarried women only. Such is Hara-san's passion for Hawaiian dance. Mori-san once stated even more clearly that she had decided to "shape [her] body" as the preliminary step to reentering society. In her interview, she admits that recently she had been feeling that raising kids, while very significant, was not enough to give her a feeling of self-fulfillment (*tasseikan*). She desires "to have something that [I] can say [I] am good at." She feels inferior looking at other women around her, especially those appearing in women's magazines, who seem "so talented." She has decided that losing weight through diet and working out will be the first step for recovering "my self-confidence" and "recharging myself" on the way to finding something that will give her some new sense of self-fulfillment and a sense of happiness.

A standard life plan as the key for being happy as a woman

Albeit the significant diversity among the women of Royal Heights, as the women narrated their lives and especially as they talked about moving through life stages, one of their striking realizations was the strength of the "natural order of things" (*atarimae*) that governed these transitions. There was no marked distinction between the women on this point. As I further explore in my previous work (Goldstein-Gidoni 2012: 58–60), for many of the women our conversations about their lives and ideas often provided a rare angle for observing the natural way in which they had made their role transitions in their lives so far, from a student to an office lady (OL) and then from a company employee to a full-time housewife (*sengyō shufu*) upon marriage.

Murakami-san can hardly be described as a model housewife. She insists that she has been always questioning her own abilities and propensity to be a good housewife. She is certainly not the domestic type; she likes being outdoors and active. Similarly to other "new-type" housewives, she enjoys swimming and going to the gym as well as going to lunch with her friends.

Nevertheless, during the interview when she talks about becoming a housewife at marriage she says:

> I have never asked myself if it's okay to be always inside the house as a housewife only. My mother was there to guard the house (*ie o mamoru*). I thought it was so natural (*atarimae*) to resign when you get married.

In her illuminating research on pregnant women, Ivry (2010: 138) found that Japanese women who could economically afford to quit their jobs when they were expecting their first child basically saw this act as replacing one full-time job with another. The stories I heard from Royal Heights women strongly support this idea. Moreover, retiring upon marriage or pregnancy did not merely mean an occupational change but surely also signified a transition into a new *social role*. I suggest that this significant transition should be regarded in the context of a general social order that has developed in corporate postwar Japan, in which individuals tend to identify themselves at each life stage with a *single role* that is clearly gendered.

Japanese women's life transitions thus seem to deeply reflect a tendency to follow a carefully written script of a strictly ordered life plan in which each life stage is firmly fixed. This tendency has been described in statistically revealing terms showing that Japanese women's entry into a position both in the educational system and in marriage is carefully timed and typically occurs once in a lifetime (Brinton 1992). In their stories, Royal Heights women gave a very significant role to their parents, especially their mothers, in decisions such as retiring from work upon marriage or during pregnancy with the first child. They also related to the way their employers or more generally their work environment influenced their decision to quit their work upon marriage by often suggesting this as the key for their happiness "as women."

This is how Sakai-san, who is considered by her neighbors and friends to be one of the leading model housewives in Royal Heights, explained how her yearning and dream of becoming a happy full-time housewife was shaped:

> Initially, I was planning to take maternity leave [and resume working]. However, even though the company's regulations offered such an option, no one had taken it before. Moreover, it was my first child and my mother strongly objected. She herself was a full-time housewife so she advised me to follow her way for the sake of the child. She said that I should first become a housewife and only after that [the years dedicated for child raising] could I think about what I would like to do next […]. Then again, I had always longed (*akogare*) to become a housewife, so I retired.

Brinton (1992) highlights the influence of "stakeholders," key adults such as parents and employers in shaping Japanese women's crucial life-course transitions. She describes this pattern as "socially embedded," as compared with the more "self-directed" lives of American women. Significant figures in the educational system such as teachers seem to also have impact on women's ideas of social roles and consequently their concepts about happiness even in early age. This impact may be more pronounced in the ultra-protective private schooling system that "good families" can offer to their daughters. Yamaguchi-san, whose firm attachment to her *shufu* role was very distinct as she declared that she saw her role as housewife as "number one and anything else is number two," was raised in such a comprehensive private and sheltered schooling system that allows students to matriculate from one school to the next without entrance examinations. When talking about how her concept of social role was shaped, she gave a significant role to the unforgettable words of her schoolmaster, who from junior high school through university strongly taught his female students that they *should* become good mothers (*ii okāsan ni nannasai, ii okāsan ni*). Her determination to become a model housewife and actually her conviction that this would surely bring happiness was accentuated by her mother's advice:

> '*Ii oyomesan ni natte, ii okāsan ni naru no wa shiawase*' [becoming a good wife and a good mother will bring [you] happiness]. All my life, since I was very small, I was [thus] told by my mother, so I accept the idea as *atarimae*, very naturally.

In 2013 I went back to Royal Heights to discuss the idea of happiness (*shiawase*) with the same women whose life I had been following for over a decade. This is how Sakai-san, the model housewife who is cited above with regard to the way her yearning (*akogare*) to become a full-time housewife was shaped, explained her idea of happiness:

> [...] but I think that if we have a job and a house we already have everything. It depends on each person how much he or she enjoys life. We got married because we wanted to become happy but besides, we wanted to make our parents content. We also were surrounded by an atmosphere suggesting that "it is better to get married."

Scientific studies of happiness seem to concur that some conditions favor happiness. Unsurprisingly, these general conditions include an economically prosperous background and social and political stability. Following this same rationale, happy persons are more likely to be married, to be part of majority or mainstream normative groups and at the top of the social ladder rather than at the bottom (Veenhoven 1991: 16). Whereas empirical research on happiness, based on the notion that happiness can be measured (Veenhoven 1984, 1988), generally attempts to locate "happy persons," the perspective of cultural studies critically offers a different approach. This critique is eloquently put by Ahmed when she suggests that instead of assuming happiness is simply found in "happy persons," we should see how claims to happiness make certain forms of happiness more valuable than others (2007: 10).

In the following I will further show how the entitlement for happiness is being formed in the lives of middle-class Japanese women. Claims for "normal" happiness are formed not only by following the expected life path, marrying the right husband, and forming a standard family. Focusing on the image of the "happy housewife," I will relate to the high involvement and impact of social and cultural agents and agencies in determining how some forms of happiness for women are more valuable than others. Special focus will be put on women's magazines that play a significant role in women's lives.

The emergence of the new "happy housewife"

As was already observed by Betty Friedan in her study of American housewives in the late 1950s, the market, the mass media, and especially women's magazines have great impact on carving the "right" female image and role ([1963] 2001: 34). Women's magazines form a large part of the Japanese print media. From early in the twentieth century, the massive publishing industry found women of all ages a good target. Studies of these magazines have revealed their vast and varied impact on women's lives. They influence women's consumption habits and play a significant role in the formation of women's identities and the cultivation of ideas of self-fulfillment (Assmann 2003; Sato 2003; Skov and Moeran 1995).

Women's magazines, especially *Very* and *Story*, which aim at women in their 30s and 40s, respectively, seemed to be very popular in Royal Heights. Some of the most enthusiastic readers went as far as to take the promise offered in those magazines as something to cherish and follow. Kudoh-san, who always made an extra effort to look fashionable and stylish even though she was not working outside the house, carried with her in her purse the embodiment of her idea of a perfect and happy housewife in the form of a scrap from an article that appeared in *Very* a few years earlier. The woman portrayed in the magazine piece, she said, was an "ordinary housewife," who, however, never neglected doing her makeup and her nails. She also took French lessons as she sometimes accompanied her husband on his business trips to Paris. "I cherish this scrap," Kudoh-san said, "as [this housewife] was so stunning (*suteki*), and moreover she looked so *totally happy* preparing good food for her husband."

Nancy Rosenberger (1996: 22–23) describes Japanese magazines targeting married women with children in the early 1990s as purposely de-emphasizing sexual attractiveness and international sophistication. Unlike those bygone publications, new ones for young married women with children, such as *Very* and *Story*, are replete with images of fashionable and attractive housewives. These women are not only exhorted to polish and paint their nails and to wear fashionable clothes, but often are also presented outdoors in the setting of the urban consumer scene, and hence are not restricted like housewives of the previous decade to finding their freedom and individuality within the home.

The changing cultural concept of happiness of Japanese housewives seems to have been largely related to the emergence of a new type of "happy housewives" as depicted in popular women's magazines. The changing point coincided with the launch of a new type of women's magazines in the mid-1990s. As observed by Ishizaki (2004), these magazines not only created a new type of housewife but also new ways for being a "happy (*kōfuku na*) full-time housewife." As Ishizaki clearly demonstrates, the magazine industry made this clever shift by using the format of young women's fashion magazines to target housewives.

Ishizaki (2004) provides an illuminating and detailed account of the gradual change in the image of the housewife as portrayed in women's magazines. She focuses on *Very*, a women's magazine that from its first issue in 1995 addressed housewives using the format of *JJ*, a popular fashion magazine for young women. Unlike the disappearing practical housewives' magazines, *Very*, targeting mainly women in their 30s, offered its housewife readers the image of a "maiden" (*shōjo*) and a fashionable housewife by using imaging and vocabulary previously closely identified solely with young unmarried women, including "cute" (*kawaii*) or "sweet" (*amai*) clothes. It also began applying the language of self-fulfillment and the pursuit of happiness through fashion and hobbies with regard to housewives.

By ascribing youth, cuteness, fashion, and self-enjoyment to housewives, *Very* seemed to have done something previously atypical of women's magazines in blurring age and social-role differentiation. However, at the same time, this shift in the housewife image can be regarded as the creation of yet another new "tribe," the tribe of happy and fashionable housewives. The latter can be explained in terms of the tendency of media and advertising people that developed in the hyper-consuming bubble years to invent age and social categories for easier targeting of fairly discrete groups, whose members can be made to think of themselves in a certain way (Clammer 1997: 10–11). This same spirit of the new happy housewife was carried over later on to other new magazines: *Story*, a magazine for women in their 40s, launched in 2002, and *Hers,* a "lifestyle magazine" targeting women in their 40s and 50s, launched in 2008. All are issued by the same publishing house, Kobunsha.

The new image bestowed on housewives since the mid-1990s has thus carried with it also new ideas of happiness. Many of these ideas, as we will shortly see, are related to the joy of consumption. The relationship between consumption and cultural ideas and ideals of happiness has been observed as related to our contemporary world at large. This should not be surprising against the background of global trends in which "the mantra of 'consumption equals happiness' is fabricated and fed to individuals from birth to death" (Johnston, quoted in Johnston et al. 2012: 15).

Consuming the promise of happiness

The first generation of proper postwar housewives was not expected to paint their nails (Goldstein-Gidoni 2012: 123). Instead, they were expected to endure and be hard working and to improve their inner beauty. This kind of beauty, which conservative social critics still esteem and wish to restore (Hayashi 1998), was often related to a "proper Japanese spirit" characterized by internal strength and stamina. This is no longer the case. As was stated by another very perceptive Royal Heights resident: "For our mothers' generation, endurance (*gaman*) was considered a virtue. A woman was expected to endure, as if it were Japanese culture. Nowadays a woman like that is no longer considered attractive (*suteki*)."

Whereas magazines for housewives even as late as the early 1990s were described as purposely promoting "Japanese femininity," or the image of the "good wife, wise mother" (Moeran 1995: 118), magazines from the mid-1990s and especially since 2000 are replete with images of fashionable and attractive housewives. This new kind of femininity is not restricted to the improvement of looks and style but has been increasingly connected with the pursuit of happiness for women and their families. Take for example Yamamoto Rikako, one of those women who "cannot stop being cool mothers" (*kakkoii okāsan wa tomaranai*), presented by *Very* (December 2007: 42–43). Rikako, 34, is a former airline stewardess and a full-time housewife "struggling" to raise four children, but nevertheless, she declares, "As a woman [I] always want to be pretty." Rikako, who never neglects doing her hair and makeup even on busy mornings, is lucky to have three daughters whom she feels obliged to teach about girls' femininity (*onna no ko rashisa*). Rikako shares with the readers her unique precious moments of pure happiness. These occur especially in the morning time when she nicely braids her daughters' hair. Rikako sometimes dresses up neatly when engaged in activities with her kids, and she even enjoys coordinating colors and sharing smart dressing (*oshare*) with her eldest daughter when they go together to a hula dance class. Nevertheless, she saves her special hairstyles and dresses exclusively for the special happy occasions when she and her husband—"just the two of us"—go out to dine.

The idea that a wife and mother should be attractive to her husband is one of the most striking recent ideas promoted by women's magazines. Until at least the mid-1990s, sexuality seemed "not to be an issue" for readers of popular housewives' magazines, in terms of their own self-image or in the way they related to their husbands (Moeran 1995: 117–18). Conversely, new magazines encourage housewives to smarten up before collecting their husbands at the train station on a rainy day and to dress fashionably when they go out to dine with them. Their own and their daughters' new fashionable femininity and smiling faces are said not only to raise their own prospects to become happy as women, but they are also encouraged as the ultimate cure and indeed a prescription for happiness for their hardworking and exhausted husbands:

> A sudden rain shower; it's the same train station as always, but today I will go to greet [my husband] dressed more fashionably and beautifully than usual. [...] What could make him [my husband] happier than getting off the crowded and exhausting train and seeing the smiling face of his daughter, fashionably dressed waiting for him? And the truth is, I also wanted [to come and] show off my newly bought fashionable high boots.
>
> (*Story* August 2009: 27)

So says the chic reader model, photographed with her cutely dressed daughter. The August 2009 issue of *Story* dedicated several pages to a number of short episodes from the lives of "real" wives and mothers. The stories, which are accompanied by full-page pictures of the women posing with a range of fashionable items (with the details of prices and where they can be purchased), allow a glimpse at the new idea of the pursuit of happiness of middle-class urban families.

The new-style magazines for housewives in their 30s and 40s urge them to stay "cute" (*kawaii*), a quality formerly related only to young, not yet married women. "It doesn't matter how old you are. For women, the best compliment is being 'cute' (*kawaii*). That is why when [a woman] enters her 40s, more than her 20s or 30s, [she] likes cute clothing, so that the romance will not end" (*Story* June 2006: 77). One of the main aims of being a "cute adult," however, is the discovery of new means for happiness that will be nourished by self-love. As was declared in *Story* "We announce a plan for 'In five years I will still love myself'" (*Happyō shimasu: "Gonengo mo I love Jibun" keikaku*) (December 2007: cover page). Women are thus encouraged to consume and be happy as wives and mothers. The feminist Ogura Chikako describes *Story*'s concept as a "trap." The magazine makes the "*Story* generation" of readers, namely women who have been living as cooperative wives and mothers, now believe that the time has come for them to start living independently, looking for "their own selves" (*jibun*). "Falling into the magazine's trap," they naively believe that they really can begin pursuing an independent and joyful lifestyle (Ogura 2003: 83). The alleged stylish independence offered to those housewives who can economically afford it can indeed be regarded as a kind of a "trap." I suggest that this is the trap of the promise of happiness. However, being entrapped in the promise that lies in fashion and consumption does not necessarily imply that the old and more common path for happiness for housewives, that which remains in the confines of the safe home, had to be extinguished. On the contrary, the joy of domesticity has had a conspicuous revival as it has gained a new fashionable aura.

The joy of female domesticity

> I have always done my housekeeping job fully, polishing each and every window, but we shouldn't perform such duties feeling it is an obligation. When you have your window polished, you can enjoy the sunlight, or even on rainy days, you feel like looking outside through a well-polished window. [On the contrary,] if you leave the window dirty, you never feel like looking outside. I believe that if you live that way [neglecting cleaning], you cannot fully enjoy your life. You are wasting your life.
>
> (Kurihara Harumi, interview, November 2007)

Despite her insistence that she is only a "simple housewife" (Goldstein-Gidoni 2012: 147–51; Newcomb 1997) who made a redebut into society after dedicating many years of her life to child raising and the home, Kurihara Harumi is in fact largely considered as "Japan's Martha Stewart" and is undoubtedly the most renowned of Japan's "charisma housewives" (*karisuma shufu*), a rather recent media invention of female idols who are leading figures of the housekeeping world. No wonder Kurihara was dubbed by the *New York Times* the "Empress of Domesticity" (Moskin 2006). Not only has she built a business empire in the field of cooking and lifestyle, she also insists on delivering the message of the joy of domesticity. The joy of polishing the living room windows while feeling the "warmth of the sunshine filling the room" (Kurihara 1999: 34) is an example of such ideas that Kurihara, though ever intimate, never preachy, nevertheless repeats in every one of her public presentations, including the so-called "private meeting" I had with her in 2007.

"Female domesticity is fun" is one of the main messages Kurihara delivers to women of the 2000s. *Mō hitotsu no okurimono: Ie no naka ni mo tanoshii koto ippai* (One more gift: In the house too there are plenty of fun things [to do]) is the title of one of Kurihara's successful books, or one of the "gifts" she has bestowed on Japanese women (Kurihara 1999). Like her numerous other books, this one is a blend of allegedly intimate accounts of scenes from her own private domestic family life, such as a quasi-poetic description of her family's house cats (title: "Just being with them makes us happy, our house cats") and tips about household management, and the like, all interwoven with Kurihara's ideologies or truths about the joy of female domesticity.

Like many women in Japan, Royal Heights women are great fans of Kurihara. Her vast popularity can be partially explained by her relative accessibility. As one of her Royal Heights fans explained, her easygoing ways and simple recipes are what make a housewife "self-confident." Others also related to her extremely simple and down-to-earth behavior, noting how "she is always smiling and has an air of happiness around her."

The message of domestic pleasure seems to be catchier (and in fact usually also cheaper to achieve) than the happiness that lies in shopping for elegance offered by women's magazines as described above. Allegedly, there is no need to do the extra step "back into society" after the years spent at home dedicated to child raising. Nevertheless, this does not necessarily imply that Kurihara is falling behind the trends that produce and promote the new happy (and happily consuming) housewife.

"I like creating things that make women smile," said Kurihara in an interview in November 2007. Admitting that the life of *shufu* has a tendency to become "boring and full of routine," Kurihara went on to relate how she had always tried to design products that would make the life of housewives enjoyable and thus meaningful. Aprons are regarded as one of the leading designer wares in her line of products. A full section in her shops is dedicated to aprons, just as it is on her official website, which chose to use a quote from the "priestess herself" to explain the significance of aprons:

> [Kurihara] Harumi says "When I tighten an apron, I feel that I am ready to work. I would like to enjoy cooking and housework, dressed fashionably. A nice apron does something to create an opportunity to enjoy daily life."[2]

Just like Kurihara's adherence to traditional values, her sense of elegance and fashion is also highly admired. In fact, one of the secrets of her success can be found in her unique ability to combine old and new. On the one hand, she is esteemed for her adherence to traditional values as she is regarded as "respectful to her own aging parents and to [Japanese] tradition," as another one of her admirers explained. But, on the other hand, this does not deny or replace Kurihara's keen eye to current trends.

Through her commercial empire of feminine domesticity, Kurihara Harumi sells both material and non-material products, beautifully adorned in the latest fashionable attire, that in fact produce, or rather reproduce, old patriarchal family values and conservative divisions of gender roles. Using the power of "traditional Japanese" values, Kurihara's unique promise of the joy of domesticity seems to carry with it deeper meanings and in fact it involves a larger promise of happiness and "Japanese-style" harmony (*wa*).

> The expression *sengyō shufu* might give foreigners the impression that we [Japanese women] are bound by our obligations, but I believe it is in fact the opposite. The housewife holds the power to make the family stick together. Some housewives may complain that they are working so hard with no one really appreciating their great contribution. However, I keep on working hard, believing that one day they [my husband and children] will understand the value of my existence. I believe that it is the mother, and not the father, who actually creates the family's peace and harmony (*wa*).
> (Kurihara Harumi, interview, November 2007)

Finally, the promise of happiness is surely vital in a time of crisis. Kurihara's message to women on the heels of the 2011 triple disaster in Northern Japan was revealing in this sense. Coming as a savior, her post-disaster basket was full not only with easy recipes carrying names such as "joyful salad plate" and "relieving potatoes." It was in fact also full with national images such as the vital "mother's smile" that will bring harmony (*wa*) not only to her own family but also to Japan at large (*Harumi* Magazine June 2011).

Conclusion

The renewed image of "the happy housewife" is surely not a Japanese invention. Sara Ahmed (2010: 52–53) describes a new generation of bloggers who take up this new identity. Very much like women's magazines, websites, and blogs in Japan, these English-speaking blogs typically include recipes, tips on doing housework, and belief statements that register the happy housewife as an important social role and duty. In the Western case as described by Ahmed, this role and duty must be defended, as with the fall of domesticity (Matthews 1987) housewives have become a minority. As explained above (see also Goldstein-Gidoni 2012), housewives in Japan have not become minority subjects. Moreover, the promoters of the image of the "happy housewife" in Japan are less bound to present counterclaims against feminist claims. Nonetheless, there is a striking similarity between the two cases with their claim that the housewife's *"duty is to generate happiness by the very act of embracing this image"* [emphasis in the original] (Ahmed 2010: 53).

This chapter offers my own reading of the "fourth dimension" of happiness as suggested in the work on happiness by Mathews and Izquierdo (2009b). My focus here is on happiness as a socio-cultural idea and on the way people in a specific cultural context *conceive* happiness. The chapter suggests that the cultural idea of happiness or the idea of what forms the promise of happiness is closely related to leading an expected and normative lifestyle and life plan. Following Mathews and Izquierdo's lead, which suggests we look at the power of national and global forces as shaping perceptions of happiness, this chapter aimed at showing the high involvement of social and cultural agents in the formation of this promise of happiness. For the women, it seems not to be enough to follow the right path and marry (right). Marriage as a common indicator for happiness seemed a good starting point from which cultural agents like women's magazines and domesticity sages and mentors suggest or rather reaffirm "if you do this or if you have that, then happiness will follow" (Ahmed 2007: 12).

Japanese women's magazines provide not only details and information, they also often tell their readers what to do and what not to do (Tanaka 1998). Magazines and other mentors provide their followers with "happiness scripts," a kind of set of instructions for what they must do in order to be happy. Certainly, the majority of those who read the magazines and follow charisma housewives like Kurihara Harumi will never reach the same level of success in their redebuts into society after child raising as the celebrities presented in the media. Chances are that the magazine readers would have to be content with dull occupations such as supermarket cashiers or other manual low-paid jobs like most women in Royal Heights, excluding the few most fortunate ones with the most "right" husbands. Moreover, the recent cracks in what was formerly experienced as a stable and secure system have obviously strengthened not only feelings of insecurity but also some kind of class awareness. However, this does not really harm the status of magazine idols and role models whom other women admire and dream of emulating.

Moreover, as Janice Winship rightly suggests in her critique of women's magazines, reality does not harm the fantasies these magazines sell to their readers. Readers are often aware that the visual and verbal representations are first and foremost fantasies for the sake of pleasure or "instant satisfaction" rather than for practical action (Winship 1983: 55). As I demonstrated in this chapter, women's magazines and other forms of media not only reaffirm what constitutes a "woman" (Winship 1983: 38), but also what constitutes a "happy woman."

Suggesting "happiness" as a cultural construct as I have done in this chapter obviously implies that the idea of what constitutes happiness is bound to gain new meanings with changing social conditions. The scripts for happiness offered to the younger generation of housewives differ from those that were bestowed upon the former generation of hardworking housewives. The new happy housewife is allowed and often even encouraged to enjoy life through fashion and consumption. However, as we could clearly see through the example of the wisdom and advice given by Kurihara, who may be dubbed the epitome of the "happy model housewife," even those of the younger generation of joyful housewives are constantly reminded that the greatest joy is indeed the joy of domesticity. Being happy as women, or wearing the "mother's smile," they are advised would finally bring happiness and harmony not only to their families but to Japanese society at large.

Notes

1 All names are pseudonyms.
2 "Yutori no kūkan," Harumi Kurihara official website. http://www.yutori.co.jp/en/products/index.html. Retrieved March 29, 2015.

References

Ahmed, Sara. 2007. "The Happiness Turn." *New Formations* 63/1:7–15.
Ahmed, Sara. 2010. *The Promise of Happiness*. Durham, NC: Duke University Press.
Allison, Anne. 1996. "Producing Mothers." pp. 135–155 in *Re-Imagining Japanese Women*, edited by A. E. Imamura. Berkeley: University of California Press.
Assmann, Stephanie. 2003. "Japanese Women's Magazines: Inspiration and Commodity." *Electronic Journal of Contemporary Japanese Studies*. Discussion Paper 6. http://www.japanesestudies.org.uk/discussionpapers/Assmann.html. Retrieved 29 March 2015.
Bourdieu, Pierre. 1977. *Outline of a Theory of Practice*. Translated by R. Nice. Cambridge: Cambridge University Press.
Brinton, Mary C. 1992. "Christmas Cakes and Wedding Cakes: The Social Organization of Japanese Women's Life Course." pp. 79–107 in *Japanese Social Organization*, edited by T. Sugiyama Lebra. Honolulu: University of Hawai'i Press.
Clammer, John. 1997. *Contemporary Urban Japan: A Sociology of Consumption*. Oxford, UK: Blackwell.
Colson, Elizabeth F. 1962. "Speaking as an Anthropologist." *Radcliffe Quarterly* November: 52–54.
Colson, Elizabeth F. 2012. "Happiness." *American Anthropologist* 114/1:7–8.
Cwiertka, Katarzyna J. 2006. *Modern Japanese Cuisine: Food, Power and National Identity*. London: Reaktion Books.
Dasgupta, Romit. 2000. "Performing Masculinities? The 'Salaryman' at Work and Play." *Japanese Studies* 20/2:189–200.
Friedan, Betty. [1963] 2001. *The Feminine Mystique*. Rev. ed. with Introduction by Anna Quindlen. New York and London: W. W. Norton and Company.
Garon, Sheldon. 1997. *Molding Japanese Minds: The State in Everyday Life*. Princeton, NJ: Princeton University Press.
Goldstein-Gidoni, Ofra. 2012. *Housewives of Japan: An Ethnography of Real Lives and Consumerized Domesticity*. New York: Palgrave Macmillan.
Gordon, Andrew. 2000. "Society and Politics from Transwar through Postwar Japan." pp. 272–296 in *Historical Perspectives on Contemporary Asia*, edited by M. Goldman and A. Gordon. Cambridge, MA and London: Harvard University Press.

Gordon, Andrew. 2002. "The Short Happy Life of the Japanese Middle Class." pp. 108–129 in *Social Contracts under Stress: The Middle Classes of America, Europe, and Japan at the Turn of the Century*, edited by O. Zunz, L. Schoppa, and N. Hiwatari. New York: Russell Sage Foundation.

Harumi Magazine June 2011.

Hayashi, Michiyoshi. 1998. *Shufu no fukken* [Restoration of the housewife]. Tokyo: Keishōdo.

Holthus, Barbara G. 2010. *A Half Step Ahead: Marriage Discourses in Japanese Women's Magazines*. PhD dissertation, Department of Sociology, University of Hawai'i at Manoa. Retrieved from ProQuest Dissertations & Theses Database, 3448644.

Ishizaki, Yūko. 2004. "Josei zasshi 'Very' ni miru kōfuku na sengyō shufu zō." [The image of the "happy" full-time housewife as portrayed in the women's magazine *Very*]. *Journal of the National Women's Education Center of Japan* 8:61–70.

Ivry, Tsipy. 2010. *Embodying Culture: Pregnancy in Japan and Israel*. New Brunswick and London: Rutgers University Press.

Johnston, Barbara Rose et al. 2012. "On Happiness and Transformative Change". *American Anthropologist* 114/1:15–16.

Kurihara, Harumi. 1999. *Ie no naka ni mo tanoshii koto ippai* [In the house too there are plenty of fun things (to do)]. Tokyo: Bunka Shuppan Kyoku.

LeBlanc, Robin M. 1999. *Bicycle Citizenship: The Political World of the Japanese Housewife*. Berkeley: University of California Press.

Love, Heather. 2007. "Compulsory Happiness and Queer Existence." *New Formations* 63/1:52–64.

Mathews, Gordon. 1996. *What Makes Life Worth Living? How Japanese and Americans Make Sense of Their Worlds*. Berkeley: University of California Press.

Mathews, Gordon. 2009. "Finding and Keeping a Purpose in Life: Well-Being and *Ikigai* in Japan and Elsewhere" pp. 167–185 in *Pursuits of Happiness: Well-Being in Anthropological Perspective*, edited by G. Mathews and C. Izquierdo. New York and Oxford: Berghahn Books.

Mathews, Gordon, and Carolina Izquierdo, eds. 2009a. *Pursuits of Happiness: Well-Being in Anthropological Perspective*. New York and Oxford: Berghahn Books.

Mathews, Gordon, and Carolina Izquierdo. 2009b. "Conclusion: Toward an Anthropology of Well-Being." pp. 248–266 in *Pursuits of Happiness: Well-Being in Anthropological Perspective*, edited by G. Mathews and C. Izquierdo. New York and Oxford: Berghahn Books.

Matthews, Glenna. 1987. *"Just a Housewife": The Rise and Fall of Domesticity in America*. New York and Oxford, UK: Oxford University Press.

Miller, Laura. 1995. "Introduction: Looking beyond the Sarariman Folk Model." *American Asian Review* 13/2:19–27.

Moeran, Brian. 1995. "Reading Japanese in *Katei Gahō*: The Art of Being an Upperclass in Japan." pp. 111–142 in *Women, Media and Consumption in Japan*, edited by L. Skov and B. Moeran. Richmond, UK: Curzon Press.

Moskin, Julia. 2006. "Empress of Domesticity Drops in." *New York Times* April 19.

Nakano, Lynne. 2011. "Working and Waiting for an 'Appropriate Person': How Single Women Support and Resist Family in Japan." pp. 131–151 in *Home and Family in Japan: Continuity and Transformation*, edited by R. Roland and A. Alexy. London and New York: RoutledgeCurzon.

Newcomb, Amalia A. 1997. "Meet Japan's Martha Stewart." *Christian Science Monitor* 90/11:1–2c.

Ochiai, Emiko. 1996. *The Japanese Family System in Transition: A Sociological Analysis of Family Change in Postwar Japan.* Tokyo: LTCB International Library Foundation.
Ochiai, Emiko. 2005. "Sekai no naka no sengo nihon kazoku" [The postwar Japanese family system in global perspective]. *Nihonshi kōza* 10:159–196.
Ogura, Chikako. 2003. *Kekkon no jōken* [Preconditions for marriage]. Tokyo: Asahi Shinbunsha.
Partner, Simon. 1999. *Assembled in Japan: Electrical Goods and the Making of the Japanese Consumer.* Berkeley: University of California Press.
Pollak, Andrew. 1993. "Japan's Taste for the Luxurious Gives Way to Utility and Frugality." *New York Times,* January 3.
Rosenberger, Nancy R. 1996. "Fragile Resistance, Signs of Status: Women between State and Media in Japan." pp. 12–45 in *Re-Imagining Japanese Women,* edited by A. E. Imamura. Berkeley: University of California Press.
Sakai, Junko. 2003. *Makeinu no tōboe* [The howl of the loser dogs]. Tokyo: Kodansha.
Sato, Barbara. 2003. *The New Japanese Woman: Modernity, Media and Women in Interwar Japan.* Durham, NC and London: Duke University Press.
Skov, Lise, and Brian Moeran, 1995. "Introduction: Hiding in the Light: From Oshi to Yoshimoto Banana." pp. 1–71 in *Women, Media and Consumption in Japan,* edited by L. Skov and B. Moeran. Richmond, UK: Curzon Press.
Story June 2006. "We Need Romantic!" pp. 77–79.
Story August 2009. "Sō da, papa o mukae ni ikō" [So, let's go to greet papa]: 27.
Tanaka, Keiko. 1998. "Japanese Women's Magazines: The Language of Aspiration." pp. 110–132 in *The Worlds of Japanese Popular Culture: Gender, Shifting Boundaries and Global Cultures,* edited by D. P. Martinez. Cambridge, UK: Cambridge University Press.
Veenhoven, Ruut. 1984. *Databook on Happiness.* Dordrecht, Netherlands and Boston, MA: Reidel.
Veenhoven, Ruut. 1988. "The Utility of Happiness." *Social Indicators Research* 20/4:333–354.
Veenhoven, Ruut. 1991. "Questions on Happiness: Classical Topics, Modern Answers, Blind Spots." pp. 7–26 in *Subjective Well-Being: An Interdisciplinary Perspective,* edited by F. Strack, M. Argyle, and N. Schwarz. London: Pergamon Press.
Very December 2007 "Kakkoii okāsan wa tomaranai" [Cannot stop being cool mothers]: 36–47.
Vogel, Ezra F. [1963] 1991. *Japan's New Middle Class: The Salary Man and His Family in a Tokyo Suburb.* Reprint, Berkeley and Los Angeles: University of California Press.
White, Merry. 2002. *Perfectly Japanese: Making Families in an Era of Upheaval.* Berkeley: University of California Press.
Winship, Janice. 1983. "'Options-for the Way You Want to Live Now,' or a Magazine for Superwoman." *Theory, Culture and Society* 1/3:44–65.
Yutori no kūkan, Harumi Kurihara Official Site. N.d. "Products." http://www.yutori.co.jp/en/products/index.html. Retrieved March 29, 2015.

6

THE WELL-BEING OF SINGLE MOTHERS IN JAPAN

James M. Raymo

Single mothers in Japan have received a good deal of recent attention in both the popular press and academic literature (e.g., Abe 2008; Nishi 2012; Raymo and Zhou 2012). To a large extent, this reflects the increasing prevalence of single-mother households and a growing awareness of their economic disadvantage. The number of single-mother families in Japan (unmarried women co-residing with a child under age 20) was 1.2 million in 2011, a 55 percent increase since 1993 (Ministry of Health, Labour, and Welfare 2012), and cross-national comparative data consistently show that Japan has the highest proportion of single-mother households living in poverty (OECD 2014). A growing body of research on single mothers focuses primarily on their economic disadvantage, stressful work circumstances, and policy efforts to support employment (Abe 2008; Shirahase and Raymo 2014; Zhou 2014). However, we currently know very little about how single mothers in Japan fare on other dimensions of well-being or about the reasons for the disadvantages faced by single mothers.

This is a major limitation in light of abundant evidence that single mothers are disadvantaged with respect to multiple dimensions of well-being across a range of other countries (Crosier, Butterworth, and Rodgers 2007; DeKlyen et al. 2006; Hughes and Waite 2009; Jayakody and Stauffer 2000; Kessler and Zhao 1999; Waite and Gallagher 2002; Whitehead, Burström, and Diderichsen 2000). In one notable exception, Abe (2008) draws upon qualitative interview data to describe high levels of stress and poor physical and emotional health among single mothers in Japan. She provides examples of mothers whose inability to provide adequate resources for their children led to depression and despair and mothers whose long work hours exacerbated physical health problems to a degree that required hospitalization. Abe's (2008) data provide compelling evidence that the disadvantages faced by single mothers extend beyond low income, highlighting potentially important implications for the well-being of children, the intergenerational transmission of disadvantage via divorce and single motherhood, and the range of policy measures that might be implemented.

Unfortunately, however, there have been no efforts to examine the emotional and physical well-being of single mothers using population data. The primary reason for this limitation is the lack of appropriate data. Sample surveys typically do not include an adequate number of single-mother households for meaningful statistical analysis. Those surveys that are large enough (e.g., *Kokumin seikatsu kiso chōsa* (Comprehensive Survey of Living Conditions in Japan)) contain detailed information about income but not about other dimensions of well-being (Shirahase and Raymo 2014). Surveys of single-mother households, including the Ministry of Health, Labour, and Welfare's *Boshi setaitō chōsa* (National Survey of Single-Mother Households) and *Boshi setai no haha e no shūgyō shien ni kan suru chōsa* (Survey on Work Assistance for Single Mothers) conducted by the Japan Institute for Labour Policy and Training, do not allow for assessment of the well-being of single mothers in comparison with married mothers.

In this paper, I address these limitations by using data from two rounds of a new survey that includes a large oversample of single mothers. These data include information on multiple dimensions of emotional and physical well-being including happiness, depressive symptoms, and self-rated health. Importantly, they also contain information on many of the factors thought to contribute to lower levels of well-being among single mothers, including mothers' own sociodemographic characteristics, economic deprivation, and work-family stress. My goals are threefold. First, I describe the extent to which single mothers report lower levels of well-being relative to their married counterparts. Second, I evaluate possible explanations for those differences. Third, recognizing the multifaceted nature of well-being, I examine three different measures of well-being: happiness, physical health, and emotional health. I do not, however, address the dimensions of societal, existential, and national institutions/global forces, articulated by Mathews and Izquierdo (2009).

Background

Single mothers in Japan

Cross-national comparative data highlight the high rates of labor force participation and low incomes of single mothers in Japan. In 2010, 85 percent of single mothers in Japan were employed, and 51 percent of single-mother households were living in poverty. Both of these figures are the highest among OECD countries (OECD 2014) and reflect public policies characterized by limited income transfers to single parents and a strong emphasis on independence through employment as well as single mothers' relatively limited earnings potential (Abe 2008; Ezawa and Fujiwara 2005; Ono 2010; Zhou 2014).

The combination of high levels of employment and low earnings also reflects the relatively weak position of women in the Japanese labor market (Brinton

2001), the fact that single mothers tend to have lower levels of education (Raymo, Fukuda, and Iwasawa 2013), and that a large majority of women leave the labor force prior to childbirth (National Institute of Population and Social Security Research 2011). Limited human capital and discontinuous work histories contribute to the tendency for single mothers to be employed in relatively unstable, low-paying jobs, often on a part-time basis (Abe and Oishi 2005; Tamiya and Shikata 2007). Single mothers' ability to engage in full-time, standard employment is also constrained by the fact that expectations of long work hours are common, commute times are often long, the operating hours of publicly provided childcare are limited, and the participation of non-custodial fathers in parenting is minimal (Abe 2008; Zhou 2008).

Furthermore, because child-support agreements are both uncommon and unenforceable (Oishi 2013), less than 20 percent of single mothers receive any financial support from their ex-husbands (Ministry of Health, Labour, and Welfare 2012), and public income support does little to compensate for the lack of private support. Japan has one of the lowest expenditures on public assistance among OECD countries; only 14 percent of single mothers receive welfare (*seikatsu hogo*) (Ministry of Health, Labour, and Welfare 2012), and recent studies have shown that single mothers' post-transfer income is actually lower, on average, than their pre-transfer income, i.e., the taxes they pay are higher than the benefits they receive (Abe 2003, 2008).

Other distinctive characteristics of single mothers in Japan include the predominance of divorce as the pathway to single parenthood and the relatively high prevalence of intergenerational co-residence (Nishi 2012; Shirahase and Raymo 2014). In contrast to the United States and many European countries where non-marital childbearing is common, the growth in single-parent families in Japan is due almost entirely to increases in divorce. The number of divorces nearly doubled between 1980 (141,689) and 2010 (251,378), and roughly one in three marriages is now projected to end in divorce (National Institute of Social Security and Population Research 2014; Raymo, Iwasawa, and Bumpass 2004). Despite growing scholarly interest in never-married mothers (e.g., Hertog 2009), the proportion of single-mother families formed via divorce was 84 percent in 2011 (Ministry of Health, Labour and Welfare 2012). The growing prevalence of single-mother families also reflects the fact that about 60 percent of recent divorces involve minor children, with the mother receiving full custody of all children in the large majority of these cases (84% in 2012; National Institute of Population and Social Security Research 2014). Only 4 percent of divorces involving children resulted in joint custody (Abe 2008; Zhou 2008).

Recent research has focused on the living arrangements of single mothers, examining the extent to which the relatively high prevalence of co-residence with (grand)parents mitigates the disadvantages associated with single-motherhood. Approximately one in three unmarried mothers is co-residing with her parent(s) (Ministry of Health, Labour, and Welfare 2012; Nishi 2012), and Raymo and Zhou (2012) find that these women report better health and economic well-being than lone-mothers. Another recent study shows that the high poverty rate for single mothers overstates the degree of economic deprivation somewhat by not accounting for the fact that so many single mothers co-reside with their parents and are thus not included in the official poverty statistics for single-mother households (Shirahase and Raymo 2014).

Single motherhood and well-being

Previous research in the U.S., Europe, and Japan suggests several reasons to expect lower levels of emotional and physical well-being among single mothers. In this paper, I consider four of the most prominent: lower socio-economic status, economic deprivation, stressful employment circumstances, and exposure to stressful life events.

Selection

A large body of research in the U.S. and elsewhere demonstrates that single mothers have lower levels of education and lower earnings potential and are characterized by several other traits associated with lower levels of well-being (e.g., strained relationships with parents, poor relationship skills, substance abuse). Research on the intergenerational transmission of divorce and non-marital childbearing also suggests that single mothers are more likely to come from disadvantaged backgrounds (Dronkers and Härkönen 2008; Högnäs and Carlson 2012). The link between low socio-economic status and worse emotional and physical health is well documented (e.g., Smith 2007).

As noted above, a similar pattern of selection characterizes single motherhood in Japan. The strong negative educational gradient in divorce (Raymo, Fukuda, and Iwasawa 2013) means a concentration of single motherhood among women with a high school education or less. Recent survey data indicate that 53 percent of unmarried mothers had a high school education or less compared to only 41 percent of married mothers (Japan Institute for Labour Policy and Training 2012). Furthermore, a recent study of poverty and intergenerational co-residence among single mothers in Japan provides strong evidence that the parents of single mothers are themselves economically disadvantaged in many cases (Shirahase and Raymo 2014).

Poverty

Economic deprivation is a well-established correlate of poor physical and emotional well-being (Kessler et al. 2003; Seccombe 2000). Multiple measures of economic circumstances, including income, relative income, poverty, food insecurity, and difficulty paying bills are associated with outcomes such as depression, unhappiness, and morbidity (e.g., Heflin and Iceland 2009; Lantz et al. 2005; Lynch et al. 2004; MacLeod et al. 2005). Studies comparing the emotional well-being of single and married mothers find that financial hardship is a particularly important factor in explaining relatively lower levels of well-being among single mothers (Crosier, Butterworth, and Rodgers 2007; Hope, Power, and Rodgers 1999).

The relatively limited economic resources of single mothers in Japan may thus contribute to lower levels of emotional well-being. Per capita income in single-mother households is about half of that in all households with children (Zhou 2008) and, as noted above, half of all single-mother households are in poverty. Abe (2008) provides suggestive qualitative evidence of the link between economic deprivation and emotional well-being, and Raymo and Zhou (2012) find that lower earnings are associated with worse self-rated health in a sample of single mothers. Other economic characteristics such as wealth, savings, consumption, and need have not been considered in analyses of single mothers' well-being in Japan.

Employment

Stressful work conditions are another possible predictor of lower physical and emotional well-being among single mothers. Several studies have documented relationships between job insecurity (e.g., non-standard employment) and worse emotional health (Ferrie 2001), shiftwork and depression (Strazdins et al. 2006), time pressure and depression (Roxburgh 2004), as well as long work hours and both physical and emotional health (Kleiner and Pavalko 2010). Work-family conflict is another established correlate of emotional health and may play a particularly important role in shaping the well-being of single parents (Chandola et al. 2004).

As noted above, the large majority of Japanese single mothers are employed, often in unstable, non-standard, low-paying jobs. They are also more likely than married mothers to work long hours and to report higher levels of work-family conflict (Japan Institute for Labour Policy and Training 2012). Abe (2008) describes single mothers whose strenuous and inflexible employment results in high levels of stress and exhaustion. In a study of marriage and health among Japanese women, Lim and Raymo (2014) find that the health advantage enjoyed by married women is due primarily to the fact that they are less likely, on average, to be employed than their unmarried counterparts. Also suggestive is evidence that long work hours and work-family conflict result in single mothers spending less time with their children (Raymo et al. 2014). Restricted time with children may contribute to lower levels of emotional well-being, especially in a setting like Japan where the social value attached to intensive mothering is high (Hirao 2001).

Stressful life events

A fourth possible explanation for lower levels of physical and emotional well-being is the experience of stressful events across the life course. There is a long history of research on the link between stressful life events and subsequent health outcomes, starting with the work of Holmes and Rahe (1967). Early life events such as exposure to poverty, death of a parent, and parental divorce, for example, have been linked to lower levels of emotional well-being (Horwitz et al. 2001; Turner, Wheaton, and Lloyd 1995). This work has also shown that the more stressful events one experiences, the greater the impact on emotional health (Thoits 2010). In addition to factors like the experience of parental divorce or poverty in childhood, evidence that domestic violence is often a precursor of divorce points to another potential life stressor among single mothers. Indeed, greater exposure to stressful events, both in childhood and adulthood, explains some of the elevated risk of depression among single mothers (Cairney et al. 2003).

To my knowledge, the linkages among stressful life events, divorce, and subsequent physical and emotional well-being have yet to be studied in Japan, but some work offers suggestive evidence. For example, Abe (2008) hints at the importance of domestic violence as a precursor to divorce and compromised emotional well-being. Shirahase and Raymo (2014) point to the possibility that many single mothers experienced economic deprivation as children or adolescents. As described below, the survey data used in this study allow for an initial examination of these relationships.

Data

Sample

I use data from the first two rounds of the *Kosodate setai zenkoku chōsa* (National Survey of Households with Children). Conducted in November of 2011 and 2012 by the Japan Institute for Labour Policy and Training, this national survey (NSHC, hereafter) of households that include parents and their minor children includes a large oversample of single-parent households. In each year, a two-stage stratified sampling based on data from the Basic Resident Registry (*Jūmin kihon daichō*) produced a target sample of 2,000 two-parent households and 2,000 single-parent households. Interviewers delivered a self-administered questionnaire to respondents' homes and returned to collect the completed questionnaires at a pre-specified date and time. In 2011, completed questionnaires were collected from 2,218 respondents, for a 56 percent response rate (61% for married parents and 50% for single parents).[1] A preference for information from mothers was emphasized both by the interviewer and in the survey instrument, but a small number of questionnaires were completed by fathers (131 married fathers and 151 single fathers). I exclude these respondents from the analyses, leaving a total of 4,137 female respondents for the two years.

The response rates of 55 to 56 percent are similar to those of other recent sample surveys in Japan but are low enough (especially among single parents) to raise concerns about the representativeness of the resulting sample. However, comparison of the characteristics of the 2011 NSHC respondents with two large, nationally representative surveys conducted by the Ministry of Health, Labour and Welfare in 2011 demonstrates that the samples are quite similar (Raymo,

Park, Iwasawa, and Zhou 2014). In both the descriptive and multivariate analyses presented below, I use weights that reflect the intentional oversampling of single mothers. These weights, provided by the Japan Institute for Labour Policy and Training, allow for generalization to the population of mothers of minor children.

Limiting the focus to mothers with at least one co-resident child age 18 or younger results in a base sample of 4053 mothers (1,296 unmarried and 2,757 married).[2]

Dependent variables

Happiness

In the 2012 survey, but not in the 2011 survey, NSHC respondents were asked to rate their happiness over the past year on a 0–10 scale. On this scale, 0 indicates very unhappy and 10 indicates very happy. The wording of the question in Japanese was "*Saikin no ichinenkan, anata wa dono teido shiawase desu ka.*"

CES-D

In both years, respondents were given a version of the Center for Epidemiologic Studies Depression Scale (Radloff 1977). The scale contained seven items in 2011 and 10 items in 2012. Because only five items were asked consistently across the two survey years, I use those items to form a modified CES-D measure. These questions asked mothers how many days during the past week they enjoyed life (*seikatsu o tanoshinde iru*), could not concentrate (*monogoto ni shūchū dekinai*), felt depressed (*ochikonde iru*), felt that everything was an effort (*nani o suru no mo mendō da*), or had trouble sleeping (*nakanaka nemurenai*). The response categories are: "rarely" (*hotondo nai*), "1–2 days," "3–4 days," and "5 or more days." These four categories were coded 0–3 so the index values range from 0–15 ($\alpha = .76$). In the analyses presented below, I rescale this measure so that those with the highest emotional well-being are coded as 0 and those with the lowest emotional well-being are coded as −15.

Self-rated health

In both years, respondents were asked to evaluate their overall health on a standard five-point scale ranging from poor (1) to excellent (5). Self-rated health is a widely used measure of well-being that reflects physical, mental, and emotional health (Singh-Manoux et al. 2006).

Independent variables

Background variables

In all models, I control for mother's age, number and age of co-resident children, and co-residence with parents(-in-law). Age is a continuous measure, number of co-resident children ranges from 1–4. The age of co-resident children is measured as a set of exhaustive, but not mutually exclusive, 0–1 indicators of the presence of a child age 0–5 (preschool), a child age 6–15 (elementary or middle school), a child age 16–18 (high school), child age 19 or older (adult), and children's ages not reported. Co-residence with parents is a 0–1 indicator distinguishing those who live with their parents or parents-in-law from those who do not. I identified mothers co-residing with parents(-in-law) from a question that asks respondents to identify their relationship to all individuals with whom they are co-residing.

Socio-economic status

To address the first hypothesis about selection into single motherhood, I use categorical indicators of mother's own educational attainment and the educational attainment of her father (as a proxy for socio-economic background and potential access to parental resources). Both measures of educational attainment distinguish six different levels of highest degree attained: junior high school, high school, vocational school, junior college, university or more, and a category for those with missing data on these questions.

Economic circumstances

To evaluate the posited role of economic deprivation of single mothers, I use measures of household income, savings behavior, and an indicator of need. Equivalent household income is the reported annual pre-tax household income (from all sources) divided by the square root of household size to account for income sharing and economies of scale (Rainwater and Smeeding 2003). Because a relatively large number of respondents did not respond to this question (n = 512 or 13% of the analytic sample), I collapsed non-missing values into quartiles and added a fifth category for missing values. Savings behavior is a six-category indicator of the frequency with which respondents report saving. The categories are: "almost every month," "sometimes," "rarely," "never," "spending down savings," and "missing." Need is a 0–1 indicator of the inability to afford food and clothing. Respondents were asked how often in the past year they were unable to buy the food or clothing they needed. I constructed a measure that distinguishes respondents who responded "frequently" to either question from those who did not.

Work circumstances

To evaluate the posited role of single mothers' stressful work conditions, I use measures of type of employment, work hours, irregular work hours, and work-family conflict. Employment type is a five-category measure of respondents' current employment: not working, part-time, non-standard employment, regular employment, and self-employed or other types of employment. Mothers' work hours are the reported number of hours per week at work (including overtime). This measure is equal to zero for those who were not employed at the time of the survey. Given the large number of zeros and a small number of missing values, I collapse responses into categories for limited employment (0–10 hours), part-time employment (11–39 hours), and full-time employment (40 or more hours). Irregular work hours is a 0–1 indicator distinguishing those who reported that their work hours were "irregular" or "often irregular" from those who did not. Work-family conflict is an index of mothers' stress calculated by summing responses to three questions asking respondents how often during the past year they felt (a) so tired from work that they could not do necessary housework and childcare, (b) that long work hours made it difficult to do housework and childcare, and (c) that the burden of domestic responsibilities made it difficult to concentrate at work. The six response options range from "never" to "every day," resulting in an index that ranges from 0–15 (α = .83). This measure is equal to zero for mothers who did not work for pay in the previous year.

Stressful life events

In both surveys, respondents were asked whether they had ever experienced the following life events: parents' divorce, receiving welfare as a child, mother's death, father's death, physical abuse by parents, physical abuse by spouse, excessive physical punishment of their child(ren), neglecting their child(ren), postpartum/childrearing depression, physical abuse of their child(ren), and thoughts of suicide. Because the majority of respondents do not report experiencing many of these events, I add the items to construct an index of stressful life events that ranges from 0–9.

Method

I estimated a series of five regression models for each of the three measures of mothers' well-being. Happiness and CES-D were estimated using ordinary least squares regression, and the ordinal measure of self-rated health was estimated using ordered logistic regression. In the first model, I included only the indicators of single motherhood, age, living arrangements, number of co-resident children, and age of co-resident children. These models provide a baseline estimate of the extent to which the well-being of single mothers differs from that of their married counterparts.

In subsequent models, I added the measures of respondents' own education and the educational attainment of their fathers (Model 2), household incomes, savings, and economic need (Model 3), employment type, work hours, irregular work, and work-family conflict (Model 4), and experience of stressful life events (Model 5). In these models, my primary interest is in the extent to which controlling for additional co-variates attenuates the posited negative relationship between single motherhood and well-being. That is, how much of the observed disadvantage among single mothers (with respect to happiness, depressive symptoms, and self-rated health) can be explained by differences in their socio-economic status (Model 2), their economic circumstances (Model 3), their work circumstances (Model 4), and their experience of stressful life events (Model 5)?

Results

In Table 6.1, I present descriptive characteristics of the sample by marital status. The first three rows indicate that single mothers have lower mean values for each of the measures of well-being. These differences are all statistically significant. The distribution of self-rated health categories (not shown) indicates stark differences in the subjective health of single versus married mothers. The proportion reporting fair or poor health was .20 for single mothers, but only .10 for married mothers.

The two groups of mothers are similar in age but differ in several ways. Single mothers had a slightly lower number of co-resident children (1.70 vs. 1.97) and were much less likely, than their married counterparts, to have a preschool age child (17% vs. 38%). Single mothers also had lower educational attainment (52% of single mothers vs. 40% of married mothers had a high school education or less), but the educational attainment of their fathers was similar. One interesting difference is the relatively high proportion of single mothers who did not report father's educational attainment (20% vs. 10% for married mothers), suggesting that single mothers may be more likely to come from single mother families or families in which the father was less involved.

Consistent with the results of existing research summarized above, single mothers face significantly greater economic disadvantage than their married counterparts do. Single mothers had significantly lower size-adjusted household income (41% vs. 13% were in the lowest income quartile), were more likely to report never saving or spending down savings (37% vs. 18%), and were more likely to report frequent economic need (9% vs. 3%). Single mothers' employment circumstances also differed from their married counterparts. They were much less likely to be not working (16% vs. 37%), more likely to be working full time (49% vs. 22%), more likely to work irregular hours (14% vs. 9%), and reported significantly higher levels of work-family conflict (5.92 vs. 3.86). Interestingly, single mothers also reported significantly more stressful life events (1.18 vs. 0.69). Tabulation of specific events (not shown) indicates that single mothers were more likely than their married counterparts to report that their parents divorced, that their (ex-)husbands physically abused them, and that they had contemplated suicide.

TABLE 6.1 Descriptive statistics, by marital status

	Single mothers		Married mothers	
Variable	Mean/proportion	s.d.	Mean/proportion	s.d.
Happiness	6.04	2.44	7.04	2.22
CES-D	-4.29	3.44	-3.05	2.77
Self-rated heatlth	3.34	1.09	3.75	1.04
Age	39.88	6.87	39.79	6.62
Coresiding with parents[a]	0.34		0.22	
Number of co-residing children	1.70	0.74	1.97	0.77
Lives with a child age 5 or younger[a]	0.17		0.38	
Lives with a child age 6–15[a]	0.70		0.67	
Lives with a child age 16–18[a]	0.27		0.22	
Lives with a child age 19 or older[a]	0.15		0.13	
Children's age missing[a]	0.04		0.04	
Educational Attainment				
Junior high school	0.09		0.04	
High School	0.43		0.36	
Vocational school	0.14		0.15	
Junior college	0.18		0.25	
University	0.09		0.17	
Missing	0.06		0.03	
Father's Educational Attainment				
Junior high school	0.29		0.27	
High School	0.34		0.41	
Vocational school	0.04		0.04	
Junior college	0.02		0.03	
University	0.12		0.16	
Missing	0.20		0.10	
Equivalent household income				
First quartile	0.41		0.13	
Second quartile	0.16		0.24	
Third quartile	0.08		0.29	
Fourth quartile	0.18		0.23	
Missing	0.17		0.11	
Savings behavior				
Saving almost every month	0.19		0.44	
Saving sometimes	0.19		0.20	
Rarely saving	0.19		0.15	
Not saving at all	0.28		0.12	
Using savings	0.09		0.06	
Missing	0.06		0.03	
Frequently unable to afford food or clothing[a]	0.09		0.03	
Type of employment				
Not working	0.16		0.37	
Part-time	0.34		0.31	

(*Continued*)

	Single mothers		Married mothers	
Variable	Mean/proportion	s.d.	Mean/proportion	s.d.
Non-standard	0.13		0.05	
Regular	0.32		0.19	
Self-employed/other	0.06		0.09	
Hours per week working				
0–10 hours	0.20		0.44	
11–39 hours	0.31		0.35	
40+ hours	0.49		0.22	
Irregular work hours[a]	0.14		0.09	
Work-family conflict	5.92	4.19	3.86	4.12
Stressful life events	1.18	1.49	0.69	1.10
N	1,254		2,708	
Weighted Proportion	0.11		0.89	

Note: a indicates 0–1 variables where 0=no and 1=yes

Results of models for each of the three measures of well-being are presented in Tables 6.2–6.4. Table 6.2 presents the results for happiness. The first column shows that single mothers score .84 (one-third of a standard deviation) lower than married mothers, on average, on the 0–10 happiness scale. Controlling for the respondent's educational attainment and her socio-economic background in Model 2 attenuates this relationship somewhat, but current economic circumstances matter much more. After controlling for income, savings, and economic need in Model 3, the magnitude of the difference between single mothers and married mothers is reduced by over 50 percent. Household income is not strongly related to happiness, but the inability to save on a regular basis and not being able to afford food and clothing are strong correlates of happiness and explain much of the observed happiness disadvantage for single mothers. In Model 4, the difference between single mothers and their married counterparts is 65 percent lower than in Model 1 but remains statistically significant. Among the work characteristics included in Model 4, work-family conflict is particularly important for understanding the lower levels of happiness among single mothers. Controlling for the lower levels of happiness among mothers who are not working (relative to those in regular employment) works in the opposite direction, increasing the negative coefficient for single mothers (who are much more likely to be employed). In Model 5, the index of stressful life events is associated with significantly lower levels of happiness, and its inclusion contributes to reduction in both the magnitude and statistical significance of the coefficient for single mothers.

Table 6.3 presents the results for emotional well-being, as measured by the five-item CES-D scale. The results are similar to those for happiness. Model 1 shows that single mothers have significantly lower emotional well-being, on average, than their married counterparts. As with happiness, the magnitude of the coefficient for single mothers is roughly one-third of a standard deviation. Controlling for socio-economic status attenuates this relationship somewhat. Respondents' own education has a strong positive relationship with CES-D, but

TABLE 6.2 OLS results for models of happiness

Variable	Model 1	Model 2	Model 3	Model 4	Model 5
Single mother[a]	-0.84**	-0.73**	-0.32*	-0.29*	-0.21
Age	-0.01	-0.02	-0.03**	-0.03*	-0.03**
Coresiding with parents[a]	-0.38**	-0.38**	-0.49**	-0.45**	-0.49**
Number of co-residing children	0.10	0.13	0.16*	0.16*	0.16[#]
Lives with a child age 5 or younger[a]	0.12	0.05	0.10	0.14	0.17
Lives with a child age 6–15[a]	-0.30[#]	-0.28[#]	-0.22	-0.23	-0.16
Lives with a child age 16–18[a]	-0.33[#]	-0.29[#]	-0.21	-0.20	-0.17
Lives with a child age 19 or older[a]	-0.55*	-0.41[#]	-0.26	-0.27	-0.25
Children's age missing[a]	-0.44	-0.32	-0.20	-0.20	-0.17
Educational Attainment					
Junior high school		-0.40	-0.05	0.02	0.22
High School (omitted)		0.00	0.00	0.00	0.00
Vocational school		0.19	0.04	0.07	0.10
Junior college		0.59**	0.29*	0.28*	0.26[#]
University		0.44*	0.09	0.20	0.19
Missing		-0.29	-0.26	-0.26	-0.35
Father's Educational Attainment					
Junior high school		-0.09	-0.05	-0.05	-0.02
High School (omitted)		0.00	0.00	0.00	0.00
Vocational school		0.23	0.32	0.25	0.30
Junior college		-0.65	-0.61[#]	-0.68[#]	-0.64[#]
University		0.17	0.20	0.20	0.19
Missing		0.01	0.11	0.11	0.13
Equivalent household income					
First quartile (omitted)			0.00	0.00	0.00
Second quartile			0.19	0.22	0.17
Third quartile			0.22	0.23	0.20
Fourth quartile			0.28	0.29	0.25
Missing			-0.82	-0.68	-0.70
Savings behavior					
Saving almost every month (omitted)			0.00	0.00	0.00
Saving sometimes			-0.56**	-0.54**	-0.53**
Rarely saving			-1.00**	-0.96**	-0.90**
Not saving at all			-1.55**	-1.53**	-1.48**
Using savings			-1.62**	-1.59**	-1.46**
Missing			0.02	-0.02	-0.12

(Continued)

Variable	Model 1	Model 2	Model 3	Model 4	Model 5
Frequently unable to afford food or clothing[a]			-1.17**	-1.05**	-0.92**
Type of employment					
Not working				-0.94**	-0.84**
Part-time				-0.11	-0.08
Non-standard				-0.01	0.02
Regular (omitted)				0.00	0.00
Self-employed/other				-0.09	-0.04
Hours per week working					
0–10 hours (omitted)				0.00	0.00
11–39 hours				-0.25	-0.28
40+ hours				-0.11	-0.15
Irregular work hours[a]				0.04	0.03
Work-family conflict				-0.11**	-0.09**
Stressful life events					-0.25**
Constant	7.49**	7.69**	8.43**	9.22**	9.36**
N	1,911	1,911	1,911	1,911	1,911
R^2	0.05	0.07	0.17	0.18	0.20

Note: a indicates variables for which omitted category is "no."
[#]p<.10, *p<.05, **p<.01

fathers' education is unrelated to women's emotional well-being. As in the models for happiness, single mothers' unfavorable economic circumstances account for much of their lower emotional well-being, and again savings and economic need are more strongly related to well-being than is household income. Controlling for work characteristics in Model 4 further attenuates the negative relationship between single motherhood and emotional well-being, and after accounting for differences in stressful life events in Model 5, the difference between single and married mothers is no longer statistically significant.

Table 6.4 presents the results for self-rated health. The estimated coefficient for single motherhood in Model 1 (-0.58) means that single mothers have 44 percent lower odds than married mothers of reporting that they are in excellent rather than good health (or in health category n rather than category n-1, more generally). The pattern of results is generally similar to that for happiness and CES-D: differences in women's own education, economic circumstances, and experience of stressful life events all explain part of the health disadvantage among single mothers. Again, differences in economic circumstances are particularly important. Two differences with the models in Tables 6.2 and 6.3 are that employment circumstances do nothing to explain single mothers' health disadvantage and that the coefficient for single mothers remains significantly different from zero in Model 5. The former reflects the fact that the negative association between self-rated health and work-family conflict (more prevalent among single mothers) is offset by the negative association between self-rated health and not working (more prevalent among married mothers). The latter indicates that there are other factors associated with single motherhood and poor self-rated health that are not included in our models.

TABLE 6.3 OLS results for models of CES-D

Variable	Model 1	Model 2	Model 3	Model 4	Model 5
Single mother[a]	-1.11**	-0.99**	-0.50**	-0.36*	-0.19
Age	0.00	-0.02	-0.02*	-0.02*	-0.03**
Coresiding with parents[a]	-0.04	-0.06	-0.17	-0.11	-0.16
Number of co-residing children	0.03	0.05	0.12	0.13	0.13
Lives with a child age 5 or younger[a]	0.26	0.16	0.24	0.38*	0.37*
Lives with a child age 6–15[a]	-0.20	-0.15	-0.08	-0.07	0.02
Lives with a child age 16–18[a]	-0.17	-0.12	-0.07	-0.09	-0.08
Lives with a child age 19 or older[a]	-0.31	-0.16	-0.06	-0.09	-0.07
Children's age missing[a]	-0.36	-0.28	-0.11	-0.03	-0.03
Educational Attainment					
Junior high school		-1.24**	-0.85**	-0.72**	-0.31
High School (omitted)		0.00	0.00	0.00	0.00
Vocational school		0.23	0.07	0.21	0.23
Junior college		0.66**	0.33*	0.39**	0.32**
University		0.41*	0.06	0.28[#]	0.25
Missing		0.23	0.15	0.13	0.00
Father's Educational Attainment					
Junior high school		0.03	0.09	0.07	0.14
High School (omitted)		0.00	0.00	0.00	0.00
Vocational school		-0.17	-0.06	-0.16	-0.02
Junior college		-0.30	-0.35	-0.39	-0.34
University		0.09	0.13	0.15	0.18
Missing		0.01	0.14	0.17	0.28
Equivalent household income					
First quartile (omitted)			0.00	0.00	0.00
Second quartile			0.14	0.12	0.04
Third quartile			0.23	0.20	0.14
Fourth quartile			0.22	0.23	0.17
Missing			-0.05	-0.04	-0.15
Savings behavior					
Saving almost every month (omitted)			0.00	0.00	0.00
Saving sometimes			-0.24[#]	-0.19	-0.21[#]
Rarely saving			-0.79**	-0.73**	-0.61**
Not saving at all			-1.52**	-1.40**	-1.23**
Using savings			-1.86**	-1.71**	-1.49**
Missing			-0.11	-0.03	-0.11
Frequently unable to afford food or clothing[a]			-1.74**	-1.38**	-1.05**

(Continued)

Variable	Model 1	Model 2	Model 3	Model 4	Model 5
Type of employment					
Not working				-1.68**	-1.50**
Part-time				-0.27#	-0.23
Non-standard				-0.12	-0.07
Regular (omitted)				0.00	0.00
Self-employed/other				-0.29*	-0.22
Hours per week working					
0–10 hours (omitted)				0.00	0.00
11–39 hours				0.37#	0.30
40+ hours				0.41#	0.29
Irregular work hours[a]				0.42*	0.38*
Work-family conflict				-0.27**	-0.24**
Stressful life events					-0.56**
Constant	-2.98**	-2.52**	-2.09**	-1.14*	-0.67
N	3,741	3,741	3,741	3,741	3,741
R^2	0.03	0.05	0.12	0.19	0.23

Note: a indicates variables for which omitted category is "no."
#p<.10, *p<.05, **p<.01

TABLE 6.4 Ordered logistic regression results for models of self-rated health

Variable	Model 1	Model 2	Model 3	Model 4	Model 5
Single mother[a]	-0.58**	-0.51**	-0.29**	-0.30**	-0.23*
Age	-0.02**	-0.03**	-0.03**	-0.03**	-0.04**
Coresiding with parents[a]	0.01	0.01	-0.04	-0.06	-0.08
Number of co-residing children	0.03	0.04	0.08	0.08	0.09#
Lives with a child age 5 or younger[a]	0.19#	0.14	0.17	0.28*	0.26*
Lives with a child age 6–15[a]	-0.13	-0.09	-0.07	-0.10	-0.07
Lives with a child age 16–18[a]	-0.05	0.00	0.02	-0.02	-0.02
Lives with a child age 19 or older[a]	-0.19	-0.11	-0.09	-0.14	-0.15
Children's age missing[a]	-0.18	-0.09	0.08	0.00	0.00
Educational Attainment					
Junior high school		-0.73**	-0.54**	-0.51**	-0.34#
High School (omitted)		0.00	0.00	0.00	0.00
Vocational school		0.14	0.09	0.11	0.12
Junior college		0.31**	0.18#	0.20*	0.17#
University		0.32**	0.18	0.26*	0.25*

(Continued)

Variable	Model 1	Model 2	Model 3	Model 4	Model 5
Missing		0.69*	0.67*	0.72**	0.63*
Father's Educational Attainment					
Junior high school		-0.09	-0.09	-0.10	-0.07
High School (omitted)		0.00	0.00	0.00	0.00
Vocational school		0.04	0.10	0.08	0.15
Junior college		-0.21	-0.23	-0.20	-0.18
University		0.07	0.08	0.08	0.10
Missing		-0.33*	-0.25#	-0.23#	-0.20
Equivalent household income					
First quartile (omitted)			0.00	0.00	0.00
Second quartile			0.19	0.20#	0.17
Third quartile			0.11	0.13	0.10
Fourth quartile			0.20	0.22#	0.19
Missing			-0.09	-0.08	-0.14
Savings behavior					
Saving almost every month (omitted)			0.00	0.00	0.00
Saving sometimes			-0.24*	-0.22*	-0.23
Rarely saving			-0.47**	-0.47**	-0.43**
Not saving at all			-0.50**	-0.48**	-0.41**
Using savings			-1.02**	-0.98**	-0.90**
Missing			-0.49**	-0.47*	-0.50**
Frequently unable to afford food or clothing[a]			-0.73**	-0.63**	-0.45*
Type of employment					
Not working				-0.71**	-0.63
Part-time				0.09	0.11
Non-standard				0.19	0.21
Regular (omitted)				0.00	0.00
Self-employed/other				0.31*	0.36*
Hours per week working					
0–10 hours (omitted)				0.00	0.00
11–39 hours				0.14	0.12
40+ hours				0.29#	0.24
Irregular work hours[a]				-0.01	-0.02
Work-family conflict				-0.10**	-0.08**
Stressful life events					-0.29**
N	3,880	3,880	3,880	3,880	3,880
F	14.46	10.38	9.74	10.11	11.39

Note: a indicates variables for which omitted category is "no."
#p<.10, *p<.05, **p<.01

Discussion

Rising divorce rates and the attendant increase in single mother families is one of the most striking, and potentially important, features of family change in contemporary Japan. While much has been made of the high labor force participation rate and high poverty rate of single mothers, little is known about other dimensions of well-being in this group. A large body of research documents a variety of disadvantages faced by single mothers in the U.S. and considers the implications of these disadvantages for overall inequality and for the intergenerational transmission of disadvantage, thus highlighting the importance of conducting similar research in Japan. New data collected by the Japan Institute for Labour Policy and Training provide a valuable opportunity to significantly expand our understanding of the extent to which single mothers are indeed disadvantaged relative to their married counterparts, whether the degree of disadvantage depends on the dimension of well-being considered, and the factors that shape the well-being of single mothers.

Results of the models presented above demonstrate clearly that single mothers are disadvantaged on all three of the indicators of well-being considered and that selection, economic disadvantage, work-related strain, and stressful life events all contribute to this disadvantage. Two findings in particular merit reiteration. The first is the powerful role that economic disadvantage plays in compromising the health and happiness of single mothers. The estimated difference between single mothers and married mothers was reduced by roughly half in the models that controlled for household income, savings behavior, and economic need. Interestingly, the inability to save and to buy necessities (food and clothing) was a stronger predictor of well-being than was household income. This highlights the importance of considering a wide range of economic indicators in models of emotional and physical well-being and suggests that subsequent research should move beyond what I have done in this paper to consider other factors such as social support (e.g., Broussard 2010; Hope, Power and Rodgers 1999). The second striking finding is evidence that single mothers are much more likely to report experiencing stressful life events and that this difference in life experiences accounts for some of the observed difference in each of the measures of well-being. Particularly striking (although not shown in the tables) is evidence of the higher prevalence of parental divorce, domestic violence, and suicidal thoughts among single mothers. Again, these are important correlates of well-being that deserve greater attention in subsequent research. Another potentially fruitful avenue for further research is to adopt a much broader definition of well-being (such as that articulated by Mathews and Izquierdo 2009) that encompasses more than the emotional and physical dimensions considered in this paper.

Taken as a whole, the results of this study shed new light on the disadvantages faced by single mothers in Japan. They suggest that policies promoting independence through employment may have unintended consequences to the extent that stressful work circumstances are detrimental to mothers' physical and emotional well-being. This is particularly true if employment does not generate sufficient income. In light of policy efforts to reduce public income transfers to single mothers (Akaishi 2011), these findings highlight the importance of other potential sources of support for single mothers and their children. Given the high proportion of single mothers who co-reside with their parents (Raymo and Zhou 2012), family is one obvious source of support. However, recent research demonstrates that, in many cases, the parents with whom single mothers co-reside are themselves in precarious economic circumstances (Shirahase and Raymo 2014).

In addition to the implications of these findings for single mothers themselves, the implications for the well-being of children also merit careful consideration. Research on academic performance, behavior outcomes, and health of the children of single parents is uncommon in Japan, but a large body of related literature in the U.S. highlights the importance of family structure for children's well-being. Considering the extreme economic disadvantages associated with single motherhood in Japan, combined with disadvantages on the other dimensions of well-being examined in this study, growth in single mother families is a potentially important mechanism for understanding variation in children's outcomes, social mobility, and the intergenerational transmission of disadvantage.

Notes

1 In 2012, the corresponding numbers were 2,201 respondents for a 55 percent response rate (61% for married parents and 49% for single parents).
2 Of the 84 mothers excluded from the sample, 77 reported no co-resident children and 7 reported that their youngest co-resident child was at least 19 years old. I retain those who did not report their co-resident children's ages. The large majority (79%) of the unmarried mothers were divorced, and small percentages were widowed (9%), never married (4%), or had missing data on the pathway to single parenthood (7%). An additional 91 observations were dropped from the analyses because they had missing values for one or more of the independent variables described below.

References

Abe, Aya. 2003. "Low-Income People in Social Security Systems in Japan." *Japanese Journal of Social Security Policy* 2:59–70.

Abe, Aya. 2008. *Kodomo no hinkon – Nihon no fubyōdō o kangaeru* [Children's poverty: A study of inequality in Japan]. Tokyo: Iwanami Shoten.

Abe, Aya, and Akiko Oishi. 2005. "Boshi setai no keizai jōkyō to shakai hoshō" [Social security and the economic circumstances of single-mother households]. pp. 143–161 in *Kosodate no shakai hoshō* [Social security and households with children], edited by National Institute of Population and Social Security Research. Tokyo: Tokyo Daigaku Shuppankai.

Akaishi, Chieko. 2011. "Single Mothers." pp. 121–130 in *Transforming Japan: How Feminism and Diversity are Making a Difference*, edited by K. Fujimura-Fanselow. New York: The Feminist Press at the City University of New York.

Brinton, Mary C. 2001. "Married Women's Labor in East Asian Economies." pp. 1–37 in *Women's Working Lives in East Asia*, edited by M. C. Brinton. Stanford, CA: Stanford University Press.

Broussard, C. Anne. 2010. "Research Regarding Low-Income Single Mothers' Mental and Physical Health: A Decade in Review." *Journal of Poverty* 14:443–451.

Cairney, John, Michael Boyle, David R. Offord and Yvonne Racine. 2003. "Stress, Social Support and Depression in Single and Married Mothers." *Social Psychiatry and Psychiatric Epidemiology* 38:442–449.

Chandola, Tarani, Pekka Martikainen, Mel Bartley, Eero Lahelma, Michael Marmot, Michikazu Sekine, Ali Nasermoaddeli and Sadanobu Kagamimori. 2004. "Does Conflict between Home and Work Explain the Effect of Multiple Roles on Mental Health? A Comparative Study of Finland, Japan, and the UK." *International Journal of Epidemiology* 33:884–893.

Crosier, Timothy, Peter Butterworth and Bryan Rodgers. 2007. "Mental Health Problems among Single and Partnered Mothers." *Social Psychiatry and Psychiatric Epidemiology* 42:6–13.

DeKlyen, Michelle, Jeanne Brooks-Gunn, Sara McLanahan and Jean Knab. 2006. "The Mental Health of Married, Cohabiting, and Non–Coresident Parents with Infants." *American Journal of Public Health* 96:1836–1841.

Dronkers, Jaap, and Juho Härkönen. 2008. "The Intergenerational Transmission of Divorce in Cross-National Perspective: Results from the Fertility and Family Surveys." *Population Studies* 62:273–288.

Ezawa, Aya, and Chisa Fujiwara. 2005. "Lone Mothers and Welfare-to-Work Policies in Japan and the United States: Towards an Alternative Perspective." *Journal of Sociology & Social Welfare* 32:41–63.

Ferrie, Jane E. 2001. "Is Job Insecurity Harmful to Health?" *Journal of the Royal Society of Medicine* 94:71–76.

Heflin, Colleen M., and John Iceland. 2009. "Poverty, Material Hardship, and Depression." *Social Science Quarterly* 90:1051–1071.

Hertog, Ekaterina. 2009. *Tough Choices: Bearing an Illegitimate Child in Japan*. Palo Alto, CA: Stanford University Press.

Hirao, Keiko. 2001. "Mothers as the Best Teachers: Japanese Motherhood and Early Childhood Education." pp. 180–203 in *Women's Working Lives in East Asia*, edited by M. C. Brinton. Stanford, CA: Stanford University Press.

Högnäs, Robin S. and Marcia J. Carlson. 2012. "'Like Parent, Like Child?': The Intergenerational Transmission of Nonmarital Childbearing." *Social Science Research* 41:1480–1494.

Holmes, Thomas H., and Richard H. Rahe. 1967. "The Social Readjustment Rating Scale." *Journal of Psychosomatic Research* 11:213–218.

Hope, Steven, Chris Power and Bryan Rodgers. 1999. "Does Financial Hardship Account for Elevated Psychological Distress in Lone Mothers?" *Social Science & Medicine* 49:1637–1649.

Horwitz, Allan V., Cathy S. Widom, Julie McLaughlin and Helene R. White. 2001. "The Impact of Childhood Abuse and Neglect on Adult Mental Health: A Prospective Study." *Journal of Health and Social Behavior* 42:184–201.

Hughes, Mary E., and Linda J. Waite. 2009. "Marital Biography and Health at Mid-Life." *Journal of Health and Social Behavior* 50:344–358.

Japan Institute for Labour Policy and Training. 2012. *Kodomo no iru setai no seikatsu jōkyō oyobi hogosha no shūgyō ni kan suru chōsa* [Survey of the life circumstances and parental employment in households with children]. JILPT *Survey Series* no. 95. Tokyo: Japan Institute for Labour Policy and Training.

Jayakody, Rukmalie, and Dawn Stauffer. 2000. "Mental Health Problems among Single Mothers: Implications for Work and Welfare Reform." *Journal of Social Issues* 56:617–634.

Kessler, Ronald C. et al. 2003. "Screening for Serious Mental Illness in the General Population." *Archives of General Psychiatry* 60:184–189.

Kessler, Ronald C. and Shanyang Zhao. 1999. "Overview of Descriptive Epidemiology of Mental Disorders." pp. 127–150 in *Handbook of the Sociology of Mental Health*, edited by C. S. Aneshensel and J. C. Phelan. New York: Kluwer Academic.

Kleiner, Sybil, and Eliza K. Pavalko. 2010. "Clocking In: The Organization of Work Time and Health in the United States." *Social Forces* 88:1463–1486.

Lantz, Paula M. et al. 2005. "Stress, Life Events, and Socioeconomic Disparities in Health: Results from the Americans' Changing Lives Study." *Journal of Health and Social Behavior* 46:274–288.

Lim, Sojung, and James M. Raymo. 2016. "Marriage and Women's Health in Japan." *Journal of Marriage and Family* 78:780–796.

Lynch, John et al. 2004. "Is Income Inequality a Determinant of Population Health? Part 1. A Systematic Review." *Millbank Quarterly* 82:5–99.

Macleod, John et al. 2005. "Is Subjective Social Status a More Important Determinant of Health than Objective Social Status?" *Social Science & Medicine* 61:1916–1929.

Mathews, Gordon, and Carolina Izquierdo. 2009. "Towards an Anthropology of Well-Being." pp. 248–266 in *Pursuits of Happiness: Well-Being in Anthropological Perspective*, edited by G. Mathews and C. Izquierdo. New York and Oxford: Berghahn Books.

Ministry of Health, Labour, and Welfare. 2012. *Heisei 23nendo zenkoku boshi setaitō chōsa kekka hōkoku* [Report on the 2011 national survey of single-mother households]. Tokyo: Ministry of Health, Labour and Welfare. http://www.mhlw.go.jp/seisakunitsuite/bunya/kodomo/kodomo_kosodate/boshi-katei/boshi-setai_h23/index.html. Retrieved March 1, 2015.

National Institute of Population and Social Security Research. 2011. *The Fourteenth Japanese National Fertility Survey in 2010, Marriage Process and Fertility of Japanese Married Couples, Highlights of the Survey Results on Married Couples*. http://www.ipss.go.jp/site-ad/index_english/nfs14/Nfs14_Couples_Eng.pdf. Retrieved March 1, 2015.

National Institute of Population and Social Security Research. 2014. *Jinkō tōkei shiryōshū* [Latest demographic statistics]. Tokyo: National Institute of Population and Social Security Research. http://www.ipss.go.jp/syoushika/tohkei/Popular/Popular2014.asp?chap=0. Retrieved March 1, 2015.

Nishi, Fumihiko. 2012. "Shinguru mazā no saikin no jōkyō (2010nen)" [Characteristics of single mothers in 2010]. http://www.stat.go.jp/training/2kenkyu/pdf/zuhyou/single4.pdf. Retrieved March 1, 2015.

OECD. 2014. *Family Database*. Paris: OECD. http://www.oecd.org/social/family/database.htm. Retrieved March 1, 2015.

Oishi, Akiko S. 2013. "Child Support and the Poverty of Single-Mother Households in Japan." *IPSS Discussion Paper Series*, No. 2013–E01. Tokyo: National Institute of Population and Social Security Research.

Ono, Hiroshi. 2010. "The Socioeconomic Status of Women and Children in Japan: Comparisons with the USA." *International Journal of Law, Policy and the Family* 24:151–176.

Radloff, Lenore S. 1977. "The CES-D Scale: A Self-Report Depression Scale for Research in the General Population." *Applied Psychological Measurement* 1:385–401.

Rainwater, Lee, and Timothy M. Smeeding. 2003. *Poor Kids in a Rich Country*. New York: Russell Sage Foundation.

Raymo, James M., Setsuya Fukuda and Miho Iwasawa. 2013. "Educational Differences in Divorce in Japan." *Demographic Research* 28:177–206.

Raymo, James M., Miho Iwasawa and Larry Bumpass. 2004. "Marital Dissolution in Japan: Recent Trends and Patterns." *Demographic Research* 11:395–419.

Raymo, James M., and Yanfei Zhou. 2012. "Living Arrangements and the Well-Being of Single Mothers in Japan." *Population Research and Policy Review* 31:727–749.

Raymo, James M. et al. 2014. "Single Motherhood, Living Arrangements, and Time with Children in Japan." *Journal of Marriage and Family* 76:843–861.

Roxburgh, Susan. 2004. "'There Just Aren't Enough Hours in the Day': The Mental Health Consequences of Time Pressure." *Journal of Health and Social Behavior* 45:115–131.

Seccombe, Karen. 2000. "Families in Poverty in the 1990s: Trends, Causes, Consequences, and Lessons Learned." *Journal of Marriage and Family* 62:1094–1113.

Shirahase, Sawako, and James M. Raymo. 2014. "Single Mothers and Poverty in Japan: The Role of Intergenerational Coresidence." *Social Forces* 93:545–569.

Singh-Manoux, Archana, Pekka Martikainen, Jane Ferrie, Marie Zins, Michael Marmot and Marcel Goldberg. 2006. "What Does Self-Rated Health Measure? Results from the British Whitehall II and French Gazel Cohort Studies." *Journal of Epidemiology and Community Health* 60:364–372.

Smith, James P. 2007. "The Impact of Socioeconomic Status on Health over the Life-Course." *Journal of Human Resources* 42:739–764.

Strazdins, Lyndall et al. 2006. "Unsociable Work? Nonstandard Work Schedules, Family Relationships, and Children's Well-Being." *Journal of Marriage and Family* 68:394–410.

Tamiya, Yūko, and Masato Shikata. 2007. "Boshi setai no shigoto to ikuji: Seikatsu jikan no kokusai hikaku kara" [Employment and housework in single-mother households: Evidence from a cross-national comparison of time use]. *Shakai Hoshō Kenkyū* 43:219–231.

Thoits, Peggy A. 2010. "Stress and Health: Major Findings and Policy Implications." *Journal of Health and Social Behavior* 51(supplement):41–53.

Turner, R. Jay, Blair Wheaton and Donald A. Lloyd. 1995. "The Epidemiology of Social Stress." *American Sociological Review* 60:104–125.

Waite, Linda, and Maggie Gallagher. 2002. *The Case for Marriage: Why Married People are Happier, Healthier and Better off Financially*. New York: Random House.

Whitehead, Margaret, Bo Burström and Finn Diderichsen. 2000. "Social Policies and the Pathways to Inequalities in Health: A Comparative Analysis of Lone Mothers in Britain and Sweden." *Social Science & Medicine* 50:255–270.

Zhou, Yanfei. 2008. "Boshi setai no 'ima' - zōka yōin, shūgyōritsu, shūnyūtō [Single mothers today: Increasing numbers, employment rates, and income]. pp. 26–38 in *Research on Employment Support for Single Mothers*, JILPT Research Report no. 101, edited by Japan Institute for Labour Policy and Training. Tokyo: Japan Institute for Labour Policy and Training.

Zhou, Yanfei. 2014. *Boshi setai no wāku raifu to keizaiteki jiritsu* [Single mothers in Japan: Attempts to balance work-care and exit poverty]. Tokyo: Japan Institute for Labour Policy and Training.

7

HAPPINESS AT WORK? MARITAL HAPPINESS AMONG JAPANESE HOUSEWIVES AND EMPLOYED WIVES

Mary C. Brinton

Marriage has long been considered one of the secrets to a happy and fulfilling life for Japanese women. In his classic study of office ladies in the late 1970s, James McLendon (1983) described the office as a "way station" for young Japanese women as they traversed the path to their final destination: marriage. Women who were not able to find a marriage partner by what was then considered the *kekkon tekireiki* (appropriate marriage age) of 25 years risked experiencing the office as a "blind alley" rather than a temporary stopping point on the way to marriage and presumed happiness. Similarly, Ogasawara's now-classic study of office ladies (OLs) in a Japanese bank described the triumph and congratulations experienced by OLs who quit their jobs to get married (1998).

These depictions of Japanese women's path into marriage imply that greater happiness is to be found as a housewife than as a wife in a *tomobataraki* (dual-earner) marriage. Does this hold true for women in 21st-century Japan, especially younger women? This question has now become a very salient one for Japanese policy makers, as they are encouraging Japanese wives to work so that the size of the shrinking labor force will be bolstered. The slow and persistent decline in the Japanese birth rate over the past 40 years has resulted in a population age structure that is an inverted pyramidal shape characterized by a small working-age population and a large elderly population. In order to address this, Japan's political elites have modified their long-held ideological support for the male breadwinner-professional housewife model of the family and now express strong support for families where wives as well as husbands are employed outside the home. At the same time, couples are being encouraged to have two children. In this way, Japanese households are being called upon to provide more labor at the present moment to the Japanese economy and to also ensure, through reproduction, a good supply of labor in the future.

These issues make it important to consider the relative marital happiness of working vs. non-working wives, especially those who are mothers. If the postwar ideal of the professional housewife (*sengyō shufu*) remains the ideal for young

Japanese and if *sengyō shufu* indeed report being happier in their marriages than working wives, then the question arises as to how Japan will reach its goal of having more married women in the labor force. If housewives are happier and if this is a well-known social fact in Japan, what will prevent Japanese women from quitting their jobs once they marry and have children, thus negating one important item on policymakers' wish list?

This chapter considers whether Japanese housewives or working wives express greater satisfaction in marriage, and explores what might account for the patterns we see. The chapter is particularly attuned to two things: 1) How recent social and economic changes in Japan may be altering the satisfaction in marriage experienced by working and non-working wives, and 2) how women's experience with the objective and subjective conditions of their marriage, especially with regard to the household division of labor and their beliefs about the value of being a housewife, affect their sense of marital satisfaction. In examining happiness within marriage, I focus not on overall happiness but on the interpersonal dimension of well-being, involving "how individuals conceive, perceive, and experience their relationship with others" (Mathews and Izquierdo 2009: 261). Consistent with the arguments that Mathews and Izquierdo make, I start with the assumption that it is important to have detailed knowledge of a society in order to understand what constitutes well-being. In addition, an understanding of social change is important—perhaps especially so if the object of concern is happiness within a particular institution, such as marriage. Despite the fact that institutions endure over time, the expectations that people hold of them can evolve over time into something different, especially if the external context is changing. As the Japanese government increasingly encourages married women and especially mothers to work, it is possible that young working mothers' satisfaction within marriage is increasing. On the other hand, if the idealized notion of the "professional housewife" lifestyle persists (Goldstein-Gidoni 2012), it may well be that even among young women, working mothers are less happy in their marriages than housewives. This may especially be the case if working mothers carry nearly as much of the housework load as non-employed mothers. This chapter sheds light on these competing possibilities.

In the first part of the chapter I focus on the question of whether Japanese housewives or working wives report greater happiness in their marriages, using data from a national survey to compare women in a recent cohort (age 35 or under) to those in an older cohort (age 36–50). I frame this comparison in the context of cross-national studies of employed and non-employed wives in an effort to "make sense" of the Japanese patterns. Comparative studies have found that Japan represents a context where wives report greater happiness if they are in marriages with strong gender-role specialization (conforming to the male breadwinner-professional housewife model; Lee and Ono 2008). I then turn to examine recent social changes in young Japanese men's and women's labor market situation that may be changing how young women evaluate happiness in marriage. Finally, I return to the comparison of housewives' and employed wives' marital happiness and explore the reasons behind the patterns.

Which Japanese wives are "happiest"?

To assess wives' marital happiness I use data from the National Survey of Families and Economic Conditions (*Ajia to no hikaku kara mita kazoku, jinkō zenkoku chōsa*; hereafter, NSFEC), a national, two-stage stratified probability sample of Japanese men and women aged 20 to 49. The survey was first carried out in 2000 and was repeated in 2009, at which point a new cross-sectional survey was conducted as well as a follow-up survey of a subset of the respondents to the 2000 survey. I combine the 2000 and 2009 cross-sectional surveys in order to maximize the sample size of married individuals. I restrict the sample to women who are in their first marriages and limit the upper age to 50 years, resulting in a sample size of 1474 women. Among these, 490 women are age 35 or under and therefore came of age in the early 1990s or later. The older cohort of women (age 36–50) numbers 984 individuals; they became adults in the 1970s and 1980s. As I describe later in the chapter, these two cohorts of women as well as their male counterparts have experienced very different employment circumstances and hold somewhat different views as to the appropriate combination of marriage and work for women. These broad social changes may well be changing what young women consider to be a "happy marriage."

The survey asked a range of questions to each individual about herself and her spouse, including questions about work and home life. I exclude self-employed women from the sample, as they constitute only 13 percent of the older cohort and 7 percent of the younger cohort; the small numbers make it impossible to analyze their situation. Appendix Table 7.3 shows the general demographic characteristics of individuals and their households, characteristics of their own employment situations and their spouses' (work hours and earnings) and the breakdown of housework hours and total work hours (housework and employment) for each spouse. The educational level of wives in the younger cohort, as one would expect, is higher than in the older cohort. Because they are younger, their household income and their husband's income is lower. Asterisks indicate statistically significant differences between the younger and older cohorts. I return to the similarities and differences in the working lives and housework hours of women in the two cohorts later in the chapter.

Marital happiness

The NSFEC survey measures marital happiness by asking individuals to state whether they are very happy, somewhat happy, so-so, somewhat unhappy, or very unhappy in their marriage. For purposes of analysis, I created a binary variable for marital happiness, with 1 indicating "very happy or somewhat happy" and 0 indicating that the respondent feels "so-so, somewhat unhappy, or very unhappy."

Figure 7.1 shows the percentage of housewives, part-time employed wives, and full-time employed wives who report being happy with their marriages. Asterisks indicate the statistical significance of the marital happiness differences between housewives and part-time working wives and between housewives and full-time working wives.

Panel A shows that of the nearly 1500 women, housewives are significantly more likely to report being happy in their marriages than either part-time or full-time employed wives; part-time employed wives are the least likely to be happy. Panel B indicates that these differences also hold when we look only at women in the older cohort (age 36–59 years). Among women in the younger cohort (age 20–35, in Panel C), more housewives report being happy than wives who are employed part-time, but the difference in marital happiness between full-time working wives and housewives is barely statistically significant (at $p<.10$). In neither cohort is there a statistical difference between the happiness of part-time vs. full-time working women. Taken together, these results indicate that the percentage of housewives who say they are happy in their marriages far exceeds the percentage for either full-time or part-time working wives. But the results for the younger cohort suggest this might be changing; the percentage of young full-time working wives who are happy in their marriages is only marginally lower (in a statistical sense) from the percentage of young housewives who are happy.

What explains these two results: that housewives are happier in their marriages than working wives, and that among young married women the marital happiness of wives who work full-time is almost as high as that of housewives? The first possible reason is economic: perhaps non-employed wives are married to men who are earning higher incomes. If most employed Japanese wives are working not because they *want* to but because it is necessary for household finances, this might lead to lower marital satisfaction among them, compared to housewives. A second reason could be the rigidity of the household division of labor. Despite the gradual increase in Japanese women's labor market opportunities and in the number of couples where both spouses work, studies continue to show that gender-role specialization within marriage remains very strong in contemporary Japan (Holthus and Tanaka 2013; Tsuya et al. 2000; Tsuya et al. 2013). International surveys consistently report that Japanese men perform less housework than men in nearly all other postindustrial societies (Fuwa 2004; Hook 2006; Knudsen and Waerness 2008; North 2009). If Japanese women shoulder nearly all of the housework whether or not they work outside the home, perhaps housewives are the happiest because they have only one job rather than a "second shift" (Hochschild 2012).

A third reason is more amorphous in the sense that it is neither strongly related to the necessity for wives to work nor related to the large share of household labor that wives perform: perhaps Japanese housewives continue to enjoy a higher social status than employed wives. As Ochiai (1997) and others have described, the "postwar family system" in Japan idealized the male breadwinner-professional housewife model of the household. Over the 30-year period up until the 1990s, the ideal life course for Japanese females was widely considered to be completion of school, full-time work for a few years, marriage and "retirement" from work, then 15 to 20 years of full-time devotion to household and children

(Brinton 1992, 1993; Yamato 2008). Many women returned to the work force only in their early 40s, once their years of intensive childrearing were completed. Even so, the expectation was that they continued to be "specialists" when it came to household work. The jobs open to women who reentered the labor force after childrearing were mainly low-paid and part-time, given that they had accumulated far fewer years of work experience than men of equivalent age (Brinton 1993; Ogasawara 1998; Yu 2009). This pattern of retirement upon marriage or childbirth, followed later by reentry into the labor market, came to be known as the "M-shaped curve of female labor force participation" across the life cycle. The pattern disappeared in the majority of Western countries by the 1980s but has persisted in male breadwinner-oriented societies such as Japan and South Korea (Ochiai and Molony 2009).

Over time, the dip in the M-shaped curve of female labor force participation in Japan has shifted, becoming more attributable to women's exit from employment when they give birth to their first child rather than to their exit from employment at the time of marriage. Table 7.1 demonstrates that McLendon's (1983) earlier characterization of employment as a "way station" for women on the path to marriage has become less and less applicable in recent cohorts—now it is much more a way station on the way to motherhood. Among women who married in 2005–2009, just 26 percent quit work upon marriage compared to 37 percent of the women who had gotten married 20 years earlier. However, this decline has been counterbalanced by an *increase* over the past 20 years in the percentage of Japanese women who quit work when their first child is born. Thus, the "dip" in the M-curve of the female labor force participation rate has not completely disappeared. Rather, it has moved to a slightly later point in the life cycle. As a result, women who quit work *either* when they marry or when they have their first child remain the strong majority (nearly 70 percent). For Japanese women to remain in the labor force throughout their early years of marriage and childrearing continues to go against the dominant social norm, despite the fact that the norm has significantly weakened in the past two decades. It may be, then, that housewives' greater happiness in marriage is due to the comfort of following prevailing social norms.

Theoretical perspectives on marital happiness, income, and the division of household labor

Where does Japan lie in the spectrum of societies that social scientists have studied when it comes to the happiness of married women, and what clues might social scientific theories offer for understanding housewives' happiness? Most research on marital happiness has been carried out in the context of Western societies, where married women's employment patterns underwent significant change earlier than in Japan (Treas et al. 2011). Talcott Parsons' structural-functional model of the family emphasized the functionality of role specialization between spouses,

TABLE 7.1 Changes in percent of Japanese women quitting work at marriage or first childbirth: Five cohorts[a]

Year of marriage	Column A Continued work after marriage	Column B Quit work upon marriage	Other status[b]	Total
1985–89	56.6	37.3	6.1	100
1990–94	56.9	34.5	8.6	100
1995–99	58.3	31.2	10.5	100
2000–04	62.4	25.6	12.0	100
2005–09	61.0	25.6	13.4	100
Year of giving birth to first child	Continued work after birth	Quit work upon birth	Other status[c]	
1985–89	24.0	37.4	38.6	100
1990–94	24.4	37.7	38.0	100
1995–99	24.2	39.3	36.6	100
2000–04	26.8	40.6	32.6	100
2005–09	26.8	43.9	29.3	100

Source: National Institute of Population and Social Security Research, *Fourteenth Japanese National Fertility Survey, 2011b*.

Notes
[a] Note that the figures that conceptually correspond to each other between the upper and lower halves of the table (such as the sum of the proportion who quit work upon marriage and "other" vs. "other" in the lower half of the table) are not precisely equal because the denominator in the upper half of the table is married women whereas the denominator in the lower half of the table is married women who have given birth.
[b] "Other status" includes being non-employed both before and after marriage, being non-employed before marriage and then becoming employed, and unknown employment status.
[c] "Other status" includes being non-employed both before and after giving birth to one's first child, and unknown employment status.

with the husband supporting the family economically through his employment and the wife focusing on household work and childrearing (Parsons 1942). The New Household Economics championed by Gary Becker and other neoclassical economists echoed this structural-functionalist view of the family, focusing on the efficiency of gender-role specialization. Especially in a labor market context such as Japan's, where women's average wages fall short of men's (either because of labor demand-side forces such as sex discrimination or supply-side forces such as women's lower human capital), the specialization of women in housework and childcare and of men in paid employment is postulated by this model to be the most efficient household division of labor (Becker 1991). While neither Parsons nor Becker explicitly addressed the issue of marital happiness per se, their model of the gendered division of labor suggest that men and women are likely to be more satisfied in male breadwinner households (households in which the wife is not employed).

But as married women's labor force participation increased from the 1970s onward in the U.S., new theories developed within sociology to predict the determinants of marital happiness. The bargaining model (Brines 1994; South and Spitze 1994) suggests that a spouse's greater access to economic resources (through employment) leads to greater bargaining power within marriage, increasing that individual's happiness. Under this model, an individual spouse's earnings should be directly correlated with their marital happiness, partly because earnings presumably give one the power to "buy out" of some of the household work. An important implicit assumption here is that neither husbands nor wives *want* to do household work; rather, it is something one tries to get out of doing. This model has been used extensively to predict the household division of labor between spouses.

Among the small number of studies that have examined marital happiness in Japan, Lee and Ono's work stands out because it is a direct comparison of the determinants of marital happiness in Japan and the U.S. (2008). They found that American women's marital happiness is not significantly related to whether they are employed or not. But among women who *are* working, those with higher earnings do report greater marital happiness, which would seem to be consistent with the bargaining model of marriage. Lee and Ono did not find a significant relationship in the U.S. between husband's income and wife's marital happiness. Their findings for Japan presented a contrast with the U.S. and conformed more closely to the role specialization model of marriage described by Parsons in the 1940s and by Becker and other economists in the 1970s. To wit, non-employed Japanese wives express greater marital happiness than employed wives. Moreover, Lee and Ono found that Japanese wives' own income appears to bear no relationship—either positive or negative—to their marital happiness. The findings for Japan therefore offer no support for the idea that higher earnings, at least for women, lead to greater marital happiness due to their translation into greater bargaining power within marriage. Rather, Lee and Ono find that Japanese wives' marital happiness is strongly related to their *husbands'* income.

Lee and Ono's data did not include information on how housework was divided within American or Japanese couples, so they were not able to examine the relationship between the household division of labor and marital happiness in order to further test the specialization model of marriage in Japan. Two recent studies have been able to do this. Yamato (2008) considered how various contributions by husbands affect Japanese wives' marital happiness: housework hours, childcare hours, playing with children and emotional support of wives. Yamato's findings are intriguing and offer further support for applicability of the gender-role specialization model to Japanese marriage. She divided her sample of married women into those who contribute no income or less than 30 percent of the household income (82 percent of the wives in her sample) and those who contribute 30 percent or more (18 percent of the sample). Wives in the first category do 93 percent of the housework, and wives in the latter category do 86 percent, so both are engaged in a high level of "specialization" in household work. Yamato found that the marital happiness of housewives and wives earning a minimal amount of income is higher if their husband is providing emotional support and spending some time playing with the children, but she found no effect of husband's housework contribution or help with childcare on women's marital happiness. In contrast, among the smaller group of women who earn at least 30 percent of the household income, marital happiness is greater when husbands help with childcare (above and beyond playing with children). Yamato concludes that "Japanese mothers regard their husbands' emotional support as essential for their satisfaction with the marital relationship; their husbands sharing housework does not appear to be necessary [... .]" (2008: 162). Along with Lee and Ono's study, this result thus supports the role specialization model of marital happiness in Japan.

Finally, a recent study by Holthus and Tanaka (2013) considered the relationship between the household division of labor and the self-reported well-being of Japanese parents with at least one child under age six. Holthus and Tanaka's study brings the *subjective* evaluation of the household division of labor into view, as they measure how satisfied women are with the division of housework. They find this to be highly correlated with wives' satisfaction with their partners. In addition, they find that part-time employed women were particularly likely to express dissatisfaction with the division of housework. Holthus and Tanaka conclude, "We cannot discuss or fully understand partnership well-being if we do not carefully analyze the satisfaction with the household chore share between the partners" (2013: 421).

In sum, studies of marital happiness in Japan have generally supported the idea that wives in marriages with a high degree of gender-role specialization (especially higher earnings by the husband) are more satisfied. But Holthus and Tanaka's study opens up the possibility that at least for young married women, satisfaction with one's spouse is closely related to satisfaction with the household division of labor. I turn now to consider recent social changes that may be altering the apparent "happiness" effect of gender-role specialization in Japan's younger generation.

Reasons for predicting changed expectations of marriage among young Japanese: The Labor Market Context

The employment situation for young single Japanese men and women has altered in complex ways since the collapse of the so-called bubble economy in the early 1990s (Brinton 2011; Fukuda 2013; Genda 2001; Genda and Kurosawa 2001). Contrary to the excellent employment prospects of young male graduates during the high-economic growth era (the era of the male breadwinner model), young men—especially those lacking a university education—faced difficult circumstances in the 1990s labor market. In order to avoid laying off middle-aged male workers who had been hired during the economic boom years of the 1970s and 1980s, many companies dramatically reduced the number of new hires (Genda 2003). The fortunes of young Japanese women shifted as well, but in somewhat different ways. Like their male counterparts, female high school graduates face an increasingly difficult job market that is characterized more and more by short-term employment contracts and a consequent lack of job security (Osawa et al. 2013). At the same time, the job prospects for highly educated young Japanese women have arguably improved. Successive government reforms have been implemented to increase the effectiveness of the 1986 Equal Employment Opportunity Law. And perhaps even more importantly, Japanese companies in the second decade of the 21st century are increasingly dealing with a labor shortage of highly qualified young workers due to the small cohorts of new graduates as a result of the low birth rate. Consequently, they turn to female graduates in addition to male graduates (Mun and Brinton 2015).

Rates of higher education attendance among young women increased from the 1990s on, and many Japanese employers now report that female Japanese university graduates equal or surpass men in their qualifications (Brinton and Mun 2015). Moreover, the government has put pressure on employers to make the workplace more conducive for women to continue working after they marry and have children. As noted earlier in the chapter, this government pressure is driven not by the underlying goal of gender equality but rather by the need to maintain the size of the labor force and to ensure the production of a future generation of workers. It is likely the government can do little to alter the continued "second shift" of housework and childcare that women perform at home, no matter how much women work in the labor market. So it is likely that employed wives have a heavy work load spread across work and home, which could lower their happiness compared to housewives.

At the same time, some recent studies suggest that young Japanese men are considering the income-earning potential of a future bride in a more positive light than was previously the case (Fukuda 2013; National Institute of Population and Social Security Research 2011a). In an analysis of the marriage patterns of several recent cohorts, Fukuda (2013) reports that the negative relationship between women's income and their probability of marriage—a stable social fact for the decades when the male breadwinner-professional housewife model reigned supreme (Ono 2003; Raymo and Iwasawa 2005; Tsuya and Mason 1995)—is not apparent in the most recent cohort. Even so, Fukuda is careful to point out that this is not translating into an increase in marriage rates overall. As he states, "marriage in recent years has become a more selective event, more likely to occur for women who are more economically independent and do not adhere to the gender role-specialized marriage." He also cautions that "[i]t is, however, too early to conclude that Japanese marriage is becoming more gender-egalitarian than before" (2013: 124).

It could be the case that because many young married women with high human capital (university education) are able to access better jobs than their older counterparts could, this is resulting in greater marital happiness among those who work full-time. Even if this is the case, whether or not they are happier in their marriages than their highly educated counterparts who are housewives is an open question. This may well depend on whether they are able to achieve a more balanced division of housework with their husbands.

Employment, housework, and the marital happiness of Japanese wives

To see how Japanese wives' marital satisfaction is related to the objective and subjective conditions of their marriages, I return now to the NSFEC data described at the beginning of the chapter for a fuller analysis. As shown in the descriptive statistics in Appendix Table 7.3, a much higher percentage of women in the younger than in the older cohort are full-time housewives (48 and 28 percent respectively), which undoubtedly reflects the fact that younger women are more likely than women in the older cohort to have at least one young child at home; in other words, the higher percentage of housewives among younger women is very likely a life-cycle effect rather than a more substantial difference between the two cohorts. Older women, by contrast, are more likely to be part-time workers. As outlined earlier, this description of the work status of the two age groups reflects the general life-cycle pattern of employment for Japanese women. For both part- and full-time working wives, there is no statistically significant difference between the weekly hours of market work across the two age groups. But older part-time working women make a particularly low percentage of the household income (17%), significantly lower ($p<.05$) than younger part-time working women.

Consistent with other Japanese surveys, the NSFEC respondents report a highly gendered household division of labor. Housework hours in the NSFEC survey are measured as the sum of weekly hours spent cooking and cleaning up after meals, cleaning house and doing laundry, and shopping for groceries and daily necessities.[1] (Unfortunately, the survey does not ask about childcare hours.) Strikingly, there is no statistically significant difference between the average number of housework hours that wives of different ages perform, although housework hours are the longest for housewives and the shortest for full-time employed wives in both cohorts. When it comes to the wife's *share* of the total housework hours (husband's plus wife's), there has been a slight reduction for the younger cohort of women who are employed full-time. On average, this group of wives performs 79 percent of the housework in their households, compared to 93 percent for similarly aged housewives. While all of the wives in the older cohort do between 84 and 90 percent of the housework in their households regardless of whether or not they work outside the home, there is a broader spread in the younger cohort according to whether they are employed or not: Young full-time working women do the lowest share of housework (79%) of any group, and young full-time housewives do the most (93%). Moving to the final rows in the table, it is clear that younger working women (both part- and full-time) are significantly happier with the way that housework is divided between themselves and their husbands than older working women. Young full-time working women, in fact, are nearly as happy with the household division of labor as their housewife counterparts; this is not at all the case for older working women.

Even though younger wives vary more than older wives in the proportion of hours they contribute to their household's total amount of housework, the gendered division of housework is very strong across all married couples. This translates into wives' total weekly work hours—the combination of employment hours and housework hours—being much higher for employed wives than housewives. Housewives in the younger and older cohorts work a total of 31–33 hours (household work) per week, compared to around 65 hours (housework and paid work) for full-time employed women. Calculated as the share of the total housework and employment hours put in by husbands and wives together, wives' share of work rises dramatically from 36 percent if they are young housewives to 55 percent if they are older full-time working wives.

As mentioned at the beginning of the chapter, the extreme disparity in weekly work hours between housewives and employed wives may account for housewives' greater happiness. Stated differently, it may be that a lower percentage of working wives are happy in their marriages because they continue to do on average more than 80 percent of the housework (higher than wives in nearly all other postindustrial countries). Additionally, it could be that working wives are less happy in their marriages because they are contributing to household income and still doing the bulk of the housework; this could be a situation that leads not so much to exhaustion as to resentment on their part.

In order to test these hypotheses I ran a series of regression analyses to predict marital happiness for women in each cohort, using as variables their educational level, the presence of at least one child under age 18 in the household, their husband's income, and a variety of specifications that reflect the amount of work hours and housework they perform. These specifications included the absolute number of hours they are employed per week, their own employment hours vs. their husband's, the absolute number of housework hours they put in, their own housework hours vs. their husbands', and finally, the total number of employment and work hours they spend per week and the relationship between this number and the same number for their husbands. In this way, I was able to look at whether wives' *absolute* expenditure of time and/or the way their *time allocation* compared to their husbands' might explain why housewives are generally happier in their marriages. I also looked at whether wives who make more income, especially relative to their husbands, seem to be less happy in their marriages;

presumably, these women are contravening an important social norm in Japan that husbands should be the primary breadwinners.

In addition to these objective conditions of women's lives, I also draw on Mathews and Izquierdo's (2009) reference to the emotional or subjective evaluation of these conditions. Similar to Holthus and Tanaka (2013), I examine how wives' *satisfaction* with the household division of labor relates to their marital happiness. Furthermore, I consider whether wives' perception of the role of housewife is fulfilling is related to marital happiness. The attitude toward being a *sengyō shufu* can be considered as a validation or invalidation of Japanese women's "traditional" role as it developed in earlier decades of high economic growth.

Table 7.2 shows the multivariate analysis for marital happiness for each age group. I use logistic regression and report coefficients as odds ratios; numbers greater than 1 indicate that the variable is positively related to marital happiness and numbers less than 1 indicate a negative relationship with marital happiness. In each model I add more variables to see how they impact the difference in marital satisfaction between housewives and employed wives. Model 1 is the basic model comparing the marital happiness of housewives (as the baseline category) to wives employed part-time or full-time. This is the equation on which Figure 7.1, discussed earlier, is based. Model 2 adds husband's income. In Model 3 I add variables indicating whether the wife is highly educated (a university graduate) and whether there is at least one child under age 18 at home.[2] Model 4 adds the wife's share of household labor and the subjective perception that being a housewife can be fulfilling. In Model 5 I add the interaction between being a university graduate and working full-time; I do so to test whether women with high human capital are happier in their marriages if they are working full-time rather than being housewives. Finally, in Model 6 I replace the actual share of household work that the wife performs with its subjective counterpart: her level of *happiness* with the household division of labor.

As was clear in the descriptive statistics, Model 1 shows that housewives are much more likely to report being satisfied with their marriages than wives who work part-time. Older housewives are also more satisfied than older full-time working wives, but among younger women, housewives are only marginally more likely to be satisfied with their marriages than wives who work full-time.

For both younger and older wives, husbands' income is strongly related to marital happiness (Model 2). Although not shown here, a wife's own income bears no relationship to her marital happiness, nor does her income *relative* to her husband's (for either the younger or the older cohort). Once husband's income is statistically controlled, the difference between the marital happiness of housewives and working wives (especially full-time working wives) in the older cohort becomes insignificant. This is consistent with the idea that older women who work full-time are doing so at least partly because their husband's income is not sufficient. In contrast, the younger women who are housewives are happier than working wives *even when* husband's income is taken into account. To test whether this might be related to having a younger child at home, I modified the variable "At least one child under age 18 at home" to a lower age, but this did not alter the result.

TABLE 7.2 Determinants of marital happiness for older and younger wives

Wives age 36–50

	Model 1	Model 2	Model 3	Model 4	Model 5	Model 6
Housewife	—	—	—	—	—	—
Employed part-time	.605***	.707*	.704*	.762	.759	.954
Employed full-time	.677*	.780	.747	.705†	.636*	.827
Husband's income		1.216***	1.208***	1.254***	1.261***	1.223***
University-educated			1.204	.974	.785	.997
At least one child under age 18 at home			.757	.760	.748	.823
Belief in value of being a housewife				2.229***	2.265***	2.112***
Wife's share of household labor				.194**	.202**	—
University-educated x employed full-time					1.816	1.806
Happiness with household division of labor						1.359***
Constant	.907	.290***	.368***	1.162	1.120	.044

Wives age 20–35

	Model 1	Model 2	Model 3	Model 4	Model 5	Model 6
Housewife	—	—	—	—	—	—
Employed part-time	.505***	.553**	.508**	.519**	.512**	.510**
Employed full-time	.657†	.621*	.548*	.578*	.433**	.458*
Husband's income		1.207***	1.208***	1.217***	1.230***	1.241***
University-educated			1.079	1.080	.790	.850
At least one child under age 18 at home			.576*	.559*	.433**	.689
Belief in value of being a housewife				2.724***	2.686***	2.280**
Wife's share of household labor				.466	.526	—
University-educated x employed full-time					2.791†	2.977*
Happiness with household division of labor						1.349***
Constant	1.273†	.549*	.888	1.400	1.325	.105***

†p<.10; *p<.05; **p<.01; ***p<.001

Panel A

Panel B

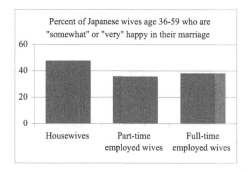

Panel C

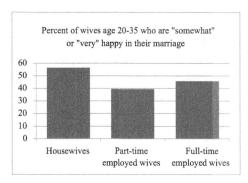

FIGURE 7.1 Marital happiness of Japanese wives

Young housewives remain more likely to report being happy in their marriages than either part-time or full-time working women even after a variety of other conditions are taken into account (in Models 3 and 4, these include husband's income, wife's education, the presence of at least one child under age 18 in the household, the wife's attitude about the fulfillment of being a housewife, and the wife's share of household labor). In contrast, the distinction between housewives' and working wives' marital happiness disappears among older women once the wife's attitude about being a housewife and the wife's share of household labor are taken into account (Model 4). Whether the household division of labor is measured as the wife's share (Model 4) or as the wife's subjective *satisfaction* with the division of labor (Model 6), it has a strong effect on older wives' marital happiness. For younger wives, only their subjective satisfaction with the household division of labor—not their actual share—is related to their marital happiness. But contrary to the situation for older wives, this still is not sufficient to render young working wives' marital satisfaction equivalent to that of housewives.

One of the most interesting findings that emerges from examining wives' employment and its relationship to marital happiness is that young women who are university graduates and are working full-time are actually *more* likely to report being happier in their marriages than all other women, including housewives (Models 5 and 6). This is not the case among older wives. There is something about this group in particular—young, highly educated wives in full-time jobs—that leads to their greater marital satisfaction.

Conclusion

Consistent with other studies that emphasize gender-role specialization in Japanese marriage, husbands' income is very strongly related to wives' marital satisfaction. This holds for both younger and older women and is a robust finding no matter what other factors are held constant. Yet there is a difference in the effect of husband's income across the two cohorts: among older women, a higher income on the part of one's husband raises the marital satisfaction of employed wives (whether they work part- or full-time) to the level of housewives. This is not the case for younger Japanese working wives, who report being less satisfied in their marriages than housewives even after husbands' income and other objective as well as subjective conditions are held constant. The one category of younger working wives likely to be as satisfied in their marriages as housewives is university-educated women who are employed full-time. This is a very specific subset of women, and further research should investigate who they are and what leads to their marital satisfaction. Full-time working wives were also the group in Holthus and Tanaka's study (2013) most satisfied with the household division of labor, leading these authors to conclude that they were probably getting the most help with housework.

Indeed, the data used in this chapter indicate that young full-time working wives have the lowest number of housework hours (22 hours per week, Appendix Table 7.3) and perform the lowest share of housework (79%) compared to all other wives.

Both the share of household labor they perform and their level of satisfaction with this amount of labor are related to older wives' marital satisfaction. For younger wives, only the subjective evaluation of the household division of labor is related to how they feel about their marriage. For both younger and older wives, believing that the role of housewife can be fulfilling is strongly related to their happiness in marriage. These findings show that not only the objective conditions of marriage but also the subjective evaluation of the division of labor and the specialized role of housewife hold significance for women's marital happiness. This reinforces the point that Mathews and Izquierdo make with regard to the influence of national institutions on well-being. Comparative studies of the household division of labor tend to look at the relative proportion of housework done by husbands and wives and to assume that wives who do *more* are *less* happy. The findings in this chapter call this into question; Japanese women's satisfaction with marriage is related to how they *feel* about the household division of labor, whatever it may objectively be. Similarly, the attitude Japanese women hold vis-à-vis being a housewife is closely related by how happy they feel in their marriage. Clearly, these findings are due at least in part to continued popular support for the cultural template of the male breadwinner-female caregiver household in Japan. As Mathews and Izquierdo point out, national institutions (e.g., male breadwinner norms) influence how individuals perceive their way of being.

It bears noting that throughout this chapter, I have interpreted the experiences of older and younger wives as reflective of cohort differences rather than life-cycle differences. Without the benefit of longitudinal data, it is not possible to know for sure whether the patterns we see among younger wives will change over time to resemble those of older wives.

What does the future hold for Japanese women's satisfaction within their marriages? The family model characterized by a breadwinner father and stay-at-home mother dominated Japan's high economic growth era (Ochiai 1997) and symbolized the successful middle-class lifestyle for millions of Japanese men and women. The findings presented in this chapter do not necessarily negate the idea that this model of marriage remains one that brings satisfaction to many Japanese women. Even so, the gendered household division of labor appears to be shifting slightly among young couples where both spouses work full-time, and highly educated wives in such couples report an even higher level of marital satisfaction than housewives do. This is a small subset of women but one that is likely to grow in the future, as Japan's labor shortage develops further, as employers strive to employ the most highly qualified workers regardless of gender, and as Japanese couples try to secure a higher standard of living.

Appendix

TABLE 7.3 Characteristics of married women: Younger and older cohorts

	Younger (Age 20–35)		Older (Age 36–50)
Demographic characteristics			
Education (percentage)			
High school or less	36.4	***	46.9
Jr. college or technical school	39.6		43.8
University	19.8	***	13.3
Household income (in ¥ million)	5.46	***	6.63
At least 1 child under age 18 living at home	81.1		78.7
Husband's yearly earnings	4.3	***	5.2
Characteristics of employment			
Employment status (percentage)			
Full-time housewife	48.3	***	28.4
Part-time employee or contract worker	30.1	***	47.3
Full-time employee	21.6		24.3
Own share of household earnings			
Part-time employed wives	.21	*	.17
Full-time employed wives	.42		.43
Employment hours (per week)			
Part-time employed wives	25.0		26.7
Full-time employed wives	42.9		42.2
Own share of total household employment hours (sum of husband's and wife's hours in dual-earner households)			
Part-time employed wives	.34		.35
Full-time employed wives	.46		.47
Housework hours per week			
Full-time housewives	30.6		32.2
Part-time employed wives	25.4		27.5
Full-time employed wives	21.9		23.2
Own share of total housework hours (wife's and husband's)			
Full-time housewives	.93	***	.90
Part-time employed wives	.89		.91
Full-time employed wives	.79	**	.84
Housework hours and total work hours (employment and housework)			
Full-time housewives	30.7		32.8
Part-time employed wives	50.4	**	54.3
Full-time employed wives	64.9		65.3
Own share of household's employment and housework hours (wife's and husband's)			
Full-time housewives	.36	**	.39
Part-time employed wives	.49		.51
Full-time employed wives	.53	*	.55
Happiness with household division of labor (0–10)			
Full-time housewives	5.72		5.81
Part-time employed wives	5.41	*	4.81
Full-time employed wives	5.68	*	5.11

*p<.05; **p<.01; ***p<.001

Notes

1 In many surveys individuals tend to slightly over-report their own housework time and under-report the time spent by their spouses. NSFEC asks respondents to report their own hours and those of their spouse. After cross-checking to see how wives report their own and their husbands' time with how husbands (from different households, as the NSFEC data are based on individual respondents, not couples) report their own and their wives' time, it appears that reporting is highly consistent, whether it is done by women or by men.
2 I also included the age of the youngest child as an alternative, with similar results.

References

Becker, Gary S. 1991. *A Treatise on the Family.* Cambridge: Harvard University Press.
Blau, Francine D., Mary C. Brinton and David Grusky, eds. 2006. *The Declining Significance of Gender?* New York: Russell Sage Foundation.
Brines, Julie. 1994. "Economic Dependency, Gender, and the Division of Labor at Home." *American Journal of Sociology* 100:652–688.
Brinton, Mary C. 1992. "Christmas Cakes and Wedding Cakes: The Social Organization of Japanese Women's Life Course." pp. 79–107 in *Japanese Social Organization*, edited by T. Sugiyama Lebra. Honolulu: University of Hawai'i Press.
Brinton, Mary C. 1993. *Women and the Economic Miracle: Gender and Work in Postwar Japan.* Berkeley and Los Angeles: University of California Press.
Brinton, Mary C. 2001. *Women's Working Lives in East Asia.* Stanford: Stanford University Press.
Brinton, Mary C. 2011. *Lost in Transition: Youth, Work, and Instability in Postindustrial Japan.* New York: Cambridge University Press.
Brinton, Mary C., and Eunmi Mun. 2015. "Between State and Family: Managers' Implementation and Evaluation of Parental Leave Policies in Japan." *Socio-Economic Review* 13:1–25.
Brinton, Mary C., and Toshio Yamagishi. 2011. *Risuku ni se o mukeru Nihonjin* [Japanese who turn their backs on risk]. Tokyo: Chūō Kōronsha.
Fukuda, Setsuya. 2013. "The Changing Role of Women's Earnings in Marriage Formation in Japan." *The Annals of the American Academy of Political and Social Science* 646:107–128.
Fuwa, Makiko. 2004. "Macro-Level Gender Inequality and the Division of Household Labor in 22 Countries." *American Sociological Review* 69:752–767.
Genda, Yuji. 2001. *Shigoto no naka no aimai na fuan* [A vague sense of job anxiety]. Tokyo: Chūō Kōron Shinsha.
Genda, Yuji. 2003. "Who Really Lost Jobs in Japan? Youth Employment in an Aging Society." pp. 103–33 in *Labor Markets and Firm Benefit Policies in Japan and the United States*, edited by S. Ogura, T. Tachibanaki and D. Wise. Chicago: University of Chicago Press.
Genda, Yuji, and Masako Kurosawa. 2001. "Transition from School to Work in Japan." *Journal of the Japanese and International Economies* 15:465–488.
Goldstein-Gidoni, Ofra. 2012. *Housewives of Japan: An Ethnography of Real Lives and Consumerized Domesticity.* New York: Palgrave Macmillan.
Hochschild, Arlie. 2012. *The Second Shift: Working Families and the Revolution at Home.* New York: Penguin.
Holthus, Barbara, and Hiromi Tanaka. 2013. "Parental Well-being and the Sexual Division of Household Labor: A New Look at Gendered Families in Japan." *Asiatische Studien* 67:401–428.

Hook, Jennifer L. 2006. "Care in Context: Men's Unpaid Work in 20 Countries, 1965–2003." *American Sociological Review* 71:639–660.

Knudsen, Knud, and Kari Wærness. 2008. "National Context and Spouses' Housework in 34 Countries." *European Sociological Review* 24:97–113.

Lee, Kristen Schultz, and Hiroshi Ono. 2008. "Specialization and Happiness in Marriage: A U.S.-Japan Comparison." *Social Science Research* 37:1216–1234.

Mathews, Gordon, and Carolina Izquierdo. 2009. "Anthropology, Happiness, and Well-being." pp. 1–22 in *Pursuits of Happiness: Well-Being in Anthropological Perspective*, edited by G. Mathews and C. Izquierdo. New York and Oxford: Berghahn Books.

McLendon, James. 1983. "The Office: Way Station or Blind Alley?" pp. 156–182 in *Work and Lifecourse in Japan*, edited by D. W. Plath. Albany: State University of New York Press.

Mun, Eunmi, and Mary C. Brinton. 2017. Revisiting the Welfare State Paradox: A Firm-Level Analysis from Japan." *Research in Social Stratification and Mobility* 47:33–43.

National Institute of Population and Social Security Research. 2011a. *Fourteenth Japanese National Fertility Survey: Attitudes toward Marriage and Family Among Japanese Singles*. Tokyo: National Institute of Population and Social Security Research.

National Institute of Population and Social Security Research. 2011b. *Fourteenth Japanese National Fertility Survey: Marriage Process and Fertility of Japanese Married Couples*. Tokyo: National Institute of Population and Social Security Research.

North, Scott. 2009. "Negotiating What's 'Natural': Persistent Domestic Gender Role Inequality in Japan." *Social Science Japan Journal* 12:23–44.

Ochiai, Emiko. 1997. *The Japanese Family System in Transition: A Sociological Analysis of Family Change in Postwar Japan*. Tokyo: LCTB International Library Foundation.

Ochiai, Emiko, and Barbara Molony. 2009. *Asia's New Mothers: Crafting Gender Roles and Childcare Networks in East and Southeast Asian Societies*. Folkestone: Global Oriental.

Ogasawara, Yuko. 1998. *Office Ladies and Salaried Men*. Berkeley: University of California Press.

Ono, Hiromi. 2003. "Women's Economic Standing, Marriage Timing, and Cross-National Contexts of Gender." *Journal of Marriage and Family* 65:275–286.

Osawa, Machiko, Myoung Jung Kim and Jeff Kingston. 2013. "Precarious Work in Japan." *American Behavioral Scientist* 57:309–334.

Parsons, Talcott. 1942. "Age and Sex in the Social Structure of the United States." *American Sociological Review* 7:604–616.

Pettit, Becky, and Jennifer Hook. 2005. "The Structure of Women's Employment in Comparative Perspective." *Social Forces* 84:779–801.

Raymo, James M., and Miho Iwasawa. 2005. "Marriage Market Mismatches in Japan: An Alternative View of the Relationship between Women's Education and Marriage." *American Sociological Review* 70:801–822.

South, Scott J., and Glenna Spitze. 1994. "Housework in Marital and Nonmarital Households." *American Sociological Review* 59:327–347.

Stier, Haya, Noah Lewin-Epstein and Michael Braun. 2001. "Welfare Regimes, Family-Supportive Policy, and Women's Employment Along the Life-Course." *American Journal of Sociology* 106:1731–1760.

Treas, Judith, Tanja van der Lippe and Tsui-o Chloe Tai. 2011. "The Happy Homemaker? Married Women's Well-Being in Cross-National Perspective." *Social Forces* 90:111–132.

Tsuya, Noriko O., Larry L. Bumpass, Minja K. Choe and Ronald R. Rindfuss. 2000. "Gender, Employment, and Housework in Japan, South Korea, and the United States." *Review of Population and Social Policy* 9:195–220.

Tsuya, Noriko O., and Karen O. Mason. 1995. "Changing Gender Roles and Below-Replacement Fertility in Japan." pp. 139–167 in *Gender and Family Change in Industrialized Countries,* edited by K. Oppenheim Mason and A. Jensen. Oxford: Clarendon Press.

Tsuya, Noriko O., Larry L. Bumpass, Minja K. Choe and Ronald R. Rindfuss. 2012. "Employment and Household Tasks of Japanese Couples, 1994–2009." *Demographic Research* 27:705–718.

Yamato, Reiko. 2008. "Impact of Fathers' Support and Activities on Mothers' Marital Satisfaction by Income Contribution during Economic Recession in Japan." *Fathering* 6:149–168.

Yu, Wei-hsin. 2009. *Gendered Trajectories: Women, Work, and Social Change in Japan and Taiwan.* Stanford: Stanford University Press.

8

THE HAPPINESS OF JAPANESE ACADEMICS

Findings from job satisfaction surveys in 1992 and 2007

Theresa Aichinger, Peter Fankhauser and Roger Goodman

According to Timothy Judge and Ryan Kinger (2007: 393) "no research on subjective well-being can be complete without considering subjective well-being at work," a view reinforced by the *World Happiness Report* of 2013 (Helliwell, Layard and Sachs 2013: 61–64). In this chapter, we look at the "subjective well-being at work" of Japanese academics through the examination of three major surveys of job satisfaction, undertaken in 1992 and 2007. These surveys are unusual in that they allow us, to an extent, to compare both how job satisfaction among Japanese academics has changed over time and how it compares with the job satisfaction of academics in other countries.

The first of these surveys was commissioned by the U.S.-based Carnegie Foundation for the Advancement of Teaching and is thus usually referred to as the Carnegie Survey of the Academic Profession or simply, as in the rest of this chapter, the "Carnegie Survey." While the project as a whole was carried out between 1990 and 1996, the raw data were collected in 1992 from 15 countries, one of which was Japan, where there were 1889 respondents.

The second survey on which this study draws was carried out between 2004 and 2014, with the raw data being collected in 2007 (Teichler 2015: 226). It was called "The Changing Academic Profession," which has in much of the literature been shortened to simply the "CAP." Eight of the 17 participating countries had also participated in the Carnegie Survey. One of those was Japan, which in the CAP had 1391 respondents.

The CAP set out to investigate what it identified as three key challenges that faced the global academic profession in 2007 and had not yet been deemed significant in 1992: the relevance of the academy in the knowledge society; internationalization as a major factor in defining and shaping academic practice; and new forms of higher education management. As a result of these three objectives, the questionnaire used in the 2007 CAP differed considerably from the one used in the 1992 Carnegie Survey, which made comparing the results over time complicated.

In order to deal with this question of comparability over time, a decision was made in Japan to undertake two surveys in 2007: one was the CAP, and a second survey that reused the exact Carnegie questionnaire of 1992. This second survey (somewhat misleadingly called the "International Survey of Academic Profession" or the "AP survey" for short (Hasegawa 2015: 136), despite the fact that it was only administered in Japan) not only used the same questionnaire as in 1992 but was also sent to the same universities as the earlier survey; therefore, it was hoped it would offer a high degree of comparability (Hasegawa and Ogata 2009: 276–77). It had 1100 respondents. As we shall see, the running of the two surveys simultaneously in Japan led to some very interestingly different outcomes.

The results of the 1992 Carnegie Survey were widely disseminated (see for example, Altbach 1996). The best-known results of the Carnegie Survey in relation to Japan published in English can be found in the work of Ehara (1998) who described Japanese academics as falling clearly into the so-called "German model" of valuing research over teaching.

The results of the CAP are still being published. Already no less than 14 edited volumes have appeared in *The Changing Academy Series*, two of which will be drawn on in particular in this chapter: the seventh volume entitled *Job Satisfaction around the Academic World* (Bentley et al. 2013) and the eleventh (Arimoto et al. 2015) entitled *The Changing Academic Profession in Japan*.

The Changing Academic Profession in Japan does draw to some extent on the AP as well as the CAP survey data, and other analyses of the AP data can be seen in publications from the Hiroshima Research Institute for Higher Education (RIHE), which undertook the original survey work. It is important to point out, however, that none of the raw data from the Carnegie Survey, CAP Survey or the AP survey are currently publicly available, and hence we are reliant on the interpretations and statistical selections of existing publications in order to make sense of them. As we shall see, some of these interpretations appear to be contradictory and the analysis incomplete, leaving plenty of questions to be explored. Nevertheless, in terms of gauging the level of happiness in one sector of Japanese society and how this has changed over time, together they offer some interesting ideas for testing Mathews and Izquierdo's (2009a) model, and we will review the data in the context of their four dimensions of well-being.

Changes in the Japanese higher education system between 1992 and 2007

In order to fully understand the comparison between the data from 1992 and 2007 in the case of Japan, it is important to examine some of the major changes that had taken place in the higher education system over that period. According to Kano (2015: 40), "[t]he change in professorship that has taken place in the past two decades reflects the 'educational revolution' that has occurred at universities in Japan." While Kano sees the U.S. as the model for this "revolution," many of the new pressures on the Japanese professoriate came from the forces of globalization more generally. It was hard for Japanese higher education—despite its size and the fact that in terms of expenditure it remains the second largest higher education system in the world—to remain as separated from the global higher education system as it had been in the past. Globalization brought pressure for marketization, corporatization, life-long learning, the emergence of the knowledge-based economy and mass higher education.

There also were pressures, however, specific to Japan, most notably the bursting of the economic bubble in 1989 and the realization that higher education needed to contribute more to the economic development of the country and the rapidly changing demography that saw the number of 18- and 19-year-olds in the population (who constitute almost all of new university entrants) decline by almost 40 percent between 1992 and 2007 (see Goodman 2005). This led to an over-supply of university places and a more demanding student population who wanted to be properly prepared for the labor force.

While research funding in Japan increased over this period, the main focus of the reforms was the improvement of university education and the student experience. Faculty development became mandatory, as did the evaluation of teaching and reform of teaching qualifications. Put simply, Japanese professors—with the exception of a minority who remained protected in government research institutions or research-intensive universities such as Tokyo or Kyoto—were forced to reevaluate their role from what the Carnegie survey of 1992 characterized as the German model (where research was paramount) to the Anglo-Saxon model (where teaching and research were of equal status) or in the case of many to the Latin American model (where teaching held primacy).

There were other features of the Japanese higher education sector that remained distinctive. While the proportion of women teaching in higher education has almost doubled since structural reforms—in particular the abolition of the faculties of Liberal Arts and Sciences in almost all universities and the relaxation of the University Accreditation Standard—were introduced into universities in Japan in 1991, Japan still has the lowest female labor participation rates in this sector in the OECD. When the CAP and AP surveys were undertaken in 2007, the figure of 18 percent of academic staff in Japan being female was half of the OECD average (Arimoto and Daizen 2013: 147). This figure also disguised major disparities within the sector: the proportion of women who were teaching in the elite former imperial universities remained less than half of the average in Japan.

A number of policy changes and social trends also combined to make permanent academic appointments increasingly hard to secure. These included governmental pressure on national universities to reduce the number of permanent appointments; the apparent desire of national universities themselves to ensure job security for senior staff by reducing the number of new junior recruitments; the huge increase of graduates from PhD programs from 4,000 in 1985 to 8,000 in 1995 to over 16,000 in 2013; the similar increase in postdoctoral positions from 6,000 in 1996 to over 15,000 in 2011. The results of these trends were, first, a huge growth in junior academics in non-secure fixed-term posts providing much of the teaching and research in universities (a group described by Minazuki (2007) as "highly qualified working poor" (kōgakureki wākingu pua)), and second a continuation of the practice of academic inbreeding despite attempts by the government to try to make the academic recruitment process more transparent and competitive (see Horta, Sato and Yonezawa 2009). The types of terms and conditions that new academics were offered were very different from those of their predecessors; particularly in medicine and the hard sciences, young academics were increasingly likely to be employed on short-term contracts, often linked to specific projects.

One way to characterize the reforms in the 1990s and 2000s was as an attempt to change the academic self-identity of academics as much as the structures in which they worked. In 2007, many universities and their professors faced a very precarious financial future. Academic self-governance, which was widely enjoyed in 1992, had become generally replaced by top-down management with a focus on productivity, efficiency, and flexibility. Many people therefore were very interested to see what the CAP and AP surveys of 2007 would show about the changing attitudes and the self-reported experiences of Japanese professors compared to those of their colleagues 15 years earlier.

An application of Mathews and Izquierdo four dimensions model

In this study, as discussed earlier, we take job satisfaction as a proxy for well-being at the workplace and adapt Mathews and Izquierdo's four dimensions to the specific context of the Japanese academic workplace. For the "physical dimension," we include the experience of stress as well as academics' experience of the built environment in terms of the facilities and equipment that are part of their workplace. The "interpersonal dimension" includes relationships with colleagues, superiors, subordinates and students combining both the perceptions of those "others" who constitute the respondents' relational environment, as well as the emotional "self" and its internal response to that environment (e.g., feeling respected or appreciated at the workplace). The "existential dimension" we translate to include both the value and meaning people find in their own work and workplace (in terms of personal achievement, pride in one's work, status and more materialistic values such as security and salary) and also how they perceive the effect of their work on others through the advancement of knowledge. According to Mathews and Izquierdo (2009b: 261), "these three dimensions are structured by a fourth dimension, involving how national institutions and global forces shape how well-being is conceived, perceived, and experienced among individuals in different societies." Thus we introduce the "structural dimension" in our analysis of the first three dimensions rather than as a separate dimension of its own.

The dimensions of academics' job satisfaction in Japan

According to the CAP survey, Japanese academics appear to have been comparatively satisfied with their work in 2007 when compared with colleagues elsewhere. As can be seen in Table 8.1, almost 69 percent chose the highest two

TABLE 8.1 Overall satisfaction with current job

	Overall satisfaction with current job (%)				
	Very high				Very low
	5	4	3	2	1
1992 (Carnegie)	7.5	46.0	32.2	11.5	2.8
2007 (AP)	5.2	46.6	32.2	13.1	2.8
2007 (CAP)	10.9	57.6	18.1	11.0	2.4

Note: Adapted from Arimoto (2011: 294), Hasegawa and Ogata (2009: 280).

categories on a five-point scale. The international average for the survey lay at roughly 65 percent and only Mexico (87%), South Korea (77%), Canada (74%) and Norway (69%) showed higher or equal overall satisfaction rates to Japan (Arimoto 2011: 294).

The AP survey, however, showed a rather different picture with only 52 percent of respondents picking the top two categories. It is interesting that this discrepancy has not yet been addressed in the literature and, as far as we can see, only the CAP data has been used in talking about Japanese academic job satisfaction in a comparative perspective. Everything that follows therefore must be read in the light of not really knowing whether Japanese academics report as more or less happy than their peers in other countries.

The physical dimension

Two key variables that need to be addressed when discussing the perception of one's physical well-being in the workplace are age and gender. According to the CAP (Table 8.2), Japanese academics' job satisfaction increases with age (Arimoto and Daizen 2013: 148), with the group aged 60 to 69 having the highest satisfaction scores (3.80), closely followed by the 50- to 59-year-olds (3.70). This is perhaps not surprising since age is closely connected to salary in the

TABLE 8.2 Overall satisfaction with current work by age

	Overall satisfaction with current work by age (%) 2007 (CAP)		
Age	Satisfied	Dissatisfied	Average
30–39	61.3	21.3	3.46
40–49	61.6	16.5	3.53
50–59	72.5	10.2	3.70
60–69	76.9	9.1	3.80
Total	70.0	13.2	3.65

Note: Adapted from Arimoto and Daizen (2013: 149). On a five-point scale from 5= "very high" to 1= "very low," those who responded with 5 and 4 are deemed 'satisfied,' those who responded with 1 and 2 'dissatisfied.'

TABLE 8.3 Overall satisfaction with current job by rank

	Overall satisfaction with current job by rank 2007 (CAP) (%)	
	Satisfied	Dissatisfied
Senior position	69.9	12.5
Junior position	59.2	18.9

Note: Adapted from Arimoto and Daizen (2013: 150). On a five-point scale from 5= "very high" to 1= "very low." Those who responded with 5 and 4 are deemed 'satisfied,' those who responded with 1 and 2 "dissatisfied."

Japanese university system (see Nanbu and Amano 2015). Age is also linked closely to the large number of younger academics who hold fixed-term contracts and have precarious working conditions (Fukudome 2011: 138–139).

Both degree level and rank (Table 8.3) also seem to be highly influential on job satisfaction: those with doctorates holding higher ranks self-score significantly higher (Arimoto and Daizen 2013: 149–150).

In the case of gender (Table 8.4), in the 1992 Carnegie Survey, female academics seem to have been slightly less satisfied with their overall job situation—although the small number of female respondents raises questions about the representativeness of the sample. The 2007 CAP survey, however, indicates the level of dissatisfaction among female academics lying 7.4 percentage points above male dissatisfaction (12.8%), which, according to Fukudome and Kimoto (2010: 153), is "about double the international average at 20.2 percent and the highest overall."

Arimoto and Daizen (2013: 148) suggest that the lower satisfaction rate among female academics can be explained by the fact that women in the Japanese academic profession are still often in lower status positions. Kimoto (2015: 93), in her analysis of the AP survey data, which also shows a higher rate of dissatisfaction among women than men, states that women still "appear to be concentrated in lower-level positions" and also that in 2007 "more men than women held

TABLE 8.4 Overall satisfaction with current job by gender

		Overall satisfaction with current job by gender (%)			
		Men		Women	
		Satisfied	Dissatisfied	Satisfied	Dissatisfied
Japan	1992 (Carnegie)	53.6	14.3	51.8	14.9
	2007 (AP)	52.4	15.2	46.2	21.5
	2007 (CAP)	69.0	12.8	62.2	20.2
International average	2007 (CAP)	66.9	9.2	60.7	10.2

Note: Adapted from Fukudome and Kimoto (2010: 154), Kimoto (2015: 99). On a five-point scale from 5= "very high" to 1= "very low." Those who responded with 5 and 4 are deemed "satisfied," those who responded with 1 and 2 "dissatisfied."

doctoral degrees." Nevertheless, we should be careful about assuming that all of the difference in male and female job satisfaction can be explained by status within the academic community. Fukudome and Kimoto (2010: 154) list further gender-based differences that may influence the satisfaction of female faculty, including the fact that women spend more time teaching when classes are in session, more women than men have the feeling that teaching and research are hardly compatible and more female academics feel the pressure to raise external funds.

The factor related to the physical dimension that has probably received the most attention in the Japanese data is stress, or "personal strain." In 1992, Japanese academics reported the highest rate of personal strain of all those surveyed, with 56 percent of the respondents choosing the top two categories in response to the statement "my job is a source of considerable personal strain" and 22 percent choosing the highest category (Arimoto 1996: 184). The CAP survey in 2007 actually showed a slight increase in personal strain from 56 to 57 percent. The AP study of the same year, however, which unlike the CAP used exactly the same questionnaire as the Carnegie survey, interestingly suggested that Japanese academics saw their work as less of a source of personal strain than 15 years before (with only about 50 percent agreeing with the statement about their job causing them strain) (Hasegawa 2015: 143). This difference in responses within the same year suggests that the survey results are not only very sensitive to *how* questions are asked but *where* they are positioned in the questionnaire. What is supported in both findings (as well as in 1992), though, is that women feel higher levels of stress at their workplace than do men (Kimoto 2015: 99; Hasegawa 2015: 145).

In relation to the built environment aspect of the physical dimension, Arimoto states that in 1992 Japanese academics complained "intensely" about facilities and equipment (1996: 189) and only library and computer facilities were assessed as either "good" or "excellent" by even a fifth of respondents (Nanbu and Amano 2015: 121). In the AP study of 2007, however, academics' ratings of classrooms, libraries, faculty offices, research equipment and computer facilities had all improved substantially, in many cases by ten percentage points or more.

The interpersonal dimension

According to Lacy and Sheehan (1997: 309), "factors related to the environment in which academics work, including university atmosphere, morale, sense of community and relationships with colleagues are the greatest predictors of job satisfaction." It is significant, therefore, that almost all of these factors were excluded from the 2007 CAP survey even though they had been included in the 1992 Carnegie Survey. It may have been because of this that the 2007 AP survey was undertaken (Table 8.5) since it does allow some comparison of Japanese academics' experience of these variables between the two dates although, to our knowledge, no correlations of these items and job satisfaction have been published, which makes it difficult to draw any definite conclusions.

The data on faculty morale and intellectual atmosphere are somewhat ambiguous. On first look, it seems that satisfaction levels in both areas have increased

TABLE 8.5 Interpersonal dimension 1992–2007

	Interpersonal dimension 1992–2007 (%)					
	1992 (Carnegie)			2007 (AP)		
	Male	Female	Total	Male	Female	Total
Faculty morale	33.7	38.5	34.1	38.5	36.9	38.4
Intellectual atmosphere	31.3	35.4	31.8	37.3	31.5	36.6
Sense of community	27.0	29.9	27.3	23.5	20.7	23.2
Relationship between faculty and administration	24.9	23.8	24.4	28.0	31.3	28.5

Note: Adapted from Kimoto (2015: 98). On a five-point scale from 5= "very high" to 1= "very low"; the proportion of those who responded with 5 and 4 are shown.

since 1992, but it becomes clear on closer inspection that this is only the case for men. In the case of female academics, they have actually become worse.

The perception of sense of community and relationships with the administration indicate significant changes since 1992. The sense of community felt by Japanese academics has diminished for both genders, with women showing a much greater reduction than men. However, appraisal of the relationship between faculty and administration has improved, with female faculty showing a stronger sense of this improvement. In truth, however, the numbers do not speak of very high levels of satisfaction with any aspects of the interpersonal dimension. Curiously, also, while women overall seemed more satisfied with these items than men did in 1992, the results were inverted in the data from 2007.[1]

Both in 1992 and in 2007, respondents were also asked about their level of satisfaction with collegial relationships (Table 8.6). It seems that the perception of collegial relationships has improved for both genders, with an increase in satisfied

TABLE 8.6 Overall satisfaction with current job and collegial relationships

	Overall satisfaction with current job and collegial relationships (%)							
	1992 (Carnegie)				2007 (AP)			
	Male		Female		Male		Female	
	Satisfied	Dissatisfied	Satisfied	Dissatisfied	Satisfied	Dissatisfied	Satisfied	Dissatisfied
Relationship with colleagues	51.3	10.2	51.4	13.4	57.1	10.3	61.0	10.7
Overall satisfaction with current job	53.6	14.3	51.8	14.9	52.4	15.2	46.2	21.5

Note: Adapted from Kimoto (2015: 99). On a five-point scale from 5= "very high" to 1= "very low" those who responded with 5 and 4 are deemed "satisfied," those who responded with 1 and 2 "dissatisfied."

respondents of 5.8 percentage points for males and 9.6 percentage points for females. This is puzzling when looking at the declining sense of community in Table 8.5 and might be due to the fact that a sense of community is a feeling that would involve most people in one's immediate work environment while, when answering the question on relationships with colleagues, respondents might be considering more restricted groups at their workplace.

In any case, it is interesting that Nanbu and Amano (2015: 123) interpret the data very positively, stating that "as a whole, it can be said that *human relationships in the university improved.*" In this context, it is notable that there is no data on academics' interactions with students, only respondents' evaluation of student quality, which is believed to be declining, with 33 percent in 2007 rating the students in their departments "poor" as opposed to 29 percent in 1992 (Ogata 2015: 82–83). In terms of our application of the happiness-model by Mathews and Izquierdo this omission of one very important form of interpersonal relation at the academic workplace represents a major hindrance for the understanding of the interpersonal dimension that will have to be addressed in future research.

The existential dimension

The relationship between job satisfaction and the value and meaning of work has been demonstrated on many occasions (Wrzesniewski et al. 1997; Rosso, Dekas and Wrzesniewski 2010) and yet it is the most difficult of Mathews and Izquierdo's dimensions to capture. To try to do so, we draw on what is the most common way of categorizing "work values" in behavioral psychology by dividing them into (1) intrinsic values, meaning personal values such as a sense of pride, interest and intellectual stimulation, and extrinsic values, defined as material values such as salary and sense of job security as well as (2) social and re-lational values, that transcend the meaningfulness of work for the individual self by pursuing societal values and the greater good (Borg 1990; Mottaz 1985; Ros, Schwartz and Surkiss 1999; Vansteenkiste et al. 2007). The Carnegie, CAP and AP surveys give us some data on which we can draw in this context.

From an intrinsic perspective, we can look at satisfaction to the extent to which work interests can be pursued. In this context, it is significant that more than half of the CAP survey respondents regard teaching and research as non-complementary or contradictory, which is the highest rate in international comparison (Fukudome 2011: 137–38) (Table 8.7).

The CAP data show that research is preferred by 71.7 percent of Japanese academics. Arimoto and Daizen (2013: 153) suggest that because the satisfaction rates in the groups *primarily* interested in teaching are lower than in those *primarily* interested in research, "satisfaction is higher among those with a research ori-entation than among those with teaching orientation." However, those who lean toward either of the two are generally more satisfied (5+4). These groups also show the lowest percentages expressing dissatisfaction (1+2). It could be argued, therefore, that preferences combining teaching and research, which are indeed closer to the academic workplace reality in Japan[2] and elsewhere, are associated

TABLE 8.7 Overall satisfaction with current job

Preferences for teaching/research	Overall satisfaction with current job 2007 (CAP) (%)					
	Very high				Very low	Average
	5	4	3	2	1	
Primarily for teaching	12.0	50.7	13.3	21.3	2.7	3.48
For both, but leaning toward teaching	10.2	61.0	18.2	8.9	1.6	3.69
For both, but leaning toward research	10.1	58.7	18.3	10.4	2.5	3.63
Primarily for research	15.4	49.7	18.5	13.3	3.1	3.61
Total	11.0	57.5	18.0	11.1	2.4	3.64

Note: Adapted from Arimoto and Daizen (2013: 154).

with higher overall job satisfaction. Looking at the AP survey data, Fukudome (2015: 175) suggests that this change might already be occurring in Japan with younger academics showing more interest in teaching.

A closely linked issue is the freedom to pursue one's own work interests. Academics in the 2007 AP survey said they felt less free than their counterparts had said they felt in the 1992 Carnegie Survey to pursue their own work interests. The CAP study also showed a significant relationship between "academic freedom" and job satisfaction, which were both described as deteriorating (Arimoto and Daizen 2013: 162). Similarly, the survey reported declining satisfaction rates when it came to university management policies. This has been especially true for national universities that do not have a research focus (Nanbu and Amano 2015: 125), as they have been both affected by major policy changes[3] and have to deal with increasing teaching demand, which has reduced research opportunities.

Although materialistic aspects are generally not seen as a top priority for those pursuing a job in the academic sector, there is an indication that such extrinsic values are rather important for Japanese academics' perception of individual job satisfaction. As Table 8.8 shows, there is a significant relation between annual gross income and satisfaction (Arimoto and Daizen 2013: 156). Academics who regard their salary as "high" have actually increased since 1992, which might suggest improving satisfaction levels (Kimoto 2015: 100). The factors that determine annual income in Japan, however, have not changed much in the recent years, despite the effects of globalization and increasing mobility and competition.

Academic rank, years of service and type and level of university all still have the greatest influence on salaries, while for example the number of institutions served, which could be a sign of competition in the market place, still has comparatively little influence (Nanbu and Amano 2015: 129–132). This can be seen in the AP data from 2007, which excluded faculty in part-time employment and was divided into four income groups of comparative size. Group 1 consisted

TABLE 8.8 Distribution of income groups according to rank and age

Distribution of income groups according to rank and age 2007 (AP) (%)					
Rank					
Group	Income (Mill ¥)	Lecturer	Ass. Professor	Professor	n
1	under 7.15	38.4	48.8	12.8	125 (100%)
2	7.15–9.10	13.2	59.5	27.3	242 (100%)
3	9.10–11.05	2.9	28.8	68.3	344 (100%)
4	over 11.05	5.8	9.9	84.3	343 (100%)
Total					1054 (100%)
Age					
Group	Income (Mill ¥)	under 39	40–49	50–59	over 60	n
1	under 7.15	51.6	30.2	10.3	7.9	126 (100%)
2	7.15–9.10	17.9	53.3	17.9	10.8	240 (100%)
3	9.10–11.05	2.3	27.5	43.3	26.9	342 (100%)
4	over 11.05	0.6	14.4	43.3	41.6	341 (100%)
Total						1049 (100%)

Note: Adapted from Arimoto (2008: 226).

of academics with an annual income of under ¥7.15 million, group 2 included salaries ranging from ¥7.15 to ¥9.10 million. Those receiving incomes between ¥9.10 and ¥11.05 million made up group 3, and group 4 consisted of employees whose annual income was higher than ¥11.05 million (Arimoto 2008: 225–227).[4]

Nanbu and Amano (2015: 130–132) confirm that academic rank and years of service are the strongest factors affecting salaries in the AP sample. The highest income group is made up of 84.3 percent of full professors, who account for only 12.8 percent in the group earning less than ¥7.15 million. While more than half of the respondents in the lowest income group are under 39 years of age, these "young" academics make up less than one percent of those in the highest wage group. Additionally, as has always been the case, private universities offer better salaries than national universities, as can be seen in Table 8.9.

Satisfaction with career prospects—above all chances for promotions—is decreasing (Kimoto 2015: 99–100). Seen from a life course perspective, this is again unfavorable for younger academics, since lower salary and poorer career prospects undoubtedly influence their satisfaction levels.

We have been unable to find any data regarding the link between societal values and academic job satisfaction, but interesting results on how Japanese academics perceive the meaning of academic work in a broader context have been shown by Yamasaki (2015: 215–217) drawing on the Carnegie and AP survey data. Responses to the surveys suggest that the single most important meaning of higher education is not the improvement of society, but rather the protection of research and scholarship. The second most important function is offering an "education

TABLE 8.9 Distribution of income groups according to institutional type

		Institutional type 2007 (AP) (%)	
Group	Income (Mill ¥)	National	Private
1	under 7.15	10.7	13.8
2	7.15–9.10	27.7	15.9
3	9.10–11.05	38.1	24.5
4	over 11.05	23.5	45.8
Total		100	100
n		625	428

Note: Adapted from Arimoto (2008: 226).

TABLE 8.10 Correlations with key variables and overall job satisfaction among Japanese academics (2007)

	Annual gross income	Hours spent on research activities in session	Percent of undergraduate instruction time	The total score of the research work
Overall satisfaction with current job 2007 (CAP)	0.141★★★	0.143★★★	−0.102★★★	0.101★★★

Note: ★★★$p<.001$. Adapted from Arimoto and Daizen (2013: 156).

for leaders." This perception of higher education is especially striking considering the fact that nowadays more than half of all high school students enter university (MEXT 2013) and may be linked with the current frustration caused by students' perceived lack of skills and quality (Ogata 2015: 82–85). Other educational aspects, such as vocational or life-long learning, are rated rather low, creating the impression that Japanese academics regard the value of their work as still lying in an orientation toward research and training the elite in society as reported in the 1992 Carnegie Survey. Societal factors, like solving social problems or conserving cultural heritage, show equally low results and have, according to the AP survey data, decreased further in importance since 1992 (Yamasaki 2015: 216).

Some tentative conclusions

It is hard to know what overall conclusions to draw from the three surveys we have examined when there is such a big difference in the key overall finding in relation to Japanese academia: the 2007 CAP survey suggests that general levels of job satisfaction in Japan are relatively high, while the AP data, which for several reasons might be considered to be more comparable to the 1992 Carnegie Survey, but offers less comparability with other countries, draws a less positive picture.

Both surveys, however, show women being less satisfied with their overall work situation, which on a structural level appears to be connected to their status and position within their institutions. Moreover, different factors seem to contribute to men's and women's sense of job satisfaction. Whereas women struggle most with the feeling that teaching and research are not compatible and worry about the rising pressure to raise external funds, men are more dissatisfied with their salary and career prospects.

Age, which in Japan is very closely linked to rank and salary, is also a factor of great importance when it comes to Japanese academics' job satisfaction. Older academics are considerably more satisfied than younger academics, a fact that attests to the major changes in academics' employment conditions in the past two decades in Japan.

According to the CAP survey, Japanese academics rank third worldwide in terms of stress and, again, women appear to feel a greater sense of personal strain than their male colleagues. Likewise, while satisfaction with the intellectual environment and enthusiasm within the faculty have increased, this also demonstrates a major gender gap, with female academics being substantially less satisfied.

Looking at work values and meanings, we can see that work interests continue to lie in research, although academics with diverse interests are generally happier than their colleagues with either only research or only teaching ambitions. When it comes to the societal context of individuals' work values, there remains a tendency in Japanese academia toward a self-perception as researchers and trainers of elites that is increasingly likely to clash with the current developments of greater teaching loads and focus on vocational learning in universities.

In this chapter, we have set out to relate the data from three major surveys on academic satisfaction to Mathews and Izquierdo's framework of well-being. The physical dimension has been discussed largely in terms of built environment. While academics seem considerably more satisfied with this environment than they were in 1992, an international comparison suggests that there still remains room for improvement. The actual perception and experience of one's own body has hardly been covered in these surveys apart from questions about levels of personal stress. Information on the interpersonal dimension lacks anything on student-teacher relationships. The existential dimension has been covered in part, with a focus on research versus teaching preferences as well as an evaluation of certain meanings academics assign to their work, but the connection to overall job satisfaction is not clear and has been given little attention.

What this all suggests is that while the quantitative data we have examined in this chapter provides some answers to the question of Japanese academics' sense of well-being and happiness, it is a long way from providing the full picture. This is perhaps not surprising. Mathews and Izquierdo (2009a: 6) warn us against setting too much store in this field on quantitative research—what they call "bald statistics placed side by side"—calling instead for a "soft comparison" that looks at happiness and satisfaction related research "in a careful, culturally sensitive way," which takes into account "the nuances of sociocultural context." It is a curious fact that despite the huge investments in both time and money that have been spent in trying to understand the levels of satisfaction of academics around the world and in Japan in the Carnegie, CAP and AP projects, there has been virtually no qualitative research that has sought to interrogate and test the data from those surveys and their subject matters. We see this study as a call for such research to begin.

One of the very few exceptions to the lack of qualitative research on faculty satisfaction is a paper by Ambrose, Huston and Norman (2005) which sets out an agenda for a qualitative approach to assessing faculty satisfaction as a means of helping institutions retain staff. By "qualitative," they mean semi-structured interviews that can be coded and compared and then used as the basis of more quantitative analysis since, as they point out, "[a]lthough survey research has the benefits of statistical power and structural modeling, the interview method allows faculty to identify, in their own words and chronology, the complex set of factors that shaped their experiences at an institution [...]. If we had initially generated a survey based on the issues commonly cited in the literature, we would have missed some issues or over-emphasized others" (Ambrose, Huston and Norman 2005: 826). We suggest that there is a strong case for arguing that this is the major weakness of the Carnegie, CAP and AP surveys and we would go one step further in arguing not only that such survey work would be greatly enhanced by the use of semi-structured interviews, but also by other qualitative methods such as ethnographic fieldwork and participation observation. We believe that other chapters in this volume, such as the chapters by Ben Ari, Yamamoto, Mathews, Kawano, and Spoden, demonstrate the strength of using such mixed methods in the study of happiness in Japan.

Notes

1 It would be informative to look at this data controlling for age and rank, but unfortunately this is not available.
2 When looking at time distribution, the academic workplace reality in Japan is very different from the stated preference for research: Time spent teaching (42%) has exceeded research time (30%) since 2007, and time spent on administrative work (13%) is steadily growing (Fukudome 2011: 135).
3 Beginning in 2004, national universities were turned into "private agencies"; faculty were no longer civil servants and lost their former employment status and job security (Goodman 2010: 72–73).
4 According to MEXT statistics from 2007, when both the CAP and the AP surveys were conducted, the average annual income for faculty at Japanese universities was ¥4,613,000 (at the mean age of 48.3). In 2013, the amount was slightly lower at ¥4,496,000 (at a higher mean age of 48.9) (MEXT 2008; 2015). The difference in these numbers is explained through the inclusion of employees with non-standard employment contracts (e.g., part-time workers) in the MEXT study, as well as the exclusion of other allowances, benefits and third-party funding.

References

Altbach, Philip G., ed. 1996. *The International Academic Profession: Portraits of Fourteen Countries.* Princeton: The Carnegie Foundation for the Advancement of Teaching.

Ambrose, Susan, Therese Huston and Marie Norman. 2005. "A Qualitative Method for Assessing Faculty Satisfaction." *Research in Higher Education* 46/7:803–830.

Arimoto, Akira. 1996. "The Academic Profession in Japan." pp. 149–190 in *The International Academic Profession: Portraits of Fourteen Countries,* edited by P. G. Altbach. Princeton: Carnegie Foundation for the Advancement of Teaching.

Arimoto, Akira. 2008. *Henbō suru Nihon no daigaku kyōjūshoku* [The changing academic profession in Japan]. Tokyo: Tamagawa Daigaku Shuppanbu.

Arimoto, Akira. 2011. "Japan: Effects of Changing Governance and Management on the Academic Profession." pp. 281–319 in *Changing Governance and Management in Higher Education* (The Changing Academy Vol. 2*),* edited by W. Locke, W. K. Cummings and D. Fisher. Dordrecht: Springer.

Arimoto, Akira, and Tsukasa Daizen. 2013. "Factors Determining Academics' Job Satisfaction in Japan from the Perspective of Role Diversification." pp. 145–165 in *Job Satisfaction around the Academic World* (The Changing Academy Vol. 7), edited by P. J. Bentley et al. Dordrecht: Springer.

Arimoto, Akira et al., eds. 2015. *The Changing Academic Profession in Japan.* (The Changing Academy Vol. 11). Dortrecht: Springer.

Bentley, Peter James et al., eds. 2013. *Job Satisfaction around the Academic World* (The Changing Academy Vol. 7). Dordrecht; New York: Springer.

Borg, Ingwer. 1990. "Multiple Facetisations of Work Values." *Applied Psychology: An International Review* 39:401–412.

Ehara, Takekazu. 1998, "Faculty Perceptions of University Governance in Japan and the United States." *Comparative Education Review* 42/1:61–72.

Fukudome, Hideto. 2011. "The Academic Profession in Japan: Work, Careers and Scholarship." pp. 133–148 in *The Changing Academic Profession in Asia: Contexts, Realities and Trends.* (RIHE International Seminar Reports No. 17), edited by RIHE. Hiroshima: Hiroshima University.

Fukudome, Hideto. 2015. "Teaching and Research in the Academic Profession: Nexus and Conflict." pp. 169–184 in *The Changing Academic Profession in Japan* (The Changing Academy Vol. 11), edited by A. Arimoto et al. Dortrecht: Springer.

Fukudome, Hideto, and Naomi Kimoto. 2010. "Teaching and Research in the Japanese Academic Profession." pp. 135–158 in *The Changing Academic Profession in International and Quantitative Perspectives: A Focus on Teaching & Research Activities* (RIHE International Seminar Reports No. 15), edited by RIHE. Hiroshima: Hiroshima University.

Goodman, Roger. 2005. "W(h)ither the Japanese University? An Introduction to the 2004 Higher Education Reforms in Japan." pp. 1–31 in *The 'Big Bang' in Japanese Higher Education: The 2004 Reforms and the Dynamics of Change,* edited by J. Eades, R. Goodman and Y. Hada. Melbourne: Transpacific Press.

Goodman, Roger. 2010. "The Rapid Redrawing of Boundaries in Japanese Higher Education." *Japan Forum* 22:65–87.

Hasegawa, Yusuke. 2015. "Working Time and Personal Strain." pp. 135–148 in *The Changing Academic Profession in Japan* (The Changing Academy Vol. 11), edited by A. Arimoto et al. Dortrecht: Springer.

Hasegawa, Yusuke, and Naoyuki Ogata. 2009. "The Changing Academic Profession in Japan." pp. 271–288 in *The Changing Academic Profession over 1992–2007: International,*

Comparative, and Quantitative Perspectives (RIHE International Seminar Reports No. 13), edited by RIHE. Hiroshima: Hiroshima University.
Helliwell, John, Richard Layard and Jeffrey Sachs, eds. 2013. *World Happiness Report*. http://unsdsn.org/wp-content/uploads/2014/02/WorldHappinessReport2013_online.pdf. Retrieved January 2, 2015.
Horta, Hugo, Machi Sato and Akiyoshi Yonezawa. 2010. "Academic Inbreeding: Exploring Its Characteristics and Rationale in Japanese Universities Using a Qualitative Perspective." *Asia Pacific Education Review* 12:35–44.
Judge, Timothy A., and Ryan Kinger. 2007. "Job Satisfaction. Subjective Well-being at Work." pp. 393–413 in *The Science of Subjective Well-being*, edited by M. Eid and R. Larsen. New York: Guilford Publications.
Kano, Yoshimasa. 2015. "Higher Education Policy and the Academic Profession." pp. 27–40 in *The Changing Academic Profession in Japan* (The Changing Academy Vol. 11), edited by Arimoto Akira et al. Dortrecht: Springer.
Kimoto, Naomi. 2015. "Gender Bias: What Has Changed for Female Academics?" pp. 89–102 in *The Changing Academic Profession in Japan* (The Changing Academy Vol. 11), edited by A. Arimoto et al. Dortrecht: Springer.
Lacy, Fiona J., and Barry Sheenan. 1997. "Satisfaction among Academic Staff. An International Perspective." *Higher Education* 34:305–322.
Mathews, Gordon, and Carolina Izquierdo. 2009a. "Anthropology, Happiness, and Well-being." pp. 1–22 in *Pursuits of Happiness. Well-being in Anthropological Perspective*, edited by G. Mathews and C. Izquierdo. New York and Oxford: Berghahn Books.
Mathews, Gordon, and Carolina Izquierdo. 2009b. "Towards an Anthropology of Well-being." pp. 248–266 in *Pursuits of Happiness. Well-being in Anthropological Perspective*, edited by G. Mathews and C. Izquierdo. New York and Oxford: Berghahn Books.
MEXT (Ministry of Education, Culture, Sports, Science and Technology). 2008. http://www.mext.go.jp/b_menu/toukei/001/002/2008/. Retrieved June 3, 2015.
MEXT (Ministry of Education, Culture, Sports, Science and Technology). 2013. *Gakkō kihon chōsa* [Basic school survey]. http://www.mext.go.jp/b_menu/toukei/chousa01/kihon/1267995.htm. Retrieved February 16, 2015.
MEXT (Ministry of Education, Culture, Sports, Science and Technology). 2015. *Chōsa kekka no gaiyō* [Overview of survey results] http://www.mext.go.jp/component/b_menu/other/__icsFiles/afieldfile/2015/03/27/1356146_3.pdf. Retrieved June 3, 2015.
Minazuki, Akimichi. 2007. *Kōgakureki wākingu pua* [Working poor with high academic qualifications]. Tokyo: Kobunsha.
Mottaz, Clifford. 1985. "The Relative Importance of Intrinsic and Extrinsic Rewards as Determinants of Work Satisfaction." *Sociological Quarterly* 26/3:365–385.
Nanbu, Hirotaka, and Tomomi Amano. 2015. "Labor Conditions." pp. 119–134 in *The Changing Academic Profession in Japan*. (The Changing Academy Vol. 11), edited by A. Arimoto et al. Dortrecht: Springer.
Ogata, Naoyuki. 2015. "Changes in University Teachers' View towards Students: Impact of Universalization." pp. 79–88 in *The Changing Academic Profession in Japan*. (The Changing Academy Vol. 11), edited by A. Arimoto et al. Dortrecht: Springer.
Ros, Maria, Shalom H. Schwartz and Shoshana Surkiss. 1999. "Basic Individual Values, Work Values, and the Meaning of Work." *Applied Psychology* 48/1:49–71.

Rosso, Brent, Kathryn H. Dekas and Amy Wrzesniewski. 2010. "On the Meaning of Work: A Theoretical Integration and Review." *Research in Organizational Behaviour* 30:91–127.

Teichler, Ulrich. 2015. "The Academic Profession: A Comparison between Japan and Germany." pp. 221–234 in *The Changing Academic Profession in Japan* (The Changing Academy Vol. 11), edited by A. Arimoto et al. Dortrecht: Springer.

Vansteenkiste, Maarten et al. 2007. "On the Relations among Work Value Orientations, Psychological Need Satisfaction and Job Outcomes: A Self-determination Theory Approach." *Journal of Occupational and Organizational Psychology* 80/2:251–277.

Wrzesniewski, Amy et al. 1997. "Jobs, Careers, and Callings: People's Relations to Their Work." *Journal of Research in Personality* 31:21–33.

Yamasaki, Hirotoshi. 2015. "Higher Education and Society." pp. 213–220 in *The Changing Academic Profession in Japan* (The Changing Academy Vol. 11), edited by A. Arimoto et al. Dortrecht: Springer.

9

DILEMMA OF FATHERHOOD

The meaning of work, family, and happiness for salaried male Japanese workers

Futoshi Taga

Introduction

During the postwar economic growth period, Japanese society held a particular image for the male standardized life course, an image that became symbolized by the *sararīman,* or salaryman. People could easily imagine the typical salaryman's lifestyle: employed by the same company his entire life, protected by permanent employment and seniority-based promotion schemes, working long hours in order to satisfy the role of breadwinner, and leaving almost all home and childcare duties to his wife. Up until the mid-20th century, "salaryman" pertained only to a small group of men who worked in the modern sectors. The standardization of employment conditions for white and blue collar employees that took place mostly in large Japanese companies (Miyake 1995; Koike 1999) and the standardization of lifestyles that came with the expanding "all-encompassing middle class mentality" (*sōchūryū ishiki*)[1] around the time of high economic growth (1955–1973) led to the term encompassing the majority of male white collar employees. Such workers grew to represent about three-fourths of the male workforce by the mid-1970s. During the period of stable economic growth (1974–1991), those who lived lives not far from the stereotypical salaryman image represented the majority of the male population (Taga 2011b). In 1980, about two-thirds of all employed persons' households were supported only by the husband's salary (GEB 2015: 9). In the mid-1980s, full-time male employees worked more than 50 hours a week on average, and those with children up to age six spent only about an hour a week doing childcare (Kuroda 2010).

Indeed, some have suggested that various types of Japanese men, such as small factory workers (Roberson 1998) and daily wage laborers (Gill 2001), lead lives and have attitudes toward life that are very different from those of the stereotypical salaryman. However, it has also been observed that the salaryman rhetoric was so powerful that it significantly influenced the way of life for Japan's entire population, becoming "a behavioral norm to aspire to" (Van Wolferen 1989: 159) or the "cultural vessel" of the general middle class consciousness (Takeuchi 1996). In research on men and masculinities, it is generally agreed upon that the salaryman embodies the concept of *hegemonic masculinity* (Connell 1995), culturally and institutionally dominating all other masculinities in postwar Japanese society (Roberson and Suzuki 2003; Hidaka 2010; Taga 2011a; Dasgupta 2012).

Rapid socio-economic changes since the early 1990s have, however, shaken the foundation of the standardized life course for Japanese men. On one hand, increasing competition for fewer regular employment positions[2] and decreasing possibility of marriage, especially among men not regularly employed,[3] seem to have enhanced the value and status of the salaryman's life. On the other hand, increasing social expectations that fathers will participate in childrearing seem to undermine men's work-centered lifestyles. Against the background of these structural changes, how have the conditions of well-being and happiness for salaried male Japanese workers changed?

Based on various survey data and in-depth interviews, this chapter examines the interrelationship of work and family life and explores continuity and change in the meaning of happiness for salaried male Japanese workers. In this chapter, I focus on the male cohort born in the 1960s and early 1970s (i.e., 20 regular employees with at least one child at the time of the interview).[4] The respondents are referred to with pseudonyms, and the listed ages, family structures, and occupations are those at the time of the interview. In the following sections, I first review existing studies and outline the conditions of salaried male workers' well-being during the period of postwar economic reconstruction and growth. Then, I show male white-collar workers' actual living conditions in the 2000s, including their attitudes toward work and family life based on existing statistics and interviews. Finally, I discuss continuity and change in the conditions and meanings of well-being for salaried male Japanese workers.

Well-being and *ikigai* for salarymen

The Japanese have often explored conditions of well-being through the term *ikigai*, meaning "that which most makes one's life seem worth living" (Mathews 1996: vii). According to Mathews and Izquierdo's (2009: 261) analytical model, well-being is divided into four dimensions—physical, interpersonal, existential and structural—in order to comprehend its complexity. *Ikigai* can be understood as primarily referring to well-being in the existential dimension.

Previous studies have suggested that male salaried Japanese workers born before the end of World War II generally claimed work to be their *ikigai* (Mathews 2003; Hidaka 2010: 139–141). This tendency has much to do with historically structured factors. In this generation, Japanese men who survived the war and witnessed the defeat of the nation to which they swore their loyalty shared a willingness to sacrifice themselves and risk their lives to rebuild the country and avenge defeat, this time in an economic war (Hazama 1999). They were proud that their generation accomplished Japan's miracle postwar restoration from ashes and rubble. Although some men in this generation listed family as their *ikigai*, most did not claim to have a deep emotional commitment to family (Mathews 2003). For this generation, family might indeed have been a source of happiness in the existential dimension because they assumed the breadwinner role as their social mission, but this was not necessarily a source of well-being in the interpersonal dimension.

Unlike the World War II generation, men born in the late 1940s and 1950s generally claimed both work and family as their *ikigai*. However, the word cannot always be taken at face value (Mathews 2003; Hidaka 2010: 141–143). In fact, these men spent most of their waking lives at work. Therefore, their social relationships tended to be established mainly around work and the company. Even in their leisure time, they often went to nightclubs with male bosses and colleagues after hours (Allison 1994) or played golf with business partners on holidays (Lockyer 2012). That they expressed spending leisure time with their family as *kazoku sābisu*, or family duties, indicates that family occupied second place.

Indeed, these attitudes and practices spurred public concern to some extent. After the 1973 oil crisis, two criticisms were raised about the standard male life course. First, there was rising disapproval with the *kaisha ningen*, or "company first person," who has a strong sense of belonging to the company and lives a work-centered life (Tao 1998). Second, complaints were heard about *chichioya fuzai*, or "father's absence," indicating the father's being absent or at least emotionally distant from his family because of his work-centered life (Kodama 2001).

However, these criticisms did not immediately translate into bringing about great changes in men's actual lifestyles. After the oil crisis, the European and American economies failed to improve, but the Japanese economy continued to grow steadily, intoxicated by the expression "Japan as number one" (Vogel 1979). Consequently, it was not until the bubble economy burst in the early 1990s that Japanese people seriously began to rethink men's work-centered lifestyles.

A shift from "work as one's life" to "a worthwhile job"

How have living conditions for salaried male workers and their attitude toward work and family life changed since the turn of the century? Let us first look at aspects related to work itself. On one hand, the lifestyles of salaried male workers, characterized by long working hours, have not changed very much. In 2006 (one of the years during which the interviews were conducted), the average working week for full-time male employees was 52.9 hours; this does not differ significantly from 52.2 hours in 1986 (Kuroda 2010). About 20 percent of full-time male workers in their 30s and 40s worked 60 or more hours a week in the late 2000s. This number is moderately lower than that of the early 2000s but is at the same level as in the late 1990s (BEG 2015: 14).

On the other hand, with regard to attitudes toward work, we can observe generational differences in at least two points. First, the younger generation seems to have a more privatized attitude toward work. Iwama (2009) has been analyzing time-series statistics about new employees' attitudes since 1969 and has observed a long trend toward the "privatization of work" in the latter half of the 20th century. Around 1980, new employees came to be more interested in "utilizing one's own ability and individuality" and thinking more about working for themselves, rather than for the company. After the burst of the bubble economy in the early 1990s, interest shifted to "having fun with work" and moved away from living a financially affluent life.

Our interviews revealed tendencies corresponding to this long-term trend. For example, Ichirō, who was born in the late 1950s and entered a general trading company in the late 1970s, said:

> I think work is primarily a means of livelihood. I'm sure that young people who insist work is primarily a means of self-expression tend to do sloppy work. A workplace is, you know, the place where you devote yourself to your duties and, in exchange for that, get a salary, rather than the place where you express yourself.

In contrast, respondents born in the 1960s and early 1970s, especially those who are single or have no children, are more likely to define work as a means of self-realization. For example, Shūichi (early 30s, married to a homemaker, no children, researcher for a pharmaceutical company) stated that his enthusiasm for his job was supported primarily by his passion for developing good medicine, rather than by his salary or membership in the company. He claimed that work is a means of self-realization and that the company is the place for that. Respondents of this generation who had children were more likely to define work as a means by which they provide for their family but are still more interested in self-realization through their job than the older generation. Ryūsuke (late 30s, married to a homemaker, one child) started work at a major electronic appliance company as an engineer just after the burst of the bubble economy and stated:

> Of course, the responsibility to feed my family is part of the reason I work, but it might not be the primary reason.... Some of my ideas have been adopted by the company, and my technological skills and originality are evaluated by people in and outside the company. If I didn't feel much about these aspects, I couldn't stand it.

He does not deny that he works to support his family and that his self-realization is inseparable from his contribution to the company and the society. Even so, he expresses self-realization as being most important in maintaining his desire to work.

Another characteristic of this generation's talk about work is that they rarely used the term *ikigai*, which has been regarded as a key term for understanding conditions of happiness for Japanese when referring to jobs as a source of well-being in the existential dimension. The only respondent who expressed his passion for his job using the term *ikigai* was Nobuo (late 30s, married to a local public employee, two children). A local public employee involved in a major Japanese city planning project, Nobuo declared that work is not only a means of providing for his family but also his *ikigai* because he dreams of continuing to contribute to the city's improvement. However, others expressed their desire to work with the term *yarigai* (worthwhile to do) or *tasseikan* (a sense of achievement). For example, Fumio (early 40s, single, systems engineer) said:

> I am not content with my salary, but I can feel a sense of achievement when I finish system construction and obtain a sense of *yarigai* when I find that I contributed to increasing the work productivity of the company. My desire to work is primarily supported by those feelings.

Masanori (late 30s, married to a homemaker, one child, salesperson) also claims that he wants to continue in his present job because he feels *yarigai* when he receives a contract as a result of his efforts.

While the term *ikigai* is usually used for continuous activities or for people with whom they have a continuous relationship, *yarigai* tends to be used for spatially and temporally limited activities. Such a tendency could be seen as a reflection of respondents' uncertain prospects for their future working conditions. As a reaction to such uncertain conditions, some respondents mention that they appreciate the present moment more than thoughts of the future. Daisuke (early 30s, single), who resigned from his first job to attend graduate school and then changed careers to work for a consulting company, stated:

> I don't think it's a good idea to stay worried about the future of your company and yourself. If you dedicate yourself to what you can do under the present conditions, you will bring yourself peace of mind, and things will go well, I think.

His attitude could be viewed as a coping strategy for uncertainty about the future. As shown above, work is still the primary influence on conditions of well-being in the existential dimension for salaried male workers. However, work seems to have become something that one throws oneself into *for oneself*, rather than for others, and from which one draws short-term satisfaction rather than that to which one devotes one's life.

Family as a source of happiness and conflict

In terms of time spent, men's participation in housework and childcare seems to have grown modestly. Male full-time workers with a child or children below six years of age spent an average of 1.1 hours on housework and 3.9 hours on childcare per week in 2006; this is a slight increase from 0.5 and 1.2 hours, respectively, in 1986. However, women in the same category spent on average 16.1 hours on housework and 12.2 hours on childcare per week in 2006 (Kuroda 2010). While percentages of female workers who gave birth and took childcare leave are between 70.6 and 90.6, the percentage of men who took childcare leave after their spouses gave birth was between only 0.5 and 1.6 during the interview period (2004–2008). Even in 2013, the percentage for men was a low 2.0 in contrast to 83.0 for women (GEB 2015: 14). This makes the fact that women still assume the majority of responsibility for household duties obvious.

In the 2000s, however, fathers with small children are experiencing quite a different social atmosphere concerning the gender division of household labor. While in 1979, 72.6 percent of Japanese completely or partly supported the idea that "the husband should work outside the home and the wife should take on domestic duties," the majority came to oppose this idea by 2002, a trend that continued until at least 2009 (Naikaku-fu 2012). Along with this change, the social expectation for fathers to be more involved in parenting has been growing. For example, in 1999, a poster and TV advertisement campaign by the former Ministry of Health and Welfare, which showed a popular TV star cradling his child and saying, "A man who does not care for his children cannot be called a father," drew people's attention. Nearly a decade later, the term *ikumen*, meaning "nice-looking man who enjoys actively participating in childcare," became prevalent, and the Ministry of Health, Labor and Welfare launched the Ikumen Project to encourage working fathers to be more actively involved in parenting. In 2008, more than 82.9 percent of all wives agreed with the idea that "the husband should share housework and childcare duties equally with the wife" (IPSS 2008). While the criticism of *chichioya fuzai* or fatherlessness, first raised in the late 1970s, had primarily required fathers to spend more time with their children for discipline, discourses on fatherhood in the 2000s have asked them to be actively involved in infant care as well. Without question, the legitimacy of a male lifestyle that leaves child raising duties to wives has been undermined.

The fact that men in their 30s and 40s generally work very long hours however remains unchanged. While in the early 2010s, about 60 percent of all households of employed persons were dual income (GEB 2015: 9), the majority of employed women are non-regular, part-time employees who are generally paid far less than regular employees and are easily discharged (ibid: 12). In addition, more than 60 percent of employed women who became pregnant resigned within a year to take care of the child (ibid: 11). These facts suggest that the majority of husbands are still the primary breadwinners. In fact, 66.6 percent of wives agree with the idea that "the husband should give high priority to the work of the company" (IPSS 2008).

These disparities in expectations on fathers bring them into conflict between work and parenting, which in the past was regarded as an issue that only working mothers faced. On the one hand, fathers who are eager to participate in childcare, but struggle to do so due to their inflexible work conditions, feel guilty or sorry for their wives who take on most of the childcare responsibilities. At least eight of twenty target respondents said that they "more or less" experienced this type of conflict. The most prominent example is Akio (early 30s), a "fast-track" bureaucrat in a government ministry and a section chief in a local office near Tokyo. His wife is a homemaker, and his two sons are four and five years old. Although his formal work schedule is from 9 a.m. to 5 p.m., Monday to Friday, he actually works until 1 or 2 a.m., sometimes staying in the office at night on weekdays, as well as often going to the office or working from home even on weekends. Although he wants to spend more time with wife and sons and do more domestic work, his working conditions do not allow it. He has a constant sense of conflict between work and family life. As he is currently the sole provider, he might avoid confronting this conflict by persuading himself that domestic work is his wife's job. In Akio's case, however, his wife is eager to work but restrains herself in order to take childcare responsibility. This fact seems to make him feel guilty and sorry for his wife and increases his feelings of conflict.

On the other hand, at least three of the 20 respondents reported having substantially reduced their working hours in order to participate in childcare and, consequently, suffered from the feeling they were not fully participating at work. The most outstanding example is Shūtarō (late 30s, employee in a manufacturing corporation), who has a homemaker wife and two daughters aged seven and eleven. Just after his first daughter was born, he experienced the most serious conflict between work and family life. At that time, he was in charge of domestic sales in Fukuoka but was sent to Osaka (about 600 kilometers away) four days every week. His wife was forced to care for their newborn baby by herself, feeling isolated and frustrated. She blamed the situation on him, and they quarreled constantly. Then he also became chronically fatigued and felt mentally unstable. He reported:

> I was so busy both at work and at home and felt I couldn't live up to my responsibility to both work and family. So, I asked the company to reassign me to an indoor service section. It was quite hard to make that decision, of course. But I felt that I couldn't stand it anymore and realized that I would lose both career and family unless I did something about it.

Although the decision was detrimental in terms of promotion, he thought it would be better than losing both career and family. After the reassignment, he had more time to spend with his family and was able to heal his relationship with his wife, but he spent some years feeling dispirited, because he felt like he was falling behind in the competition for promotion.

Another example is Atsushi (late 30s, married to an airline company employee, two children) who is a researcher in a government-affiliated think-tank. His wife is a cabin attendant for an international airline and is absent from home for about ten days at a time when she is flying. During the time his wife is away he takes their daughter to and from the childcare center. Because his work allowed him to arrange his hours at his own discretion to some extent, he was able to do so. However, this choice produced stress:

> When I was single, I lived a work-centered life while doing research on favorite subjects, but after having a child, I was no longer able to do so. I used to feel that I sacrificed myself for my family, because by devoting time and energy to my family I was hindering my career prospects under conditions of escalating free-competition. Until recently, I envied single colleagues who could devote their time and energy to working freely.

Carefully examining these examples indicates that reducing work hours has not seriously obstructed the salarymen's employment conditions and or levels of income at the time of the interview. What they "sacrifice" by reducing working hours seems to be "achievement," "face," or "the chance of promotion." Indeed, the possibility that their "sacrifice" might negatively influence their job security and long-term income cannot be denied. It is evident, however, that their dissatisfaction is not a result of concern regarding income, but rather that reducing work hours interferes with their self-realization and social success.

In brief, to be happy at work, contemporary male salaried workers appear to need to realize themselves through work. In addition, to be happy in their family lives, they also need to build intimate relationships with their families. Such expanding conditions for happiness, both in work and family life, seem to increase chances that salaried fathers are faced with a dilemma.

Reflexive definition of work, family, and happiness

As previously stated, contemporary male salaried workers who have a child or children are currently more likely to experience a conflict between work and family life than those of previous generations. This reflects that having a child has become more likely to be a burden for salaried men, not only financially but also practically. In addition, the practice of having children after marriage seems to have been changing from a standard to an option. The proportion of people who support the idea that "people do not necessarily have to have children after marriage" increased from 30.6 percent in 1992 to 42.8 percent in 2009. Notably, 63 percent of people in their 20s and 59 percent in their 30s supported this idea in 2009 (Naikaku-fu 2009). Against the backdrop of such a social climate, some respondents admitted they have avoided having a child in order to maintain their liberated lifestyle or professional career.

Shigeto (late 30s, employee for a casualty insurance company, married to a homemaker wife for over ten years, without children) said:

> I don't mean that I don't want children, but I don't need to have them now. Actually, I'm worried about that. While I want to have a person to whom I pass down my way of thinking and life, I don't want to lose my current

relaxed lifestyle. I am justifying the current conditions partly by utilizing what my wife says, "I don't want a child for now," and then persuading myself, "It's good enough."

Shigeto has refrained from having a child not because of strong feelings against it, but because he has not been able to make up his mind. In contrast, Manabu (early 50s, married to a homemaker wife, no children) explains that he intentionally avoided having children to give his career priority:

> There are two reasons why I didn't have children. One is that I wanted to get ahead rapidly and successfully in my life. The other is that I think only about twenty percent of parents would be perfectly happy about having children without any problems. If you have more than one child, at least one won't grow up well, not only do poorly but also make trouble at home. So, I claimed that I didn't want to have a child when I got married, and my wife agreed with me.

As Manabu said, he devoted his energy to work and gained promotions in the company at the fastest pace possible. He later changed careers, working for a U.S.-affiliated company, where he reached senior-level management. These two cases suggest that the weight of the decision whether or not to have children has increased when managing risk in private life. In contrast, other male salaried workers who experienced a conflict between work and family life have tried to address and overcome it. Again, let us use the examples of Shūtarō and Atsushi.

As explained in the previous section, Shūtarō changed his position at work to one less advantageous to career promotion in order to help his wife with childcare. Thereafter, he spent some years in low spirits. However, when his second daughter passed the infant stage and his wife's responsibilities became less stressful and demanding, he began to think about returning to a sales position more beneficial for promotion. As returning to a position from which one had intentionally resigned was not allowed, he asked the company to relocate him to another division's sales department and received permission for this move. Then he began to work hard again and was promoted to chief of one of the most important sections. Although he has a heavy workload and must work around 12 hours every weekday, he can spend the whole weekend with his family, picking up and dropping off his children at cram schools, going shopping, and dining out with his wife and daughters. He says:

> I don't sacrifice my family life to devote myself to work anymore. I think I can balance work and family now. I feel what I do in my current job is worthwhile, and my daughters motivate me to work. I want to earn enough money for them to be able to take cultural and sport lessons as much as possible.

While Shūtarō returned to a life pattern of prioritizing work, at least in terms of time allocation, Atushi overcame the conflict between work and family in a different way. Although he was frustrated that he had to sacrifice his professional career for his childcare responsibilities when his first child was small, he gradually came to have second thoughts:

> If I wanted to be a great success as a researcher, I could choose a lifestyle in which I put my entire heart and spirit into research without having a family. But the fact that I got married means that I didn't choose that way of life. Recently, I came to stop thinking about carrying out a big job at the cost of my family life.

He claims that he decided to have the second baby ten years after the first because of a change in his viewpoint on family life:

> Recently, I came to feel grateful to my family who made me feel the significance of my existence outside of my work, and now I pity people who can find this significance only through work. Thinking in terms of profit and loss, you would never be able to make a choice to have a child. Now I feel that bringing up children gives me pleasure for which there is no other substitute.

Although he has prioritized his family life, he still maintains passion for his work and strives to do the best job he can within his limited time.

Conclusion

This chapter examined change and continuity in the living conditions of salaried male Japanese workers in the 2000s and their attitudes toward work and family life in terms of happiness. On the one hand, we can observe a considerable degree of continuity in current life patterns among contemporary salaried male workers and those of the older generation. Despite some progress in participation in housework and childcare, the life patterns of salaried male Japanese workers in the 2000s are generally not very different from the stereotypical images of the "salaryman," characterized by long hours of work and short hours of participation in household and childcare duties.

Moreover, the definitions of work and family life have broadened and diversified. For contemporary salaried male workers, work has become not only a means of livelihood and contribution to the company and society but also something that should be worthwhile. The family has become not only the people for whom they provide, but also the people with whom they establish intimate relationships. As a result of this broadening and diversification of the meaning of work and family life, salaried male workers more frequently face a dilemma while balancing the two. They will continue to do so unless they succeed in realigning their life patterns and redefining the meaning of work and family life.

From what I discussed above, we can conclude that the de-standardization of happiness is progressing. The conditions of happiness for salaried male Japanese workers, once standardized by a socially defined salaryman image, are now continuously reformed by persistent choices and are reflexively redefined during various periods of one's life, against the backdrop of multiple conflicting discourses on happiness in an increasingly individualized Japanese society.

Notes

1 According to a 1975 national opinion poll, the total percentage of people who recognized their living standard as "upper middle," "middle of the middle," and "lower middle" reached 89.9 percent (Taga 2011b).
2 Although the proportion of regularly employed male workers was more than 90 percent until the mid-1990s, it had dropped to less than 80 percent by 2013 (GEB 2015: 12).
3 Although the proportion of never married was below 5 percent for both genders until the mid-1980s, this has been on an upward trend, rising to over 10 percent for women and over 20 percent for men in 2010 (GEB 2014: 5–6). See also MHLW (2009: 8) for differences in probability of marriage according to employment position.
4 Interviews were conducted during my first project, funded by KAKENHI (2004–2006), and during a follow-up project by Yohei Murata, Masanori Sasaki, Mitsunari Higashino, and me, supported by Raewyn Connell, University of Sydney (2006–2008). Details on respondents are shown in Taga (2011a: 219–231).

References

Allison, Anne. 1994. *Nightwork: Sexuality, Pleasure, and Corporate Masculinity in a Tokyo Hostess Club.* Chicago: University of Chicago Press.
Connell, W. R. 1995. *Masculinities.* Cambridge: Polity Press.
Dasgupta, Romit. 2012. *Re-reading the Salaryman in Japan: Crafting Masculinities.* London: Routledge.
GEB (Gender Equality Bureau, Cabinet Office). 2014. *Danjo kyōdō sankaku hakusho Heisei 26 nenban* [White paper on gender equality 2014]. Tokyo: Gender Equality Bureau, Cabinet Office.
GEB. 2015. *Men and Women in Japan 2015.* Tokyo: Gender Equality Bureau, Cabinet Office.
Gill, Tom. 2001. *Men of Uncertainty: The Social Organization of Day Laborers in Contemporary Japan.* Albany: State University of New York Press.
Hazama, Hiroshi. 1999. *Keizai taikoku o tsukuriageta shisō: Kōdo keizai seichō-ki no rōdō etosu* [The philosophy that built up the economic superpower: The labor ethos of the high economic growth period]. Tokyo: Kōshindō.
Hidaka, Tomoko. 2010. *Salaryman Masculinity: Continuity and Change in Hegemonic Masculinity in Japan.* Leiden: Brill.
IPSS (The National Institute of Population and Social Security Research). 2008. *Daiyonkai zenkoku katei dōkō chōsa: Kekka no gaiyō* [Fourth national survey on family in Japan: Summary of results]. http://www.ipss.go.jp/ ps-katei/j/NSFJ4/NSFJ4_gaiyo.pdf. Retrieved May 31, 2015.
Iwama, Natsuki. 2009. "Shinnyū shain no yonjūnen" [Trends in new employees' attitude for 40 years]. pp. 161–184 in *Wakamono no hatarakikata*, edited by R. Kosugi. Kyoto: Mineruba Shobo.
Kodama, Ryoko. 2001. "Chichioyaron no genzai," [Contemporary trends of the discourse on fatherhood]. pp. 122–148 in *Nihon no otoko wa doko kara kite doko e iku no*

ka: dansei sekushuaritī keisei kyōdō kenkyū, edited by Ningen to Sei Kyōiku Kenkyū Kyōgikai Dansei Keisei Kenkyū Purojekuto. Tokyo: Jūgatsusha.
Koike, Kazuo. 1999. *Shigoto no keizaigaku* [The economics of work]. Tokyo: Tōyō Keizai.
Kuroda, Sachiko. 2010. "Seikatsu jikan no chōkiteki na suii" [Measuring trends in allocation of time over two decades]. *Nihon Rōdō Kenkyū Zasshi* 599:53–64.
Lockyer, Angus. 2012. "From Corporate Playground to Family Resort: Golf as Commodity in Post-War Japan." pp. 284–305 in *The Historical Consumer: Consumption and Everyday Life in Japan, 1850–2000,* edited by P. Francks and J. Hunter. Basingstoke: Palgrave Macmillan.
Mathews, Gordon. 1996. *What Makes Life Worth Living: How Japanese and Americans Make Sense of Their Worlds.* Berkeley: University of California Press.
Mathews, Gordon. 2003. "Can 'a Real Man' Live for His Family? *Ikigai* and Masculinity in Today's Japan". pp. 109–125 in *Men and Masculinities in Contemporary Japan: Dislocating the Salaryman Doxa,* edited by J. E. Roberson and N. Suzuki. London: RoutledgeCurzon.
Mathews, Gordon, and Carolina Izquierdo, eds. 2009. *Pursuits of Happiness: Well-Being in Anthropological Perspective.* New York and Oxford: Berghahn Books.
MHLW (Ministry of Health, Labor and Welfare). 2009. *Heisei 21 nenban kōsei rōdō hakusho* [Annual health, labor and welfare report 2008–2009]. Tokyo: Ministry of Health, Labor and Welfare.
Miyake, Akimasa. 1995. "Nihon ni okeru howaito karā no ichi: Rekishiteki sekkin" [The position of white-collar in Japan: Historical approach]. *Annals of the Society for the Study of Social Policy* 39:3–18.
Naikaku-fu (Cabinet Office). 2009. *Danjo kyōdō sankaku shakai ni kan suru yoron chōsa Heisei 21nen 10gatsu* [National opinion poll on gender equal society, October 2009]. http://survey.gov-online.go.jp/h21/h21-danjo/index.html. Retrieved May 31, 2015.
Naikaku-fu (Cabinet Office). 2012. *Danjo kyōdō sankaku shakai ni kan suru yoron chōsa Heisei 24nen 10gatsu* [National opinion poll on gender equal society, October, 2012]. http://survey.gov-online.go.jp/h24/h24-danjo/index.html. Retrieved May 31, 2015.
Roberson, James E. 1998. *Japanese Working Class Lives: An Ethnographic Study of Factory Workers.* London: Routledge.
Roberson, James E., and Nobue Suzuki. eds. 2003. *Men and Masculinities in Contemporary Japan: Dislocating the Salaryman Doxa.* London: RoutledgeCurzon.
Taga, Futoshi. ed. 2011a. *Yuragu sararīman seikatsu: Shigoto to katei no hazama de* [The changing life of the salaryman: Between work and family life]. Kyoto: Minerva Shobo.
Taga, Futoshi. 2011b. "Yuragu rōdō kihan to kazoku kihan: Sararīman no genzai to kako" [Changing family and work norms. Past and present of the salaryman]. pp. 1–13 in *Yuragu sararīman seikatsu: Shigoto to katei no hazama de,* edited by F. Taga. Kyoto: Minerva Shobo.
Takeuchi, Yo. 1996. "Sararīman to iu shakaiteki hyōchō" [The salaryman as social symbol]. pp. 125–142 in *Nihon bunka no shakaigaku,* edited by S. Inoue et al. Tokyo: Iwanami Shoten.
Tao, Masao. 1998. *Kaisha ningen wa doko e iku* [Where does the company-first person go to?]. Tokyo: Chūō Kōronsha.
Van Wolferen, Karel. 1989. *The Enigma of Japanese Power: People and Politics in a Stateless Nation.* London: Macmillan.
Vogel, Ezra F. 1979. *Japan as Number One: Lessons for America.* Cambridge, MA: Harvard University Press.

PART III
Old age

10
HAPPINESS PURSUED, ABANDONED, DREAMED OF, AND STUMBLED UPON

An analysis of 20 Japanese lives over 20 years

Gordon Mathews

Happiness and aging in the Japanese life course

As the introduction to this book discusses, cross-cultural surveys consistently show that Japan has a lower rate of reported happiness than many other societies in the world (see, for example, the *World Happiness Report* (Helliwell, Layard and Sachs 2015)), despite the fact that by objective measures such as life expectancy and education, Japan is among the world's most well-off societies (see, for example, the United Nations Development Programme 2014; Coulmas 2010: 1–2). Why might this be? Some have argued that this is due to an unwitting bias in cross-cultural surveys (see Mathews and Izquierdo 2009a: 7). But it seems also that Japanese society has a particular inflexibility in its social and institutional structures that may serve to create unhappiness in some of its members.

There has been, for example, a marked division of gender roles in postwar Japan (Yamada 2004: 129), whereby men are expected to work outside the home to economically support their families and women, after marriage and the birth of a child, to stay home and raise their children and do the housework. A woman who sought a career faced—and still faces, to a degree—considerably greater obstacles, such as discrimination and lack of recognition and promotion, than her counterparts in most Western societies. By the same token, a man who has sought to devote himself to family has typically not been able to do so, due to the demands of work (Mathews 2002). For those men and women who have sought happiness through the standard gender division of "men at work, women at home," this situation may be optimal, but for those who seek an alternative path, the lack of gender-role flexibility may be a source of considerable unhappiness.

There has also been the structural rule that young people, and particularly men, must find career-track employment by their mid-20s, immediately after graduation, or else they will probably never have a career-track job in their lives

(Genda 2001: 82). A young person who has sought to "find himself/herself" for a few years before entering the workplace, something quite common in societies with more flexible patterns of employment, would face potential career suicide in Japan and may have taken a job he or she felt unsuited for because of a sense of having no other choice. Here too, a lack of structural flexibility—in this case, in terms less of gender than of life course—may create unhappiness in those individuals who do not fit their lives within the established pattern.

Both of these structural inflexibilities have been giving way to some extent in Japan over the past two decades (see Rebick 2006 on changing gender norms in Japanese corporate employment; see Mathews 2004 on changing youth employment attitudes). However, in their wake, new sources of unhappiness have emerged. One is the loss of secure career-track employment for many people—particularly young people—in Japan's 25 years of economic stagnation since the early 1990s. Another is changing marriage norms, whereby marriages once based on playing one's gender role now require communication and emotional intimacy, to the chagrin and confusion of some men of an earlier era, as we will shortly discuss. First, however, let me briefly discuss retirement and old age in Japan in the context of happiness.

Ruth Benedict noted long ago that "the arc of life in Japan is plotted in opposite fashion to that of the United States," with Japanese young children and the very old having freedom in social life, and adults in the prime of life laboring under great social restrictions (1974 [1946]: 253–254), unlike the United States, where those in the prime of life may be seen to be freest. This rings true in Japan today—the social pressures and structural inflexibilities faced by those in the prime of life in Japan may be immense, and being old may represent freedom from the social pressures of company and family. However, freedom does not necessarily mean happiness. The Japanese market is saturated with advice books on how to live a happier and more meaningful life for those who are older (for example, Kanemaru 1999; Shibata 2002; Saitō 2004; Yanagisawa 2007) and books more or less darkly describing old people's social situations and psychology (Inoue 2005, Takenaka 2000, 2005). These books reveal that personal freedom to live as one likes may, for some older Japanese, lead not to happiness but to ennui.

Contemporary ethnographic writings in English on aging in Japan include Plath's by-now classic work on maturity (1983: 218), discussing how "the Japanese archetype [is]…a self that can feel human in the company of others"; Hashimoto's (1996) discussion of attitudes about elderly care in Japan and the United States; Traphagan (2000, 2004) on the cultural construction of senility in Japan, and on religious rituals as expressions of concern over well-being and aging; Thang (2001) on a social welfare institution designed for both the very old and the very young; and White (2002) discussing the elderly in the context of changing Japanese familial structures. These, and numerous other books and articles, have specific arguments about the state of being old in Japan today. However, for my purpose in this chapter, I point out only that these give broad suggestions that despite the pressures and rigidities of the Japanese prime of life, it provides intense social meaning that in old age may become lost. Outside the social embrace of company and family/child raising, it may be hard for some older people to find something to live for.

Mathews and Izquierdo (2009b: 263) have discussed four experiential dimensions of well-being: the physical, the interpersonal, the existential, and the institutional. In the Japanese adult life course, physical well-being and pleasure are approved of within limits, as can be seen in areas from toleration of drinking to love of bathing in hot springs. The problems for happiness in the prime of Japanese adult life stem from the interpersonal—the eyes of other people and society (*sekentei*) upon one, judging one's conduct in life (a force that is less powerful than in the past but remains potent)—and the institutional: societal rules that because of their inflexibility may be particularly likely to create unhappiness, as discussed above. However, these interpersonal and institutional pressures in the prime of life may be accompanied by a powerful sense of belonging—a full sense of "feeling human in the company of others," in Plath's formulation. Those who have retired from work or who have seen their children become self-sufficient adults have left behind the interpersonal and institutional pressures that earlier may have shaped their life choices, to enter instead a realm of existential uncertainty: "Now that I have finished my social role of work/childrearing, what should I live for?" They may experience freedom from social pressure and institutional constraints, but also a sense of loss, for they have in effect been expelled from the most meaningful social networks of their lives. This is typically more the case for men than for women: work may end abruptly, while family ties continue. The above formulation is too simple—Japan has 126 million people living a multitude of complex individual lives—but has a grain of truth to it, I think.

In this paper, I build off the arguments offered above to examine the individual lives of a few people I have known for 20-some years. In 1989–1990, I conducted research on *ikigai* in Japan, interviewing 50 Japanese at length about their lives, hopes and anxieties and about happiness (Mathews 1996). Over the intervening years I have stayed in contact with many of these people and have had the chance to see how their lives have unfolded; in 2011, I formally re-interviewed 21 of them. My sample is of course small. However, because no researchers that I know of have ever looked at happiness chronologically in Japan through ethnographic interviews, I share what I have found in this chapter. It is now two-plus decades since my original interviewing, and everyone I re-interviewed in 2011 was 40 or above, in the second half of their lives. Of the 50 people I interviewed in 1989–1990, at least eight had died (I interviewed people between the ages of 20 and 80 in 1989–1990, so this is not surprising). Close to half of those I re-interviewed were "retired," in the sense of being no longer involved in full-time work or no longer having children living at home for whom they were the primary caretaker. In this paper, I explore how, for the people I interviewed, the social roles in family and work and their departure from these roles are linked to senses of personal happiness over the past two decades. What my interviews show is the socio-cultural context of Japanese happiness and unhappiness; I can depict why the few Japanese I have spoken with over 20 years are happy or unhappy with how their lives have unfolded.

For the people I interviewed, happiness was immediate and personal and not related to large catastrophic events like the March 2011 Tōhoku earthquake and tsunami—none of the people I interviewed knew anyone who had been a victim of that disaster. Had their marriage succeeded, or failed? Did their children grow up happy, or were there dropouts or suicides? Had they themselves sought happiness as corporate employees or mothers/housewives, or had they sought alternative routes to happiness? If they left these roles behind as they aged, were they able to make fulfilling new lives for themselves, or was this a problem for them? These questions are personal, but this does not mean that the large-scale course of events in Japan over the past 25 years has had no effect on them. Some I interviewed had lost their "lifetime employment"; others have been divorced because they or their spouses could not make enough money to support their families. To what extent can we unravel the mystery of why some Japanese people lead lives in which happiness flourishes, and others in which happiness shrivels? In this chapter, I first examine marriage and family; then I look at work and retirement; finally I consider the actual experience of happiness among the people I interviewed.

Marriage, family and happiness

There has been a shift in Japan in the nature of marriage and what is expected of marriage. Several of the wives I interviewed in 1990 mentioned the saying *teishu wa jōbu de rusu ga ii*—"it's good when the husband is healthy and absent," jokingly referring to their own marriages. In these marriages, the separate roles of husband and wife were central: if the husband was off at work, and reliably bringing home his paycheck, that was all that mattered. Today, however, particularly among those in their 40s and younger, but across the range of the life course, more may be required of a husband: not just his financial contribution to the family but his emotional contribution as well. As Nakano (2011: 135) notes, in Japan in recent years there has been "[…] a shift in understandings of marriage, from the idea that marriage involves social duty and the fulfillment of social roles, to the companionate model in which love, individual choice, and companionship form the basis of marriage." But this may be difficult for marriages that date from an earlier era. How do you learn to communicate once you are already in the middle of your marriage? (Mathews 2014: 66–67; Kawano, Roberts and Long 2014: 15).

The two happiest marriages of anyone I interviewed (as far as I can judge from interviews) were that of a blue-collar worker and his part-time working wife and of a husband-and-wife manager of a school sending children overseas for university education. In both cases, the parents had left aside the fraying but still extant middle-class model of husband at work, wife at home, to be more or less equal partners in work and family. On the other hand, however, it seemed particularly difficult to find happiness within marriages following the standard middle-class model, because, as earlier mentioned, the rules have changed (see Yamada 2001: 194). As one unhappy salaryman in his 40s maintained to me, "When I married my wife, I never knew it would become like this." He married her because she was good looking and sweet. The cultural rules for marriage have changed over the past 20 years in Japan, leaving his wife disgruntled at his lack of communication, and leaving him bewildered that such a thing would now be required of him.

In 1990, I interviewed a housewife in her 50s, married to a teacher. Twenty-two years later, in 2012, she was more critical toward her husband than she had been in our earlier interview: "He recently asked me whether, if there were reincarnation, I would want to be with him again. I told him no. The way he treated me in our marriage was just too inconsiderate." Her husband could only make light of his wife's discontentment in his comments to me. All his working life as a teacher, his family life was secondary, something that he took for granted and largely ignored; his work was everything to him. As he told me in 1990, "In my house, my wife was like a widow; I was busy, even on Sunday, with my school clubs. So now, if I'm not home, everyone feels more relaxed." Since his retirement, he is at home much of the time. His wife and he lived in separate worlds for so long that now that they live in the same world, what in the world is there to talk about? She later offered a softer view of her husband: "Over the years I began to understand how he really was kind at heart; now I can be more relaxed with him, and have a warmer feeling. That wasn't really the case until fairly recently, after he stopped being so busy at work: it's no longer a matter of man and woman, but a human feeling." His retirement has made her relationship with her husband better, by her account; but her discontentment over the long-term course of their relationship remains.

In other cases among the people I interviewed, unhappiness specifically arose because of children. One man I interviewed, an elite salaryman in his 50s, has two sons in their 20s living at home with him, one who has been *hikikomori*, a stay-at-home dropout (see Borovoy 2008; Horiguchi 2011) and another who quit his career-track job to come home to live. In retrospect he blames himself: "I wanted them to go to top universities and enter top companies, but I see that I was putting too much pressure on them." The fact that his children are in conventional terms failures weighs upon him heavily: a shadow over his life. For a number of years, he and his wife quarreled over their children, but both finally seem to have accepted their situation. Another salaryman I interviewed insisted that he did not want his children to follow a conventional path in life, unlike his wife: "She wants them to go to work for big companies, but I think that's a bad idea—they need to find their own paths," he said. Those I interviewed who were happiest about their children were accepting of alternative career paths. This includes a mother, happy that her son in his late 20s was a sound technician for rock bands in Tokyo, despite the fact that he had to work at other odd jobs to support himself—"He's doing what he loves to do." This also includes a father, happy that his son, also in his late 20s, is able to find work as an illustrator in Sapporo: "Finally, this year, for the first time I didn't have to help him pay his rent!"

I interviewed five people who had divorced (see Alexy 2011)—in several cases, a wife divorced a husband who had lived for his dreams rather than for his family. An executive for a well-known company, who expressed nothing but love for her husband in 1989 divorced him a few years thereafter, telling me that he didn't really care about her. In fact, he cared more for his dream of being a renowned artist than for her, and so she asked him to leave. She proclaims her happiness as a single person now and also says, "I know no one among my work colleagues or friends who is happily married." A man I interviewed in 1990 was on the cusp of getting married to a woman who disapproved of his dreams; he became a salaryman but then quit after a decade to start a coffee shop. His wife accused him of abandoning the family. "I wasn't her husband anymore, she said, because I wasn't earning enough money. She didn't want to lose her high standard of living like she had when I was working for a company." He had not seen his children in three years—his wife would not let him see them, to his dismay, and Japanese courts do not typically grant joint custody of children to divorcing couples. It was clear, in interviewing these people, that even if they themselves had initiated the divorce, it was a profound source of unhappiness, for it signified that their previous dream of deep life-long linkage to another human being had been dashed.

All in all, happiness through family has become harder to find than it was two decades ago for two reasons. There is 1) the raising of expectations of what a good marriage should be—it must now include compatibility and communication between husband and wife, as it did not 30 years ago. This is a demand more on the part of wives than of husbands, but it is profound, due to Japanese cultural shifts in gender roles and expectations; the happiest couples I interviewed were those who did not seek to fit those roles and expectations. There is also 2) the increasing pessimism about raising children in a Japan where the old models of having a salaryman son and a full-time housewife daughter do not seem promising anymore. New, more nimble models are necessary but are also highly uncertain in an economically straitened society (see Nagase 2006). The happiest couples I interviewed were those who only hoped that their children would be happy—but what will happen as these children become older and perhaps in pursuing their poorly paid callings might be unable to ever support families of their own?

Work, retirement and happiness

A few of the people I interviewed in 1989–1990 sounded similar to the stereotypical salaryman of that era. A worker for Takugin bank told me, "I can't separate myself from Takugin. I am what I am because of Takugin." The bank was his identity. However, the bank collapsed in 1997, and this man's identity and pride could only have been severely shaken. I unfortunately could not locate him for a re-interview, but I did find his subordinate, who said in 1990, "I'll spend the next forty years with the bank, the best part of my adult life. I feel awful, but if I were asked what else I wanted to do, I couldn't answer." But he spent only eight years with the bank before it collapsed. He then went to work for another bank, and has had a standard salaryman's life, but Takugin's collapse profoundly affected him—he owns several apartments, without his company's knowledge, as a way to ensure that he has money just in case he were to lose his job once again. As he told me, "Japan is now in decline. The biggest lesson I've learned is to never depend upon a company, because you cannot know what will happen to it...."

This man became detached from his company because of Japan's recent history—the once taken-for-granted lifetime employment of white-collar workers in large companies has become increasingly less reliable in Japan. However, others I interviewed were detached because they were going to retire soon and were well aware that the company to which they had devoted most of their lives would soon vanish from their lives. A female executive I know well has always heaped scorn upon her male co-workers, although not on her company itself; she has carved out her own career niche, allowing her to escape some of the more inflexible aspects of corporate life. She says, "I am happy as I get closer to retirement, because I can relax: I don't have to worry so much anymore." She has been cultivating various hobbies for her post-retirement life, and insists that she will be quite happy in retirement. Another executive soon to retire, a man who was extraordinarily pessimistic 22 years ago about his life, now speaks with great optimism because, as he said, "I've learned to accept that there's nothing I can do about things, so why worry?" He dreams of how, in his upcoming retirement, he will read lots of books and travel overseas, which, since his wife does not speak English, he will do alone. In our earlier interview, he was pessimistic because of the bonds of work and the bonds of family that forced him to work. In retirement, he will be free from one of these bonds, and at least when he travels, free of the other bond as well, or at least so he envisions. Only time will tell whether, once these two people have left behind the interpersonal and institutional pressures and belonging that work provides, they will indeed be able to find happiness within their dreams of retirement.

The female executive quoted above stated that "[...] women are better off than men after retirement. Men, after they lose their titles, they're lost. Women have things they spend time on—household stuff, and many other things." Indeed, two recently retired men I interviewed seemed to have trouble filling up their days: they did not seem to know what to do with themselves now that work was no longer their dominant daily necessity. For some retired men, it is as if, having expended all of themselves for their work over the course of decades, they have no selves left beyond work and no energy left to find such a self.

For most people I interviewed, work was not a calling—simply, they happened to have wound up in a company to which they gave their lives. There were several exceptions. One was a male coach of a female high school basketball team who lived for basketball and continued coaching well into his 70s when I interviewed him. Another was a former salaryman for a large telecommunications company who, during the decades he worked, also played Japanese musical instruments and became a Buddhist priest. While he worked, he told me, he faced the constant criticism of his bosses who said, "Why are you doing those other things? You should be devoting all your time to the company!" He retired early so that he could indeed devote himself to those other pursuits and now has his own temple in his home and a small Buddhist congregation: he seems a fulfilled and happy man, although, as a Buddhist, he insists that happiness does not matter. A third was a teacher for an alternative school sending students discontent with the Japanese educational system overseas to study. His work has always been a financial struggle—a few years ago, he lost ownership of his company, because he could not pay the bills—but nonetheless he continues into his late 60s, because this is work he believes in. Only these three men seemed truly happy in their ongoing work.

It has always surprised me how little happiness all the Japanese salarymen I know seem to have derived from their work. This seems to be partly because of the lack of a sense of personal calling, partly due to the interpersonal and bureaucratic pressures inherent in working in a large Japanese organization (which seem to be significantly greater than in other societies) and partly due to the possibility that any Japanese willing to expose his or her life to a foreign anthropologist in such depth in 1990 and thereafter may be somewhat unusual and detached from conventional Japanese life as compared to his or her fellows. I do not know how these factors may intertwine; I only know that I have never met a Japanese salaryman who is happy in his job. This is reflected in the literature, most memorably by, in the 1990s, Miyamoto's caustic book (1995) and less extremely, in Ogasawara's account (1998), both describing an era in which my informants worked and depicting why personal fulfillment in corporate or bureaucratic work is so hard to find.

Whether in a new Japanese era of change mainstream work may become more of a source of happiness than it has been in the recent past very much remains to be seen. Whether in a new Japanese era of change more Japanese will be able to find fulfillment in retirement also remains to be seen, but I sense this is already taking place for people such as the two discussed above, who have apparently been foresighted enough not to let themselves become consumed by their work.

The mystery of happiness

Among the people I interviewed, Japanese women seemed happier than Japanese men. I cannot make large-scale generalizations from this, nor can I completely discount the possibility that the women I spoke with were more likely to express themselves emotionally than were men; but this is what I have found. One woman told me in 1990:

> What women live for is closer to themselves; it lasts all their lives. But a man's work at his company doesn't last; he'll have to retire. Some men

realize that in their work they're just a cog in a machine, but others don't; they believe that they're essential, that without them the company couldn't survive. These men are being fooled, I think. But family is different. It's not like a company; you can't simply exchange one mother for another; a member of a family is not just a replaceable cog.

(Mathews 1996: 74)

Western feminists sometimes assume that Japanese women are oppressed because they are treated unequally in the workplace; but from this woman's point of view, work is intrinsically inferior to family as a source of happiness. Two older women I interviewed in 2011 spoke nostalgically about when they were raising their children, as if those were the best years of their lives; but they and others continued to have closer relations with children and grandchildren than their husbands. One woman in her 70s devoted herself to her mentally and physically handicapped grandson, giving her, she said, a reason for living that her husband, a retired civil servant, could not enjoy. Indeed, because men have been expected to be immersed in work, they are often cut off from a range of other human relations and interactions—sources of happiness beyond work. This may be changing generationally, with gender role division increasingly giving way to some extent at home and in the workplace (see Nagai 2009), but is true for the people I interviewed: men often seem to lack the resources that women have for living a happy and fulfilled old age. This may lead to a range of further conjectures—if Japanese women become more equal to men in the Japanese workplace, more immersed in work, might they become less happy? But let me in conclusion go in a different direction: what does it mean to be happy?

In 1990, I spoke with a young woman of 22, working for a government office, with dreams of being a writer and world traveler. She said "If I married a good man and had two kids, working at the same job I have now, would I be disappointed? Yes, I'd be disappointed!" When I interviewed her 21 years later, in 2011, I found that this is exactly her situation: she had indeed married a good man, had two children, and was working at the same place she was working two decades past. "My life is good—I'm 90% satisfied—but I'm not fully happy," she said. "My children were an accident, at least the first one. But once you have children, they become your life." She now seems resigned to living the middle-class Japanese life she'd dreamed of avoiding, a life like that of their parents. She went to a fortune teller who scolded her when she told of her discontents: "Just live your life! Be a good mother and good worker and be happy in that!" But still, she seeks something more in her life. She e-mailed me after our interview, to ask, "What's the difference between those who enjoy their lives and those who don't? If I'm not content enough with my present life, is the problem my personality? With a different way of thinking, could I feel totally happy? Maybe."

I also re-interviewed the wife of a construction manager in her 50s. Today her children are grown and practicing their own blue-collar trades; she works part time and sees her husband only intermittently, due to his work in different places, although she obviously is deeply attached to him. The dominant feeling in interviewing her was that she seemed so unassumingly happy. She said that she simply enjoys every day, the food she eats, the view from her apartment, fresh air, the taste of a tangerine; and while from some people such claims might seem dubious, from her I have no doubt that they are entirely genuine. She told me of how, when she met her friend, who likes to look at the hidden side of things, she feels like a child: "She thinks I'm not very smart. When I talk with her, I want to be more adult-like. ... But then, I'm happy. I look at the surface of things, and accept them. That's OK, I think. I'm just happy in my life each day!"

The one woman, following a standard middle-class life path, after dreaming of more, wonders, "Why aren't I completely happy?" The other, following a standard working-class path, says, "Wow, am I happy!" Perhaps these contrasting interviews simply reveal that while raising children one does not have time to be happy; that only comes after children have left. But I think there is more: why is one person happy with the ordinary things in life and another not? One explication is social class. For an intellectual college graduate in Japan, like the first woman, middle-class life should be transcended, and if it is not, it is a life disappointment. For a woman of working-class background, like the second woman, her present is a better life than she might have expected—and expectations are extraordinarily important in shaping happiness. Beyond this, some psychologists estimate that 50 percent of happiness is genetic (Layard 2005: 55–58). Perhaps the second woman has the genetic endowment to be able to think, "Wow, this tangerine tastes good!" while the first woman, genetically less blessed, can only think, "Oh, it's just a tangerine...."

And this last comparison leads to questions far beyond what this chapter can answer. Is happiness false consciousness? If we are happy, are we enlightened or merely stupid? Would we be better off if we all asked fewer questions and simply accepted life as it is? But then, is happiness really an ultimate good? Is it better to be unhappily aware of life or very happily enjoying the surface of things? I do not know the answers to these questions but raise them at the end of this chapter because they are so fundamentally important. One thinks, in this context, of Aldous Huxley's *Brave New World* (1977) with its soma, a drug making all in Huxley's novel happy except for its malcontented protagonist. Happiness is not the highest human value, philosophers argue (see Baggini 2004: 97–101). And yet, who among us, Japanese or otherwise, would choose to be miserable rather than happy in our lives?

In this chapter, on the basis of longitudinal interviews with a few people over 20-some years, I have examined marital expectations, employment and retirement as sources of happiness or its lack. I have found that changing Japanese marital ideals have left some of the people I interviewed less than happy in their marriages, that Japanese corporate life has been consistently unfulfilling for many and that retirement is a source of hope that may or may not actually be fulfilling. Finally, I have considered two Japanese people I interviewed, one habitually searching for happiness and not finding it and the other habitually happy in the tiny pleasures of day-to-day life.

Japanese society could be restructured to make more of its members happier. I discussed at the start of this chapter some of the structural inflexibilities of postwar Japanese society, and believe that if society were to become more flexible in its demands on individuals, this might create more optimal conditions for happiness. But as to whether happiness should be a societal or even an individual goal, I am skeptical, believing in a statement attributed to C. P. Snow that "if you pursue happiness you'll never find it" (see also Ehrenreich 2009 on "how positive thinking is undermining America"). Reflecting on the two women discussed in the last section of this chapter, it may be that within our own lives, the less we think about happiness, the better.

References

Alexy, Allison. 2011. "The Door My Wife Closed: Houses, Families, and Divorce in Contemporary Japan." pp. 236–253 in *Home and Family in Japan: Continuity and Transformation*, edited by R. Ronald and A. Alexy. London: Routledge.

Baggini, Julian. 2004. *What's It All About? Philosophy and the Meaning of Life*. Oxford: Oxford University Press.

Benedict, Ruth. 1974 [1946]. *The Chrysanthemum and the Sword: Patterns of Japanese Culture*. New York: Meridian.

Borovoy, Amy. 2008. "Japan's Hidden Youths: Mainstreaming the Emotionally Distressed in Japan." *Culture, Medicine, and Psychiatry* 32/4:552–576.

Coulmas, Florian. 2010. "The Quest for Happiness in Japan." Kwansei Gakuin University, *Annual Review of the Institute for Advanced Social Research* 2:1–25.

Ehrenreich, Barbara. 2009. *Bright-Sided: How Positive Thinking Is Undermining America*. New York: Picador.

Genda, Yūji. 2001. *Shigoto no naka no aimai na fuan* [The vague uneasiness of work]. Tokyo: Chūō Kōron Shinsha.

Hashimoto, Akiko. 1996. *The Gift of Generations: Japanese and American Perspectives on Aging and the Social Contract*. Cambridge: Cambridge University Press.

Helliwell, John F., Richard Layard and Jeffrey Sachs, eds. 2015. *World Happiness Report 2013*. New York: Sustainable Development Solutions Network.

Horiguchi, Sachiko. 2011. "Coping with Hikikomori: Socially Withdrawn Youth and the Japanese Family." pp. 216–235 in *Home and Family in Japan: Continuity and Transformation*, edited by R. Ronald and A. Alexy. London: Routledge.

Huxley, Aldous. 1977. *Brave New World*. London: Granada.

Inoue, Katsuya. 2005. *Kōreisha no shinri ga wakaru* [Understanding old people's psychology]. Tokyo: Chūō Hōki Shuppan.

Kanemaru, Hiromi. 1999. *Jibun no tame no ikigai zukuri: Nakama ga iru to konna ni chigau gojūdai kara no ikikata* [Creating ikigai for yourself: Life after fifty will be very different when you have friends]. Tokyo: Ichimansha.

Kawano, Satsuki, Glenda S. Roberts and Susan Orpett Long. 2014. "Introduction: Differentiation and Uncertainty." pp. 1–24 in *Capturing Contemporary Japan: Differentiation and Uncertainty*, edited by S. Kawano, G. S. Roberts and S. Orpett Long. Honolulu: University of Hawai'i Press.

Layard, Richard. 2005. *Happiness: Lessons from a New Science*. London: Allen Lane.
Mathews, Gordon. 1996. *What Makes Life Worth Living? How Japanese and Americans Make Sense of Their Worlds*. Berkeley: University of California Press.
Mathews, Gordon. 2002. "Can 'a Real Man' Live for His Family? *Ikigai* and Masculinity in Today's Japan." pp. 109–125 in *Men and Masculinities in Contemporary Japan: Dislocating the Salaryman Doxa*, edited by J. E. Roberson and N. Suzuki. London: RoutledgeCurzon.
Mathews, Gordon. 2004. "Seeking a Career, Finding a Job: How Young People Enter and Resist the Japanese World of Work." pp. 121–136 in *Japan's Changing Generations: Are Young People Creating a New Society?*, edited by G. Mathews and B. White. London: Routledge.
Mathews, Gordon. 2014. "Being a Man in a Straitened Japan: The View from Twenty Years Later." pp. 60–80 in *Capturing Contemporary Japan: Differentiation and Uncertainty*, edited by S. Kawano, G. S. Roberts and S. Orpett Long. Honolulu: University of Hawai'i Press.
Mathews, Gordon, and Carolina Izquierdo. 2009a. "Introduction: Anthropology, Happiness, and Well-Being." pp. 1–19 in *Pursuits of Happiness: Well-being in Anthropological Perspective*, edited by G. Mathews and C. Izquierdo. New York and Oxford: Berghahn Books.
Mathews, Gordon, and Carolina Izquierdo. 2009b. "Towards an Anthropology of Well-being." pp. 248–266 in *Pursuits of Happiness: Well-being in Anthropological Perspective*, edited by G. Mathews and C. Izquierdo. New York and Oxford: Berghahn Books.
Miyamoto, Masao. 1995. *Straitjacket Society: An Insider's Irreverent View of Bureaucratic Japan*. New York: Kodansha USA.
Nagai, Akiko. 2009. "Otto no kaji sanka [Husbands' participation in housework]." pp. 115–121 in *Gendai Nihon no kazoku* [Family patterns in contemporary Japan], edited by S. Fujimi and M. Nishino. Tokyo: Yūhikaku.
Nagase, Nobuko. 2006. "Japanese Youth's Attitudes towards Marriage and Child Rearing." pp. 39–53 in *The Changing Japanese Family*, edited by M. Rebick and A. Takenaka. London: Routledge.
Nakano, Lynne Y. 2011. "Working and Waiting for an 'Appropriate Person': How Single Women Support and Resist Family in Japan." pp. 131–151 in *Home and Family in Japan: Continuity and Transformation*, edited by R. Ronald and A. Alexy. London: Routledge.
Ogasawara, Yuko. 1998. *Office Ladies and Salaried Men: Power, Gender, and Work in Japanese Companies*. Berkeley: University of California Press.
Rebick, Marcus. 2006. "Changes in the Workplace and Their Impact on the Family." pp. 75–93 in *The Changing Japanese Family*, edited by M. Rebick and A. Takenaka. London: Routledge.
Saitō, Shigeta. 2004. *'Toshiyori' no udemakuri* ['Old people,' rolling up our sleeves]. Tokyo: Naminorisha.
Shibata, Hiroshi. 2002. *Hachiwari ijō no rōjin wa jiritsu shite iru!* [Over 80 percent of old people are independent!]. Tokyo: Bijinesusha.
Takenaka, Hoshirō. 2000. *Kōreisha no koritsu to yutakasa* [Old people's isolation and affluence]. Tokyo: NHK Books.
Takenaka, Hoshirō. 2005. *Kōreisha no sonshitsu taiken to saisei* [Old people's experiences of loss and rebirth]. Tokyo: Seitōsha.
Thang, Leng Leng. 2001. *Generations in Touch: Linking the Old and Young in a Tokyo Neighborhood*. Ithaca, NY: Cornell University Press.

Traphagan, John W. 2000. *Taming Oblivion: Aging Bodies and the Fear of Senility in Japan*. Albany: State University of New York Press.
Traphagan, John W. 2004. *The Practice of Concern: Ritual, Well-Being and Aging in Rural Japan*. Durham, NC: Carolina Academic Press.
United Nations Development Program. 2014. http://hdr.undp.org/en/content/human-development-index-hdi-table. Retrieved March 21, 2015.
White, Merry. 2002. *Perfectly Japanese: Making Families in an Era of Upheaval*. Berkeley: University of California Press.
Yamada, Masahiro. 2001. *Kazoku to iu risuku* [The risk called family]. Tokyo: Keisō Shobō.
Yamada, Masahiro. 2004. "Pātonā erabi to kekkon senryaku" [Choosing one's partner and using marriage strategies]. pp. 121–126 in *Kazoku kakumei* [Family revolution], edited by H. Shimizu et al. Tokyo: Kōbundō.
Yanagisawa, Isamu. 2007. *Ikigai aru jinsei kōhan o dezain suru* [Designing the second half of your life to be a life with purpose]. Tokyo: Hōzuki Shoseki.

11
SENIOR VOLUNTEERS AND POST-RETIREMENT WELL-BEING IN JAPAN

Satsuki Kawano

Introduction

Yokoyama-san, a male volunteer in his mid-60s, told me: "I enjoy my days now since I started volunteering at the Grave-Free Promotion Society (Sōsō no Jiyū o Susumeru Kai; GFPS[1]). Before I began volunteering, I used to go to a local library every day." Thinking of my university's research library, I responded, "Oh, you like reading." For a moment, he stared at me, as if to say, "You didn't get what I said." Then Yokoyama-san explained: "Don't you know what kind of place a library is? People who have nothing else to do go there to take a nap!"

Paying special attention to the transformation of older workers into GFPS volunteers, this chapter examines the relationship between seniors' post-retirement volunteering experiences and their senses of well-being. The GFPS is a citizens' movement that promotes people's freedom to choose their own mortuary practices. The group conducts ash scattering ceremonies for its members, who prefer not to follow the social expectations of interring cremains in a grave. The GFPS sees ash scattering, unlike conventional interment in a grave, as an environmentally friendly practice (see Kawano 2010). Being part of this citizens' movement is an important source of identity for its volunteers. Although volunteers receive little or no monetary compensation, they are expected to be committed and to perform tasks that are no easier than paid work. Clearly, monetary gain itself cannot be considered the primary reason volunteers contribute their efforts to the movement. The stories of GFPS volunteers reveal that the loss of their employment status due to retirement has spoiled their senses of well-being in a significant way. For them, retirement initially implies that they do not have a place of belonging beyond their families or a useful engagement in the eyes of society. "Being idle" after retirement is considered to harm their physical health, spousal relations, and existential well-being. By joining the group, serving as volunteers and receiving appreciation from non-family others, senior volunteers have developed new identities and senses of well-being as mature adults.

In their volume *Pursuits of Happiness: Well-being in Anthropological Perspective*, Gordon Mathews and Carolina Izquierdo (2009: 257) suggested that we study diverse experiences of well-being in a particular culture by highlighting the significance of socio-economic status, age, and gender. By examining their interpersonal, physical, existential and institutional dimensions of well-being among middle-class seniors, particularly retired salaried men, this chapter aims to provide a nuanced, gendered description of well-being in Japan.

Understanding seniors' volunteerism and well-being

A number of previous studies indicate that volunteering is positively associated with seniors' well-being (Wilson 2000). Volunteering provides seniors with a role that protects them "from hazards of retirement, physical decline and inactivity" (Fischer and Schaffer 1993: 9). Volunteering is associated with seniors' physical well-being (Stephan 1991), higher functional abilities (Moen et al. 1992: 1628), and lower risks of mortality (Rogers 1996). Wheeler et al. (1998) note, in a meta-analysis of 37 studies of senior volunteers' well-being, that volunteering is positively related to life satisfaction. A recent meta-study of 16 research projects conducted in the U.S. indicates that "volunteering in old age predicted better self-rated health, functioning, physical activity and life satisfaction, as well as decreased depression and mortality" (von Bonsdorff and Rantanen 2011: 167).

The literature on volunteering reveals multiple reasons seniors take on voluntary activities. These reasons can be divided into social benefits and personal benefits, which include feeling useful, using one's skills, and exploring one's own interests (Narushima 2005: 575). For example, American seniors volunteer to "help others" (83%), to "feel useful or productive" (65%) and to "fulfill a moral responsibility" (51%) (Okun 1994). Maintaining self-esteem is another reason for some seniors to volunteer (Okun 1994). Compared with younger adults, seniors are more likely to feel a moral obligation to engage in voluntary activities (Narushima 2005: 570).

A recent study by Matz-Costa and colleagues (2014: 279) further deepens our understanding of the benefits of volunteering in later life. Rather than "mere involvement" in volunteering, it is important to examine "the degree to which this involvement is experienced as positive, fulfilling, meaningful, and interesting." Building on Kahn's work (1990), which employed Goffman's concept of role embracement (1961) to examine individuals' work roles, Matz-Costa and colleagues note the importance of shifting away from role occupancy toward role embracement in their analysis of volunteering. Rather than examining whether social actors occupy particular roles, previous studies have illustrated that their subjective role experiences must also be explored (McMunn et al. 2009). Their study is particularly useful, as it illustrates an association between participants' (workers', volunteers', and caregivers') assessments of the rewards received for their investments in these roles and their self-reported subjective well-being.

Although previous studies have constructively classified different reasons among seniors for volunteering, a number of questions still remain. As most of the studies on volunteering and seniors' well-being are quantitative, they tend to provide limited accounts of the process through which and the socio-political contexts in which seniors take voluntary roles. The literature also provides limited accounts of volunteering experiences, including the types of rewards related to the participants' different levels of investment in volunteering. Moreover, little is known about how different types of volunteering affect participants' health (Harris and Thoresen 2005). Wilson (2000: 232) notes that "most of the health benefits accrue to those who volunteer in moderation and who volunteer in connection with a church." By examining detailed subjective volunteer experiences and engagement in Japan, where Christianity remains a minor religion, this study will further refine our understanding of volunteering and seniors' senses of well-being.

Well-being in late adulthood in Japan: Second careers, retirement, and volunteerism

"Eighty years of life" is a phrase heard in both popular and official rhetoric to characterize the life course in Japan. With prolonged post-retirement life, retirement (*teinen*)[2] no longer marks the end of one's productivity and engagement; instead, it has been increasingly reconfigured as the beginning of one's second life (*daini no jinsei*; see Thang 2006). For example, *Post-retirement*, a collection of essays on retirement published by a leading publisher, Iwanami Shoten, aims to teach recent and future retirees how to lead fruitful lives (1999: v). Not only the popular discourse of retirement but also the official discourse of aging promoted by policy makers encourages the young-old—in particular, new retirees—to take the initiative, enrich their lives and keep themselves engaged, whether through employment, volunteerism, learning or leisure activities. In the era of 80 years of life, this official discourse aims to resocialize the retired population and make it productive, though this productivity is defined much more broadly, that is, not solely in terms of economic employment. Interestingly, there is an assumption that the retired-to-be will be required to consciously transform themselves from employees into active retirees.

Before exploring my informants' experiences, it is useful to briefly sketch the ways in which state policies and programs shape seniors' lifestyles by linking their active engagement through employment or social activities with their well-being. Security in old age is one of the important objectives shaping these policies regarding employment and social engagements in later life. The Japanese government is particularly anxious about the declining birthrate because a shrinking number of future workers will have to support an increasing number of seniors. The policies regarding senior workers thus address the issue of seniors' economic dependence on the dwindling younger population. Given this context, it makes sense that one of the characteristics of Japanese senior-related policies is that the state encourages seniors to remain employed (Campbell 1992: 18). This trend contrasts with the situation in many European and American societies (Mitani 2001: 355) in which the percentage of male workers aged from 55 to 64 continuously fell between 1970 and 1990 (Guillemard and Rein 1993: 473).

In postwar Japan, the mandatory retirement age rose significantly. Until the 1980s, the mandatory retirement age was 55 (Sasajima 2002: 88). As the minimum pensionable age for company employees rose from 55 to 60 between 1954 and 1974, the time lag between the age at which one qualified for pension benefits and the mandatory retirement age became an issue for workers and the state. The state thus encouraged employers to increase the retirement age to 60. In 1998, the government prohibited a mandatory retirement age of younger than 60. To encourage people in their early 60s to stay employed, pension reforms in 1989 and 1994 ceased to reduce social security benefits when earned income exceeded a stipulated amount set by the government (Mitani 2001: 351). In 2000, these changes were applied to those in their late 60s as an attempt to further reduce economic dependence and raise the retirement age (Sasajima 2002: 93–94). In 2000, approximately nine out of ten companies with mandatory retirement systems set 60 as the retirement age (Mitani 2001: 247). Most firms (92.2%) had mandatory retirement systems (Cabinet Office 2004). According to a 2004 survey on employment among seniors, slightly more than two-thirds of men aged from 60 to 64 and half of men aged from 65 to 69 were employed (Ministry of Health, Labour, and Welfare 2004). The government thereafter continued to encourage employers to give their older employees the option of working longer and to raise the retirement age further. As a result, persons in their 60s were increasingly incorporated into the labor force.

To provide seniors with part-time work opportunities in their communities, the state also initiated the Silver Human Resource Center project in 1974 (Weiss et al. 2005: 50). Retired persons register at these centers and perform tasks, ranging from domestic work to clerical jobs, for below-the-market rates. Since 1980, the program has been expanded further (Sasajima 2002: 346) "to build vital local communities, to reconnect the retirees to their locales and tap their expertise, and to promote health and well-being [...] by providing senior citizens with opportunities for paid work on a part-time, temporary basis in their locales" (Roberts 1996: 116). The jobs provided by Silver Human Resource Centers tend to be low-paying, manual labor jobs or skilled blue-collar jobs, which do not necessarily match the needs of retired white-collar professionals who are looking for a "cleaner," meaningful post-retirement activity.

Volunteerism is another activity that the state considers appropriate for seniors who wish to stay active in their post-retirement years. Volunteerism (*borantia*)[3] dates back to the early postwar period and is distinguished from a system of mutual support among community members, which had existed in prewar Japan (Keizai Kikakuchō 2000: 19). *Borantia*, a loanword derived from the English word "volunteer," took root in the 1960s, when volunteerism became a way for university students to achieve individual self-realization (Ri 2002: 74). In the 1970s, the government established programs to encourage volunteerism (Ri 2002: 67) through which homemakers played central roles. In the 1980s, volunteerism attracted people from a wide range of backgrounds; the number of volunteers increased steadily from 1.6 to 3.9 million people.

By the 1980s, the negative effects of the aging population on future health care and pension budgets became urgent issues in the minds of policy makers. In this context, seniors' life-long learning and civic engagement were seen to promote healthy and independent lifestyles in later years (Chen 2013: 101). Seniors were urged to make use of their abilities and participate in their communities through volunteering (Kuroiwa 2001: 230). In the 1980s, the state advanced volunteerism among seniors as part of their *ikigai seisaku*—policies aimed at providing activities that make life meaningful (*ikigai*) and thus enrich seniors' lives. In 1986, seniors' clubs (community organizations for the seniors) were encouraged to engage in volunteer activities that enhanced community welfare (Kuroiwa 2001: 232). Despite the state's efforts to promote volunteerism, it is unclear whether volunteerism was integrated into seniors' lives during the 1980s. Between 1982 and 1983, Kinoshita and Kiefer (1992: 164) studied a Japanese retirement community and found that its Christian retirees regularly volunteered at a local nursing home. In this context, volunteerism clearly had a religious significance, and volunteerism was not part of a regular routine for the general retiree population in this community.

By the 1990s, seniors' clubs were made into hubs for the promotion of a social ideal that pushed healthy seniors to support those in need (Kuroiwa 2001: 237). As part of these welfare programs, club members helped seniors with domestic chores and eldercare. In 1995, the Great Hanshin-Awaji Earthquake further popularized the notion of volunteerism, which also stimulated seniors' participation in volunteerism (Chen 2013; Thang 2006). To further promote citizens' voluntary activities, the Non-Profit Activity Promotion Law was established in 1998, which enabled voluntary groups to obtain legal status.

Volunteerism in late adulthood has been more systematically promoted in recent policies. For example, the white paper published by the Cabinet Office in 2000 states that, since 1999, the state has been supporting volunteer consultation programs to encourage newly retired salaried employees and those soon-to-be retirees to use their experience for social welfare. Community social welfare councils match prospective volunteers and local non-profit organizations to facilitate seniors' participation in civil society (Chen 2013: 104; also see Thang 2006: 241). According to a government survey conducted in 2011, approximately half of the respondents who were 60 years old and older reported that they had participated in community and voluntary activities during the previous year (Cabinet Office of Japan 2012).

In short, the state has redefined people's normative activities in late adulthood in many ways. State policies urge seniors to maintain meaningful societal engagements through second careers and volunteerism to ensure that they remain self-reliant and healthy. Such state policies aim to reduce government spending on the social security system, which is taxing the budget due to a rapidly growing older generation. Meanwhile, the media and popular culture construct seniors' post-retirement years as a potential void that retirees must manage to fill to lead meaningful lives. Some seniors become GFPS members to transform themselves in these cultural and historical contexts.

Grave-Free Promotion Society

The GFPS is a citizens' movement that promotes a new mortuary practice of *shizensō* (natural mortuary practice), or the scattering of ashes, in contemporary Japan. Founded by Yasuda Mutsuhiko, a former *Asahi Shinbun* journalist, the group attempts to fight for the freedom to choose one's mortuary practice, which Buddhist institutions and the state have long suppressed. Buddhist institutions have long exerted control over matters of death, including ritual performances and burial practices in postwar Japan (Kawano 2010; Smith 1974; Suzuki 2000). Although graves are not automatically tied to religious institutions, in many communities these institutions continue to have control over the performance of funerals and ancestor rituals to venerate the family dead. Today, family graves, in which generations of ancestors are expected to rest, are often found in cemeteries in Buddhist temple compounds, municipal cemeteries, or large-scale for-profit cemeteries that are designed for people regardless of their religious affiliations. In urban areas such as Tokyo, there are people who move away from the influences of Buddhist institutions and attempt to forgo Buddhist funerals and ancestor rites. Nonetheless, Buddhist mortuary authority has not completely waned, even in urban areas. In the public's eyes, joining and volunteering for the GFPS, a non-profit, non-religious organization run by volunteers, can be a challenge to the enduring Buddhist mortuary authority.

The mainstream mortuary option since the Shōwa period (1926–1989) has been to inter the deceased persons' cremains in a family grave (Makimura 1996: 12), which is ideally transmitted from the household head to only one child (successor) in each generation. The ideal successor to a family grave is a married son with child(ren), who lives close to his parents; he and his wife can thus easily maintain the family's grave. However, due to declining birthrates, declining marriage rates, mobility, urbanization, and changing household compositions, it is difficult for some families to secure a successor to a family grave (Kawano 2010). Some families have no sons, while others have sons who remain unmarried. Other families have married sons, but they may not live close to their parents. Ash scattering emerged during the 1990s and provides a practical option for people—many of whom are aging urbanites—who lack a successor to maintain a family grave. My research (2010) indicates that many GFPS members lack memorial assets and/or a culturally preferred successor (a married son with at least one child) to maintain a family grave. Those who do not own their memorial site are in the position to secure their own site, although a family grave plot is expensive and the investment in such a ceremonial asset may not be considered sensible if the family has no successor. Once acquired, generations of descendants are expected to maintain the grave, and a grave without a successor has to be "returned" to the plot provider without a refund.

Although many ordinary GFPS members adopted ash scattering because they lack a memorial site and/or a successor to a family grave, the environmental focus of the GFPS also plays a role in attracting supporters. Founder Yasuda Mutsuhiko, who used to work as a journalist specializing in water conservation issues, finds the development of large-scale cemeteries problematic. In his view, ash scattering with the GFPS is environmentally friendlier than the interment of cremains in a grave. To build cemeteries, trees are cut down and the ground is covered with concrete. A large amount of pesticide is used to maintain cemeteries. Mr. Yasuda originally conceived of the project of ash scattering when he was investigating developmental projects in an area that supplied drinking water to Tokyo residents. During his visit, he realized that burial was still practiced in that area. He came up with an idea of establishing a "forest of rebirth" that could be protected from development and used as a scattering site for Tokyo residents. His plan was to solve two urban problems: the high cost and shortage of graves in Tokyo and the limited availability of drinking water.

Although ash scattering is considered to provide practical solutions to a number of problems surrounding graves, the aesthetics of scattering ceremonies cannot be underestimated when evaluating the group's appeal. A number of research participants noted that rather than "going into a dark, small space" after death, they wanted to "return to nature." Founder Yasuda once discussed his experience of hosting a scattering ceremony at sea and commented that the ocean was breathtakingly beautiful, which made him want to "go into the water just like that" (*sono mama umi ni haitte ikitai*). He noted nature was "Mother" to him. His characterization of ash scattering as a journey to the sea, the mountains and the sky certainly speaks to the aesthetic appeal of ash scattering.

Members' reasons for joining the GFPS vary—many of them had a combination of reasons, including cost, the availability of successors, aesthetics and/or environmental concerns. The volunteers whom I met tended to emphasize the group's desire to challenge the control that for-profit Buddhist institutions and the death industry maintained over mortuary practices. The volunteers did not want to promote ash scattering as a second-best solution for families without successors. They considered the issues surrounding mortuary practices to be social problems that need to be addressed by citizens.

Retirement and gender among middle-class urbanites

Before diving into the narratives of GFPS volunteers, it is important to consider the ways in which seniors' engagement in post-retirement lives is patterned according to gender and how these patterns shape well-being in late adulthood.

Homemakers do not necessarily retire in their 60s when their middle-class salarymen husbands retire. Although not a paid position, in Japan, full-time homemaking is typically considered to provide a woman—in particular, a salaryman's counterpart—with an occupational status. A salaryman's post-retirement well-being, therefore, must be examined in relation to his wife's well-being.

Most GFPS volunteers whom I encountered were either middle-class retired salarymen or homemakers in their 60s or early 70s living in the Tokyo area, though a few were retired female workers. The male volunteers were formerly employed in a variety of positions: a municipal-level civil servant, a journalist at a major news company, a ship captain, a manager of a major department store, a manager at a major trading company, a banker, a bureaucrat at a national-level institution, an electronic company employee and members of executive boards. Most of the female volunteers were full-time homemakers, but they typically had experiences in volunteering via other venues before becoming GFPS volunteers. For example, one woman used to work for a suicide crisis hotline, while another woman was involved in support work for foreign students. Few female volunteers had full-time careers. This is not surprising, given the common path for this generation of middle-class women to become full-time homemakers.

Among many GFPS volunteers who were in their 60s and 70s during my fieldwork in the early 2000s, the middle-class ideal of gender complementarity defined married men as full-time workers and their wives as homemakers responsible for housework, domestic finances and the education of children. Husbands and wives, therefore, had complementary roles: men serving in the public sphere and women in the domestic. Though both roles were essential and important, a man's position as breadwinner weighed more heavily in the eyes of society. Retirement, however, reshaped the balance of power and gender division of labor in a married couple.

Due to the complementary division of labor between husbands and wives, during the major portion of their adult life, men and women examined in this chapter built their identities through different channels. As homemakers, older female informants tended to develop social networks outside the home through part-time jobs, hobby groups, volunteering or regularly traveling with other women when their children were old enough. Therefore, by the time they reached their 60s, they had already established enjoyable social networks to sustain themselves. Meanwhile, during their careers, senior male informants were socialized to construct their primary identities as loyal workers. A divorced GFPS member in her early 60s described her former husband: "He was so devoted to work, and his personal self seemed inseparably fused with the company where he worked. He had no individual self." We cannot assume that people generally experienced such a complete absorption of their personal self by the resocialization process at work (Plath 1983). Nevertheless, although contested in many ways, the idea of company-as-family encouraging the fusion of private self and self as worker did shape workers' identities in postwar Japan, not only in mainstream society, but also in smaller businesses (Kondo 1990). We also need to remember that, in the early postwar period of rapid recovery and economic prosperity, "killing oneself" for the sake of the company did not mean self-sacrifice with no gain. On the contrary, such an act was considered a sure path to personal success and eventual individual satisfaction, since, in the strong economy of early postwar Japan, employers were expected to reward long-term, loyal employees with seniority-based raises and promotion.[4] This is the context in which many GFPS volunteers were socialized in employment.

A new male retiree thus must go through a process of adjustment and resocialization, exploring a new identity different from that of loyal worker, which often poses a potential threat to marital relations. Due to the public/domestic division of labor between husband and wife, a middle-class man in his 60s or 70s in the 2000s was typically unskilled in housework before retirement. His wife tended to have complete control over the domestic sphere, in which the husband may have been treated like a helpless child (Lebra 1984: 133). This division of labor was maintained as long as the husband was serving his role as the principal earner. Once he ceased to serve that role due to retirement, however, the complementary gender division of labor was thrown out of balance. Having a retired husband at home often means additional work for the wife, such as the necessity to stay home and prepare lunches for him every day. If the wife has been unhappy with the husband's total devotion to his work and his subsequent lack of attention to the family for the many years of his employment, his retirement can signal his loss of privilege—the official reason that exempted him from domestic chores. Husbands' retirement, therefore, potentially leads to a restructuring of marital relations.

In the collection of rank-and-file retirees' essays on their post-retirement lives mentioned earlier (Iwanami Shoten 1999), several highlight marital conflict arising from husbands' retirement. One essay entitled "Wife Strikes Back, and Then," describes the explosion of a wife's anger that had accumulated over many years. On the day of his retirement, the writer comes home late at night with a bouquet of flowers from a retirement party hosted by his company. Instead of receiving words of gratitude from his wife for the years of his service, he finds a note left on the dining room table: "As of today, my life is my own. I retire from the position of a housewife" (Mochizuki 1999: 308). After reading the note, the writer discovers that his wife has not reheated the bathwater for him so it remains tepid. Stereotypically a good Japanese wife stays up late until her husband comes home, cooks him a meal, and prepares a nice hot bath so that he can relax. The cold bath thus signifies her rebellion, which did not end the wife's revenge, but was only the beginning of their long marital turmoil.

We should not assume that a husband's retirement always weakens his position at home, however. He might try to claim an authoritative position there to compensate for his loss of power and authority as a breadwinner by, for example, attempting to take over home finances or make other major domestic decisions that were previously in his wife's hands. In such a case, the wife might unwillingly face the loss of her authority and control over the domestic sphere. In either case, a husband's retirement can create a serious shift in marital power relations and division of labor.

Studies of retired couples in North America report similar problems of retired husbands "getting in the way" at home (e.g., Myers and Booth 1996). Yet, unlike North America, in Japan a married couple's spending time together is not as important a part of marital relations, and marital strain is much more publicly tied to husbands' retirement in the popular consciousness. A "wet leaf" (*nure ochiba*), for example, is a rhetoric that became popularized in the media to refer to a retired husband at home. Like a wet leaf, he sticks to his wife, even though his wife tries to shake him off. Symbolizing lack of agency, independence and direction, the wet leaf conveys the purposelessness and uselessness of a retired husband in the domestic sphere. In the media, strained domestic relations in post-retirement life are often tied to rising divorce rates in older couples.

These negative stereotypes surrounding husbands' retirement contribute to making middle-aged and older workers more conscious of the need to plan their post-retirement lives. It is considered particularly important to have "something to do" after retirement, whether a hobby or not. A 72-year-old GFPS member told me: "When I was in my fifties, a neighbor's wife complained to me that her husband stays home all day after retirement and her freedom had been severely curtailed. I had no hobby then, so I started taking photographs. I thought I needed to find something to do after retirement. I did not want to cause trouble (*meiwaku*) to my family." A lack of the husband's engagement in post-retirement years is seen to harm family relations and thus interpersonal well-being.

In order to guide recent and future retirees through the major restructuring of their lives upon retirement, a number of how-to books are available. Interestingly, these manuals do not assume that people naturally and effortlessly develop hobbies and social networks outside their workplaces. These activities and networks must be consciously cultivated over time. Men are encouraged to become independent social actors outside their workplaces, and along with traveling, learning and hobbies, volunteering is recommended as a meaningful post-retirement activity. At the GFPS, this gendered discourse of post-retirement life is evident. Male members are more likely to have been encouraged by their families to participate in volunteering activities.

From workers to volunteers

My informants typically told me that they were either asked or encouraged to volunteer at the GFPS by the group's founder, fellow members or their own families. Male informants were more likely to state that their families encouraged them to participate in volunteering. Moreover, several male volunteers I interviewed had wives who had served as volunteers at the GFPS or were active volunteers at other organizations. The following accounts of male volunteers illustrate that wives' encouragement plays a role in shaping men's post-retirement lifestyles. Furthermore, the following accounts delineate the significance of cultivating ties with non-family others in the absence of their public role in employment.

Mori-san

Mori-san, an energetic man in his late 60s, volunteers at the GFPS office twice a week and also serves as a ceremonial director at scattering ceremonies. When I asked him if he had started new activities in his post-retirement life, he told me that he had begun to cook: "I am pretty good at making eggs sunny-side-up and fried rice. I do not like to look at books when I cook. When I first stewed fish, I burnt it. When I did it the second time, to prevent the fish from burning, I placed a sheet of kelp underneath the fish. The stew produced a lot of bubbles, so I punched holes in the kelp with a driver. Then it went really well!" Mori-san likes to discover new ways of doing things on his own, not only in cooking, but also as a volunteer.

Mori-san told me that volunteering is good for his family and his health. When he first retired from his job, he stayed home for a while. He told me, "I did not have much to do, so I started drinking more. This made my family worried." Mori-san first began volunteering at the suggestion of his family when the ward office established a group for promoting health among seniors: "Older persons pay unnecessary visits to hospitals and turn them into social clubs. The health group was formed to reduce the medical expenses spent by the elderly, to give them a place to socialize, and to encourage them to exercise regularly." Participants in the health group meet once a week at the ward's community center to stretch and dance. As a volunteer, Mori-san dances with older women, and he says they are thankful for his service as a volunteer: "If older persons stay home all the time, they develop problems, such as bad knees. Then they go to hospitals and get medicine. It's good for them to get out of their homes. In fact, many people in my group improved their health."

When I asked Mori-san if he is satisfied with voluntary activities, he told me, "Volunteering gives me a chance to get out. If I stay home all the time, I spend too much time drinking. Volunteering keeps me healthier and my family happier." Mori-san's wife has been volunteering for a much longer period of time as a storyteller, routinely performing at nursing homes. Currently, both husband and wife enjoy volunteering.

Sekine-san

Sekine-san, a volunteer in his early 70s, did not experience a period of relative inactivity before beginning his volunteering career. He first became an elder-care volunteer at the suggestion of his wife, who had already been a volunteer in the program he joined. She had also been serving as a volunteer at the GFPS. Sekine-san said, with a sense of humor, "My wife told me to volunteer and see what kinds of people are loved or hated in old age." As a result of his observation, he realized that everybody hates arrogant people who dwell on past accomplishments such as their jobs and statuses, while everybody loves people with good personalities. Presumably due to his discovery, Sekine-san is modest about his past accomplishments, and I learned much later from others that he used to be an executive at a major corporation. Sekine-san told me: "I learned quite a bit from volunteering. Once I took an older woman in her wheelchair out to a department store, and I did not realize that she wanted to go to the lady's room. She was embarrassed to ask me to take her to the lady's room because I am a man. I should have asked, but it never occurred to me." Sekine-san said that volunteering gave him an opportunity to discover the dynamics of social relations in old age and learn to be attentive to other people's needs.

Sekine-san began volunteering at the GFPS because Founder Yasuda recruited him soon after he had retired. At the GFPS, he assists with bookkeeping. He also keeps track of members who have left the organization. When there is no bookkeeping work, he folds flyers and deposit slips just like other volunteers do. Sekine-san also serves as a ceremonial director at scattering ceremonies twice a month. He enjoys trekking, and his love of nature contributed to his choice of serving as a ceremonial director.

Sekine-san said that at first he considered volunteering, or doing something for others, to be a little embarrassing. Eldercare is conventionally a woman's job, and crossing the gender line might have contributed to Sekine-san's feeling. He said he had previously approached volunteering more formally by reading a book about it, adding: "I am no longer embarrassed. I now feel that I volunteer for my own benefit, not for others." Though Sekine-san was modest in evaluating his voluntary activities, he seemed to find them worthwhile. In addition to volunteering at two organizations, he pursues painting as a hobby.

As the two cases above illustrate, the transformation of former workers into volunteers may or may not occur swiftly and painlessly. The transition is more difficult when retirees experience a period of relative inactivity after retirement, in which they are "sitting around" and "having nothing to do" at home. Voluntary activities may also provide seniors with new learning experiences by developing ties with non-family others.

In both of these cases, family played a role in restructuring the retirees' identities. Sekine-san's wife strongly encouraged him to take part in eldercare so that he might discover a way of being a good person in late adulthood. He emphasized the importance of not clinging to his previous career or status in post-retirement life. In Mori-san's case, his family encouraged him to volunteer to get him out of his house and lead a healthier life. Another male volunteer was recruited as a volunteer because his wife, a former GFPS volunteer, had told Founder Yasuda that her husband had nothing to do after retirement.

A retiree, therefore, does not always find a new place in society according to his own plan or through individual will alone. The transformation of a retiree's identity—from a worker to a volunteer—is not the outcome of one isolated individual's action. Such change is likely to occur in a context of interactions among "convoys" (Plath 1980)—significant others aging along with a person in his or her life course. Similarly, well-being is not simply determined by an individual's blood pressure levels or functional limitations; it is collectively shaped among convoys. In the cases above, volunteering reportedly benefited the volunteer's physical and existential well-being, which, in turn, contributed to his family's well-being.

Rewards and frustrations

One day, a female staff member and I were talking about how salaried employees cannot say what they think to their bosses because they have to keep their jobs and seek promotions. She told me that she says whatever she wants because she is not employed (by the GFPS). She described her status as being that of a helper rather than an employee. Permanent staff members received some money, but they were not considered to be wages; they were instead similar to stipends in return for the help that they provided. Ceremonial directors (volunteers) received some compensation (5000 yen per day; US$50), plus the cost of transportation when they conducted a ceremony. Therefore, certain expenses were reimbursed, and ceremonial directors received some monetary compensation; however, this compensation resembled allowances more than salaries. Volunteers who worked in the main office were not paid, even though their tasks were, in many ways, no different from paid work in Japanese society. Nevertheless, GFPS volunteers took their assigned tasks seriously. They regularly arrived at the office on time. Occasionally volunteers noted a mistake that had gone unnoticed by staff members, thereby contributing to quality control. Ceremonial directors tested their new ideas and customized their ceremonies. If monetary compensation was not the main reward for their efforts, what made volunteering worthwhile on a personal level?

Most often volunteers reported that they were given a chance to be appreciated by others, and some even maintained that volunteering gave them the opportunity to use their skills in public contexts and to gain social recognition. One ceremonial director told me, "It makes me feel good when people for whom I conducted a scattering ceremony write to me and thank me for my effort." Many volunteers told me that such appreciation is a special moment in their volunteering experiences. Similarly, a GFPS member in her 60s told me, "I volunteer at a nursing home. I also take care of my mother at home. It makes me happy when people at the nursing home thank me—I do exactly the same thing at home, but nobody thanks me!" Appreciation from non-family others was a primary source of satisfaction for many volunteers.

Voluntary activities offered some people the chance to use their specialized skills. A computer specialist at the GFPS, who meticulously maintained the society's home page, was proud of his contribution. The ability to make and maintain a home page was a much needed but rare skill among GFPS volunteers.

Volunteering, therefore, can give people an opportunity to win personal recognition and gratitude.

For some volunteers, GFPS involvement provided them with a social identity. A member of the executive board told me that he was pleased to be serving on the board: "When the GFPS was established, people knew nothing about us. Today, the organization is recognized by many people." Therefore, this informant enjoyed the social recognition given to the organization and to him as a board member.

Because GFPS volunteers were not employees—they were instead supporters of a citizens' movement—they did not like to be ordered around (*meirei sareru*). Ordering someone to do something also went against the spirit of egalitarianism that was valued in day-to-day interactions. Rather than being given orders, volunteers expected others to ask them to help. On one occasion, a ceremonial director said, "I like the name of our organization; it embodies what we do. I will quit if the GFPS becomes an organization that simply takes care of scattering ceremonies. I am here to help because of our ideology—the freedom to choose mortuary practices." To appreciate the importance of this statement, it is necessary to note that ash scattering was widely believed to be illegal before the establishment of the GFPS in 1991. After a public announcement was made regarding the group's first scattering ceremony, the Ministry of Health and Welfare acknowledged that it did not break the national law regarding cemeteries and burial, as ash scattering was not anticipated under that law and thus fell beyond its scope (Yasuda 2010: 13–14). From the perspective of the GFPS and its core members, their social movement thus provided a significant step toward promoting the plurality of mortuary practices in post-industrial Japan. Despite their breakthrough, however, the interment of cremains in family graves remains the norm in the early 21st century, and GFPS volunteers still felt that there was a strong need to further develop their movement. Outsiders, however, often failed to understand such attitudes among volunteers. Volunteers were often frustrated when callers treated them as salespeople, as though they were doing their jobs for money. One day, a caller inquired into the GFPS's activities and asked how much it cost to have a scattering ceremony. The volunteer who received the call did not quote a price, saying that it depended on the kind of ceremony, which upset the caller. He yelled at the volunteer and asked why she did not know the price of the ceremony she was selling. The volunteer was quite distressed. Outsiders' lack of understanding sometimes made volunteers feel undervalued.

Nevertheless, negative experiences with outsiders did not necessarily cancel the positive effects of receiving appreciation from non-family others, given that none of the volunteers seemed to quit due to negative experiences with outsiders. During the two-year period of my research, one volunteer stopped coming to the group's activities and events; in another volunteer's words, this person did not feel valued by the group. This suggests the need to evaluate volunteering experiences and post-retirement well-being by considering seniors' interactions with both insiders and outsiders.

Discussion

The well-being of older volunteers must be examined by considering social and cultural contexts in which seniors choose to volunteer. The cultural scripts for volunteers, which are gendered, shape the processes through which individuals become volunteers. In Japan's post-industrial society, policy makers and popular culture construct post-retirement years as a potential void to be filled. In particular, retired salarymen are urged to transform themselves into new retirees by consciously adopting meaningful activities. In some cases, the making of a new volunteer involves the process of unmaking a salaryman, which is considered to be an important transition that affects post-retirement well-being. New volunteers go through a period of readjustment, while interacting with their peers who have already abandoned their salaryman identity. Rather than focusing on role occupancy alone, this study provides insight into the complex process by which older individuals come to occupy the volunteer role. In some cases, the adoption of the volunteer role involves the encouragement of family members, especially wives. This point is worth emphasizing, as the involvement of family members has received limited attention in the literature on older volunteers' well-being.

In her ethnographic study of community volunteers in Japan, anthropologist Lynn Nakano provides reasons for volunteering among retired men; volunteering not only helps "solve the problem of the aging of society" in Japan and "solve the problem of [not having] *ikigai* [what makes life worth living]," but it also allows retirees to do their "part for society" and earn "the right to receive [elder]care" in the future (2005: 58). Similarly, the senior volunteers examined in Thang's study (2006: 241) emphasized the importance of self-sacrifice—serving others and giving back to society. Similar to my informants, these participants emphasized the sense of fulfillment that comes from the social significance of their work as volunteers. Furthermore, Nakano described the transformation of a male worker into a volunteer, which is somewhat similar to the cases discussed in this study. This participant used to do blue-collar shop work and became an unpaid eldercare assistant/volunteer in later life. In adopting a new caregiver role, he reconstructed his masculine identity, as eldercare work is stereotypically a woman's job. Nakano's informant stressed the social significance of this work, and he chose to perform his work in a public place—an eldercare center (Nakano 2005: 57; also see Thang 2006: 236). By stressing the public significance of his work, the informant thus separated it from the domestic caregiving associated with women. The male volunteers examined in this study, however, did not need to make sense of their performance of "feminine" tasks, as their work at the GFPS was not clearly classified as women's work.

By exploring the subjective experiences of volunteering in detail, this study provides insight into the types and quality of rewards gained through volunteering, rather than simply assessing its investment-reward balance. Although non-family outsiders' appreciation plays a significant role in shaping the sense of fulfillment among senior volunteers, peer volunteers' recognition may also play an unexpectedly important role in defining volunteers' well-being. However, the issue of peer appreciation was not fully explored in this study. This issue obviously requires further research.

Conclusions: Well-being in post-retirement life

Volunteering gives retirees a way of being appreciated by others in a new social context, which, in turn, provides them with a productive way of coping with the loss of employee status and discovering a new post-retirement existence in the public sphere. My informants did emphasize some key Japanese values—productivity, cultivating maturity, reciprocity, and mutual aid—in discussing their volunteering experiences. Getting out of the house and doing something useful in the community were considered valuable. By volunteering and helping others, one may become more sensitive to other people's needs. Volunteering provides an opportunity to give but also an opportunity to learn from non-family others and to gain a sense of value through having interactions with them. Volunteers feel that they receive something in return from those whom they help. In the narratives of senior volunteers examined in this chapter, we find that the ideals of interdependence and reciprocity are often emphasized in different facets of life in Japan. Older volunteers' well-being, therefore, is in part generated from their engagements with and cultivation of ties with non-family others, which, in turn, are thought to positively benefit volunteers' physical well-being and their interpersonal well-being in a family context.

To the casual observer, the retirees examined in this chapter may seem to align themselves with the state's program of producing more independent, healthier and more socially engaged seniors to reduce the burden on public spending on eldercare. The state's efforts constitute part of the fourth dimension of well-being discussed by Mathews and Izquierdo, which focuses on the ways in which national institutions and global forces shape individual conceptions and experiences of well-being (2009: 261). Just as the raised mandatory retirement age is expected to reduce the older populations' economic dependence on a shrinking younger population, so too can volunteerism be a way of directing seniors' labors for the state's benefit. However, the senior volunteers examined here are far from being docile reproducers of the well-being idealized by the state. As observed, by advocating their freedom to choose an end-of-life ceremony and promoting a new memorial form of scattering that radically departs from the conventional interment of cremains in family graves, GFPS volunteers promote a social change that the state had neither imagined nor planned to initiate (Kawano 2010). These seniors do not volunteer to simply fill their time or to obtain extra money; they help create a new ideal in society—the freedom to choose mortuary practices. This engagement, which contests state-sanctioned mortuary conventions, has certainly contributed to the volunteers' senses of existential well-being and fulfillment in late adulthood.

Acknowledgments

The Social Science Research Council—Japan Society for the Promotion of Science fellowship (2002–2004) generously funded the fieldwork for this project. I would like to thank Glenda Roberts of Waseda University for her kindness and generosity during my tenure of the fellowship, as well as the staff at the Asia-Pacific Studies Department. I would like to express my deep gratitude to Mr. Mutsuhiko Yasuda of the Grave-Free Promotion Society (GFPS), volunteers at the GFPS Tokyo Office and other GFPS members who participated in this study.

Notes

1 All the data for this study come from my extended fieldwork conducted in Japan between 2002 and 2004. Recently, the founder Yasuda Mutsuhiko stepped down, and the group changed its English name to Japan Sōsō Society. However, I have kept the original English group name in this chapter, as it was used during my term of research, and it succinctly refers to the group's ideal. My data do not cover the period of the recent transition to new leadership.
2 *Teinen* refers to the year in which one stops working and leaves one's primary job. However, people are commonly given second jobs in the same workplace or a subsidiary. Thus, *teinen* does not imply a complete withdrawal from the labor force. This issue will be discussed in detail later.
3 There is a terminological issue here. Common community activities in Japan can be considered voluntary activities (see Nakano 2005), and leadership roles are often assigned to seniors. Neighborhood associations in Japan organize residents to participate in cleaning, patrolling, and planning of local festivals, for example. However, when my informants discussed their prior experiences as volunteers (*borantia*), they did not always include these activities.
4 The prolonged recession since the 1990s led to major restructuring, layoffs, and promotion by merit rather than seniority. Compared with the situation of my senior informants, workers in contemporary Japan are much more skeptical as to whether their total devotion to their companies will in fact lead to their promotion and stable lifelong careers.

References

Cabinet Office of Japan. 2004. *Kōrei shakai hakusho* [White paper on the aged society]. http://www8.cao.go.jp/kourei/whitepaper/w-2004/zenbun/html/G2311100.html. Retrieved March 1, 2015.
Cabinet Office of Japan. 2012. *Kōrei shakai hakusho* [White paper on the aged society]. http://www8.cao.go.jp/kourei/whitepaper/w-2012/zenbun/pdf/1s4s_2.pdf. Retrieved April 24, 2015.
Campbell, John. 1992. *How Policies Change: The Japanese Government and the Aging Society.* Princeton, NJ: Princeton University Press.
Chen, Li-Mei. 2013. "Senior Volunteerism in Japan: A Policy Perspective." *Aging International* 38:97–107.
Fischer, Lucy, and Kay Schaffer. 1993. *Older Volunteers.* Newbury Park, CA: Sage.
Goffman, Erving. 1961. *Encounters: Two Studies in the Sociology of Interaction.* Oxford, UK: Bobbs-Merrill.

Guillemard, Anne-Marie, and Martin Rein. 1993. "Comparative Patterns of Retirement: Recent Trends in Developed Societies." *Annual Review of Sociology* 19:469–503.

Harris, Alex H., and Carl E. Thoresen. 2005. "Volunteering Is Associated with Delayed Mortality in Older People: Analysis of the Longitudinal Study of Aging." *Journal of Health Psychology* 10:739–752.

Iwanami Shoten. 1999. *Teinengo* [Post-retirement], edited by Iwanami Shoten. Tokyo: Iwanami Shoten.

Kahn, William. 1990. "Psychological Conditions of Personal Engagement and Disengagement at Work." *Academy of Management Journal 33*:692–724.

Kawano, Satsuki. 2010. *Nature's Embrace: Japan's Aging Urbanites and New Death Rites*. Honolulu: University of Hawai'i Press.

Keizai Kikakuchō, Kokumin Seikatsukyoku 2000. *Kokumin seikatsu hakusho: Yōshi* [Annual report on the people's life: A summary]. Tokyo: Keizai Kikakuchō.

Kinoshita, Yasuhito, and Christie W. Kiefer. 1992. *Refuge of the Honored: Social Organization in a Japanese Retirement Community*. Berkeley: University of California Press.

Kondo, Dorinne K. 1990. *Crafting Selves*. Chicago: University of Chicago Press.

Kuroiwa, Ryōko. 2001. "Ikigai seisaku no tenkai katei" [Changes in quality of life politics]. pp. 215–241 in *Ikigai no shakaigaku*, edited by Y. Takahashi and S. Wada. Tokyo: Kōbundō.

Lebra, Takie Sugiyama. 1984. *Japanese Women: Constraint and Fulfillment*. Honolulu: University of Hawai'i Press.

Makimura, Hisako. 1996. *Ohaka to kazoku* [Grave and the family]. Tokyo: Toki Shobō.

Mathews, Gordon, and Carolina Izquierdo. 2009. *Pursuits of Happiness: Well-being in Anthropological Perspective*. New York and Oxford: Berghahn Books.

Matz-Costa, Christine et al. 2012. "Differential Impact of Multiple Levels of Productive Activity Engagement on Psychological Well-Being in Middle and Later Life." *The Gerontologist* 54/2:277–289.

McMunn, Anne et al. 2009. "Participation in Socially Productive Activities, Reciprocity and Wellbeing in Later Life: Baseline Results in England." *Ageing & Society* 29:762–782.

Ministry of Health, Labour, and Welfare. 2004. *Kōreisha shūgyō jittai chōsa* [Survey on employment among older persons]. http://www.mhlw.go.jp/toukei/itiran/roudou/kokyou/keitai/04/kekka-k1.html). Retrieved March 1, 2015.

Mitani, Naoki. 2001. "Kōreisha koyō seisaku to rōdō juyō" [Employment policies for the aged and labor demand]. pp. 339–377 in *Koyō seisaku no keizai bunseki*, edited by T. Inoki and F. Ōtake. Tokyo: Tokyo Daigaku Shuppankai.

Mochizuki, Yoshirō. 1999. *Tsuma no gyakushū, soshite* [Wife strikes back, and then]. pp. 308–313 in *Teinengo*, edited by Iwanami Shoten. Tokyo: Iwanami Shoten.

Moen, Phyllis, Donna Dempster-McClain and Robin Williams. 1992. "Successful Aging: A Life Course Perspective on Women's Multiple Roles and Health." *American Journal of Sociology* 97:1612–1638.

Myers, Scott M., and Alan Booth. 1996. "Men's Retirement and Marital Quality." *Journal of Family Issues* 17:336–358.

Nakano, Lynne. 2005. *Community Volunteers in Japan: Everyday Stories of Social Change*. London and New York: RoutledgeCurzon.

Narushima, Miya. 2005. "'Payback Time': Community Volunteering among Older Adults as a Transformative Mechanism." *Ageing & Society* 25/4:567–584.

Okun, Morris A. 1994. "The Relation between Motives for Organizational Volunteering and Frequency of Volunteering by Elders." *Journal of Applied Gerontology* 13/2:115–126.

Plath, David W. 1980. *Long Engagements: Maturity in Modern Japan*. Stanford, CA: Stanford University Press.
Plath, David W. 1983. "Introduction: Life Is Just a Job Résumé?" pp. 1–13 in *Work and Lifecourse in Japan*, edited by D. W. Plath. Albany: State University of New York Press.
Ri, Kenen. 2002. *Borantarī katsudō no seiritsu to tenkai* [Establishment and development of volunteering]. Kyoto: Minerva Shobō.
Roberts, Glenda S. 1996. "Between Policy and Practice: Japan's Silver Human Resource Centers as Viewed from the Inside." *Journal of Aging & Social Policy* 8/2-3:115–133.
Rogers, Richard. 1996. "The Effects of Family Composition, Health, and Social Support Linkages on Mortality." *Journal of Health and Social Behavior* 37:326–338.
Sakamoto, Fujiyoshi. 1977. *Nihon koyōshi* [Japan's history of employment]. Vol. 2. Tokyo: Chūō Keizaisha.
Sasajima, Yoshio. 2002. *Gendai no rōdō mondai* [Contemporary labor issues]. Tokyo: Chūō Keizai Sha.
Smith, Robert J. 1974. *Ancestor Worship in Contemporary Japan*. Stanford, CA: Stanford University Press.
Stephan, Paula E. 1991. "Relationships among Market Work, Work Aspiration and Volunteering: The Case of Retired Women." *Nonprofit Volunteer Sector Quarterly* 20:225–236.
Suzuki, Hikaru. 2000. *The Price of Death*. Stanford, CA: Stanford University Press.
Thang, Leng Leng. 2006. "Defining a Second Career: Volunteering among Seniors in Japan." pp. 227–263 in *Perspectives on Work, Employment and Society in Japan*, edited by P. Matanle and W. Lunsing. Basingstoke: Palgrave Macmillan.
von Bonsdorff, Mikaela, and Taina Rantanen. 2011. "Benefits of Formal Voluntary Work among Older People." *Aging Clinical and Experimental Research* 23/3:162–169.
Weiss, Robert S. et al. 2005. "Japan's Silver Human Resource Centers and Participant Well-being." *Journal of Cross-Cultural Gerontology* 20:47–66.
Wheeler, Judith, Kevin Gorey and Bernhard Greenblatt. 1998. "The Beneficial Effects of Volunteering for Older Adults and the People They Serve." *International Journal of Aging & Human Diversity* 47:69–80.
Wilson, John. 2000. "Volunteering." *Annual Review of Sociology* 26:215–240.
Yasuda, Mutsuhiko. 2010. *Haka wa kokoro no naka ni: Nihonhatsu no shizensō to shimin undō*. [Build a grave in your heart: Japan's first "natural mortuary ceremony" and a citizens' movement]. Tokyo: Gaifūsha.

12

WELL-BEING AND DECISION-MAKING TOWARDS THE END OF LIFE

Living Wills in Japan

Celia Spoden

In this chapter, I explore how people who have signed a Living Will conceptualize their understanding of a meaningful life, under which circumstances death becomes more desirable than life and how these notions are connected to the concepts of happiness and well-being. Therefore, rather than focusing on the decision-making process in end-of-life situations, I concentrate on the decisions people make in advance, in the event that they might no longer be able to make their own decisions on medical treatments.

Drawing on the life stories of middle-aged and elderly Japanese who have written Living Wills, I analyze my interviewees' perceptions using Mathews and Izquierdo's four dimensions of well-being (2009b: 261): physical, interpersonal, existential and institutional. Starting with an introduction to the institutional dimension, I will provide a brief overview of changes that have been made to medical practices and decision-making processes applied in end-of-life situations and review discussions of Living Wills in Japan. I will then turn to my empirical data and consider how signing a Living Will is related to the critical awareness of life-sustaining treatments, considering the physical, interpersonal and existential dimensions of well-being.

Overall, my interviewees' accounts are not directly related to well-being during their final days. Instead, they are concerned about potential negative conditions that could arise at the end of their lives and about situations they want to avoid. The Living Will, as I will show, is a strategy available to people in Japanese society that allows them to maintain agency in end-of-life situations, to avoid situations associated with the irreversible loss of well-being and happiness and prevent themselves from becoming a burden to relatives and negatively affecting the latter's well-being and happiness.

The institutional dimension: How death became a matter of individual decision-making

At an institutional level, medical practices and interactions with terminally ill patients have undergone enormous changes in Japan since the second half of the 20th century. As a result, the process of dying is now perceived as belonging to the realm of self-determinant decision-making, although it was not considered a matter of personal choice until recently.

With improvements in medicine, healthcare and hygiene, the main causes of death have now become cancer and cerebrovascular diseases. As Long and Long (1982) have shown in their study of cancer diagnoses in Japanese hospitals, in the 1970s, non-disclosure of a terminal cancer diagnosis was understood to be in a patient's best interests. This assumption was accompanied by a medical practice that advocated using all means available to prolong a patient's life as long as possible. Disclosing the diagnosis, or "truth-telling," was believed to cause harm to the patient, leading him or her to lose hope, stop fighting and give up on life. A cancer diagnosis was thus widely perceived as equivalent to a "death-sentence" (Long and Long 1982: 2101; Ohnuki-Tierney 1984: 61).

In order to die a "good death," all parties involved were expected to do everything possible to keep the patient alive, and the patient was not to accept death until the very end. Lacking awareness of his or her condition, the dying person was therefore unable to make decisions about his or her final days. Furthermore, terminally ill patients were not seen as being capable of making decisions. In general, physicians would obtain the approval of the patient's family before making treatment decisions, but in cases where there was no mutual agreement, the decision-making authority lay with the physician.

Only a decade earlier, Glaser and Strauss (1965) reported similar findings in American hospitals with regard to the "awareness context" of dying patients, where it was also common for patients to be unaware of their impending death. Long and Long were well aware of the rapid changes in truth-telling that medical practice had undergone in the United States and presumed that with advances in medical technologies, and possibilities to cure some cancers, attitudes and behavioral patterns would also change in Japan in the coming years. At the time their study was published, the first critical voices were questioning whether the practice of fighting death with every means available was really in the best interest of the patient.

Although these changes did not take place as rapidly as in the United States, criticism of the medical system in Japan grew louder during the 1990s. Public surveys showed shifting evaluations of disclosure, and a growing demand to be told the truth, in order to be able to make decisions about one's final days (Kimura 1998: 188; Leflar 1996: 90). At the same time, the hospitalization of old and dying people increased and became a matter of public debate, together with the implementation of policy measures for dealing with Japan's aging society.

This critical awareness is also reflected in the still small but rising number of people who had signed a Living Will by the end of the 1980s in order to reject life-sustaining medical technologies for end-of-life situations in advance (Igata 2006: 76, 81, 86; JSDD 2012; Yomiuri Shinbun 2009: 4). Living Wills were first introduced in Japan by the Society for Euthanasia (*anrakushi kyōkai*), founded in 1976, and renamed the Japan Society for Dying with Dignity (JSDD, *nihon songenshi kyōkai*) in 1983. The JSDD considers itself the founder and main actor of the Japanese right-to-die movement. The main goals of the organization are to gain legal recognition for the right to die and to make Living Wills available throughout Japan (Igata 2006:10; JSDD 2013; Tateiwa 2005: 24).

The JSDD provides a Living Will registration system for its members. All members sign the same standardized Living Will form, which states the following three preferences: 1) the rejection of life-sustaining treatments in the event of a terminal illness; 2) the request for palliative care, even though it may shorten the life of the patient; and 3) the demand that all life-sustaining treatments be withdrawn after several months in the event of an irreversible coma (JSDD 2005: 80, 81; Masuda et al. 2003: 248). So far, however, Living Wills are not yet legally binding documents.

As Mathews and Izquierdo (2009) note with regard to a new understanding of the concept of well-being among medical professionals, the former practices of shielding patients from the truth and keeping them alive as long as possible are no longer considered appropriate. Instead, "medical professionals have increasingly come to realize that keeping people alive, in an era in which medical technology has been rapidly developing, is insufficient; rather individuals' well-being must also be closely considered" (Mathews and Izquierdo 2009a: 3). This altered perception of the appropriate way of dealing with end-of-life care and treatment is reflected in several guidelines issued by medical associations and Japan's Ministry of Health, Labour, and Welfare (MHLW) (Akabayashi 2002: 519–21; MHLW 2012: 5–6).

Nonetheless, the situation cannot be simply described as a shift from paternalism to patient autonomy. As shown by the reactions to the parliamentary debate on death-with-dignity legislation, which is still ongoing as of 2016, there are several actors arguing against the right to die. This opposition can be traced back to the founding of the right-to-die movement in 1976. Several NGOs have formed a counter-movement demanding greater recognition of the right to life and the pursuit of happiness for disabled people and chronically ill patients, as granted by the Japanese Constitution (Anrakushi songenshi hōseika o soshi suru kai 2005; Songenshi no hōseika o mitomenai shimin no kai 2012). In their opinion, there are no situations in which death should be preferred over life, if life is still possible (Tateiwa 2008: 17; Tateiwa 2005: 23).

The arguments of right-to-die opponents often seem to center around the assumption of an intrinsic value of life, whereas proponents of Living Wills see themselves as defending humanist values and promoting the human right to die with dignity. One of the strongest criticisms of right-to-die policies is that, under the guise of humanistic values, people in need of assistance or care will be subjected to social pressures to choose an early death in order to avoid becoming a burden on society (Otani 2010: 58). As the discussion about the legislation of Living Wills shows, there is an ongoing struggle regarding values and new rules for how society should deal with the chronically ill, disabled, old and dying and how appropriate it is to end a life.

This dilemma is also felt on the personal level. Since decision-making is no longer perceived as an objective medical judgment concerning the best interests of the patient, the individual must decide which treatment suits his or her personal well-being. Individual decision-making often occurs in a situation of crisis, where the person is confronted with conflicting or ambivalent thoughts and desires. Therefore, a process of self-reflection, taking into account the patient's physical state, social relationships, values and social norms, accompanies the decision-making. When people talk about their decisions, they present them as being embedded in their life stories and draw on shared socio-cultural patterns to exemplify and legitimize their choices.

Empirical data

The empirical data discussed in this paper are derived from an in-depth case study of Living Wills in Japan (Spoden 2015) conducted in August and September 2009. I used snowball sampling to identify study participants, and interviewed about 25 people, including experts and people who signed a Living Will. For the analysis, I selected five women and five men between 45 and 88 years of age. The interviews lasted between 45 and 135 minutes. In most cases, I met with the interviewee only once. The majority of my informants are members of the middle and upper-middle classes and lived in one of Japan's major cities. With two exceptions, they did not suffer from a severe illness but signed a Living Will for several reasons. All names have been made anonymous.

Of primary interest in all interviews were the interviewees' subjective views of life and death and their acceptance or rejection of life-sustaining treatment. In order to give my interviewees as much space as possible to voice their own thoughts, I used the method of narrative interviews (Schütze 1983). With the initial question, my interview partners were asked to tell their stories and describe why they had decided to sign a Living Will.

The physical dimension: Critical awareness of life-sustaining treatments

Based on their personal experiences, my interviewees had developed a critical awareness of life-sustaining treatments. For example, they had witnessed the disease progression or the dying of someone close to them, which moved them to think about their own final days. According to their narratives, writing a Living Will seemed to be a means of coping with their fears, through which they could make arrangements for situations in which they might no longer be able to voice their own wishes.

Most interviewees spoke of a specific occasion (*kikkake*) that prompted their critical awareness of life-sustaining treatments or the need to sign a Living Will. These occasions varied in degree of personal involvement, but all provoked a feeling of insecurity. My interviewees thus perceived the Living Will as providing a chance to feel secure again, as Mrs. Chibana from Tokyo, a 73-year-old widow and mother of two daughters, said: "When I received the Living Will it was like an *omamori* (talisman) for me. I have felt very secure ever since."

When my interviewees spoke about a "good death," they meant either a sudden death (*ikki ni* or *pin pin korori*) or a natural death due to old age (*rōsui*). By signing a Living Will, they wanted to avoid dying slowly in a hospital in a condition they call the "spaghetti state" (*supagetti jōtai*), referring to the tubes connected to medical devices.

Mrs. Chibana cited the example of her aunt, who fell into an irreversible coma. Her cousins did not agree about what should be done with their mother. The son wanted everything possible done to prolong her life, but the daughter wanted the machines to be turned off, to allow her mother to die. In the end, the physician decided to keep the aunt alive. He told the children that turning off the machines would be the equivalent of killing their mother. As a result of this decision, the aunt was kept alive, in an irreversible coma, for five years.

Mrs. Chibana referred to her aunt as being in the condition of a "human vegetable" (*shokubutsu jōtai*), thereby equating life in a persistent vegetative state with the biological status of a plant. From her point of view, such a life is no longer a human life and is thus no longer desirable. She remembered how she tried to imagine what she would want for herself if she were in the same situation as her aunt. After these reflections, she signed a Living Will, documenting her own wish to not be kept alive if in such a physical state.

Mrs. Ono, an 88-year-old widow, provided a similar account. She lives on the same estate as her son and his wife in a quiet neighborhood in Tokyo and wishes to die a natural death. She refers to life-sustaining treatments such as artificial nutrition and respiration as new technologies that were not available in her younger days and differentiates between situations in which these measures save lives and others in which the same devices merely prolong the process of dying. In her opinion, life prolongation is not desirable in a condition close to death, because it means trouble and sorrow for the family. Her statement emphasizes the artificial character of technological devices. This often-used dichotomy of artificial versus natural equates the artificial with inhumane practices that cause suffering for the patient and the family.

Mrs. Chibana and Mrs. Ono both want to avoid the irreversible loss of consciousness or a slow process of dying in a hospital. Mr. Kondo, a childless English high school teacher, named Alzheimer's disease as his biggest fear. However, there are also other physical states in which the cognitive capabilities are not affected, yet still they are subject to the perception that death is preferable to life. Mr. Kondo referred to a relative who is completely paralyzed, lives on an artificial respirator, and communicates with his eyes and a syllable-board. Mr. Kondo stated that his uncle is kept alive even though he cannot participate in life anymore, and his existence causes trouble for other people. He differentiated between "being alive" (*ikite iru*), and "being kept alive" (*ikasarete iru*). In his opinion, there is no justification for ending someone's life if that person is able to live, but he draws a line at the point in time when the physical condition reaches a point at which there is no life force left (*jibun de ikite iru chikara*) and the person cannot stay alive without the assistance of medical technology. What keeps his uncle alive is an artificial respirator, a device Mr. Kondo said he would oppose in the first place. If someone is on such a machine and conscious, he explained, then there is no alternative but to continue living. However, before reaching this juncture, there is a point in the course of the disease where one can decide for or against the machine, and he would decide against it.

Mrs. Minami, another interviewee, was diagnosed at the age of 50 with the same disease that Mr. Kondo's uncle has: amyotrophic lateral sclerosis (ALS), an incurable degenerative motor neuron disease. As the motor neurons decline, the patients increasingly suffer from paralysis and experience difficulties swallowing, speaking and breathing. On average, three to five years after the onset of symptoms, the respiratory capacities are affected, and patients must decide whether they want to carry on living on an artificial respirator or die from respiratory insufficiency (Borasio, Gelinas and Yanagisawa 1998: S7; Smyth et al. 1997: S93).

At the time of the interview, Mrs. Minami was 53 years old, but she explained that in order to cope with the diagnosis, she had decided to live every remaining year of her life as if it were ten years:

> It is three years ago that I was told about my diagnosis. Since I was 50 at that time, I decided to make this year to be my 50s decade, the following year to be my 60s, and the following my 70s. I thought, if I lived the amount of ten years in one year, wouldn't that be great?

Mrs. Minami decided against artificial respiration and added personal notes concerning her disease to a copy of her Living Will. She referred to a prominent ALS-patient and opponent of the death-with-dignity movement, Hashimoto Misao, who has lived with an artificial respirator for over 20 years and, using her lifestyle to exemplify that an active and meaningful life is possible in a state of almost complete paralysis (Yamazaki 2006), encourages other patients to decide in favor of life and the machine. Hashimoto has compared the artificial respirator to a pair of glasses, though she needs the device to stay alive (Tokyo Shinbun 2009). She argues that when eyesight diminishes, one uses glasses to support this weakened bodily function, and the ventilator provides the same functionality for weakened respiration. Mrs. Minami rejects this metaphor, however. In her opinion, humans breathe in and out without a machine, and when this is no longer possible, the course of the disease will have reached the point where she wants to die.

As these examples show, physical condition and age are not considered in "objective" terms. Rather, the interviewees use common metaphors to interpret physical conditions. These interpretations of the physical are subject to complex social negotiations. A closer look reveals that "nature's way" is only desired in situations that are perceived as hopeless or close to death, such as those involving irreversible loss of consciousness and subjectivity or the loss of physical capabilities needed for social interactions. "Nature's way" is equated with the withholding of treatment and appears to be a strategic argument to legitimize the preference for death by defining a point in time when inaction seems justifiable.

The interpersonal dimension: Not being a burden or living an independent life

Physical or medical conditions often serve as triggers for the consideration of a Living Will. When interviewees speak about the intended impact of their Living Wills, it becomes clear that making arrangements for one's final days is of utmost importance on an interpersonal level. Interpretations of Living Wills vary: people may use them as a tool to avoid becoming a burden on others, to guide the family in decision making, to anticipate and avoid deathbed conflicts between relatives and physicians or to prohibit family members or physicians from trying to override the patient's personal wishes.[1]

Not becoming a burden (*meiwaku o kakenai*) is a central issue. At 88, Mrs. Ono wants to be as self-reliant as possible, even though she cannot avoid being a burden to her family at times, due to her age and physical condition. To avoid becoming a permanent burden, in her opinion, it is crucial to make up her mind about her last days and to arrange everything, in order to cause as little trouble and sorrow for her family as possible.

The need to think about her own life and make plans for herself is something she first realized in old age. She compared her own generation to the younger ones and explains that women of her age were raised to become good mothers and wives who think about the family first and define their own happiness as secondary to the happiness of their children:

> For people nowadays their own concerns are most important, and thus they also [think] about their final days. In my day, we didn't think about ourselves, almost like idiots (*baka mitai ni*). [...] When I talk to my old friends from school, we often say that in our generation we did not think about our own things. That's what we say. Actually the happiness (*shiawase*) of our children—I don't know if it really was the happiness of our children—but that they will become happy [was most important for us]. We ourselves didn't matter. That's how we thought. Being a parent meant this. And therefore we didn't think about our future. But this is no longer possible. I think it was really a mistake. In the end, if you don't think about it, in the end you will become a burden.

Mrs. Ono drafted a Living Will when she turned 70. In her family, she explained, almost everyone died around the age of 60, and she never expected to live much longer. When she reached 70, she thought that this age was the maximum length of time she would live and that it was enough. Her age became an occasion for her to talk to her family to explain her thoughts about life-sustaining treatments and to express her wish to die naturally.

According to Susan O. Long, in Japan death is accepted and seen as a sad but unavoidable natural fact when it occurs in old age (Long 2002: 311). Using this rationale, it might not be particularly surprising that an 88-year-old woman who has outlived her husband, one of her sons, and many friends, would say she thinks she has already lived long enough. However, much younger 51-year-old Mr. Kondo provides similar thoughts:

> I am not really attached to the idea of living a long life. I don't want to live a long life. It's not such a good thing. [...] I don't want to live long. I only think that I should live as long as I still have responsibilities. Therefore I want to live. Now I am 51 years old. When I was younger, I always thought that I would die around 50. [...] I have already lived a longer life than I ever expected.

Mr. Kondo did not explain why he never expected to grow older than 50, but he did explain what he meant by living as long as he has responsibilities: he does not want to die before retirement. As a high school teacher, more than a hundred people, including his colleagues, students and their families, would have to attend his funeral if he died mid-career. Mr. Kondo is strongly motivated to lead a self-reliant life, to take responsibility for his own affairs and to make his own decisions until the very end, as he has always done throughout the course of his life. For this reason, Mr. Kondo made a note in his handwritten Living Will that he wants a secret funeral (*missō*) to be attended only by his closest relatives and friends. This is consistent with Long's (2004) explanation that the interpretation of death at old age as a sad but unavoidable event is not related to a certain age limit. Rather, the evaluations are based on the duties and responsibilities one has according to his or her social roles (Long 2004: 922).

Mr. Kondo has no children. He lives with his wife, whom he describes as sharing his values and lifestyle. On the other hand, he describes his mother and brother as "conservative" and explains that they share neither his independent lifestyle nor his decision to reject life-sustaining treatment:

> We do not live together, but for example my older brother and my mother, who is still alive, my relatives, they have a completely different way of thinking. They are more conservative; they have an old way of thinking. Therefore, if something happened to me, my wife and my relatives wouldn't agree [about the treatment]. That is unfavorable (*mazui*).

In this context, his Living Will is intended to prevent a situation in which his family could override his wishes. His wife shares his values, and the Living Will is intended to support her as his surrogate and to avoid possible future conflicts between her and his relatives.

The interviewees draw on their life stories in order to connect their decisions to earlier stages of their lives and to construct a coherent and consistent biography. This can also be seen in the case of Mrs. Minami, who recounted how she had always lived an independent life. She signed her Living Will when she was healthy, years before she was diagnosed with ALS. The event that prompted her to do so was her mother's stroke. At the time, Mrs. Minami ceased working in her husband's restaurant in order to take care of her mother. She described her mother's lifestyle before the stroke as self-reliant. Her mother used to run her own small shop, and Mrs. Minami remembered how difficult it was for her to watch her mother being dependent on support for her basic physical needs. She promised her mother to act as her surrogate and communicate her wish not to undergo life-prolonging measures if she suffered another stroke. As a result of the conflicts her mother's wishes caused between relatives, herself and the physicians, she herself decided to sign a Living Will.

Mrs. Minami described her ability to take care of other people, exemplified by her decision to work as a nurse before she married her husband, and as a care-manager after her mother's death. She used her caregiving experiences to explain that, in her opinion, life alone does not mean happiness:

> When I saw the state of my mother, and also later the situation of patients and their families through my work as a care helper and care manager, I wondered whether just being alive really means happiness (*shiawase*)? If I had to say what I want for myself, I would not choose it.

A selfish person (*wagamama*) like herself, she continued, cannot bear the thought of being reliant on the help of other people. Ever since she was diagnosed with ALS, she has used the time to relinquish her social roles and withdraw from social life by saying goodbye and thanking others for their support. This was part of her strategy to prepare herself for death:

> I thought about what I could do and that I have to take care of my things, to write my last will, to arrange everything, throw away things and give away my belongings, for example my jewelry. [...] I thought about what I should do with my kimonos, wear them myself or give them away? I thought I would feel better if I gave them away. So I altered my kimonos. I did this in a dream-like condition. During this time my pain was eased. All in all I had 100 pieces. It took me one year to alter half of them. About 50 pieces remained, but the other half I gave away to relatives, siblings, friends and people who have done me a favor. I fitted the kimonos to these people and altered them. This was what I was able to do. Now I cannot use my hands anymore.

She often referred to the Buddhist phrase *shūchaku ga nai*, saying that she no longer feels attached to life. Regarding family relationships, she explained that her parents are dead, she has no children and her husband is able to care for himself. She further described her relationship with her husband as an equal partnership; he encourages her to make her own decisions, and, in his words, each partner must go his or her own way (*kimi ni wa kimi no michi ga atte, boku ni wa boku no michi ga aru*).

In addition to their interpretations of physical conditions and age, the interviewees explained how social interactions affected their decision to sign a Living Will. They wanted to avoid becoming a burden and living in circumstances that cause suffering to others. At the same time, the Living Will also appears to serve as a tool for preventing conflict at the deathbed and for taking precautions in the event their families might someday become surrogates in the final decision-making process. Although they do not speak about well-being per se, it can be reasonably assumed that they saw the decision to sign a Living Will as necessary to prevent entering a state of non-well-being—both for the person who signed the Living Will and for the family.

The existential dimension: *Jibunrashisa*, or "in accordance with myself"

Personal values, interpretations of a "good death," and perceptions of a meaningful life underlie my interviewees' thoughts concerning the physical and interpersonal dimensions. Ultimately, these thoughts form the existential dimension. Based on their experiences, and in a manner consistent with their lifestyles, my interview partners presented their understanding of various situations in which life is no longer desirable. They want to maintain their self-reliance until the very end and die according to their own wishes. In this section, I will explore the importance of the concept of dying one's own death (*jibunrashii shi*).

Mrs. Kondo, a 45-year-old nurse who works in a hospice, stressed the importance of dying with dignity:

> Dying with dignity (*songenshi*) is exceptionally highly ranked for me. But I know that there are also people who do not think so. I don't know why, but there are women who married and were only housewives during their lives. They ask their husbands about everything, and their husbands have the right to decide. I learned through my work at palliative care and in the hospice that there are people who cannot decide their own things for themselves.

Concerning her own way of life, Mrs. Kondo pointed out that deciding for herself is an ability she learned in childhood. It continues to lead her through life, especially in situations of life crises. To overcome a difficult situation, and to create a meaningful life, she always asks herself, "What do I want to do?" or "What should I do?" This is the lifestyle she wants to maintain until she dies, she said. When asked what dying with dignity means to her, she answered:

> I think it means dying in accordance with oneself (*jibunrashiku*). If there is someone who supports this sense of being oneself [laughs] then it isn't necessary to become a member of this organization [JSDD]. If one meets such a person who supports oneself then it is good like this. But if this is not the case, then it is better to decide one's own things for oneself and become a member of this organization.

Mrs. Kondo's explanation shows how closely "dying with dignity" is associated with the JSDD and Living Wills.[2] She explained dying with dignity as a death that unfolds in accordance with that person's personality (*jibunrashii shi*). To die one's own death means to respect and support that person's personality throughout the process of dying. The difficulty lies in finding out which decision fits the notion of oneself.

Compared to my other interviewees, Mr. Jōmon is an exception as he has no Living Will. He is a 48-year-old father of two sons, and his situation is similar to that of Mrs. Minami: he was diagnosed with ALS and must decide whether he wants to be put on an artificial respirator in the near future in order to continue living. Although he said he thinks that advance directives such as Living Wills can be important instruments for communicating a patient's wishes, he does not have one because he cannot decide whether or not he wants to be put on a respirator.

He described the time after his diagnosis as a period during which his past, present and future condensed (*gyōshuku sareta*) and that he had to find new meaning in his life in order to cope with the diagnosis. He reflected on what he would like to think about at the moment of his death and realized that he would like to be told by his children and wife that he had been a good father and husband. While thinking about the best death possible, he suddenly began to consider how he could lead a good life:

> When I thought about how I could attain this, I realized that if I wanted to be the best father possible until this very last moment, I have to be a good father while I am alive. And if I really wanted to be told by my wife at the last moment that I was a good husband, I would have to be a good husband right now, from every moment to the next. And as I thought with all my effort about dying and how I could die the best death possible, I thought about how I should live my life.

According to Mr. Jōmon, he has to make the decision by himself, but his decision cannot be solely based on his own wishes. If he chooses the respirator, his family will have to care for him for a long time, meaning that the decision also affects their lives. Therefore, a truly good decision must be good for him *and* for his family. He said that he has not yet reached a conclusion that is consistent with his way of life. He formulated questions such as, "What is a lifestyle consistent to myself (*bokurashii ikikata*)?" and "Which lifestyle is consistent with Mr. Jōmon's lifestyle (*Jōmon-san rashii*), one on a machine or that of a natural death?" And on a more abstract level, he asks, "Which decision is really me (*jibunrashisa wa dochi darō*)?"

At the time of the interview, Mr. Jōmon portrayed his life as happy (*shiawase*). In comparison to other ALS patients, the course of his disease is very slow, giving him time to cry and adjust to the gradual loss of his physical abilities to the disease. He has found a job as an office assistant in a small clinic, where special work arrangements have been provided to support his physical condition. Being employed is important to him, as he feels connected with society through his work, and it allows him to contribute to his children's education. If he could, he would like to live long enough to see his sons become fathers and to take care of his wife as long as she lives.

In contrast to the other interviewees, Mr. Jōmon did not voice a fear of being bedridden and dependent on the care of his family. Instead, he is afraid of losing himself:

> To express oneself is the most human characteristic (*ichiban ningenrashii*). This is the most outstanding characteristic of a human being. Human beings have several ways to express themselves. This is remarkable, isn't it? I will lose all these possibilities because of my disease. My senses will stay normal, I will feel or think as every other person. […] But when I lose the possibility to express myself, then I will lose my individuality, my personality. If I think about how Mr. Jōmon will get lost being Mr. Jōmon, it is very painful.

In comparison to the interviewees who signed a Living Will, Mr. Jōmon's acceptance of physical decline and dependency goes further. His case shows how the diagnosis of a disease disrupts one's life course. To overcome this existential crisis, he had to find new meaning in his life. This led him to a process that involved searching for a decision that is in accordance with his notion of self. For Mr. Jōmon, the experiences of other ALS patients are a very important part of the decision-making process. From their stories, as well as from his own experiences, he learned that his own decision might change during the course of the disease or due to social relationships. His example shows the difficulties involved in making a decision about one's own death in advance and how closely connected the physical, interpersonal and existential dimensions are when it comes to the evaluation of one's own situation and the available institutional options, in order to overcome a crisis and regain the ability to act on one's own behalf.

Discussion

My interviewees spoke about what a meaningful and humane life means to them on a personal level, based on their own experiences and the possibilities available to them for making sense of their physical state, interpersonal relationships and values. They approached this topic from a negative point of view, as they are concerned about situations in which they would choose death over life.

As I have shown, the institutional framework of medical decision-making had to undergo several changes so that making decisions about the process of dying could become an individual matter. Due to these changes, the individual became the authority to evaluate and to make medical decisions concerning his or her own personal well-being. This shift of responsibility is especially apparent at the interpersonal and existential levels on which the individual considers his or her social and family roles, related responsibilities, values and notions of self. In this context, instruments such as Living Wills can be seen as tools to empower patients and to communicate their wishes. Although the number of people who have signed a Living Will is still small, several surveys (Akabayashi, Slingsby and Kai 2003; Miyata, Shiraishi and Kai 2006; Yomiuri Shinbun 2009)[3] have indicated the growth of an attitude in which the Living Will is seen as an important provision for a "good death."

Furthermore, as the examples from my case study show, the Living Will functions mostly as a precaution against potential problems in future medical decision-making. Due to a critical awareness of life-sustaining treatments in the present, my interviewees took action to avoid possible unwanted situations in the future, and, at the same time restore the feeling of being secure and able to act on their own behalf in the present. One might say that their sense of well-being follows a dual time axis: making preparations for future well-being means acting in the present, which in turn contributes to a present sense of happiness. In addition, their notion of personal well-being is closely connected to the presumed happiness and well-being of their social environment: to act on one's own behalf without interfering with the happiness and well-being of others is crucial to maintaining or regaining a sense of well-being.

On one hand, this development can be described as an increase in freedom for the individual, who is allowed to actively engage in his or her own personal well-being until the very last days. From the perspective of my interviewees, it seems unlikely that a state of well-being can be achieved in circumstances of irreversible loss of consciousness, altered subjectivity, a prolonged process of dying, or a state in which social interactions are no longer possible. It is for these reasons that they signed a Living Will.

On the other hand, Traphagan (2004: 58) has pointed out the normative power of concepts such as health and well-being, which impose personal responsibility on the subject to engage in activities in order to stay healthy and maintain a state of personal well-being. By engaging in activities that increase health and well-being on a personal level, the individual contributes to the well-being of the social group. This implies a moral duty to stay healthy and maintain one's well-being and conversely to also avoid (prolonged) illness and/or state of non-well-being:

> Well-being and illness are not only states of the body, they are also embodied states of knowledge and power that are often used to index the possession of cultural capital—the degree to which one is perceived as "fitting in" with ideals of selfhood and normative behavior.
> (Traphagan 2004: 62)

Here, the Living Will is being used as a tool not only to avoid situations of personal non-well-being, but also to act in accordance with social norms not to interfere with the well-being of the social group. In this context, the normative implications of the concept of well-being and happiness serve as one legitimation strategy among others, for rejecting medical technologies and giving up on living.

This resembles the arguments of the opponents of the right to die, who say that Living Will legislation would pressure disabled, elderly or severely ill people to choose death even when life is still possible, in order to avoid being a burden on society. They also say the emphasis on the individual as a self-reliant and responsible person would lead to a society where only the happy, or people in a state of well-being, have lives worth living (see for example Kawaguchi 2012; also Tateiwa 2008: 32 and 2005: 25). It is further argued that people who refer to the above-mentioned strategies to legitimate their decisions have already internalized the values of such a "sustainable society" (Otani 2010: 58).

In fact, the narratives indicate several social problems, especially in relation to the family as caregiver and the lack of institutional support for people who need help to lead independent lives, despite their disability, age, or disease. But one should not forget that people are not solely determined by social norms and values. Rather, my study shows how individuals struggle to reach a decision; one that they perceive is in accordance with their notions of self. Caught up in a complex and ambivalent decision-making process, they draw on norms and values that are consistent with their way of life and reject, question or distance themselves from others. Life crises, such as the diagnosis of an incurable disease, and/or the experience of caring for ill or dying family members, are occasions that prompt people to think about their own lives and to solve problematic situations.

The example of Mr. Jōmon suggests that without having experienced a particular physical condition, it is difficult to anticipate what might represent another person's well-being, or even one's own future well-being. He is well aware that over the course of his disease he may alter his view of his physical and interpersonal situation, as well as his values concerning a good lifestyle. This can be understood as a fundamental problem of advance decision-making. Therefore, it seems important to regard the decision to make a Living Will as a solution to a problematic situation that will restore agency and a sense of well-being in the present, keeping in mind that this decision might be altered in the future by new interpretations of one's physical state, social relationships, changing values and norms or notions of self, as well as by the institutional framework.

Notes

1 In cases where the Living Will is conceptualized as a tool of resistance to family members or physicians who could try to override the patient's personal wishes, my interviewees rely on at least one person they are close to as surrogate, who they trust to advocate on behalf of their wishes. Although all of them know that the Living Will is not legally binding on the physician, they voice only a minimum of uncertainty that their wishes could be ignored. Furthermore, in most cases the formulations in the Living Will are broad and leave a wide scope of interpretation in an actual situation, which is entrusted to the physician (except in the example of Mrs. Minami where additional notes have been added). This is consistent with survey results concerning the attitudes of middle-aged and senior adults (40–65) in Tokyo toward Living Wills, where 59.8 percent prefer to indicate treatment preferences in broad terms and only 5 percent demand that their preferences should be strictly observed (Miyata, Shiraishi and Kai 2006; Akabayashi, Slingsby and Kai 2003).
2 For a further examination of how "dying with dignity" was translated into *songenshi* at the end of the 1970s and has become closely associated with the JSDD, Living Wills, and passive euthanasia since the 1980s, see Spoden 2015.
3 In these surveys the general acceptance of Advance Directives varies from 60 to 80 percent, whereas the percentage of participants who have actually written one remains under 10 percent.

References

Akabayashi, Akira. 2002. "Euthanasia, Assisted Suicide, and Cessation of Life Support: Japan's Policy, Law, and Analysis of Whistle Blowing in Two Recent Mercy Killing Cases." *Social Science and Medicine* 55:517–527.
Akabayashi, Akira, Brian Taylor Slingsby and Ichiro Kai. 2003. "Perspectives on Advance Directives in Japanese Society: A Population-Based Questionnaire Survey." *BMC Medical Ethics* 4/5:w.p.
Anrakushi songenshi hōseika o soshi suru kai. 2005. "Seimei" [Statement]. http://soshisuru.fc2web.com/seimei.html. Retrieved April 8, 2015.
Borasio, Glan Domenico, Deborah F. Gelinas and Nobuo Yanagisawa. 1998. "Mechanical Ventilation in Amyotrophic Lateral Sclerosis: A Cross-Cultural Perspective." *Journal of Neurology* 245/2:(Supplement) 7–12.
Glaser, Barney G., and Anselm L. Strauss. 1965/2009. *Awareness of Dying*. New Jersey and Chicago: Aldine.
Igata, Akihiro. 2006. *Nenpyō ga kataru kyōkai 30nen no ayumi* [The association's 30-year history as told by the chronicle]. Tokyo: Nihon Songenshi Kyōkai.
JSDD / Japan Society for Dying with Dignity. 2005. *Sekai no ribingu uiru / Living Wills Around the World*. Tokyo: Nihon Songenshi Kyōkai.
JSDD / Japan Society for Dying with Dignity. 2012. "Kaiinzu no suii." [Membership trend]. http://www.songenshi-kyokai.com/about/purpose.html. Retrieved December 5, 2014.
JSDD / Japan Society for Dying with Dignity. 2013. "Kyōkai no katsudō: Nihon Songenshi Kyōkai no setsuritsu no mokuteki." [The activities of the organization:

The founding aims of the Japan Society for Dying with Dignity]. http://www.songenshi-kyokai.com/. Retrieved July 12, 2013.

Kawaguchi Yumiko. 2012. "Ima watashitachi ni 'shinu kenri' wa hitsuyō nanoka?" [Do we need 'the right to die' now?"] *Songenshi no hōseika o mitomenai shimin no kai.* http://mitomenai.org/message. Retrieved April 19, 2013.

Kimura, Rihito. 1998. "Death, Dying, and Advance Directives in Japan. Sociocultural and Legal Points of View." pp. 187–208 in *Advance Directives and Surrogate Decision Making in Health Care: United States, Germany, and Japan,* edited by H. Sass, R. M. Veatch and R. Kimura. Baltimore/London: The Johns Hopkins University Press.

Leflar, Robert B. 1996. "Informed Consent and Patients' Rights in Japan." *Houston Law Review* 33/1:1–112.

Long, Susan Orpett. 2002. "Life Is More Than a Survey: Understanding Attitudes towards Euthanasia in Japan." *Theoretical Medicine* 23:305–319.

Long, Susan Orpett. 2004. "Cultural Scripts for a Good Death in Japan and the United States: Similarities and Differences." *Social Science and Medicine* 58:913–928.

Long, Susan Orpett, and Bruce D. Long. 1982. "Curable Cancers and Fatal Ulcers. Attitudes toward Cancer in Japan." *Social Science and Medicine* 16:2101–2108.

Masuda, Yuichiro et al. 2003. "Physician's Reports on the Impact of Living Wills at the End of Life in Japan." *Journal of Medical Ethics* 29:248–252.

Mathews, Gordon, and Carolina Izquierdo. 2009a. "Introduction: Anthropology, Happiness, and Well-Being." pp. 1–19 in *Pursuits of Happiness: Well-Being in Anthropological Perspective,* edited by G. Mathews and C. Izquierdo. New York and Oxford: Berghahn Books.

Mathews, Gordon, and Carolina Izquierdo. 2009b. "Conclusion: Towards an Anthropology of Well-being." pp. 248–266 in *Pursuits of Happiness: Well-Being in Anthropological Perspective,* edited by G. Mathews and C. Izquierdo. New York and Oxford: Berghahn Books.

MHLW (Ministry of Health, Labour and Welfare/kōsei rōdō shō). 2012. "Shūmakki iryō no arikata ni kan suru kentōkai no secchi ni tsuite: Kore made no keii to dōkō." [About setting up a study group on the current state of terminal care: history and trends] Materials 2. *Iseikyoku Shidōka,* 27.12.2012, 1–15. http://www.mhlw.go.jp/stf/shingi/2r9852000002sarw-att/2r9852000002sawq.pdf. Retrieved July 1, 2013.

Miyata, Hiroaki, Hiromi Shiraishi and Ichiro Kai. 2006. "Survey of the General Public's Attitudes toward Advance Directives in Japan: How to Respect Patients' Preferences." *BMC Medical Ethics* 7/11:n.p.

Ohnuki-Tierney, Emiko. 1984. *Illness and Culture in Contemporary Japan: An Anthropological View.* Cambridge: Cambridge University Press.

Otani, Izumi. 2010. "'Good Manner of Dying' as a Normative Concept: 'Autocide', 'Granny Dumping' and Discussions on Euthanasia/Death with Dignity in Japan." *International Journal of Japanese Sociology* 19:49–63.

Schütze, Fritz. 1983. "Biographieforschung und narratives Interview." *Neue Praxis* 13/3:283–293.

Smyth, Angela et al. 1997. "End of Life Decisions in Amyotrophic Lateral Sclerosis: A Cross-Cultural Perspective." *Journal of Neurological Sciences* 152/1:(Supplement) 93–96.

Songenshi no hōseika o mitomenai shimin no kai. 2012. "Seimei" [Statement]. http://mitomenai.org/. Retrieved April 8, 2015.

Spoden, Celia. 2015. *Über den Tod verfügen. Individuelle Bedeutungen und gesellschaftliche Wirklichkeiten von Patientenverfügungen in Japan.* Bielefeld: transcript.

Tateiwa, Shinya. 2005. "Tasha o omou shizen de watashi no ichizon no shi [Altruistic, natural and autonomous death]." *Shisō* 976:23–44.

Tateiwa, Shinya. 2008. *Yoi shi* [Good death?]. *Tokyo Shinbun*: Chikuma Shobō.
Tokyo Shinbun. 2009.11.27. "Shi no songen yori mo mazu ikiru koto." [First of all to live is more important than the dignity of death]. *Tokyo Shinbun* Evening Edition: 4.
Traphagan, John W. 2004. *The Practice of Concern. Ritual, Well-Being, and Aging in Rural Japan*. Durham, NC: Carolina Academic Press.
Yamazaki, Maya. 2006. *Madonna no kubikazari. Hashimoto Misao, ALS to iu ikikata.* [Madonna's necklace. Hashimoto Misao and the lifestyle called ALS]. Tokyo: Chūō Hōki Shuppan.
Yomiuri Shinbun. 2009.15.1. "Muri na enmei kyohi. Ribingu uiru no kadai." [Rejection of unreasonable life-prolongation. The issue of living Wills]. *Yomiuri Shinbun* Evening Edition: 4.

13

FEAR OF SOLITARY DEATH IN JAPAN'S AGING SOCIETY

Tim Tiefenbach and Florian Kohlbacher

Introduction

Loneliness is an important social issue negatively affecting the well-being of both individuals and societies. It is also a widely researched area of study, particularly in the context of aging and old age. The current demographic shift in many countries around the world toward aging populations makes this topic even more prevalent and important. In Japan, a related issue has received increasing attention in recent years: *Kodokushi*—a lonely (or solitary) death—is the phenomenon of mostly older people dying solitarily and unnoticed in their homes, only to be found days or even weeks later by neighbors or the authorities. Solitary deaths in Japan are receiving substantial media attention and also have become an issue in the social policy debate (Cabinet Office, Government of Japan 2010; NHK 2010).

This paper is the first to analyze determinants and correlates of worries about solitary death. Using data from the *Heisei 25nen seikatsu no shitsu ni kan suru chōsa* (2013 Survey of Quality of Life; N=7,538) this paper sets out to (1) confirm whether social isolation is the main driver of worries about solitary death, to (2) investigate what other determinants are influencing worries about dying alone and to (3) examine whether different age groups show similar determinants. With older people more likely to die and being more exposed to the risk of dying alone, we are especially interested in identifying age-specific variables predicting worries about solitary death in old age. We assume worries about solitary death (1) to show higher levels in older age, (2) to show a higher negative correlation with happiness in old age and (3) to be correlated to a different set of independent variables over the age groups.

The occurrence of a new term: *"Kodokushi"*

The first appearance of the word *kodokushi* can be traced back to 1970, when on April 16 the leading newspaper *Asahi Shinbun* (1970) reported that a man was found dead in his apartment in Tokyo's Arakawa district, after not coming to work for almost one week. While 40 years later *kodokushi* is understood as a phenomenon of mainly older people, the first appearance in the media was related to the death of a 20-year old man. Only five days later, on April 21, the *Yomiuri Shinbun* (1970) reported the solitary death of a 38-year-old taxi driver, noting that this incidence was already the sixth "solitary death" in the inner city of Tokyo that year. It is important to note that although the word *kodokushi* appeared in 1970 for the first time, the media reported incidences of people dying unnoticed in their home already since the Meiji period (Kotsuji and Kobayashi 2011). In the following section, we explore how it came to the emergence of a new term for an old problem.

Solitary deaths in the wake of disasters, societal change and policy responses

Although the problem of people dying alone might be an old one, Japan in the 21st century is facing a rapid rise in incidents of solitary death as well as an increasing awareness of the problem (see Figure 13.1 below). The growing media attention is related not only to the rising number of cases, but also to the fact that in some cases the solitary deaths remained unnoticed for several days or even weeks. An increase in the number of cases of solitary death was observed after the Great Hanshin Earthquake in January 1995. After the disaster, many victims moved to temporary housing facilities where they had been cut off from their social network. In the first five months after the earthquake, six people were reported dying a solitary death in their temporary accommodations (Asahi Shinbun 2000). When the temporary facilities were finally closed down five years after the disaster in January 2001, the *Asahi Shinbun* reported that over the years 233 of the inhabitants had died solitary deaths. Even among people who moved out of the temporary facilities into newly constructed public housing facilities (*fukkō jūtaku*) in Kobe, the lack of social ties led to a substantial number of solitary deaths: 190 cases were reported between 1995 and 2003 alone (Kaji and Kimura 2010: 11).

Despite the tremendous increase in numbers, solitary deaths were first considered to be a long-term effect of the Kobe Earthquake and therefore not perceived as a societal problem. However, this changed after a documentary was broadcast in September 2005 on Japan's national public broadcaster. The NHK documentary reported a series of solitary deaths that happened—unrelated to any disaster—in Tokiwadaira, a settlement in Chiba prefecture not far from Tokyo. The cases of solitary death in Tokiwadaira received increased attention since the deceased were found several weeks after their actual death. NHK (2010) put the increasing incidences of solitary death into a larger perspective by linking them to the weakening of social ties. In a "society without bonds" (*muen shakai*) more and more people lose the bonds to their relatives, neighborhood, and workplaces and run the risk of dying a "disconnected death" (*muen shi*).

Following these developments and especially the rising media attention, the issue was picked up by Japan's Cabinet Office in its *Annual Report on the Aging*

Society in 2010. The report states that being found days after one's death violates the human dignity of the deceased and causes mental distress and financial costs not only for the relatives, but also to neighbors and landlords. To prevent solitary death, the report concludes, the phenomenon needs to be understood as the result of social isolation during the lifetime of the deceased that only becomes visible at the time of dying. Therefore, any kind of countermeasures to the problem need to be aimed at preventing older people from becoming lonely and isolated in the first place (Cabinet Office 2010: 58–59). Emphasizing the preceding period of isolation from society before the actual death, official authorities in Japan chose to use the term *koritsushi*, an "isolated death," instead of *kodokushi*. Some authorities also distinguish between an isolated death (*koritsushi*), defined as the death of a person isolated from his or her relatives and neighbors who is found several days later in her home, and a lonely death (*kodokushi*), defined as the death of a person who is connected to friends and relatives but dies at home or in a hospital alone (see for example Sapporo City (2013)). In the media and in large parts of the academic literature, the word *kodokushi* prevails, although most cases can be considered "isolated deaths." In English, however, the expression "solitary death" captures both (1) the state of being isolated and (2) the act of dying alone.

Recently, the phenomenon has gained attention in foreign media. Since 2010 solitary deaths in Japan have become a topic in *Time Magazine* (Nobel 2010), *The New York Times* (Makohara 2012; McDonald 2012), *BBC News* (BBC 2012) and *The Guardian* (Waterson 2014). Considering that Western countries show similar developments in terms of population aging and growing number of single households, it seems only a matter of time until solitary deaths become a problem in other societies as well. In the U.S., a first row of solitary deaths occurred during the Chicago heat wave in 1995 in which several hundred people died alone in their homes (Klinenberg 2002: 15). Analyzing the social and structural causes behind this disaster, Klinenberg identified social isolation as a major cause for the many lonely deaths the heat wave caused. Apart from disaster-related solitary deaths, an increase in people dying alone has been reported for San Francisco (Nieves 2000) and Wales (Hughes 2012). Against this backdrop, we assume that *kodokushi* is likely to be adapted into the English language in a similar way as *karōshi*, which was added in 2002 to the Oxford English Dictionary Online as "death caused by overwork or job-related exhaustion" (*Japan Times* 2002).

Despite the growing awareness of the problem, a clear definition of solitary death is still lacking, which is why no reliable numbers exist regarding how many people actually die a solitary death in Japan. Each municipality has its own way of defining solitary death, but a statistic often referred to is provided by the Bureau of Social Welfare and Public Health of the Tokyo Metropolitan Government (Shimizu 2014; Shibukawa 2014). The Medical Examiner's system of Tokyo's 23 wards allows for identifying unnatural deaths in single households. The resulting number is used by the Bureau of Social Welfare and Public Health as a proxy for solitary deaths. Figure 13.1 shows the development of solitary death in inner Tokyo (23 wards) from 1987 to 2013. As depicted in this figure, the number of

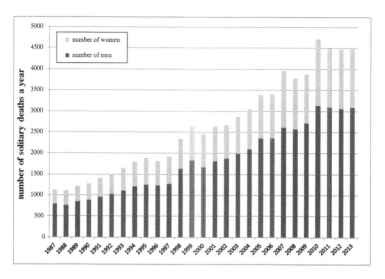

FIGURE 13.1 The number of solitary deaths in inner Tokyo from 1987 to 2013
Source: Own calculation based on data from the Bureau of Social Welfare and Public Health (BSWPH 2015b).

solitary deaths rose constantly over the last 25 years. In 2013 around 4500 people died a solitary death in inner Tokyo. For later analysis and discussion it is important to note that more than a two-thirds of the victims are male. Considering that in the same area 75,332 people died that same year (BSWPH 2015a), this yields a 6 percent rate of solitary deaths for the inner part of Tokyo city.

The social context of death and dying in Japan

When looking at the increasing number of solitary deaths reported by the media, the question arises as to whether these numbers represent a real trend or whether the issue is nothing more than a media hype. A look at the statistics reveals that solitary death is indeed a phenomenon that is correlated with the weakening of traditional social bonds.

An institution said to be eroding, not only in Japan (Kingston 2013), is the family. Data from the *2010 Japan Census* (Statistics Bureau of Japan 2010) shows marriage is not only increasingly delayed but sometimes foregone altogether. The steepest drop in marriage rates occurred around the time of Japan's bubble economy between 1980 and 1995. Nowadays 31.9 percent of men and 23.3 percent of women aged 40 have never married. At age 50, the percentage of unmarried adults drops to 20.1 among men and 10.6 among women.

Directly related to the erosion of the family is the changing housing situation in Japan, with a steady linear increase in the percentage of single households since 1960. Single households made up more than 30 percent by 2010, and about one-third of these comprise people over the age of 65. These numbers help us understand the social context in which *kodokushi* emerged as a new term for a problem already known since the Meiji period. In the following we look at the implications of these social changes on death and dying in Japan.

Japan's society remains rooted in a collectivistic ideology with a strong tendency to place importance on social ties and community (Sugimoto 2010; Hendry 2012). This applies also to matters of death and dying. Until the years after the Second World War, death was shared collectively within the household and community (Suzuki 2013b). This changed with rapidly progressing urbanization as well as the concomitant attenuation of communities. Indicative for this change is the emergence of professional funeral services. The funeral industry arose in the 1960s and developed into a commercialized service industry by the mid-1990s (Suzuki 2003). The implication of this development was that "[t]he locus of the funeral was no longer in the community and the household, but independent families and their member's social relationships" (Suzuki 2013b:10).

Although nowadays the funeral industry is providing a variety of services with different mortuary rites, funerals are still an integral part of Japanese society (Inoue 2013; Valentine 2010), yet they vary significantly due to economic status and the family situation of the deceased (Suzuki 2013b). The most basic form of funeral is the so-called "direct funeral" (*chokusō*), where the deceased is sent for cremation within one day (Suzuki 2013b). The funeral itself is stripped to its core and is held without a wake, priest or mortuary ritual. About 30 percent of "direct funerals" are for people without family and relatives—the typical case of solitary death. The growing awareness of social change and weakening social bonds causes feelings of ambiguity and uncertainty in individuals facing death (Suzuki 2013a). In this context, a new form of funeral has emerged: the "funeral-while-alive" (*seizensō*) is a self-executed ceremony that gives the "deceased-to-be" the chance to bring his or her life to a close within a well-chosen circle of friends and relatives. At the heart of this new trend lies the worry of having no one to rely on in the face of death (Suzuki 2013a). The emergence of this new kind of funeral is indicative of not only the social importance of death and dying in Japan, but also the increasing worries about dying alone.

Approaching the issue: Modeling worries about solitary death

To approach the analysis of worries about solitary death, we apply two working assumptions. First, based on research findings that high death anxiety is associated with poor subjective health (Mullins and Lopez 1982), we assume that people who are in a less healthy condition worry more about dying in general. Second, we assume that people extrapolate their current situation when thinking about the future (Klayman and Schoemaker 1993). We assume that this also holds true for thinking about one's own death. Specifically, we assume that people who feel lonely or who are socially isolated are extrapolating their situation into the future, resulting in higher worries about dying a solitary death. Taken together, we understand worries about solitary death as a function of subjective health, subjective feelings of loneliness and social isolation.

Academic research on the critical issue of loneliness and its antecedents and consequences is abundant (e.g. Jong-Gierveld 1987; Cacioppo et al. 2015; Parigi and Henson 2014). This is especially the case for social isolation and loneliness among older people as these problems are particularly pervasive in later life (Fees, Martin and Poon 1999; Coyle and Dugan 2012; Simon et al. 2014; Pinquart and Sorensen 2001). In terms of consequences, their impact on mortality (i.e., lonely adults have increased risks of dying) is particularly striking (Perissinotto, Stijacic Cenzer and Covinsky 2012; Luo and Waite 2014; Luo et al. 2012).

Academic studies on solitary death are scarce, and those that are available tend to be fairly descriptive in nature and focus on special cases. Fukukawa (2011) for instance, briefly outlines the case of an incident in a settlement in Chiba prefecture. The first *kodokushi* victim in this complex, a man aged 69, was found dead in 2001, three years after his death at his residence (Fukukawa 2011). Other studies have focused on solitary deaths in connection with natural disasters, such as the Great Hanshin-Awaji Earthquake in 1995 and the Great East Japan Earthquake in 2011 (Maeda 2007; Shinfuku 2004; Iuchi, Maly and Johnson 2015). Most of these studies focus on available support such as local health professionals, self-help among residents and housing construction after a disaster and thus cover only one specific aspect in the complex set of factors that may be connected to solitary deaths. Overall, the phenomenon of solitary deaths, despite its increasing importance, remains an under-researched topic.

Conceptually our approach differs from previous studies on solitary death in two ways. First, instead of focusing on single incidents, case studies or disasters, we analyze the effect of solitary death on the entire Japanese population represented by a large-scale national probability sample. Second and related to the first, we do not study the direct mental and material effects of solitary death on relatives, neighbors or landlords. Instead, we are interested in the indirect effects of solitary death in terms of worries. Methodically, our approach is part of a broader body of literature applying econometric models to outcome variables of subjective well-being, especially life satisfaction and happiness (for a review of the literature see Dolan, Peasgood and White 2008).

In this context, it is important to mention that worries about solitary death are related to happiness across three dimensions. Since worries about solitary death are a proxy for subjective feelings of loneliness and social isolation, they are directly linked to feelings of (un)happiness. This is supported by international studies showing interpersonal relations to be a major component of subjective well-being across most cultures (Delle Fave et al. 2011). Similarly, Mathews and Izquierdo (2009) conclude that among their four identified dimensions of happiness "the social/interpersonal is the most pivotal realm of well-being" (Mathews and Izquierdo 2009: 262–263). At the same time, worries about solitary death tap into another important dimension of (un)happiness: long-term physical well-being (Mathews and Izquierdo 2009). A poor health status not only leads to higher worries about dying alone but also is directly related to one's level of happiness. Studies show that subjective health is a major determinant of general life satisfaction and happiness (van Praag, Frijters and Ferrer-i-Carbonell 2003).

Finally, Mathews and Izquierdo (2009) show that meaning of life is another important dimension related to well-being. Considering that death and dying are directly related to meaning of life (Mathews 2013), worrying about a death in solitude means worrying about a meaningful life as well.

Data and variables

The present study uses data from the *2013* Survey of Quality of Life (*Seikatsu no shitsu ni kan suru chōsa*) (thereafter SQL), a representative nationwide survey commissioned by the Japanese Cabinet Office and initiated in 2012. The survey can be considered as the successor to the National Survey on Life Style Preferences (*Kokumin seikatsu senkōdo chōsa*), which ran from 1972 to 2012. The sample is generated via a three-stage randomized stratified procedure and includes 4,950 households targeted at a population including men and women in Japan above 15 years of age. The sample contains 7,717 individuals nested in 3,086 households, which corresponds to a response rate of 62.3 percent. Further details of the survey are described in Kuwahara et al. (2013). Note that we only use data of respondents between 20 and 85 years of age, since we focus our analysis on the comparison of three life stages: young (20–39 years), middle age (40–59 years) and old age (60–85 years).

As a dependent variable, we use a question on worries about solitary death. The corresponding survey question asks: "To what extent do you feel worried about the items below? Please circle the appropriate number for each corresponding item." The list of worries contains the following items: (1) unemployment, (2) food safety, (3) future of the children, (4) public order and security, (5) natural disasters, (6) radioactive pollution, (7) the financial situation after one's retirement, (8) death from overwork (*karōshi*) and finally (9) solitary death. The answer options range from 1 to 5 on a 5-point Likert scale. The answer items read: "1: I usually feel worried," "2: I feel somewhat worried," "3: Cannot say," "4: I don't feel very worried," and "5: I do not feel worried at all." For our analysis, the scale is recoded in reverse order with 5 indicating the most, and 1 indicating the least worries.

Since we understand worries about solitary death to be influenced by one's subjective health, feelings of loneliness and social isolation, we include single-item measures of the former two variables, and proxy social isolation with the number of social contacts as well as measures of social and emotional support. The feeling of loneliness is a self-reported single item measure, and the number of social contacts ("How often do you meet family members, relatives, friends …" etc.) as well as social support ("In case you are in trouble or ill, how many people in the following categories will help you?") are calculated as summed scales. We calculated emotional support as the average of five items asking to what extent respondents can share their emotions when they feel blue or happy, etc. In line with the literature on subjective well-being, we further control for several standard variables such as gender, income, age, education, marital and employment status and number of children as well as for geographic region and city size.[1] We especially expect the number of children and marital status to correlate with worries about solitary death. Further, income allows people to receive care services and engage (more) in social activities, which is why we also expect income to be related to worries about solitary death. In addition to these basic variables, we include items assessing the housing situation (time of living in same place, type of home, substandard housing), the living situation (living alone, living with a patient, patient in family) and the neighborhood (access, neighborhood dissatisfaction) into our analysis. The reason for including these variables is two-fold. First, solitary death occurs, almost by definition, at home, which is why living conditions (especially of single households) are of special interest. Additionally, Klinenberg (2002) shows in his analysis of lonely death during the Chicago heat wave in 1995 that the quality of the neighborhood systematically affected the death toll. The two neighborhood measures in the SQL regard convenient access to ten basic facilities and subjective neighborhood dissatisfaction. We take the row sum of neighborhood dissatisfaction with noise, air, water and litter pollution, the provision of green areas and the experience of crime and vandalism as a general proxy for the quality of the neighborhood.

Before turning to the empirical analysis, we take a short look at the descriptive data of our variable of interest. We provide summary statistics of all other variables in the appendix (Table 13.3). To better understand age differences in changes about the worries about solitary death we plot the average value (on a scale of 1 to 5) over age in Figure 13.2.

It is interesting to note that worries about solitary death rise from the age of 20 years (mean of 2.64) constantly until they peak at the age of 43 years (3.17). They stay on this elevated level until the age of 79 years, after which they abruptly drop to a lifetime low of 2.4 points at the age of 85. A likely interpretation for this is that with increasing age people get a better idea of how—that is in what kind of

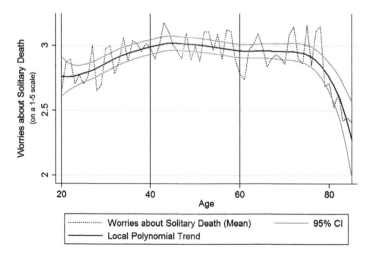

FIGURE 13.2 Worries about solitary death over the life course

TABLE 13.1 Different worries and their correlation with happiness in the 2013 SQL

		Age groups		
	All	20–39	40–59	60–85
Unemployment	-0.25	-0.26	-0.29	-0.25
Food safety	-0.07	-0.06	-0.07	-0.08
Future of the children	-0.10	-0.02	-0.10	-0.15
Public order and security	-0.10	-0.10	-0.11	-0.11
Natural disasters	-0.04	-0.01	-0.04	-0.05
Radioactive pollution	-0.05	-0.03	-0.05	-0.02
Financial situation after retirement	-0.22	-0.15	-0.22	-0.31
Death from overwork	-0.21	-0.18	-0.21	-0.26
Solitary death	-0.27	-0.29	-0.28	-0.28

environment—they will face death. Given that the percentage of solitary death is rather low, people might realize that their worries about dying alone were unnecessary. Thus, we see that worries about solitary death are not a unique problem of people in old age.

While the actual numbers of solitary deaths presented in Figure 13.1 may seem large, they also suggest that most people do *not* die a solitary death; however, many worry about it. The 2013 SQL shows that 32 percent of the respondents are somewhat or very concerned about dying alone. These worries, in turn, are negatively correlated with subjective well-being. As seen in Table 13.1, worries about solitary death show one of the highest negative correlations with happiness (-0.27) among the list of nine different worries, even before unemployment (-0.25). A closer look at three different age groups reveals that, counterintuitively, the youngest age group (20 to 39 years) shows the highest negative correlation with happiness for worries about solitary death (-0.29), while for people in middle and old age solitary death ranks on number two (-0.28), behind unemployment (-0.29) in middle age and behind worries about finances after retirement (-0.31) in old age.

Analysis and results

For the empirical analysis, we apply weighted OLS regressions against the data and variables described above. Following quantitative approaches dealing with subjective well-being data (Ferrer-i-Carbonell and Frijters 2004), we chose OLS regression instead of ordered probit estimations for the sake of interpretability. Re-estimations using ordered probit models, however, yielded qualitatively similar results. Further, to compensate for the under-sampling of single households we used weighted regressions. While, according to the 2010 Population Census of Japan, 32.4 percent of all households are single households, the 2013 SQL only comes to a ratio of 7.5 percent. Since we expect that people living alone are more likely to be worrying about solitary death we applied weighted regression, adjusting the sample to the ratios measured in the 2010 Population Census of Japan. Finally, for a better interpretation of the results, we chose to standardize not only our outcome variable, but also all variables measured on randomly defined Likert scales.

Model statistics

Table 13.2 reports the results of our three regression models, one for each age group. The number of observations ranges from 1,549 (old age) and 1,672 (young age) to 2,063 (middle age), and all models turn out to be statistically significant. The variance explained (r-squared) ranges from 26.8 and 26.2 percent for the young and middle aged to 28.7 percent for the old aged, indicating that the goodness of fit of the prediction model is almost stable across age groups. Considering that models with outcome measures of subjective variables, such as happiness or worries, normally yield an explained variance between 3 to 20 percent, we consider the predictive power of our models to be fairly good (for a comparison we refer to the literature reviewed in Dolan, Peasgood and White 2008).

To answer our first research question, whether social isolation is the main driver of worries about solitary death, we re-estimated all models using *only* the variables for social isolation, that is: feelings of loneliness and social connections as well as social and emotional support (see Appendix, Table 13.4). The variance explained (r-squared) for the re-estimated models is 16.7 percent for the youngest age group, 18.5 percent for people in middle age and 16.5 percent for the oldest age group.[2] Comparing the goodness of fit of both model specifications shows that in all age groups the four measures of social isolation alone predict more than half of the variance of the full model. We therefore can conclude that social isolation is the main driver of worries about solitary death, but other variables still have a significant influence.

Taking a closer look at subjective health and social isolation, we find that for people in middle age all of the respective variables are significant predictors of worries about solitary death (Table 13.2, Model 2). Given that a change of one standard deviation of the measures is associated with a 0.08 to 0.12 standard deviation change of worries about solitary death, we can say that in terms of effect size all measures are almost equally important. For people in old age, the number of social connections does not turn out to be statistically significant, while feelings of loneliness and social support show coefficients that are double in size compared to subjective health and emotional support (Table 13.2, Model 3). For the youngest age group, however, the two latter turn out to be non-significant, while feelings of loneliness have the highest coefficient for this age group (Table 13.2, Model 1).

Regarding the standard socio-demographic variables, two findings have to be highlighted. First, in old age, people with low household incomes report higher worries about solitary death compared with respondents from the middle-income group.[3] Interestingly, similar income effects are not observed for the young and middle age groups. Second, despite controlling for a variety of variables, a gender gap in worries about solitary death can be observed in the young and middle age

TABLE 13.2 OLS regression predicting worries about solitary death (standardized)

Age groups	Model 1 20–39 years	Model 2 40–59 years	Model 3 60–85 years
Health and isolation			
Subjective health *(stand.)*	−0.032	−0.091***	−0.066*
Feelings of loneliness *(stand.)*	0.227***	0.099***	0.138***
Social connections *(stand.)*	−0.096*	−0.127***	−0.064
Social support *(stand.)*	−0.095**	−0.083**	−0.135***
Emotional support *(stand.)*	−0.017	−0.094***	−0.061*
Socio-demographics			
Household income: Low	0.072	0.018	0.167**
Household income: Medium	reference group		
Household income: High	−0.002	0.010	−0.111
Age	−0.067	0.012	0.326***
Age-squared	0.002*	−0.000	−0.002***
Female	0.140**	0.173***	0.055
Number of children	−0.080	−0.084***	−0.085**
Single	0.300**	0.076	0.106
Married	reference group		
Divorced	−0.170	0.039	0.260
Widowed	−0.642***	0.123	0.089
Working	0.001	−0.066	−0.035
Education: Low	−0.181	−0.107	0.115
Education: Medium	reference group		
Education: High	−0.041	−0.074	−0.092
Education Other	−0.159	0.144	0.269
Housing and living			
Time living in same place	−0.001	−0.003	0.004
Type of home: Detached house	reference group		
Type of home: Apartment house	−0.195**	−0.119	0.047
Type of home: Other	−0.079	−0.023	−0.267
Substandard housing	0.081*	0.024	0.003
Living alone	0.180	0.388**	0.143
Patient in family	0.049	0.064	0.058
Living with patient	0.010	−0.031	0.034
Neighborhood access *(stand.)*	−0.016	0.041	0.083**
Neighborhood dissatisfaction *(stand.)*	0.176***	0.155***	0.216***
City size: 1 million and more	−0.003	−0.000	0.043
Regional controls	yes	yes	yes
Observations	1,672	2,063	1,549
R-squared	0.268	0.262	0.287
F-test model	$F(34,1215)=$ 18.335***	$F(34,1445)=$ 16.237***	$F(34,1113)=$ 18.145***

*** $p<.001$, ** $p<.01$, * $p<.05$
Note: (stand.) = standardized variables. Constant is omitted.

groups: women worry more than men about dying alone. However, for people in old age, the coefficient becomes non-significant, indicating that the gender gap eventually declines. While similar gender differences in the perception of worries and risks have been reported in other areas, such as food safety (Dosman, Adamowicz and Hrudey 2001; Miles et al. 2004) or crime and terrorism (Brück and Müller 2010), those studies have not investigated whether age works as a moderator on this gender effect (i.e., gender differences decline with increasing age). Regarding family structure, we find that for people in middle and old age the number of children has a negative effect on worries about solitary death. A somewhat counterintuitive finding is that only people of young age report significant differences in worries about solitary death depending on their marital status. Here, single persons report 0.3 standard deviations more worries about dying alone compared to married respondents.

Finally, we looked at several variables regarding housing and living. The most noteworthy finding is that in all age groups dissatisfaction with one's neighborhood is significantly associated with worries about solitary death. In terms of effect size, a one standard deviation change in neighborhood dissatisfaction of older people leads to a 0.22 standard deviation change in worries about solitary death, which thereby is one of the highest correlates. Although the survey items asked for the dissatisfaction with measures of air, water and noise pollution etc., the overall dissatisfaction index is likely to tap into the social quality of the neighborhood as well. In a similar vein, but with a smaller effect size, convenient access to ten basic facilities including post office, banks, supermarkets, etc. is an important determinant of worries about solitary death, at least for people in old age. For respondents of young and middle ages, however, neighborhood access is not a significant predictor, which suggests that mobility becomes more of an issue for the elderly. Regarding the housing situation, older people do not show a statistically significant correlation, while people in young age report higher worries about solitary death when they are living in inconvenient places ("substandard housing" includes, for example, apartments without a bathtub, balcony or flush toilet, etc.). Similarly, young people report far less worries about solitary death if they live in an apartment building compared to respondents who live in a detached house. Finally, our analysis shows that living alone is highly associated with worries about solitary death, but only for people in middle age. For them, it is the most important predictor with an effect size of a 0.39 standard deviation in worries about solitary death.

Conclusion

In this chapter, we analyzed worries about solitary death using recent survey data from Japan. We have three key findings that answer the questions we posed at the beginning. First, we find that social isolation and feelings of loneliness are the main drivers of worries about solitary death, especially for people between the ages of 40 and 59. This is an important finding in an aging society with an increasing number of middle-aged and aged persons. Second, we find that these factors are not the only drivers: age, household income, marital status, number of children, type of home and household type, as well as neighborhood access and dissatisfaction are likewise important determinants of worries about solitary death. Third, some variables show similar effects across all age groups, whereas others exhibit age- or cohort-specific effects. The measures of social isolation show slight differences across the three age groups with young people being more vulnerable to feelings of loneliness and older people putting an emphasis on social support. Neighborhood dissatisfaction shows very stable results across all three age groups indicating that the less satisfied people are with their neighborhoods the more they worry about dying alone. Furthermore, women worry more strongly than men in the young and middle-age group, and the number of children negatively affects worries about dying alone in the middle- and old-age group. Age-specific determinants are: neighborhood access and low household income for people in old age, living alone for people in middle age and type of home and being single for people in young age.

This chapter focused on identifying age-specific variables predicting worries about solitary death in different age groups. With older people being more likely to die and thus being more exposed to the risk of dying alone, we assumed worries about solitary death (1) to show higher levels in older age, (2) to show a higher negative correlation with happiness in old age and (3) to be correlated to different variables over the age groups. However, contrary to our expectations, worries about solitary death (1) decrease in old age (see Figure 13.2 above), (2) show a constant negative correlation with happiness over the age groups (see Table 13.1 above) and (3) share—to a certain extent—a common set of determinants.

The gender effect reported above is of particular interest when considering that most of the cases of solitary death in the inner city of Tokyo were male. For the case of the Chicago heat wave, in which isolation was the greatest risk of heat-related mortality, Klinenberg (2002: 20) reported age-adjusted death rates showing that men were twice as likely to die in the heat wave, while women were usually more likely to report being lonely and isolated (Gibson 2000: 50). These findings are supported by research on death anxiety, which shows a similar gender-effect of women being more concerned about dying in general (Russac et al. 2007).

As explained earlier in this chapter, worries about solitary death are related to happiness across three dimensions of the well-being framework by Mathews and Izquierdo (2009). First, worries about solitary death are a proxy for subjective feelings of loneliness and social isolation, and they are directly linked to feelings of (un)happiness. By studying these worries we contribute new knowledge to the "most pivotal realm of well-being," the social/interpersonal dimension (Mathews and Izquierdo 2009: 262–263). Second, worries about solitary death are related to long-term physical well-being measured as subjective health. However, this holds only true for people in middle and old age. Third, worries about solitary death are connected to issues of meaning of life and as such affect yet another important dimension of the well-being framework.

Appendix

TABLE 13.3 Summary statistics

Variable	Obs	Mean	SD	Min	Max
Worries about solitary death	5,284	2.880	1.213	1	5
Subjective health	5,284	3.642	1.084	1	5
Feelings of loneliness	5,284	2.618	2.614	0	10
Social connections	5,284	29.218	8.318	0	72
Social support	5,284	11.829	6.779	0	30
Emotional support	5,284	3.692	0.804	1	5
Household income: Low	5,284	0.304	0.460	0	1
Household income: Medium	5,284	0.336	0.472	0	1
Household income: High	5,284	0.360	0.480	0	1
Age	5,284	48.773	16.124	20	85
Female	5,284	0.526	0.499	0	1
Number of children	5,284	1.613	1.166	0	5
Single	5,284	0.204	0.403	0	1
Married	5,284	0.731	0.444	0	1
Divorced	5,284	0.032	0.175	0	1
Widowed	5,284	0.034	0.180	0	1
Working	5,284	0.725	0.446	0	1
Education: Low	5,284	0.105	0.307	0	1
Education: Medium	5,284	0.389	0.488	0	1
Education: High	5,284	0.503	0.500	0	1
Education: Other	5,284	0.002	0.041	0	1
Time living in same place	5,284	17.373	9.898	0.5	98
Home: Detached house	5,284	0.806	0.395	0	1
Home: Mansion	5,284	0.150	0.358	0	1
Home: Other	5,284	0.043	0.204	0	1
Substandard housing	5,284	0.461	0.695	0	4
Living alone	5,284	0.028	0.164	0	1
Patient in family	5,284	0.205	0.404	0	1
Living with patient	5,284	0.167	0.373	0	1
Neighborhood access	5,284	13.912	3.708	10	30
Neighborhood dissatisfaction	5,284	14.525	4.856	5	30
Region: Hokkaidō / Tōhoku	5,284	0.133	0.340	0	1
Region: Kantō	5,284	0.310	0.463	0	1
Region: Hokuriku / Higashiyama	5,284	0.098	0.297	0	1
Region: Tōkai	5,284	0.126	0.332	0	1
Region: Kinki	5,284	0.146	0.353	0	1
Region: Chūgoku / Shikoku	5,284	0.082	0.274	0	1
Region: Kyūshu / Okinawa	5,284	0.105	0.307	0	1
City size: 1 million and more	5,284	0.180	0.384	0	1
City size: Less than 1 million	5,284	0.820	0.384	0	1

TABLE 13.4 Loneliness predicting worries about solitary death

	Model 1	Model 2	Model 3
Age groups	20–39 years	40–59 years	60–85 years
Social isolation			
Feelings of loneliness *(stand.)*	0.245★★★	0.146★★★	0.203★★★
Social connections *(stand.)*	−0.161★★★	−0.219★★★	−0.190★★★
Social support *(stand.)*	−0.109★★★	−0.108★★★	−0.205★★★
Emotional support *(stand.)*	−0.046	−0.133★★★	−0.046
Observations	1,672	2,063	1,549
R-squared	0.167	0.185	0.164
Change in R-squared compared to full model	Δ0.101★★★	Δ0.077★★★	Δ0.124★★★
F-test model	F(34,1215)= 60.39★★★	F(34,1445)= 82.30★★★	F(34,1113)= 54.75★★★

★★★ $p<.001$, ★★ $p<.01$, ★ $p<.05$
Note: (stand.) = standardized variables. Constant is omitted.

Notes

1 Although we split the sample into three age groups, we still include age and age-squared in the single regressions to filter out quadratic age trends within each age group.
2 The differences between the two model specifications (social isolation only model vs. full specified model) are statistically significant at the 1% level in each age group.
3 We use three income classes: "low" = up to JPY 4 million a year (34,000 USD); "middle" (reference group) = JPY 4–7 million a year (59,000 USD); and "high" = more than JPY 7 million a year.

References

Asahi Shinbun. 1970. "Mata Tōkyō no kodokushi isshūkanme hakken" [Again a solitary death in Tokyo – Found after the first week]. *Asahi Shinbun* Evening Edition, April 16: 11.
Asahi Shinbun. 2000. "Hanshin daijinsai no kasetsu jūtaku kodokushi, 233nin" [Solitary death in temporary housing facilities of the Great Hanshin Earthquake, 233 People]. *Asahi Shinbun* Ōsaka Edition, January 14:30.
BBC. 2012. "Japanese Authorities Concerned about 'Lonely Deaths'." *BBC News,* February 24. http://www.bbc.com/news/world-asia-17152949. Retrieved June 3, 2015.
Brück, Tilman, and Cathérine Müller. 2010. "Comparing the Determinants of Concern about Terrorism and Crime." *Global Crime* 11:1–15.
BSWPH (Bureau of Social Welfare and Public Health). 2015a. *Jinkō dōtai tōkei* [Demographic statistics]. http://www.fukushihoken.metro.tokyo.jp/kiban/chosa_tokei/eisei/jinkou.html. Retrieved September 15, 2015.
BSWPH (Bureau of Social Welfare and Public Health). 2015b. *Tōkei dētabēsu* [Statistics database]. http://www.fukushihoken.metro.tokyo.jp/kansatsu/database/index.html. Retrieved September 16, 2015.

Cabinet Office, Government of Japan. 2010. *Heisei 22nendo kōrei shakai hakusho* [Fiscal year 2010 white paper on the aging society] http://www8.cao.go.jp/kourei/white paper/w-2010/gaiyou/22indexg.html. Retrieved April 13, 2015.

Cacioppo, John T. et al. 2015. "The Neuroendocrinology of Social Isolation." *Annual Review of Psychology* 66:733–767.

Coyle, C. E., and E. Dugan. 2012. "Social Isolation, Loneliness and Health among Older Adults." *Journal of Aging and Health* 24:1346–1363.

De Jong-Gierveld, Jenny. 1987. "Developing and Testing a Model of Loneliness." *Journal of Personality and Social Psychology* 53:119–128.

Delle Fave, Antonella et al. 2011. "The Eudaimonic and Hedonic Components of Happiness: Qualitative and Quantitative Findings." *Social Indicators Research* 100:185–207.

Dolan, Paul, Tessa Peasgood and Mathew White. 2008. "Do We Really Know What Makes Us Happy? A Review of the Economic Literature on the Factors Associated with Subjective Well-being." *Journal of Economic Psychology* 29:94–122.

Dosman, Donna M., Wiktor L. Adamowicz and Steve E. Hrudey. 2001. "Socioeconomic Determinants of Health- and Food Safety-Related Risk Perceptions." *Risk Analysis* 21:307–318.

Fees, B. S., P. Martin and L. W. Poon. 1999. "A Model of Loneliness in Older Adults." *The Journals of Gerontology Series B: Psychological Sciences and Social Sciences* 54B: P231.

Ferrer-i-Carbonell, Ada, and Paul Frijters. 2004. "How Important Is Methodology for the Estimates of the Determinants of Happiness?" *The Economic Journal* 114:641–659.

Fukukawa, Yasuyuki. 2011. "Solitary Death: A New Problem of an Aging Society in Japan." *Journal of the American Geriatrics Society* 59:174–175.

Gibson, Hamilton B. 2000. *Loneliness in Later Life*. Houndmills, Basingstoke/New York: Macmillan/St. Martins.

Hendry, Joy. 2012. *Understanding Japanese Society*. New York: Routledge.

Hughes, Brendan. 2012. "Revealed: Growing Number of Elderly Dying Alone with No Relatives." *Wales Online,* 21 August. http://www.walesonline.co.uk/news/wales-news/revealed-growing-number-elderly-dying-2026097. Retrieved June 07, 2015.

Inoue, Haruyo. 2013. "Contemporary Transformation of Japanese Death Ceremonies." pp. 123–137 in *Death and Dying in Contemporary Japan*, edited by H. Suzuki. New York: Routledge.

Iuchi, Kanako, Elizabeth Maly and Laurie Johnson. 2015. "Three Years after a Megadisaster: Recovery Policies, Programs and Implementation after the Great East Japan Earthquake." pp. 29–46 in *Advances in Natural and Technological Hazards Research, Post-Tsunami Hazard*, edited by V. Santiago-Fandiño, Y. Kontar and Y. Kaneda. Cham: Springer International Publishing.

Kaji, Shintarō, and Shunsuke Kimura. 2010. "Kōsōkai, 'inochi' no koritsu – 'kodokushi 2 shūkan' tosshutsu" [Isolated life in higher floors – Solitary death above 2 weeks stand out]. *Asahi Shinbun* Ōsaka Evening Edition January 14:11.

Kingston, Jeff. 2013. *Contemporary Japan. History, Politics, and Social Change since the 1980s.* Chichester: John Wiley & Sons.

Klayman, Joshua, and Paul J. H. Schoemaker. 1993. "Thinking about the Future: A Cognitive Perspective." *Journal of Forecasting* 12:161–186.

Klinenberg, Eric. 2002. *Heat Wave. A Social Autopsy of Disaster in Chicago*. Chicago: University of Chicago Press.

Kotsuji, Hianori, and Muneyuki Kobayashi. 2011. "History of News Reports on Lonely Death." *Core Ethics* 7:121–130.

Kuwahara, Susumu, Michiko Ueda and Shiho Kono. 2013. *Seikatsu no shitsu ni kan suru chōsa (setai chōsa: hōmon ryūchihō) no kekka ni tsuite* [Regarding the results of the survey of Quality of Life (household survey: drop-off version)]. *ESRI Research Note*. http://www.esri.go.jp/jp/archive/e_rnote/e_rnote030/e_rnote023.pdf. Retrieved June 12, 2015.

Luo, Ye, and Linda J. Waite. 2014. "Loneliness and Mortality among Older Adults in China." *The Journals of Gerontology Series B: Psychological Sciences and Social Sciences* 69:633–645.

Luo, Ye et al. 2012. "Loneliness, Health, and Mortality in Old Age: A National Longitudinal Study." *Social Science & Medicine* 74:907–914.

Maeda, Kiyoshi. 2007. "Twelve Years since The Great Hanshin Awaji Earthquake, a Disaster in an Aged Society." *Psychogeriatrics* 7:41–43.

Makohara, Kumiko. 2012. "Afraid of Dying Alone." *The New York Times,* April 9. http://www.nytimes.com/2012/04/10/opinion/afraid-of-dying-alone.html. Retrieved June 3, 2015.

Mathews, Gordon. 2013. "Death and 'the Pursuit of a Life Worth Living' in Japan." pp. 33–48 in *Death and Dying in Contemporary Japan.* edited by H. Suzuki. New York: Routledge.

Mathews, Gordon, and Carolina Izquierdo. 2009. "Towards an Anthropology of Well-Being." pp. 248–266, in *Pursuits of Happiness. Well-being in Anthropological Perspective,* edited by G. Mathews and C. Izquierdo. New York and Oxford: Berghahn Books.

McDonald, Mark. 2012. "In Japan, Lonely Deaths in Society's Margins." *The New York Times,* March 25. http://rendezvous.blogs.nytimes.com/2012/03/25/in-japan-lonely-deaths-in-societys-margins/?_r=0. Retrieved June 3, 2015.

Miles, Susan et al. 2004. "Public Worry about Specific Food Safety Issues." *British Food Journal* 106:9–22.

Mullins, Larry C., and Martha A. Lopez. 1982. "Death Anxiety among Nursing Home Residents: A Comparison of the Young-old and the Old-old." *Death Education* 6:75–86.

NHK "muen shakai purojekuto" shuzaihan [NHK "society without bonds project" news crew]. 2010. *Muen shakai. "Muenshi" sanman nisen nin no shōgeki* [Society without bonds]. Tōkyō: Bungei Shunjū.

Nieves, Evelyn. 2000. "In San Francisco, More Live Alone, and Die Alone, Too." *The New York Times,* 25 June. http://www.nytimes.com/2000/06/25/us/in-san-francisco-more-live-alone-and-die-alone-too.html. Retrieved June 07, 2015.

Nobel, Justin. 2010. "Japan's 'Lonely Deaths': A Business Opportunity." *Time,* April 6. http://content.time.com/time/world/article/0,8599,1976952,00.html. Retrieved June 3, 2015.

Parigi, Paolo, and Warner Henson. 2014. "Social Isolation in America." *Annual Review of Sociology* 40:153–171.

Perissinotto, Carla M., Irena Stijacic Cenzer and Kenneth E. Covinsky. 2012. "Loneliness in Older Persons: A Predictor of Functional Decline and Death." *Archives of Internal Medicine* 172: 1078–1083.

Pinquart, Martin, and Silvia Sorensen. 2001. "Influences on Loneliness in Older Adults: A Meta-Analysis." *Basic and Applied Social Psychology* 23:245–266.

Russac, R. J. et al. 2007. "Death Anxiety across the Adult Years: An Examination of Age and Gender Effects." *Death Studies* 31:549–561.

Sapporo City. 2013. *Koritsushi bōshi ni mukete* [Towards a prevention of isolated deaths], Sapporo City. https://www.city.sapporo.jp/koreifukushi/koritsushi/documents/h25chirashi.pdf. Retrieved September 15, 2015.

Shibukawa, Kiko. 2014. "Koritsushi risuku no takai kōreisha e no shien no arikata: Setagaya-ku no koritushisha zensū 147ken no keikō o tōshite." [The state of support for the elderly with high risk of dying an isolated death: Looking at the trend of Setagaya District's 147 cases], in *Setagaya Jichi Seisaku 6 [Local Government Policy Vol. 6]*, edited by K. Morioka.

Shimizu, Fumiko. 2014. "Tōkyō 23ku dake de 4500 nin – kodokushi to wa nani ka" [4500 people alone in Tokyo's 23 wards – What is solitary death]. *Shūkan Tōyō Keizai*, 19 July: 58–59.

Shinfuku, Naotaka. 2004. "The Experience of the Kobe Earthquake." pp. 127–136 in *Disasters and Mental Health*, edited by J. J. López-Ibor et al. Chichester: John Wiley & Sons.

Simon, Melissa A. et al. 2014. "The Prevalence of Loneliness among U.S. Chinese Older Adults." *Journal of Aging and Health* 26:1172–1188.

Statistics Bureau of Japan. 2010. *2010 Japan Census*. http://www.stat.go.jp/data/kokusei/2010/index.htm. Retrieved September 15, 2015.

Sugimoto, Yoshio. 2010. *Introduction to Japanese Society*. Cambridge: Cambridge University Press.

Suzuki, Hikaru. 2003. "McFUNERALS: The Transition of Japanese Funerary Services." *Asian Anthropology* 2:49–78.

Suzuki, Hikaru. 2013a. "Funeral-while-alive as Experiential Transcendence." pp. 102–122 in *Death and Dying in Contemporary Japan*, edited by H. Suzuki. New York: Routledge.

Suzuki, Hikaru. 2013b. "Introduction: Making One's Death, Dying, and Disposal in Contemporary Japan." pp. 1–30 in *Death and Dying in Contemporary Japan*, edited by H. Suzuki. New York: Routledge.

The Japan Times. 2002. "'Karoshi', 'keiretsu' on Oxford List." January 18. http://www.japantimes.co.jp/news/2002/01/18/national/karoshi-keiretsu-on-oxford-list/#.VW7DbFKGnjO. Retrieved June 3, 2015.

Valentine, Christine. 2010. "The Role of the Ancestral Tradition in Bereavement in Contemporary Japanese Society." *Mortality* 15:275–293.

van Praag, Bernhard, Paul Frijters and Ada Ferrer-i-Carbonell. 2003. "The Anatomy of Subjective Well-being." *Journal of Economic Behavior & Organization* 51:29–49.

Waterson, Hannah. 2014. "No More Lonely Deaths: Our Promise to the Older People of Adachi in Japan." *The Guardian*, April 29. http://www.theguardian.com/local-government-network/2014/apr/29/no-more-lonely-deaths-older-people-adachi-japan. Retrieved June 3, 2015.

Yomiuri Shinbun. 1970. "Mata kodoku no shi, 17 nichime" [Another lonely death, found on the seventeenth day]. *Yomiuri Shinbun*, April 21:14.

14
RECONSIDERING THE FOUR DIMENSIONS OF HAPPINESS ACROSS THE LIFE COURSE IN JAPAN

Wolfram Manzenreiter and Barbara Holthus

Japan may be unhappy as a society, if we go by what the international surveys quoted in the introduction state. But the studies of particular subgroups and subdomains of happiness that we collected for this volume suggest otherwise for reasons that are awaiting explanation. Without exception, the Japanese that our authors studied at specific stages of their life course have hardly been identified as disheartened, miserable or outright unhappy. Some were found to have a harder time finding happiness, compared with their peers within the same subgroup. Our authors have inferred from differences in health conditions, material resources, exposure to social norms, conflicting role expectations and freedom of choice that the reasons for the differences in happiness and unhappiness can be well described (but hardly explained) by factors of relevance for Mathews' and Izquierdo's four-dimensional model of happiness, which we also discussed in the introduction. Our conclusion attempts to identify the dimensions that have been most salient throughout the case studies and to understand possible connections among the discrete dimensions. We ask if the weight and meaning of particular dimensions have shifted over the life course, and if age-specific patterns emerge from the comparison of the studies from our authors. By pointing to similarities and dissimilarities among the studies, we also ask for continuities and discontinuities that characterize the trajectory of happiness across the life course in Japan, ultimately evaluating the usefulness of merging the model with the inventory of life course theory.

The great unknown: The physical dimension

As social scientists, we are naturally prone to expect that the interpersonal dimension will emerge as the most influential out of the four throughout the life course. After all, human beings are by nature social beings that need others for support, shelter and guidance, and cultural patterns of sociality such as interdependence, collectivism, and consideration for others have often been identified as distinctive characteristics of Japanese sociality. However, it is also not unlikely that we force the social dimension to be of central importance because our research design is biased toward social phenomena that can be classified, counted, measured and compared. By comparison, the existential dimension including mores, ethics and aesthetics is much more difficult to observe and approach. Only at special occasions and in highly ritualized dramatic presentations can we directly observe the emanation of people's belief systems, convictions and moralities. To make up for this shortcoming, social scientists can draw on reflexivity as another basic human capability and ask people about the purpose of life, the coordinates of their world view, and the nature of the magnetizing forces of their ethical compass. Even more challenging is the question of how to research the social aspects behind the physiological as well as psychological experiences of being in the world. The body as a social construct and the corporeality of human beings have only recently been acknowledged as fields worthy of investigation in social sciences.

The lack of appropriate tools and theories might be a major reason why the physical dimension does not feature very prominently in this book. Positive corporeality is touched upon only in the two chapters by Ben-Ari and Goldstein-Gidoni that point at happiness emanating from the joy of children playing and the household beautification work of modern housewives. The physical dimension is strikingly missing in the biographical accounts Mathews has summarized for this volume. His emphasis on family and work life in the reflections of adults in the prime of their life is certainly due to the centrality these domains and trajectories have in their lives. Skinship, intimacy and sexual pleasures, which other authors identified as dearly valued factors of family life (Moriki 2017), do not feature prominently in the memories of Mathews' matured informants. Positive accounts of work life, in which the materiality of the body, its sensuality and conscious operation may feature as contributing factors to people's subjective well-being, are nearly non-existent. Rare exceptions of work-related happiness appeared in the narratives of a sports coach and a Buddhist monk, both professionals for whom the body and its physicality arguably are more important than for the average salaryman. This is an interesting observation for the poor emotional reward people gain from their work, and this is particularly troubling for a society in which social status and gratification are closely linked to the institution of work that is demanding so much of its members' time and attention.

Even though the positive impact of corporeality on happiness is largely absent from the studies of this volume, it does not mean that the body does not appear at all in the survey or interview data of other chapters. The physical dimension of happiness is prevalent in the form of physical and mental health issues throughout most chapters, and more specifically in relation to illness and distress. Health has been identified as such a powerful contributor to well-being that quite a few studies have used health as an approximation of overall happiness. Raymo has done this, too, in his study on the happiness of single mothers. In the regard that health conditions turn into health concerns only when something is wrong or could be wrong with the body, the relation between positive effect and cognitive awareness strikingly resembles the usual lack of awareness of happiness in the moment of greatest joy, just as Ben Ari explained with the concept of "flow." During a "flow" experience, one is so immersed in an activity that one does not stop to reflect on it, but afterwards does call it a happy occurrence.

Narrative accounts of health by contrast are likely to show that objectively similar health conditions lead to different health concerns, as their assessment is inflected by age and aging, social conditions and the environment. Furthermore they reveal that human beings have astonishing capabilities of adapting to severe changes of physical conditions and that different cultures have specific ideas of health and illness that are played out in terminology, diagnostic procedures and treatment and by extension also in the sensual, pre-cognitive assessment of health. While there is no reason to doubt the significance of health for happiness, it must be stated that its contribution differs very much across the life cycle. Physical pains will have an equally constraining effect at every life stage, but young and old people are inclined to assess smaller and larger changes in body proportion, skin elasticity, physical strength and agility differently, depending on age and the individual capability of reading decay and fragility as natural coincidences of aging and therefore less troublesome. Still we must take into account that agility and mobility are of crucial importance for senior Japanese, too, because without the capability of moving the body freely it becomes rather impossible to maintain an active life of meaning and sustain a broader web of interpersonal relations.

Happiness as co-production: The interpersonal dimension

As expected, the interpersonal dimension features highly throughout all chapters and the life course. Ben-Ari's study of preschoolers discusses how group-oriented play and communicative and reflective processes are used to give direction to their sense of well-being by linking the preconscious experience of play and fun to cooperation, caring and group membership. Ben-Ari argues that from an early age a child's mindset is carefully molded by self-enhancing didactical devices and for objectives that are common in many institutional settings through which the child will go in later life. That "being alone" is good for neither one's immediate well-being nor one's further progress in life is widely accepted already by elementary school children, finds Yamamoto. For the children she studied, going to school is a source of happiness as school provides the setting where one meets friends and receives the support needed to advance skills and knowledge to become an adult.

Interpersonal relations are even of significance for the well-being of those who choose to withdraw from society, as Horiguchi's contribution demonstrates. Frustration about the poor quality of friendship relations and a breach of trust in group embeddedness are frequent triggers for the determination to live a life in isolation from the world at large. The *hikikomori* lifestyle of extremely minimalized social contacts often turns into an extremely prolonged transitional state that links youth and adulthood, prior to the reintegration of the socially withdrawn. It is impossible to know how long the retreat may last. The possibility of such a moratorium from interpersonal relations may make the *hikikomori* happy, but has a detrimental effect on family members whose willing or unwilling support in providing food, shelter or financial resources facilitates and sustains the state from which all family members suffer. The capability of having family members carry out such essential roles on one's behalf is an indicator of agency exerted by the *hikikomori*, and the source of the power is rooted in the special quality of social relations among nuclear family members.

The significance of peer groups for moving along the early stages of the life course in Japan has been widely documented, and some of these relations outlast the social context for which they were crafted, turning into friendship (see also Dales 2017 and Nakano 2017 on friendship relations as surrogate of romance partnerships). For the well-being of young adults, however, Hommerich shows that feeling connected to the larger world of society is even more influential than the web of relations that forms their smaller world of friends and family. Goldstein-Gidoni demonstrates that sharing the bright lifestyle (*akarui seikatsu*) of happy housewives with other women of similar age and class background is a source of well-being for women who are not tied to employment; this is rather different from their husbands and men in general, for whom workplace relations are of more significance. Aichinger, Fankhauser and Goodman demonstrate that the quality of relations with peers, superiors and students enhances the workplace happiness of Japanese academics. Taga's study reveals that the well-being of married men can be dampened by conflicting expectations from the two life worlds of work and family and that those who escape the multiple demands by sticking to the normative lifestyle of the breadwinner appear to be less stressed and dissatisfied. The difficulties of combining work life and family life is a problem that resonates through all accounts of Japanese happiness along the adult years of the life course. Brinton shows that married working women are less happy than housewives are. Only for those rare cases in which both husband and wife hold a similar view on the equal distribution of domestic and employed labor the married working wives are able to report higher levels of well-being than housewives. Raymo's study about single mothers' happiness rarely touches upon their social relations, but it appears that the badly paid and precarious jobs they are confined to offer less opportunities for socializing.

Because of the centrality of work and family within the highly gendered patterns of everyday life in Japan, retirement and the time when grown-up children move out of the family home are crucial turning points in the life course of many men and women. Mathews' interview partners reflect about such life events and weave them into their biographical narratives. We also learn from Kawano that male retirees find difficulties in maintaining social relationships once they lose their workplace-centered network. Volunteering enables them to fill the void and find a new space to be (*ibasho*) that provides them with a sense of belonging, meaningfulness and a new public identity. Wives are usually better positioned to accommodate the transition to old age because of the lasting relationships that they retained from their former role of child caretaker and the head-on start they had on appropriating new spaces, activities and identities after their children moved out. The trajectory of happiness understood and experienced as a collective and joint project that started in preschool resonates through the thoughts and feelings of people at all life stages until they approach a stage when it comes to thinking about one's death. Spoden as well as Tiefenbach and Kohlbacher show that reflections about death and its impact on others are not necessarily happening when one's biological time is coming to its end. Feelings of loneliness and social isolation from communal life are main drivers of the increasingly reported fear of dying a lonely death; these anxieties are even more widespread among young adults because of the greater importance they attach to social embeddedness.

Interpersonal relations therefore are a prominent feature of well-being throughout the life course. Data from most surveys give proof to the assumption that marriage impacts positively and divorce negatively on happiness (Holthus et al. 2015). However, in the narrative accounts of Mathew's longitudinal study it also becomes clear that marriage per se is not a provider of happiness, having its ups and downs over the years. The impact of children, that in quantitative happiness surveys seem to have more of a downgrading effect on overall well-being (Holthus et al. 2015), similarly appears to be more complex in its effects, with children being both a source of joy and sorrows. The studies in this volume suggest that idealized notions of the family, gendered life scripts and incomplete support systems in combination with a dynamic sense of self, which is realized with and in opposition to the needs and demands of others, are most of all responsible for the diversity of well-being in interpersonal relations. Fulfilling role obligations in interdependent social relationships, creating and maintaining a balance of interpersonal harmony, and striving to promote the welfare and prosperity of the family cannot be achieved independently by single, autonomous agents, but only in cooperation and coordination with others. If collective well-being truly is a dependent variable for subjective well-being, and we think there still is such a thing, readjusting the research design in order to include the multiple levels of social well-being at the nodes of an ego-centered network would greatly improve the accuracy of social surveys of well-being, in Japan and wherever else relational well-being exists.

Meaningful happiness: The existential dimensions

As interpersonal relations are embedded into collectively shared moralities, it is perhaps not surprising that the existential dimension equally attracts focused attention throughout the life course. Again, the prevalence of this might be an effect that is exaggerated by research design and the focused inquiry into the underlying rationalities of observable behavior and structures. But we conclude from the observations that coherency of behavior and personal values is of some significance for subjective well-being and that social action and positions, if incongruent with deep convictions about how life should be, eventually generate dissatisfaction and unhappiness. We already mentioned how young children are taught to appreciate the experience of belonging as a source of happiness and the responsibilities that come with it. Language is a crucial tool that teachers use to guide them through the transition from an egocentric life stage to one in which they develop a greater understanding of the self as part of the group. Performative routines and the internalization of key concepts contribute to acquiring a commonly shared sense of self whose well-being is contingent on the well-being of the group. School life in Japan is not unlike a "total institution" that comprehensively cares for its dependent members. Next to the family, schools are the most important setting and social institution in which children acquire new social roles and an understanding of responsibility toward the world outside the family. Many children are confronted with positive and negative sanctioning only at school and in the family.

The dominance of the institution of school over the life of its members may have dramatic consequences for those who are singled out for various reasons or stand at the margin of the school community. Bullying and skipping school are typical and frequent triggers for the *hikikomori* phenomenon studied by Horiguchi. She argues that social withdrawal is an existential crisis of young Japanese that have heightened expectations of friendship norms and performance. Questions about oneself, the relations to the world and one's future are common elements of the life stage of youth. But some young Japanese expand these questions to a degree as to transfer them into the underlying rationale of a new social identity. Taking time out from society is interpreted by Horiguchi as a challenge of social norms, which may be positive in itself. However, it rather creates a number of consequential problems due to the strict patterns of social life in Japan. "Falling behind" one's age cohort inevitably minimizes chances of obtaining a standard career path, and alternatives are so rare that they usually go hand in hand with lower income prospect and social status. This problem of being "out of sync" with one's generation also affects the well-being of young adults who have lost track of the uniform progress of their peers after graduating from school or university. The bleak outlook of the future that Hommerich reports for young adults is particularly gloomy when seen in relation to the career prospects of others, such as their parents' generation.

The rapid transition through life stages, often marked by life events that are accompanied by the adoption of new roles and an extended understanding of self, does not slow down after the educational years but rather picks up speed with marriage and childbirth. Employment and career mobility are part of a largely standardized life plan, which however, is by now only available to a minor proportion of a cohort. For others of the same generation who have to secure their livelihood from changing jobs of limited duration, payment and status, precarity and the concomitant reduced options for timely marriage and family formation or adequate social security benefits emerged as collaterals of a trajectory gone astray. For the more privileged peers, however, marriage and starting a family multiplies the number of life events that may become turning points. A major reason for this is the increase of family members and the impact their life courses is having on one's own sense of self. We will come back to the overlapping of "private" time and family time at a later stage. First we want to explain the meaning of the dominant public identities available and desired for by most male and female adults in Japan.

Even though the past decades have seen an increasing diversity of family types and employment patterns, the gendered division of labor and work, for example, stubbornly resists change. Femaleness remains largely tied to household chores and childcare, whereas male self-appreciation is foremost based on work-related achievements and the ability to provide as the single breadwinner. As we already discussed, Taga and Mathews show how recent expectations that men will become involved in family activities, caregiving, and paying attention to the needs of their wives have decreased the happiness of many men. New conceptions of work and family have created a role conflict between being the breadwinner and supporting wife and family at home. Work is no longer seen as having value in itself, defined by its income-generating function in the service of the family; rather, as Taga explains, a new generation places the conversations about the meaning of work into broader debates. In contrast to the father generation that fulfilled its obligations by going to work and subjugated the self to corporate well-being, the sons tend to reinterpret work in existential terms as something that is supposed to be fulfilling and enriching. The pursuit of self-realization that is tied into larger debates about the plasticity of the self and the individual's responsibility of managing its own happiness, however, is at conflict with new fathering roles and expectations from the family.

Goldstein-Gidoni describes how consumption and self-work is propagated by the mass media as existential sources of happiness for modern full-time housewives. Brinton is marred by the idea that the traditional promise of happy housewives is actually putting women who aim to stay in the labor market while they are married and have children at a disadvantage. Her analysis highlights the fact that wives' career ambitions are largely dependent on husbands' support, which therefore is tantamount to increase the happiness of working married women. A very significant finding for understanding the impact of competing role demands and life paths on happiness is the degree to which women willingly subscribe to the gendered division of household labor. Therefore women who cannot accept the implicit demands of the traditional gender order report less happiness. All of this is however beyond reach for single mothers who are often forced to cope with the cumulative disadvantages of low education; experiences of existential crises, including abuse and domestic violence; weak employability and a general lack of material and immaterial resources. Raymo's study demonstrates how their struggle to make ends meet fuels a general sense of insecurity and vulnerability.

The loss of certainties impacts not only the present well-being of the vulnerable and marginalized sections of society but also individual life trajectories. The same forces also affect the educated elite, as Aichinger, Fankhauser and Goodman discuss. The university reform of the 1990s has largely redefined the role spectrum of academics that turned from independent researchers into administrators and teachers. It is an interesting finding that the fundamental redefinition of what it means to be an academic has more negative consequences for the well-being of the younger cohort. Apparently it is less the pressures of efficiency and productivity that make them feel less at ease, but rather the lack of stability and security that academic employment had promised and still safeguards the life plans of senior colleagues and superiors.

The existential dimension also looms large at the later stage of life and particularly in accounts of the transition from work to retirement. This is a major turning point in the life of many male Japanese who lose not only their social network, as previously discussed, but also the core of their public identity. Kawano shows the high significance of collective agency involving wives and other family members for easing the transition and keeping it short. The role of "senior volunteer" provides the retired with a new public identity that is acknowledged for service to the public good. The Japanese state has been promoting volunteering particularly for the purpose of smoothing the transition to post-retirement and for capitalizing on the unpaid services provided by the retiree workforce. But as Kawano's study demonstrates, senior volunteers are not simply duped into prefabricated role functions. Furthermore, in the case of Kawano's study, the seniors are volunteering for a new type of funeral, namely ash scattering practices. By this they also support a new and progressive way of dealing with one's posthumous life through propagating a burial practice that exemplifies refusal or avoidance of the obligatory and highly regimented posthumous rites to which the family members have to adhere. Challenging established routines they interpret as curtailing individual freedom and engaging in volunteer activities that are at odds with state objectives is eventually a further source of pleasure.

Volunteering provides a new dimension of meaning in life through the gratitude of those on whose behalf the volunteers act. By realigning with society in a publicly acknowledged role, the senior volunteers escape the nagging threat of inactivity and disorientation, which they and others see as detrimental for health and self-esteem, and which eventually would make them a burden on their families. Hence their sense of well-being is directly linked to family well-being. The fear of being a burden to others is deeply engrained in Japanese culture. Preventing others from the troublesome role of care in times of terminal illness is also the main motivator for Spoden's informants to take precautions against the potential loss of agency at a time when they are still able to make the necessary decisions by themselves. Signing a Living Will is an act of regaining control in the face of a potential loss of subjectivity. It reduces anxieties, affirms their individuality (*jibunrashisa*) and contributes to their present well-being by foreseeing different possibilities of well-being of the self and others in the future as Spoden demonstrates.

The Japanese researched in the studies that we have summarized here find happiness in a meaningful life, in activities that further enhance self-realization. Subjective well-being is premised on caring for others, the awareness of support one receives in reciprocity from others and a behavior that takes the needs of significant others into consideration. The dominant norms and values of Japanese society are used as benchmarks to critically reflect on the question of how to live a good life. Living in tune with the behavior script facilitates the well-being of those who largely agree with social norms; for others, however, they are a potential source of unhappiness. Being oneself and having the liberty to live an autonomous life are perhaps contradicting a subjective well-being rooted in interdependence. But these are factors that are equally valued by many in Japan, and for some to a degree that they overrule the dominant norms and values. That contemporary Japan is offering more leeway to opt among different choices is related to the historical time of the studies, as they have been conducted at a time of larger social transformations spurred by the forces of globalization.

Changes of the larger backdrop: The structural dimension

Throughout the previous sections, we have occasionally hinted at the role of state politics, global forces, the media and cultural institutions that may have an enhancing or constraining impact on happiness: education, work, marriage and family have been most prominent in this regard. In fact, as much as the other three dimensions are neatly interwoven with each other, it is impossible to discuss well-being at the level of the body, the social and the ideational without taking the impact of governing regulations into account. Preschool and elementary school education, social welfare and the labor market are, like family and marriage, institutionalized by the power of state legislation and administrative control; at the same time, these forces of government are not immune to changes spurred by the power of globalization. We agree with Mathews (2017) about the far-reaching consequences of two decades of neoliberal politics. The development, starting in the financial sphere and eventually reaching labor relations, the education system, and state politics, among others, neatly demonstrates how the change of any institution suspends the equilibrium of institutional integration and inflicts the burden of adjustment on affected institutions. As institutions, due to differing degrees of formality and complexity, adjust at different speeds, the diversity of accepted and preferred lifestyles is likely to increase in that period. While the increase in options to select from is nascent only and infers new challenges and uncertainties, it is safe to conclude that this will have an impact on the diversity of life paths and ideas of happiness. The consequences of the pursuit of happiness in Japan are promising: Greater diversity offers more possibilities to find a life plan tuned to one's own rhythm and tastes. Those who are willing— and able—to see the unlocking of institutions as an opening of possibilities will benefit; those who shun the responsibility of agency will see their well-being decline due to the loss of certainties.

In summarizing this section, we argue that the strong grip of institutionalized structures and norms of interdependency are responsible for the U-shaped happiness curve over the lifetime that the literature reports. Because the options of escaping structural pressure and choosing alternative life paths are most limited in the years of adulthood, with offering less leeway to those who must negotiate family and work life, it is understandable that happiness is lower for those who are battling the complexities of life and the expectations of others on two fronts. The young and the old are by comparison able to enjoy a life of fewer constraints. However, are they really happier because they have less social responsibilities to shoulder and less institutional obligations to bear? Children and teens are, as we have seen in the studies of this volume, also subjected to massive pressure from social relations at school and the institutionalized demand of high commitment to the goals of the educational system. We do not have enough data and case studies here to fully appreciate age-specific differences of happiness in the physical and existential dimension. Previous findings suggest that excitement and diversion, which lean more toward the physical, are quite crucial for the experience of happiness of the young. Happiness of the older generations, by contrast, is more associated with a sense of simplicity and contemplative serenity. Given that these generations have distinctive emotional states in mind when they refer to and reflect on happiness, and that these states are linked to specific causal and conditioning factors, we might also ask if it makes sense to compare two so different experiences that only in the cognitive practice of recollection happen to be labeled in the same way.

In general we struggle with formulating answers to the question of which of the four dimensions of well-being is more influential throughout the life course and how each domain is related to the turning points in the life course and broader social change. We assumed that the effect of Japanese institutions may be the primary answer for why subjective happiness in Japan is lower than objective indicators of health, wealth and equality would suggest, and this is certainly the case for adulthood, as many studies have shown. However, more than institutions alone, it is the particular relation between individuals and the institutional context that determines the impact institutions have, with gender playing a significant role. The family system binds women more than men; the employment system constrains men more than women. Workers that cannot share the burden of household labor with a partner are less likely to be happy, and those who have no partner at all are even less well off. Taking into consideration the differences in social status, material riches and public support opportunities, the question of happiness in Japanese society boils down to the individual's relationship to structures and agency, or more specific to its positioning between constraining and empowering factors that enable people in Japan to live the life they want. There are many different ways to the experience of happiness: People might equally gain a sense of well-being from staying within the system—sticking to the rules, going with the flow, and making ends meet within institutional limits (see Laurent 2017). Or they might find it only when stepping out of the track, resisting the pressure to follow the normative patterns of standardized life plans and embarking on alternative life paths (see also Steinhoff 2017 or Lieser 2017). To understand the different outcomes of seemingly identical choices and the same outcome of apparently different choices on experiencing happiness, we must take into account agency and the congruency of individual and societal norms and values.

Living shared lives: Reflections on happy life course theory

The particular emphasis that agency receives in life course theory is only one reason we have indexed our research to life course theory and referred to its key concepts throughout the book. None of the studies in the book are researching life course in the proper sense of the term, with the possible exception of Mathews' close-up on the meaning of lives of Japanese adults whom he had studied two decades earlier by re-interviewing the same individuals after a 20-year hiatus. Based on the kind of survey data used for this volume, two more studies have the potential to qualify as longitudinal analyses of understanding happiness in the domains of work and family life at different points of time. Aichinger, Fankhauser and Goodman base their research of academic work satisfaction on a cross-sectional study that was repeated after 15 years. Brinton also uses data from two different rounds of a cross-sectional study, but she merges the data into one file to increase the number of working married women. The gap between the two rounds of their respective surveys is too narrow to speak of generational differences anyway. Using data from two different points of time allows separating the impact of historical time and therefore offers an improved way of assessing cohort-specific attitudes, preferences and patterns of behavior. Studies that are just using the variable of age in cross-sectional studies, which is quite frequently done in life course research and in happiness research, too, can only attempt to model possible cohort effects. Cross-sectional studies cannot discriminate between possible generational effects of aging and cohort-specific experiences that are shaped by their environment and family histories.

The main reason we added life course terminology to the book is that the key concerns of life course theory—agency, the interdependency of human lives, historical time and private time—seem to us highly significant for understanding the complexity of happiness. The issue of interdependency has been running through most chapters to a degree that it appears to be a key motif of sociality, sense of self and happiness in Japan. Particularly in Mathews' study, but also in Yamamoto's and Spoden's studies on private views and visions of human life closer to the start and end points of the life course, we see how the cultural lens is tainting the working of institutions such as the family, schooling and work in Japan. Life course theory would also suggest explaining differences in happiness that people express by the lasting impact of early life experiences and their power for shaping mental responsiveness. We saw in Ben-Ari's study of daycare centers how the institutional setting of early childhood education outside the family framework is instrumental for drawing such mental maps. The positive gratification that children realize when they consciously relate the pleasure of play activities to the interests and objectives of the group prepares ground for a life-long predisposition to feel consideration for and concern by others. Yamamoto shows that the slightly older children in elementary school are already capable of imagining the effects of such a causal relationship. In Spoden's study we are reminded that interdependency comes with a price if individuals eventually lose their subjectivity rooted in mental health, reflexivity and control.

Life course theory also places a particular focus on the family as the cardinal place where individuals embark to acquire a sense of self and commonly shared values and norms. Our book does not feature contributions that look at happiness socialization in the context of time spent together within young families. But the importance of the family is not restricted to intergenerational exchanges that take place during the early childhood years. Rather the interdependency of lives within the family endures over the entire life course, as we have seen in different life stories, interviews and survey data (see also Umegaki-Costantini 2017). Life events are quite often significant for individuals in relation to the common understanding of their social roles within the family. Families change through the influence of effects by either anticipated or real major and/or regular life events such as graduation from school, marriage, childbirth, divorce or death of a family member. Other life events, for example a romance, a driver's license, an internship or an illness might be of a different nature, sometimes less significant, rather acute than enduring and not always controllable. But still most life events have a shaping impact on the family, particularly if they eventually are grasped as turning points, because they redefine the collective inventory of roles and responsibilities of the family. Family collaboration is needed to adjust to life events of its members and also for crafting a collectively shared understanding of the historical conditions under which their family relations are shaped. Hence, as a common element, the studies in this volume feature the family as collective framework for the experience or enhancement of happiness. For example, the Living Will signed by Spoden's informants is a demonstrative affirmation of subjectivity and autonomy in light of family relations. The process of signing the document symbolically expresses caring for others as the desired legal status takes the future well-being of oneself and of the family equally into consideration. Kawano's study of volunteering as a new public identity of retirees also demonstrates how family members care for others and take precautions in order to protect the family well-being from future deterioration that might come along with crucial turning points in the life of other members.

Larger transformations of the environment also require the collaborative efforts of family members. Historical events, man-made in kind like revolutions or natural in kind like disasters, severely affect the lives of families and their members, and they typically require collaborative responses and the adjustment of individuals' reactions to the challenges that the changed environment brings along for their families. The changes of the labor market in the aftermath of the burst bubble economy, for example, curtailed the options of entire cohorts to find a new status after graduation and embark on an autonomous life as a fully recognized adult capable of sustaining a family. Typical life events of a cohort at this stage of life, including graduation from school or university and the subsequent entrance to the workforce, often followed by marriage and already less frequently by childbirth, continued to be part of a more or less smooth transition for some. As their work and family trajectories developed in line with commonly held age norms, others, by contrast, saw themselves falling behind. Delaying or avoiding marriage, postponing childbearing, and having fewer children are perhaps strategies to cope with the economic challenges of the lost decades. But not everybody is similarly willing to embrace alternative life models, and the comparison of well-being within a generation clearly shows that not an entire cohort is able to find positive strategies for coming to terms with the competition for limited resources.

The happiness of the young generation, whether distancing itself from age norms or fully complying with normative life plans, is inseparably tied to the happiness of its parent generation. Those at the prime of their life might enjoy the extended comfort of intergenerational cohabitation and the prospect of future elderly care provided by their own adult dependents. Alternatively, and the U-shaped pattern of happiness across the life course rather suggests this reading, the divergence of their children's life paths from age norms might become a source of unhappiness. Parents might be worried simply because of concern for the well-being of their children. But they also might take a cross-generational perspective and feel concerned about the future trajectory of the family name and ancestor worship. Finally, they may see their own well-being impaired by the prolongation of their own family roles as providers of material means, security and services. Mathews has shown how the willingness to accept alternative patterns of work and life style decisions made by their children effectively increases the happiness of parents, particularly fathers.

Many more studies hint at the way in which different lifelines and time horizons of family members are intertwined with each other. Raymo has argued that previous experiences of domestic violence and physical abuse are quite frequently observed among single mothers who struggle economically and have lower consumption power, worse health records and less opportunities of social participation. Low education status, minimal welfare support and precarious working conditions are other commonly observed factors that contribute to what life course theorists have discussed as "cumulative disadvantages." Similar effects characterize the working poor among Hommerich's sample of young adults and threaten their future trajectories of work, family and happiness. The socially withdrawn discussed by Horiguchi are equally exposed to accumulated disadvantages and to structural conditions under which they have made their choices; these conditions are likely to have a lasting impact on their own future prospects and possible life chances of the next generations. It is reasonable to assume that we can trace back similar cumulative effects, albeit with positive outcomes, among those with a stable home, positive childhood experiences, good academic performances and work records. Within this book, Goldstein-Gidoni's informants of middle-aged housewives are an example of a group of Japanese that collectively benefits from family background, educational achievements and their husbands' employment status. Their narratives provide evidence for the reproduction of normative life plans by consecutive generations of homemakers, continuities of peer group expectations across the generations and the intergenerational transfer of cumulative advantages in the context of the "promise of female happiness."

Summarizing these observations and reflections, we believe that a "happy life" course theory should try to combine the particular perspective of life course theory on social life with the sociological findings of happiness research. "Happy life" course theory hence projects the ideas of interdependent lives, synchronized time and agency on the notion of happiness as a socially co-produced state of being that is experienced within physical, interpersonal and existential dimensions, which are all impacted by institutional forces of various scales. How families change and adapt under changing historical conditions and how individuals and families synchronize their lives to accommodate to changing social conditions impacts their subjective sense of happiness. This impact is difficult to measure (as the huge share of unexplained variation in the quantitative models by our sociological authors equally implies) but can be expressed in qualitative terms (as expressed by the nature of interview data that help put even contradictory and incoherent statements into perspective).

We do not propose the integration of two strands of social theory as a fundamental step toward improving the current state of theorizing and model-building. However, when comparing the chapters of this edited volume we noticed differences in the degree of engagement with the model drafted by Mathews and Izquierdo (2009). Some authors use it as a heuristic tool to isolate specific domains of well-being, others to separate different levels of observation from each other. Some just used it for framing the discussion of happiness as a research problem, if that. The variation is primarily stemming from the nature and quality of data that our authors rely on. Reanalyzing and reinterpreting data and findings that originally were collected for answering different research questions is by design not capable of grasping happiness in its entire complexity. Yet we also realized a kind of methodological divide, as authors in the quantitative tradition felt less capable to post-facto incorporate a model that originally had been drafted for the purpose of soft comparison of well-being in different cultural settings. Authors in the qualitative tradition were much more prone to appreciate the advantages of a descriptive model that is primarily interested in giving order to the various dimensions of social life that have an impact on well-being.

Future research should take the study of happiness seriously enough to develop research methodologies that are capable of capturing the difference between subjective well-being and relational well-being. The cultural lens, including the preferences for shared commitment, the responsibility of feeling concerned for others, and the hesitance to possibly put a strain on others, supports the assumption that relational well-being as a social phenomenon will be more prevalent in Japan than in the United States. Without testing a model that locates its primary object of interest in relational well-being as the result of collaborative efforts, it is impossible to say how the prototypical characterization of Eastern selves that are bound by their social relationships and agency residing in these relationships between the selves, are responsible for such an understanding of happiness.

We think that this volume is one more first step (see Ishida and Slater 2000 in this series) toward developing a research agenda that is benefiting from the different strengths of divergent methodological approaches. Why people differ in their subjective appreciation of a structurally identical situation, how they understand happiness and what makes them be more interested in pleasure, meaningfulness or satisfaction are all questions asking for explanations. These explanations are situated within the reasoning of the individual, and therefore ethnographic or in-depth interviews are well suited to elicit them. However, there is no way to prove for sure how far these explanations can be generalized, and this strategy is also prone to glossing over factors of which the interviewer and interviewee are not aware. Cohorts and the basic conditions of their happiness in and across particular domains can be systematically grasped and compared with each other by quantitative measurement tools only. But these survey techniques fail to explain their larger trajectories over different points in time, and they would need many additional variables to come to terms with differences in the subjective appraisal of objectively similar conditions, which by contrast qualitative methods such as life histories or biographical narratives are better qualified to extract. Quantitative studies are better at picturing the situation at large, as they are focusing on institutions and the positioning of the individual within structures. Qualitative studies are better equipped for taking a close-up at the micro level, leading eventually toward a fuller understanding of how individuals make sense of their positioning within the structures and how they achieved both position and assessment over the history of their lives. We also expect that a comparison of happiness in Japan with other countries, if using the same mixed-methods approach, would prove useful to further our understanding of different happiness regimes around the world and ultimately the influences of a neoliberal world order.

Finally, in closing this concluding chapter and the book, we think it is useful to build a bridge between the unmediated happiness experiences of children absorbed in the flow of play and the conscious appraisal of happiness by senior Japanese approaching the final stages of the life cycle. We reckon from the comparison of accounts along the life course that the appreciation of "small happiness" is highest at both extremities of human life paths, which might be a valuable lesson for putting the significance of "big happiness" into perspective. What we also may learn from the experience of small happiness is that whatever the circumstances of living are, might they be good or bad, benevolent or harsh, empowering or constraining, the less one thinks about happiness, the higher the likelihood is of being happy, just in this very moment.

References

Dales, Laura. 2017. "Intimate Relationships: Friendships, Marriage and Gender in Japan." pp. 67–85 in *Happiness and the Good Life in Japan*, edited by Wolfram Manzenreiter and Barbara Holthus. London and New York: Routledge (JAWS series).
Holthus, Barbara, Mathias Huber and Hiromi Tanaka. 2015. *Parental Well-Being in Japan.* (Miscellanea 19) Tokyo: Deutsches Institut für Japanstudien.
Ishida, Hiroshi, and David Slater, eds. 2010. *Social Class in Contemporary Japan: Structures, Sorting and Strategies.* London and New York: Routledge (Nissan Institute/Routledge Japanese Studies series).
Laurent, Erick. 2017. "Japanese Gays, the Closet and the Culture-dependent Concept of Happiness." pp. 106–122 in *Happiness and the Good Life in Japan*, edited by Wolfram Manzenreiter and Barbara Holthus. London and New York: Routledge (JAWS series).
Lieser, Martin. 2017. "'My Life is Taiyō Kōmuten': On the Relationship between Organized Football Fandom and Happiness in Japan." pp. 195–210 in *Happiness and the Good Life in Japan*, edited by Wolfram Manzenreiter and Barbara Holthus. London and New York: Routledge (JAWS series).
Mathews, Gordon. 2017. "Happiness in Neoliberal Japan." pp. 227–242 in *Happiness and the Good Life in Japan*, edited by Wolfram Manzenreiter and Barbara Holthus. London and New York: Routledge (JAWS series).
Mathews, Gordon, and Carolina Izquierdo. 2009. "Towards an Anthropology of Well-Being." pp. 248–266 in *Pursuits of Happiness. Well-being in Anthropological Perspective*, edited by G. Mathews and C. Izquierdo. New York and Oxford: Berghahn Books.
Moriki, Yoshie. 2017. "Physical Intimacy and Happiness in Japanese Families: Sexless Marriages and Parent-child Co-sleeping." pp. 41–52 in *Happiness and the Good Life in Japan*, edited by Wolfram Manzenreiter and Barbara Holthus. London and New York: Routledge (JAWS series).
Nakano, Lynne. 2017. "Happiness and Unconventional Life Choices: Views of Single Women in Japan." pp. 53–66 in *Happiness and the Good Life in Japan*, edited by Wolfram Manzenreiter and Barbara Holthus. London and New York: Routledge (JAWS series).
Steinhoff, Patricia G. 2017. "Makers and Doers: Using Actor-network Theory to Explore Happiness in Japan's Invisible Civil Society." pp. 125–143 in *Happiness and the Good Life in Japan*, edited by Wolfram Manzenreiter and Barbara Holthus. London and New York: Routledge (JAWS series).
Umegaki-Costantini, Hiroko. 2016. "Grandfathering in Contemporary Japan: Altruistic and Self-serving Means to Happiness." pp. 86–105 in *Happiness and the Good Life in Japan*, edited by Wolfram Manzenreiter and Barbara Holthus. London and New York: Routledge (JAWS series).

INDEX

3/11 2, 17, 90, 111, 192, 243; *see also* earthquake

academics: academic competition 54; academic inbreeding 161; academic performance 46, 54, 134, 269; junior 160–1, 163, 167–8, 170; professors 101, 159–61, 168; self-identity 161
adolescents 47, 62, 101–2, 121; *see also* youth
aesthetics 14, 37, 208, 257
agency 3, 10–11, 13, 15, 23, 106, 211, 221, 234, 259, 263, 265–6, 269–70
aggression 49
aging: discourse 204; old age 22–3, 72, 76, 86, 190–1, 197, 203–4, 212–13, 222, 224–5, 227–8, 238, 244, 246–7, 249–50, 258; 260; society 16, 66–8, 72, 206–7, 216, 222, 238, 240, 249; *see also* senior citizens
Alzheimer's disease 225
amae 58
ancestor worship 207, 268
anger 49, 210
anxiety 8, 17, 20, 23, 37, 52–4, 58, 60–2, 64–6, 68, 73–4, 80–1, 83, 85–8, 90, 191, 204, 224–5, 232, 242, 250, 260, 263; about future 16, 20, 68, 73–4, 77, 81, 85–7;
Asahi Shinbun 207, 238–9
aspirations 2, 12, 15, 47, 103
autonomy 8–9, 14, 65, 223, 260, 264, 267–8

bargaining model 144
basic needs 7–8, 45, 59, 65
belonging 63, 77–8, 80, 89, 177, 191, 195, 202, 222, 260–1
benefits: personal 203; social 19, 51, 53, 203, 262; *see also* welfare
Better Life Index 2
Bhutan 1–2
birth of a child *see* childbirth
birth rate 67, 138, 146, 204, 207
body: bodily activities 37, 61; decoration 14; *see also* physical
bonds: work 195; family 195; social 20, 72, 241–2
breadwinner 16, 20, 86, 102, 138–9, 141–2, 144, 146, 149, 153, 175, 177, 180, 209–10, 259, 262
Buddhist institutions *see* religion
bullying 46, 62, 261
burial practice 207, 215, 242, 263; *see also* funeral

Cabinet Office 2, 7, 73–5, 77, 90, 206–6, 238–40, 244
capital: cultural 234; human 66, 118, 143, 147, 149; social 72, 75, 77–8, 86, 88
care: caregiving 32, 153, 204, 216, 229, 234, 262; caretaker 32, 34, 38, 40, 191, 260; elderly 190, 206, 212–13, 216–17, 268; palliative 223, 230; services 245; *see also* childcare
career: alternative career path 193; ambitions 262; career-track job 189–90,

193; mobility 261; prospects 168, 170, 182, 261; second 207
Carnegie Survey of the Academic Profession 158–60, 162–9, 171
cemeteries 207–8, 215
Changing Academic Profession study 158–9
chichioya fuzai 177, 180
childbirth 16, 118, 142–3, 180, 189, 261, 267–8
childcare 118, 124, 143–4, 146–7, 175, 180–1, 262; daycare centers 19, 31–4, 37, 39, 267; institutions 10, 181; leave 180; men's participation 145, 175, 179–81, 183–4; *see also* care
childhood 12, 40, 62, 101, 121, 230; early 32–3, 38, 267; experience 42, 269; stages 32
child poverty 18, 59
childrearing 124, 142–3, 176, 191
children: elementary school 19, 35, 54, 258, 267; middle-class 47, 54; parental demands 52, 54, 193; self-esteem 20, 62–3, 73–4; working-class 47, 51, 54
Christianity *see* religion
citizen's movement 202, 207, 215; *see also* civil society
civil society 7, 206; civic engagement/ activism 7, 17, 206; invisible civil society 18; political demonstrations 18; protest 18
class background 47, 54, 198, 259; *see also* social class
cohabitation 268
colleagues 11, 22, 161, 164–6, 170, 177, 182, 194, 228, 263
collectivism 8, 242, 257
communal life 7, 260
community 14, 51, 63, 164–6, 205–6, 212, 216–18, 242, 261
companionship 192
connectedness 34, 39, 61, 63–4, 78, 232, 240, 247–8, 251–2, 259
consumption 1, 15, 19, 100, 102, 106–7, 109–110, 113, 120, 262, 268
corporate life 22, 195, 198
corporeality 13, 257
creativity 9, 53
crime 245, 249
culture: cross-cultural comparison 5, 8–9, 13, 46–7, 75, 99, 189; cultural differences 7, 12; cultural forces 14; cultural folk theories 8; cultural institutions 5, 13, 264; specifics 3, 5

daily life 32, 72, 81, 110
daycare center *see* childcare
death: causes of 73, 222; from overwork (*karōshi*) 240, 244, 246; process of dying 23, 222, 225, 231, 233; reflections on 224, 242, 260; right to die 223, 234; solitary (*kodokushi*) 23, 238–51, 260
decision-making 11, 23, 221–2, 224, 227–35, 263, 268
deflation 15
demographic change 6, 16, 72, 160, 238
depression 21, 60, 72, 116, 119–22, 203; after childbirth 124
despair 21, 116; frustration 49, 169, 181, 184, 215, 258
dignity 223, 226, 230–1, 235, 240
dimensions of happiness 5, 13–14, 19, 57, 74, 82, 87, 98, 116–17, 133, 159, 161, 176, 191, 221, 243, 250, 256, 265, 269; existential 5, 13–14, 19, 22, 53, 57, 64, 68, 74–5, 77, 81, 83, 86, 98–9, 161, 166, 170, 176–7, 179, 191, 203, 221, 230, 232, 244, 250, 257, 260, 263, 265, 269; interpersonal 5, 13–14, 19, 21–2, 33, 51, 53, 57, 61, 63, 64, 68, 74–5, 77–8, 83, 86, 98, 139, 161, 164–6, 170, 176–7, 191, 203, 221, 227, 232, 243, 250, 256–8, 269; multidimensionality of happiness 5–6, 74, 98; physical 5, 13–15, 19, 33, 37, 55, 57, 59–60, 68, 74, 117, 161–4, 170, 176, 191, 203, 221, 224, 232, 243, 250, 256–7, 265, 269; structural 5, 13, 15, 53, 58, 68, 74, 98–9, 112, 161, 176, 191, 203, 217, 221–2, 264, 269
disaster 2, 10, 17, 90, 111, 192, 239–40, 243–4, 246, 267; technological 1; *see also* 3/11
discrimination 143; 189
disillusionment 82
distress 62–3, 65, 68, 73, 215, 240, 257
divorce 10, 117–19, 121, 124–5, 133–4, 192, 194, 209, 211, 260, 267
domestic chores *see* housework
domestic violence 121, 133, 262, 268
domesticity 109–13
dying *see* death

earthquake 17, 192, 206, 239, 243; *see also* 3/11
economy: American 15, 177; bubble burst 15, 72, 74, 98, 100, 145, 160, 177–8, 268; economic change 6, 22, 139; economic disadvantage 21, 116, 119–20, 125, 133–4, 262, 268; economic downturn

Index **275**

68, 76; economic growth 15, 98, 146, 149, 153, 175–7; economic power 15, 17; economic problems 18; stagnation 15, 17, 67, 74, 76, 190
education: early childhood 32–3, 264, 267; educational career 9; higher 9, 21, 158–60, 169, 168; educational revolution 159; educational status 9, 77, 140; institution 10; low education 118–19, 262, 268; educational system 9, 19, 46, 104–5, 159, 196, 264–5; university 48, 146, 160, 192; women in higher 146–7; *see also* school
egalitarianism 46, 54, 147, 215
elderly care *see* care
elementary school *see* school
emotions: emotional support 144–5, 244, 247; negative 6; positive 6–7, 54; social contextualization 38
empathy 38–9, 62
employee *see* employment
employment: blue-collar 175, 192, 197, 205, 216; finding 20, 73; full-time 21, 118, 125, 140–1, 147–9, 152–3, 175, 177, 179, 209; job transfer 101; lifetime 175, 192, 195, 218; long-term 210; married women 138–42, 144–9, 152; non-regular 83, 86, 120, 171, 176, 180; part-time 66, 118, 140–2, 145, 147, 149, 152, 167, 171, 180, 192, 197, 205, 209; permanent 16, 175; precarious 16, 18, 22, 67–8, 72, 75–6, 83, 146, 161, 163, 259, 261, 268; regular 22, 76, 78, 83, 102, 124, 127, 176, 180, 185; security 86, 146, 160–1, 166, 171, 182, 204, 263; self-employment 67, 124; stability 16, 86, 263; system 16, 265; unstable 118, 120; white-collar 175, 176, 181, 195, 205; youth 190; unemployment 16, 20, 67–8, 72, 78, 83, 141, 144, 246
end-of-life stage 11, 23, 221, 223
enjoyment: active 36; passive 36, 39
environment 202, 208; enjoyable 32, 40; housing and 18, 45; safe 64, 102; schooling 47, 53; social 233; work 104, 161, 164, 166, 268; *see also* nature
Equal Employment Opportunity Law 67, 146
equal partnership 192, 230
era of high growth 76
existential crisis 232, 261–2
existential dimension of happiness *see* dimensions of happiness
eyes of society *see* sekentei

failure 19, 52–4, 66, 68, 193
family: background 47–8, 59, 102, 269; extended 62; life 12, 22, 66, 76, 99, 110, 176–7, 181–2, 184, 193, 257, 259, 265–7; members 59–61, 216, 227, 234–5, 244, 259, 262–3, 267–8; nuclear 97–8, 259; obligations 76; pattern 66, 97, 265; postwar system 141; role 60, 233, 268; single-parent 116, 118, 125, 133–4; structure 134, 176, 190, 249
fashion 14, 21, 97, 100, 106–11, 113
fatherhood 180; fathering 262
fears *see* anxieties
female homemaker 20, 178–9, 181–3, 206, 209, 269; *see also* housewife
femininity 108, 111, 216
feminism 109, 112, 197
financial hardship *see* economy
flexibility 161; gender-role 189; social structures 22, 190; time and space 63; *see also* inflexibility
flow 19, 36–7, 39–41, 258, 270
free play 19, 32–6, 40
freedom 7, 14, 22–3, 32, 106, 167, 190–1, 202, 207, 211, 215, 217, 233, 256, 263
freeter 66
friend 34–5, 55, 57, 62–4, 74, 77–80, 86–7, 102–4, 194, 198, 227–9, 240, 242, 244, 258–9; friendship 35, 62, 64, 68, 258–9, 261
frustration *see* despair
Fukushima catastrophe *see* 3/11
full-time work *see* employment
funeral 207, 228, 242, 263; *see also* burial practice
furītā see freeter
fushiawase see unhappiness
futōkō see school refusal
future: chances 73; expectations 74, 81–2, 86–7; goal 74; life 12, 45, 87; orientations 11; prospects 16, 18, 73, 77, 83, 261, 268; *see also* anxiety

gakkyū hōkai 47
gap society *see kakusa shakai*
GDP 1, 16
gender: difference 59, 83, 164, 247, 249; division of gender roles 20–1, 102, 111, 139, 141, 143–8, 152–3, 180, 189–90, 197, 209–10, 262; equality 18, 146–7; everyday life 11, 260; flexibility 189; shift of gender norms 190, 194
generation: generational change 11, 197; generational gap 100, 102, 178, 266;

older 75, 178, 182, 184, 207, 265; post-war 15, 58, 98, 107–8, 177, 261; young 72, 88, 111, 113, 145, 178, 268
globalization 15, 159–60, 167, 264
government 1, 10, 15, 17–18, 63, 66, 72–3, 78, 98, 139, 146, 160–1, 181, 197, 204–7, 264; political elites 138
graduation 10, 15–16, 48, 61, 67, 78, 90, 101, 145–6, 149, 152, 160, 179, 189, 198, 261, 267–8
gratitude 210, 215, 218, 263
Great East Japan Earthquake *see* 3/11
Great Hanshin Earthquake 206, 239, 243; *see also* earthquake
Gross Arakawa Happiness Project 2
Gross National Happiness 1
group: activity 19, 215; embeddedness 258; enjoyment 39–40; membership 258; group-oriented culture 40; group-oriented play 258

habitus 11
Hanako tribe 100
hanseikai 38
Happiness League 2
happiness ranking 5, 7
harmony 8, 111, 113, 260
hate speech 17
health: concern 258; emotional 21, 116–17, 120–2; mental 20, 58, 66, 73, 122, 257, 267; physical 21, 60, 116–17, 119, 122, 202; problems 60, 116; *see also* ill-being
hegemonic masculinity *see* masculinity
hikikomori 19–20, 57–68, 193, 259; discourse 57–9, 66; lifestyle 259; recovery 57, 60, 63–4, 68; support organizations 63–6; treatment 63, 66; *see also* tojikomori
homogeneity 5, 16
hobby 103, 107, 195, 209, 211, 213
hope 16, 22, 68, 73–4, 87, 191, 198, 222
hospice 230
hospitalization 116, 222
household: budget 73, 141; changing composition 207; chores 142–5, 147–9, 152–3, 180, 184, 195, 262, 265; composition; consumption 15; division of labor 21, 139, 141, 143–5, 147–9, 152–3; single 116–17, 119–21, 240–1, 245–6; three generation 76; *see also* income
housewife 5, 20–1, 59, 98–113, 138–42, 145–9, 152–3, 192–3, 210, 230, 259, 262, 269; full-time 97–8, 101–5, 107, 147–8, 194, 262; middle-class 20, 98; modern 103, 107, 257; role 35, 100, 102, 105, 149, 153

housework 110–11, 124, 139–41, 143–8, 152–3, 155, 180, 189, 209; men's participation 141, 145, 148, 153, 179–80, 184, 210
human capital *see* capital
Human Development Index 5, 7
human relations 32, 62, 166, 197

ibasho 63, 260
identity: masculine 216; public 100, 260, 262–3, 267; retiree 213; salaryman 194, 209–10, 216; social 215, 261; volunteer 22, 202–3; women 106, 111, 209
ijime see bullying
ikigai see meaning of life
ikumen 180
ill-being 8, 19–20, 57, 68
illness 224, 234, 257–8, 267; terminal 223, 263; *see also* health
inactivity 61; retirement 203, 212–13, 263
income 5, 16, 21, 83, 102, 116–20, 123, 134, 140–1, 144–6, 148–9, 152, 167–9, 171, 180, 182, 205, 245, 262; daily wage 175; household 15, 78, 120, 123–5, 127, 129, 133, 140, 144–5, 147–8, 247, 250; level 7; prospect 46, 261; *see also* salary
independence 8, 14, 51, 109, 206, 211, 217, 228–9, 234, 242, 260, 263; financial 64, 72, 76, 117, 133, 146
individual: lives 6, 10, 14, 191, 263; achievement 8; choice 10, 192; self 166, 209; individualism 8, 100, 185; individuality 106, 178, 232, 263
industrialization 15; industrial society 1, 5, 8, 46; post-industrial society 141, 148, 215–16
inequality 16, 20, 67, 72, 133; social inequality 16, 72
inferiority complex 61
inflexibility 20, 120, 180, 190, 195; social and institutional structures 189–91, 199; *see also* flexibility
insecurity *see* security
interdependence 8, 14, 23, 217, 257, 260, 264–7, 269
International Day of Happiness 2
internationalization 158
internet 60, 63, 68
interpersonal: communication 57, 67; relations 20, 58, 61–4, 68, 83, 166, 233, 243, 258–60
interpersonal dimension of happiness *see* dimensions of happiness

intimacy 63, 110, 190, 257; intimate relationship 61–2, 182, 184; intimate sexual encounters 61
isolation *see hikikomori*

Japan Institute for Labour Policy and Training 117, 119–22, 133
Japan National Survey on Family and Economic Conditions 180
jibunrashisa 230–2, 263
jokes 37, 61
Journal of Happiness Studies 4
juku 47

kaisha ningen 177; *see also* work-centered lives
kakusa shakai 16; *see also* inequality
karōshi see death
kawaii 101, 107, 109
kazoku sābisu 177; *see also* family
kindergarten 32, 39, 46, 50, 53
kodokushi see death
Korean minorities 17
koritsushi see death
Kumamoto Happiness Index 2

labor force 67, 138, 146, 160, 205, 218; M-shaped curve of female labor force participation 142; participation 117; women's labor force participation 118, 133, 139, 142, 144, 160; *see also* household
labor market 11, 15, 18, 66–7, 72, 76, 86, 117, 139, 141–3, 146, 262, 264, 268; access 9, 59
late adulthood 206, 208, 213, 217; *see also* retirement
leisure: activities 204; time 177
life choices 99, 191
life course 12, 18, 20, 23, 40, 65, 86, 104, 120, 141, 168, 175–7, 190–2, 204, 214, 232, 257–60, 262, 265–8, 270; approach 5; male standardized 175; research 10–11, 266; stages 73, 76, 256, 259; theory 6, 13, 256, 266–9
life crises 230, 234
life cycle 1, 10–12, 66, 142, 147, 153, 258, 270; middle 12; transitions 20, 66–8; perspective 9
life expectancy 189
life satisfaction 4–8, 12–13, 20, 74–8, 81, 83, 86–8, 90, 99, 203, 243
life-sustaining treatments *see* medical treatments
Living Will 23, 221, 223–35, 263, 267

loneliness 23, 39, 238, 242–4, 247, 249–50, 260
lonely death *see* death
lost decades 15, 67, 74, 76, 268; *see also* economy
love 109, 192, 194, 213

male breadwinner *see* breadwinner
male workforce 175
marriage: expectations 22, 192, 194, 198; ideal 22, 198; late 16, 241; marital happiness 98, 100, 138–49, 152–3, 260; marital relations 202, 210–11; marital satisfaction 21, 139, 141, 147, 149, 152–3; marital status 125, 244, 249–50; married women 97, 103, 106–7, 120, 139, 141–5, 147, 262, 266; norms 190; rates 146, 207, 241; *see also* divorce
masculinity 61, 176; hegemonic 98, 176
mass media *see* media
maternity leave 104
maturity 61, 65, 190, 217
meaning of life 6, 13, 20, 23, 54, 57, 64–5, 74, 81, 82, 232, 244, 250, 257–8, 263, 266
meaningful life 190, 206–7, 221, 226, 230–1, 233, 244, 260, 264
media 15, 19, 21, 46–7, 54, 59, 68, 72, 100, 106–7, 110, 112, 207, 211, 239–41, 262, 264; attention 3, 238–40; discourse 16, 23, 57–8, 66; publishing industry 106; social 63, 68
medical treatments 221; life-sustaining treatments 221, 223–5, 228, 231, 233
meiwaku 51, 211, 227
mental disorder 57, 60, 72, 197; *see also* health
middle-class 5, 20, 31, 40–1, 47–8, 54, 59, 98–102, 106, 109, 203, 209–10; consciousness 16, 97, 176, 209; life 153, 197–8; mentality 175; model 192–3; new 98; upper middle-class 59, 224; *see also* class background
Ministry of Education 32, 46
Ministry of Health, Labor and Welfare 32, 58, 116–18, 121, 180, 205, 215, 223
minority 16–17, 19, 21, 73, 111, 160
monster parents 47
morality: moral appreciation 9; moral panic 66; moral responsibility 53, 203, 234; mores 257
moratorium 259
mortuary rites *see* burial practices

mother: mothering 120; never-married 118, 134, 241; single 21, 116–29, 133–4, 258–9, 262, 268
muen shakai 239

National Institute of Population and Social Security Research 16, 118, 143, 146
national institutions 53, 98, 117, 153, 161, 217
National Survey of Households with Children 21, 121
National Survey on Lifestyle Preferences 7, 77, 244
nationalism 17
natural disasters *see* disaster
nature 208, 213, 227
NEET 66; *see also* employment
neighborhood 61, 101–2, 218, 225, 239; dissatisfaction 23, 245, 249–50; middle-class 48, 99–100
neoliberalism 68; ideology 1; politics 16, 264; world order 270
Non-Profit Activity Promotion Law 206
non-profit organization 206–7
norms 23, 31, 46, 153, 190, 233, 235, 261, 265, 267–8; challenge 65, 261; normative behavior 176, 234; normative expectations 65; normative lifestyle 65, 86, 99, 112, 259, 266, 268–9; social 20, 65, 68, 142, 149, 224, 234, 256, 261, 264, 266
nuclear disaster *see* 3/11

OECD 2–3, 5, 12, 45, 68, 116–18, 160
OECD Better Life Initiative 7; Index 2, 5
office lady 101, 103, 138
old age *see* aging

parent 20, 45, 47–9, 51–2, 54, 57–60, 63, 68, 72, 102, 104–5, 111, 117, 119–21, 124–5, 133, 145, 183, 192, 197, 207, 227, 230, 261, 268; coresidence with 118–19, 134; parenting 118, 180; relationship 119
part-time work *see* employment
paternalism 223
patient autonomy 223
peer: appreciation 217; competition 54; group 259, 269; relationship 51, 216
pension system 16, 72, 76; budget 206
personality 197, 213, 231–2
physical abuse *see* violence
physical condition 226–7, 230, 232, 234, 258; *see also* health
physical decline 203, 232; *see also* illness

physical dimension of happiness *see* dimensions of happiness
pleasure 57, 59, 61, 110, 112, 184, 191, 199, 263, 270; school 31, 35–8, 40–1, 267
pollution 245, 249
population: working population 16, 138; shrinking population 16, 205; *see also* demographic change
post-retirement: life 195, 204, 208, 210–13; discourse 211
postwar Japan 67, 98, 104, 189, 199, 205, 207, 209–10; economic growth 97, 175–6; family system 141
poverty 1, 15, 18, 59, 78; single mothers 116–17, 119–21, 133
precarious jobs *see* employment
preschool *see* school
pressures: academic 46, 54; bureaucratic 196; institutional 191, 195; interpersonal 191; social 59–60, 62, 65, 190–1, 224, 265
pride 35, 161, 166, 194
productivity 15, 17, 20, 60, 64, 67–8, 161, 179, 203–4, 217, 263
professional housewife *see* housewife
promotion 168, 175, 181–3, 189, 210, 214, 218
PTA 102
public: agencies 66; health centers 63; housing facilities 239
publishing industry *see* media
punishment 52, 124
purpose of life *see* meaning of life
pursuit of happiness 2, 39, 99, 107–9, 203, 223, 264

quality of life 3, 4, 6–7, 23, 238, 244

radiation 17; *see also* 3/11
recession 67, 72; *see also* economy
relationship: colleagues 161, 164–6; family 55, 230; human 32, 166; social 177, 224, 232, 235, 242, 259–60, 270; student-teacher 51, 170; workplace 259
relatives 58, 62, 221, 226–9, 239–40, 242–4
religion 14, 36, 190, 206–7; Buddhism 196, 230; Buddhist institutions 207–8; Christianity 204, 206
retirement 10, 22, 76, 78, 190–8, 202–13, 215–17, 228, 259, 263; discourse 204; financial situation 244, 246; marriage 141–2; *see also* aging
retreat from society *see* hikikomori
right-to-die movement *see* death

risk 18, 86, 121, 138, 176, 183, 203, 238–9, 243, 249–50; social 20, 72
rite of passage 10, 61
ritual 9, 36, 190, 207, 242, 257; *see also* religion
role: conflict 256, 262; housewife 35, 100–2, 105–6, 149, 153; obligation 8, 63, 194, 260; social 10, 89, 104–5, 107, 111, 191–2, 228–9, 261, 267; *see also* gender
romance 61, 109, 259, 267
routines of daily life 32, 36, 55, 61

sabishisa see loneliness
safety 7, 17–18, 45, 249; safe environment 64, 109
salary 15–16, 64, 143, 161–2, 166–8, 170, 175, 178–9, 214; *see also* income
salaryman 20, 22, 97–8, 101–2, 175–6, 182, 193–6, 209, 257; lifestyle 175–6, 195; image 175, 184–5; retirement 209, 216
school: alternative schooling 196; attendance 31, 45–54, 57, 179; elementary/primary 19, 46, 54, 258, 264, 267; extra-curricular 46–7, 183; high 46, 77, 119, 125, 146, 169, 195, 225, 228; learning experiences 48, 213; life 45, 48, 53, 261; preschool 18–19, 31, 35–42, 47, 52, 125, 258, 260, 264; private schooling system 105; public 47–8; schooling 10, 15, 19, 46–9, 52–5, 266; types 9
sciences: hard 99, 161; social 31, 257
security 17, 160–1, 263, 268; food 18; insecurity 72, 112, 119–20, 225, 262; in old age 204; social 205, 207, 262; *see also* employment
sekentei 191
self: appreciation 262; control 35; esteem 20, 62–3, 73–4, 203, 263; expression 178; fulfillment 8, 103, 106–7; hatred 61; identity 161; image 108; realization 9, 178, 182, 206, 262, 264; reflection 14, 90, 224; reliance 207, 227–30, 234; sacrifice 176, 182, 210, 216
sengyō shufu see full-time housewife
senility 190
senior citizen 22, 202–210, 212–13, 215–18, 258, 270; seniors' clubs 206; volunteer 22, 202–18, 259, 263, 267
service industry 67, 242
sex: discrimination 143; sexual attractiveness 106; sexual desires 61; sexual pleasures 257; sexuality 108
shame 20, 52–3, 60–1
shopping 50, 110, 147, 183

shufu see housewife
single women 21, 97
skinship 35, 257
sleeping 32, 60, 122
sōchūryū ishiki see middle-class
social benefits 19, 51, 53, 203
social bonds 20, 72, 241–2
social capital *see* capital
social change 10–11, 20–1, 68, 100, 139–40, 145, 217, 242, 265
social class 16, 75, 198; *see also* class background
social embeddedness 260
social environment *see* environment
social expectations 19, 54, 65, 176, 180, 202
Social Indicators Research 3
social institution 15, 18, 99, 261
social isolation 23, 59, 68, 238, 240, 242–4, 247, 249–50, 260; *see also hikikomori*
social media *see* media
social movement 18, 215; *see also* civil society
social network 11, 13, 20, 78–9, 191, 209, 211, 239, 263
social problems 16, 57, 66, 169, 208, 234
social recognition 214–15
social roles *see* role
social sanctions 52
social security system *see* security
social status *see* status
social ties 239, 242
social uncertainties 72; *see also* security
social welfare *see* welfare
social withdrawal *see hikikomori*
sociality 14, 68, 257, 266
socialization 31, 38, 40; 42, 46, 53, 209, 267; resocialization 204, 210; socializing 19, 40, 57, 209–10, 212, 259
socially withdrawn youth *see hikikomori*
societal rules 191, 224; *see also* norms
socio-economic: background 19, 54, 123, 127; changes 22, 176; conditions 5, 76, 77; differences 48–9, 51, 54; gap 47; resources 59; *see also* status
solidarity 7
solitary death *see* death
spousal relations *see* marriage
standard of living 7, 82, 87, 98, 153, 194
status: economic 242; social 141, 257, 261, 265; socio-economic 51, 54, 77, 83, 86–8, 119, 125, 203
stress 20–2, 61, 63, 65, 73, 116–17, 120, 124, 161, 164, 170, 182, 183, 259; stressful life events 119–21, 124–5, 127,

129, 133; work conditions 116, 119–20, 123, 134, 164
structural dimension of happiness *see* dimensions of happiness
structure 3, 10–11, 15–16, 21, 99, 161, 260, 265, 270; social 10–11, 22, 189; structural change 6, 22, 58, 68, 72, 160, 176; structural circumstances 5, 74, 240, 268
students 19, 46–9, 51–5, 61, 103, 105, 160–1, 166, 169, 196, 206, 209, 228, 259
suburban Japan 20, 99–100
suicide 65, 124–5, 133, 192, 209; suicide rate 73
Survey of Quality of Life 23, 238, 244; *see also* quality of life
Survey on Japanese Attitudes 73
sustainable society 234

tasseikan 103, 179
teacher 45–7, 50–1, 105, 193, 196, 225, 228, 261, 263; daycare center 19, 32–41
Tōhoku earthquake and tsunami *see* 3/11
tojikomori 59; *see also hikikomori*
tradition 7, 14, 16, 111, 149, 241, 262
traveling 195, 197, 209, 211
triple disaster in Northern Japan *see* 3/11
trust 20, 79, 86–7, 90
tsunami 17, 192 *see also* 3/11

unemployment *see* employment
UNICEF 18
urban area 17, 34, 106, 207–8
urbanization 207, 242
U-shaped happiness curve 12, 77, 90, 265, 268

value: change 22, 235; extrinsic 166–7; individual/personal 166, 223, 230, 261; materialistic 161, 166; social 120, 166, 234; societal 90, 166, 168, 264, 266; system 13, 15; traditional 14, 111; *see* norms
violence 19, 60; domestic 121, 133, 262, 268; physical abuse 124, 268; *see also* domestic violence
volunteering *see* senior citizen

wa see harmony
wages *see* salary
welfare 67, 118, 124, 260; benefits 76, 205; community 206; government 72; mental 66; social 16, 60–1, 190, 206, 240, 264
well-being: collective 260; material 18, 77, 83; national 2–3
women's magazines 21, 100, 103, 106–12
work: colleagues 11, 22, 161, 164, 166, 170, 177, 182, 194, 228, 263; long work hours 116, 118, 120, 124; shiftwork 120; trouble 73; work-centered life 176–7, 182; work-family conflict 120, 123–5, 127, 129; workplace relations 259; *see also* employment
working class 47–8, 51, 54, 198
working poor 16, 160, 268
work-life balance 7
World Happiness Report 2, 5, 7, 158, 189
World Map of Happiness 4

yarigai 179
young adults 19, 72–3, 259–61, 268
youth 19–20, 47, 57–68, 72–4, 88, 90, 107, 190, 259, 261